CONTRACTS

SIXTH EDITION

STEVEN L. EMANUEL

Founder and Editor-in-Chief, the *CrunchTime* series,
Emanuel Law Outlines, and *Emanuel Bar Review*

Harvard Law School, J.D. 1976
Member, NY, CT, MD and VA bars

The *Emanuel CrunchTime*® Series

ASPEN PUBLISHING

To contact Customer Service, e-mail customer.service@aspenpublishing.com, call 1-800-950-5259, or mail correspondence to:

> Aspen Publishing
> Attn: Order Department
> PO Box 990
> Frederick, MD 21705

Printed in the United States of America.

9 0

ISBN 978-1-4548-7017-3

This book is intended as a general review of a legal subject. It is not intended as a source for advice for the solution of legal matters or problems. For advice on legal matters, the reader should consult an attorney.

Certified Chain of Custody
Promoting Sustainable Forestry
www.sfiprogram.org

About Aspen Publishing

Aspen Publishing is a leading provider of educational content and digital learning solutions to law schools in the U.S. and around the world. Aspen provides best-in-class solutions for legal education through authoritative textbooks, written by renowned authors, and breakthrough products such as Connected eBooks, Connected Quizzing, and PracticePerfect.

The Aspen Casebook Series (famously known among law faculty and students as the "red and black" casebooks) encompasses hundreds of highly regarded textbooks in more than eighty disciplines, from large enrollment courses, such as Torts and Contracts to emerging electives such as Sustainability and the Law of Policing. Study aids such as the *Examples & Explanations* and the *Emanuel Law Outlines* series, both highly popular collections, help law students master complex subject matter.

Major products, programs, and initiatives include:

- **Connected eBooks** are enhanced digital textbooks and study aids that come with a suite of online content and learning tools designed to maximize student success. Designed in collaboration with hundreds of faculty and students, the Connected eBook is a significant leap forward in the legal education learning tools available to students.

- **Connected Quizzing** is an easy-to-use formative assessment tool that tests law students' understanding and provides timely feedback to improve learning outcomes. Delivered through CasebookConnect.com, the learning platform already used by students to access their Aspen casebooks, Connected Quizzing is simple to implement and integrates seamlessly with law school course curricula.

- **PracticePerfect** is a visually engaging, interactive study aid to explain commonly encountered legal doctrines through easy-to-understand animated videos, illustrative examples, and numerous practice questions. Developed by a team of experts, PracticePerfect is the ideal study companion for today's law students.

- The **Aspen Learning Library** enables law schools to provide their students with access to the most popular study aids on the market across all of their courses. Available through an annual subscription, the online library consists of study aids in e-book, audio, and video formats with full text search, note-taking, and highlighting capabilities.

- Aspen's **Digital Bookshelf** is an institutional-level online education bookshelf, consolidating everything students and professors need to ensure success. This program ensures that every student has access to affordable course materials from day one.

- **Leading Edge** is a community centered on thinking differently about legal education and putting those thoughts into actionable strategies. At the core of the program is the Leading Edge Conference, an annual gathering of legal education thought leaders looking to pool ideas and identify promising directions of exploration.

TABLE OF CONTENTS

Preface

Thank you for buying this book.

The *CrunchTime®* series is intended for people who want Emanuel quality, but don't have the time or money to buy and use the full-length *Emanuel Law Outline* on a subject. We've designed the series to be used in the last few weeks (or even less) before your final exams.

This book includes the following features, most of which have been extracted from the corresponding *Emanuel Law Outline*:

- *Flowcharts* — We've reduced most principles of *Contract* law to a set of 16 Flowcharts. We think these will be especially useful on open-book exams. The Flowcharts begin on p. 1.

- *Capsule Summary* — This is a 119-page summary of the subject. We've carefully crafted it to cover the things you're most likely to be asked on an exam. The Capsule Summary starts on p. 41.

- *Exam Tips* — We've compiled these by reviewing dozens of essay and multiple-choice questions asked in past law-school and bar exams, and extracting the issues and "tricks" that surface most often on the exams. The Exam Tips start on p. 165.

- *Short-Answer* questions — These questions are generally in a Yes/No format. In the case of the present Contracts volume, they've been adapted from the *Law in a Flash* flash-card deck on Contracts. (We've re-written most answers, to better mesh with the *Emanuel Law Outline*'s approach.) The questions start on p. 235.

- *Multiple-Choice* questions — These are in a Multistate-Bar-Exam style, and are taken from *Strategies & Tactics for the Finz Multistate Method*, which is also published by Wolters Kluwer Law & Business. They start on p. 293. Answers explaining why one answer option is correct and the others are not are provided.

- *Essay* questions — These questions are actual ones asked on law school exams. They start on p. 319. Sample answers are provided.

We hope you find this book helpful and instructive. Good luck.

Steve Emanuel
Larchmont, NY
September 2016

FLOWCHARTS

TABLE OF CONTENTS
To FLOWCHARTS

Note: The cross-references in the Flowcharts' footnotes (e.g., "See Ch.6, V(B)") are to the full-length *Emanuel Law Outline* on Contracts (10th Edition, © 2012, published by Wolters Kluwer Law & Business).

I got an A in Contracts with Spann my 1L year.

Figure 1-1
Analyzing Contracts Questions

Use this chart to help you spot issues when analyzing any contracts exam question. Skim the questions along the far left for the general issues, and follow the body of the chart where needed for more detailed analysis.

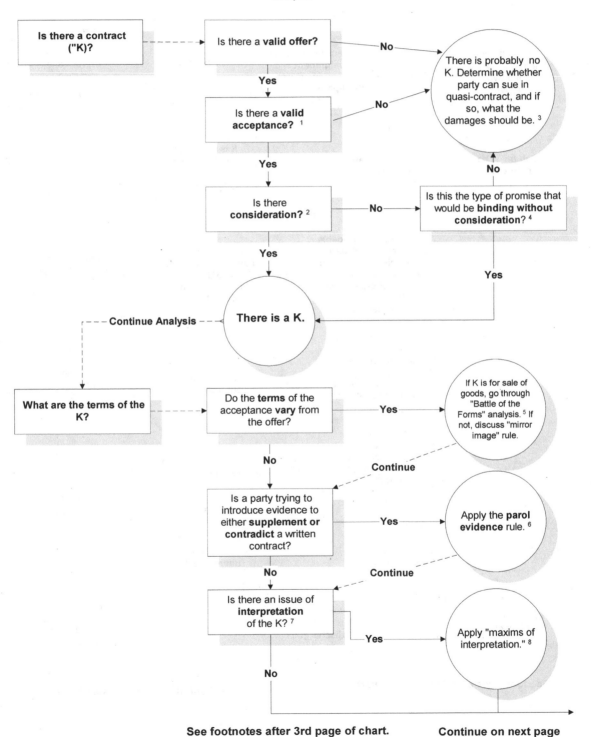

See footnotes after 3rd page of chart.   **Continue on next page**

Figure 1-1
Analyzing Contracts Questions (cont.)

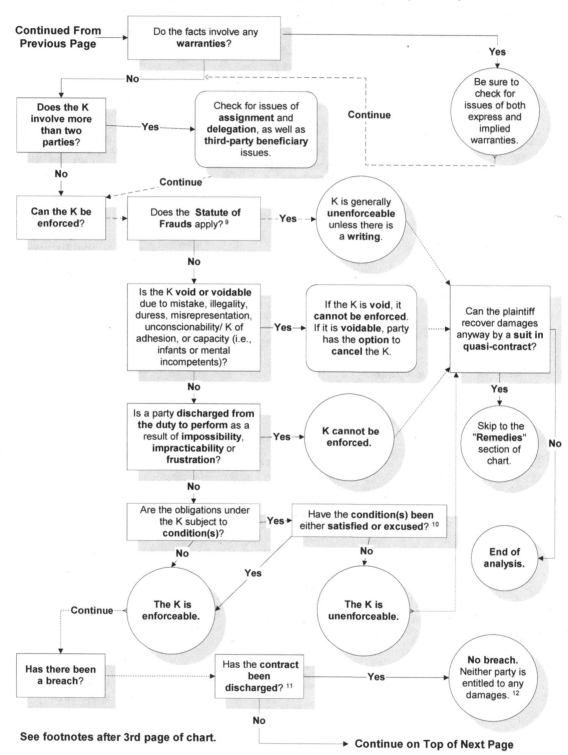

See footnotes after 3rd page of chart.

Figure 1-1
Analyzing Contracts Questions (cont.)

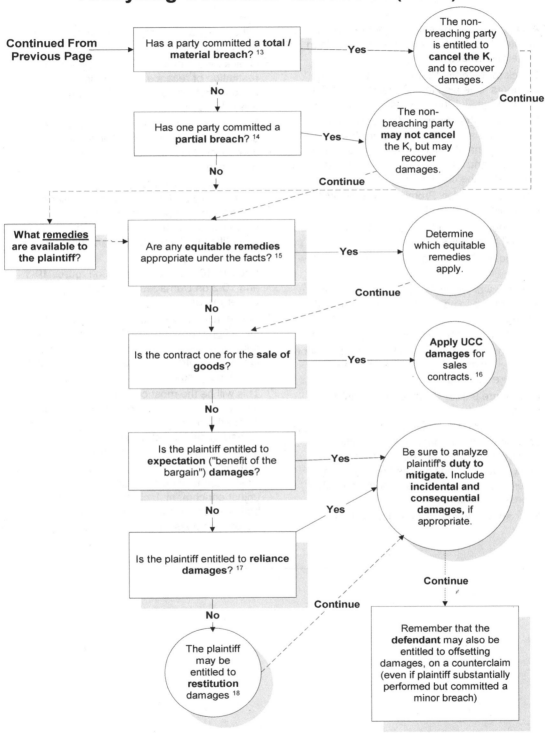

See footnotes on next page

Notes to
Figure 1-1 (Analyzing Contracts Questions)

[1] Acceptance can be either by performance (in unilateral contract) or by promise to perform (in bilateral contract).

[2] Check for both the "bargain" and "detriment" elements. See also the "Consideration" flow charts, Figs. 3-1 through 3-4.

[3] But even in the absence of a specific valid offer and/or acceptance, consider the possibility that the parties' later actions may have recognized the existence of a contract, in which case the court will enforce that contract.

[4] See Figure 4-1 for "Promises Binding Without Consideration" flow chart.

[5] See Figures 2-3 and 2-4 for "Battle of the Forms" flow charts.

[6] See Figure 6-1 for "Parol Evidence Rule" flow chart.

[7] Your answer will be "yes" if a party is trying to show the meaning of a term contained in the writing.

[8] See Ch. 6, V(B). Remember that if the conflict concerns the meaning of a key term, it may be that there was no "mutual assent" and therefore no contract.

[9] See Figure 9-1 for "Statute of Frauds" flow chart.

[10] Check for: (1) "substantial performance" of the condition (that's enough, if the condition is constructive rather express) or (2) facts that show that the condition has been waived or otherwise excused (that's enough, for either express or constructive condiitions).

[11] Your answer will be "yes" if, for example, there has been a rescission or an accord and satisfaction.

[12] Check for the possibility of a non-contractual restitution or reliance award (common where the contract was discharged for impossibility, frustration, etc.)

[13] Your answer will be "yes" if a party has not substantially performed her obligations. Be sure to include cases of anticipatory repudiation here.

[14] Your answer will be "yes" if a party has substantially performed, but nonetheless failed to comply perfectly with the contract's requirements. In that case, the other party will be entitled to damages to compensate for the non-conformity.

[15] See Ch. 10, sec. XIII. See also Figures 10-1 and 10-2 on Damages in Sales Contracts Under the UCC.

[16] These include specific performance and injunctions. Equitable remedies are rare in contracts cases. They are used most often in land sale contracts, and occasionally for sales of unique goods.

[17] This will be the most common form of damages in: (1) suits brought on the contract, where the plaintiff's lost profits (expectation measure) can't be shown with sufficient certainty; and (2) suits brought in quasi-contract.

[18] Restitution is used most often to prevent unjust enrichment, including cases in which both parties have been discharged (e.g., cases of impossibility or frustration).

Figure 2-1

Offer and Acceptance #1
(The Offer)

A valid offer is one that instills in the offeree the power to enter into a contract simply by making his acceptance. Use the chart below to help determine whether or not there is a valid offer under your facts.[1] (The chart uses the word "offer" to refer to expressions that may or may not be true offers. Where an expression is a true offer -- i.e. a statement that if accepted will automatically form a contract -- the chart calls that expression a "valid" offer.)

handwritten annotations (top right):
- See Notes
- Not relevant
- EXPRESS INTENT BY OFFEROR;
- RETAIN POWER OF ACCEPTANCE IN OFFEREE;
- AND ALL NECESSARY TERMS OF DEAL

IS THERE A VALID OFFER?
To find out, start here

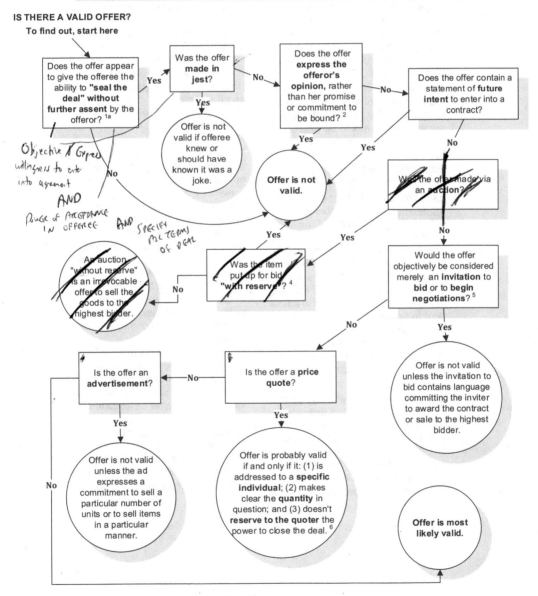

handwritten annotations (left/center):
- Objective / Express willingness to enter into agreement AND
- POWER OF ACCEPTANCE IN OFFEREE AND SPECIFY ALL TERMS OF DEAL

See footnotes on next page

Notes to
Figure 2-1 (The Offer)

[1] This flowchart (and Figs. 2-2 through 2-5 below) will help you determine whether a contract can be based on the parties' respective offer and acceptance. However, keep in mind that sometimes the parties never make a true "offer" and/or a true "acceptance," but a contract is created anyway by their conduct. For instance, several UCC provisions allow the court to find a contract based solely on the parties' conduct. See Ch. 2, V(I).

[1a] This box explains a threshold requirement that any expression has to meet in order to be a valid offer: the expression has to be worded by the "offeror" in such a way that the "offeree" can cause a contract to come into force without any further action or consent by the offeror.

Example ("no futher assent needed" requirement met): *A* writes to *B*, "I'll sell you my 2014 Honda Civic for $8,500. To accept, deliver a cashier's check for this amount to my house before Saturday." Since *A*'s language indicates that a contract of sale would come into force as soon as *B* delivers the check (without *A*'s having a final right to approve or disapprove the deal once *B* delivers the check), the "no further assent needed" requirement imposed by this box is satisfied -- therefore, *A*'s statement is a valid offer.

Example ("no futher assent needed" requirement *not* met): *A* writes to *B*, "I'm probably willing to sell my 2014 Honda this week, if I can get at least $8,500. If you're interested, send me an email with your proposed price and warranty terms by Saturday, and let's discuss your proposal by phone if and when I get it." By this language, *A* has indicated that even if *B* sends a proposal by the Saturday deadline to buy the car for $8,500 without warranties, *A* wants to have a follow-up phone conversation before any deal becomes final. The need for this phone conversation (something that can't happen without *A*'s participation) means that *A* has *not* authorized *B* to "seal the deal" without further action by *A*; therefore, *A*'s writing is not a valid offer. (Instead, it merely solicits *B* to make an offer, which *A* might or might not "accept" in the follow-up conversation.)

[2] For example, a surgeon's statement, "if I operate, it will take about four days for the boy's hand to heal" is an opinion, not a promise. See, e.g., *Hawkins v. McGee.*

[3] This and the two succeeding auction-related boxes assume that you're analyzing whether a seller has made an offer. If you're analyzing whether a bidder (a would-be buyer) has made an offer, the general rule is that the bidder has the right to withdraw his bid at any time before the gavel goes down. Therefore, the mere act of bidding involves no commitment and thus no valid offer.

[4] "With reserve" means the auctioneer can withdraw the goods without consummating the sale to any bidder.

[5] For example, "I would consider $50 for this necklace" is an invitation to begin negotiations, not an offer.

[6] An example of (3) might be a statement in the quote, "All orders are subject to seller's home office approval." See Ch. 2, III(D), et seq, for more factors concerning quotes.

— See Notes

Figure 2-2
Offer and Acceptance #2
(The Acceptance)

In order for an acceptance to be valid: (1) it must be made to someone intended by the offeror to have the right to accept; and (2) it must become effective during the time in which the offeree still has the power to accept. Use the chart below to help figure out whether your facts fit these requirements. [1]

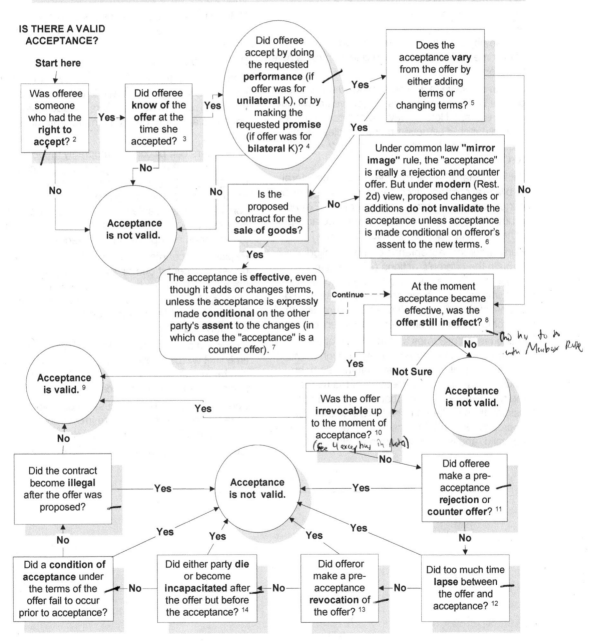

IS THERE A VALID ACCEPTANCE?

Who has to do with Mailbox Rule

(See 4 exceptions in note)

See footnotes on next page

Notes to
Figure 2-2 (The Acceptance)

[1] In addition to the requirements stated in the flowchart, the acceptance will not be valid if: (1) the deal is void for <u>indefiniteness</u>; or (2) the parties have had a fatal <u>misunderstanding</u> about a key term. See Ch. 2, sections VIII and IX, for further discussion of these issues.

[2] Use an objective test to determine whether the offeror meant for the person in question to be able to accept.

[3] Use an objective test to determine whether the offeree had knowledge. His subjective knowledge is not relevant. Note however that "standing offer" rewards offered by governmental bodies do not require advance knowledge. See Ch. 2, IV(C)(2)(a).

[4] If it is unclear whether the offer is for a unilateral or bilateral contract, acceptance can be <u>either</u> by performance or by promise to perform. (*Example:* A buyer's order for goods can usually be accepted either by shipping or by promising to ship.)

Remember that acceptance can be <u>implied</u> through the offeree's <u>actions</u> (e.g., keeping goods), under the objective theory of contracts. Also, make sure the <u>method</u> of acceptance (e.g., phone, mail, etc.) is as allowed by the offer -- the offeror is "master of his offer" in this sense.

[5] This question assumes that the terms of the "acceptance" correspond closely enough to those of the offer that it's fair to say that there's been "mutual assent," i.e., a "meeting of the minds." If the two diverge so much that there's no mutual assent, then under both the UCC and the modern approach for non-UCC cases, the "acceptance" is not valid, and is at most a counter-offer.

[6] See Rest. 2d, §§ 59 and 61, and V(N) of this chapter.

[7] See Figures 2-3 and 2-4 for UCC "Battle of the Forms" issues, then return to this chart for further analysis.

[8] Determine when acceptance became effective by referring to Figure 2-5, "The Mailbox Rule" flow chart.

[9] But see Note 1, supra.

[10] Note that an offer is still revocable even though it contains language like "I will hold this open for two weeks." True irrevocable offers include option contracts and "firm offers" by merchants under the UCC.

Also, offers can become <u>temporarily irrevocable</u> as a result of the offeree's <u>part performance</u> or <u>detrimental reliance</u>. See Ch. 2, VI(J). For instance, <u>sub-contractor bids</u> are usually considered irrevocable during the reasonable time necessary for the general contractor to obtain the job and then accept the sub-contractor's bid.

[11] Rejection or counter offer will not terminate the power to accept if offeror specifically indicates that the offer still stands, or if offeree says that although he does not now intend to accept he wishes to consider the offer further. See Rest. 2d, §§ 38(1) and (2).

[12] If offeror did not set a time limit, a "reasonable" time limit will be implied. Also, a late acceptance can be treated as a counter offer which the original offeror can then accept or reject.

[13] See Ch. 2, VI(G), for a discussion on revocation. Note that option contracts are irrevocable offers, even if the offeror purports to revoke.

[14] See Ch. 2, VI(H), and Rest. 2d, § 48.

Figure 2-3
Battle of the Forms (Part I)

Use this chart when the offer and acceptance for the sale of goods are communicated by way of **standardized forms** (i.e., purchase order for the offer and acknowledgment for the acceptance). The chart will help you most if the acceptance varies from the offer; in that situation, the chart will help you determine whether a contract has been formed, and if so, what its terms are under UCC § 2-207. (In cases involving a confirmation of an oral agreement, use Figure 2-4.)

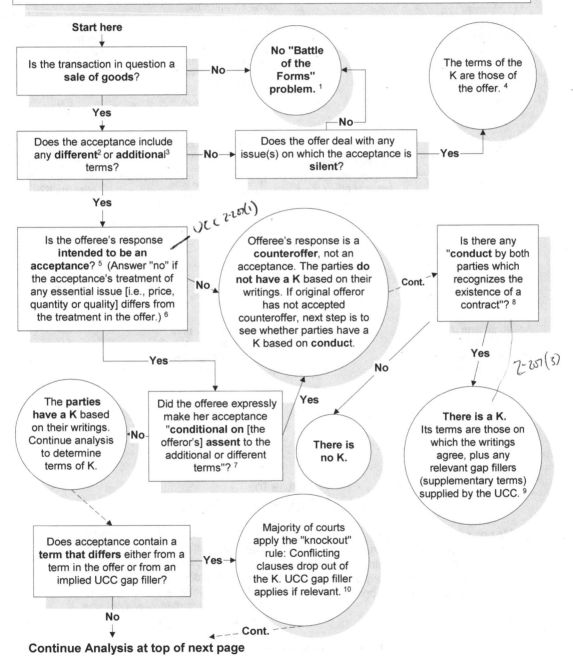

Continue Analysis at top of next page

Figure 2-3
Battle of the Forms (Part I, Cont.)

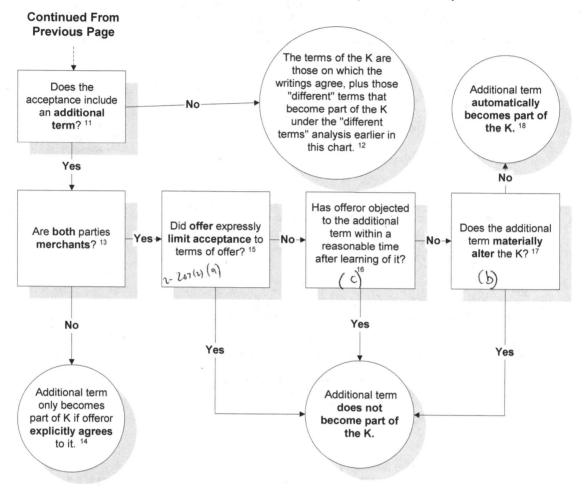

Notes to
Figure 2-3 (The Battle of Forms)

[1] In non-sale-of-goods cases where the parties have used standardized forms, a court might follow the common-law "mirror image" rule. However, many courts use the UCC's battle-of-the-forms principles in non-UCC cases.

[2] A "different" term is one that <u>directly contradicts</u> either a term in the offer or a term supplied by a UCC gap-filler. (Example of different term: purchase order [offer] says delivery to occur April 1, acknowledgement [acceptance] says delivery to occur April 15.)

Footnotes cont. on next page

Notes (cont.) to
Figure 2-3 (The Battle of Forms, Pt. I)

[3] An "additional" term is one that deals with an issue that is neither: (1) dealt with explicitly by the offer; nor (2) covered by a UCC gap-filler.

[4] The offeree is deemed to have accepted all terms of the offer, not just those addressed by the acceptance. (But check to make sure that the offeree's document matches the offer closely enough to constitute a true acceptance rather than a counter offer; see the issues covered in fn. 5, 6 and 7 below.)

[5] UCC § 2-207(1) requires a "definite and seasonable expression of acceptance."

[6] There is no gap filler regarding subject matter or quantity. Failure to agree on these terms will result in the K's being deemed unenforceable due to indefiniteness, even under the UCC.

[7] UCC § 2-207(1). To qualify, the offeree must make it clear that she does not intend to be bound at all unless the offeror agrees to the new or different terms. (Note that if the offeror does assent, the changes become part of the K and your inquiry is over.)

[8] UCC § 2-207(3) (1st sentence). *Example:* Seller's and Buyer's forms diverge too much to be offer-and-acceptance. Seller then ships goods, and Buyer receives them and uses them. The shipment and usage will together be conduct "recognizing the existence of a contract," even though there's no document that's an offer or an acceptance.

[9] UCC § 2-207(3) (2nd sentence). Examples of gap fillers include price, place/time of delivery or payment, and warranty. They can be found in UCC §§ 2-305 to 315.

[10] See Ch. 2, V(G)(1)(a). See also footnote 9 supra. Note that if the offeree's term conflicts with a gap filler, most courts hold that both are initially knocked out, but that the gap filler comes back to fill in the hole.

[11] If proposed term is "additional" to the explicit terms of the offer, but would conflict with an implied UCC gap filler, you should not treat it as an "additional" term but rather as a "different" term, and go through that analysis instead. See box that includes footnote 10.

[12] For the different-terms analysis, see the part of the chart that includes footnote 10.

[13] A "merchant" is defined in UCC § 2-104 as "a person who deals in goods of the kind or otherwise by his occupation holds himself out as having knowledge or skill peculiar to the practices or goods involved in the transaction[.]" UCC Comment 2 suggests that almost every person in business will be considered a merchant, for offer-and-acceptance purposes.

[14] Otherwise, it becomes a separate offer made by the offeree, in which she proposes additions to the K.

[15] UCC § 2-207(2)(a). Language like "acceptance of this offer is limited to the terms of this offer" will suffice.

[16] UCC § 2-207(2)(c). Note that silence by the offeror regarding the additional terms added by the offeree will act as an acceptance of those terms.

[17] UCC § 2-207(2)(b). See Comments 4 and 5 for examples that do and don't materially alter the offer; also Ch. 2, V(F)(4)(b). Many issues are gray areas that will have to be argued both ways on an exam.

[18] UCC 2-207(2), 2nd sentence.

Figure 2-4
Battle of the Forms (Part II):
Confirmation of an oral agreement, under UCC § 2-207 [1]

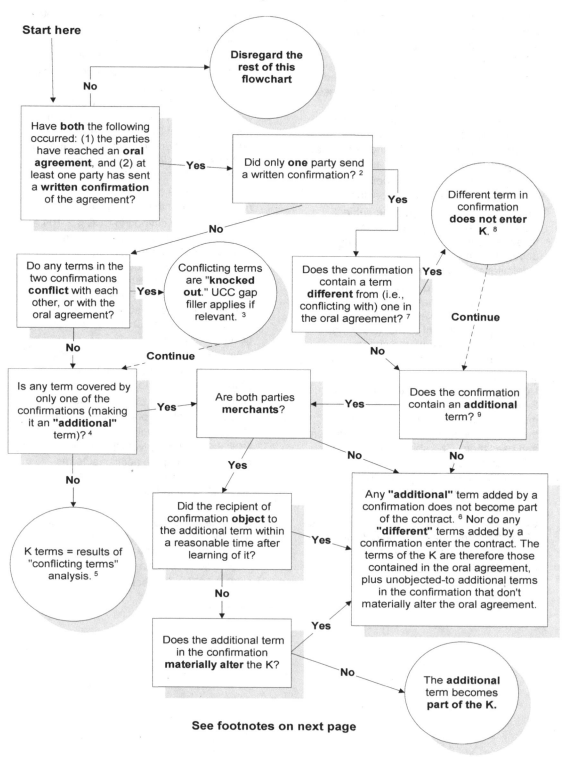

Start here

Disregard the rest of this flowchart

No

Have **both** the following occurred: (1) the parties have reached an **oral agreement**, and (2) at least one party has sent a **written confirmation** of the agreement?

Yes → Did only **one** party send a written confirmation? [2]

No

Do any terms in the two confirmations **conflict** with each other, or with the oral agreement?

Yes ▶ Conflicting terms are "**knocked out**." UCC gap filler applies if relevant. [3]

Yes → Does the confirmation contain a term **different** from (i.e., conflicting with) one in the oral agreement? [7]

Different term in confirmation **does not enter K**. [8]

Continue

No (from "Do any terms...")

No (from "Does the confirmation contain a term different...")

Is any term covered by only one of the confirmations (making it an **"additional"** term)? [4]

Continue

Are both parties **merchants**?

Yes ← Does the confirmation contain an **additional** term? [9]

Yes →

No

No

No (from "Is any term covered...")

K terms = results of "conflicting terms" analysis. [5]

Yes (from "Are both parties merchants?")

Did the recipient of confirmation **object** to the additional term within a reasonable time after learning of it?

Yes → Any **"additional"** term added by a confirmation does not become part of the contract. [6] Nor do any **"different"** terms added by a confirmation enter the contract. The terms of the K are therefore those contained in the oral agreement, plus unobjected-to additional terms in the confirmation that don't materially alter the oral agreement.

No

Does the additional term in the confirmation **materially alter** the K?

Yes →

No → The **additional** term becomes **part of the K.**

See footnotes on next page

Notes to
Figure 2-4 (Battle of the Forms, Part 2)

[1] The major source within § 2-207 on the effect of confirmations is Official Comment 6 to that section.

[2] Ignore any "expressly conditional" language in confirmations (e.g., "The deal is expressly conditional on assent to the additional or different terms contained in this confirmation"). Such language has no effect. See Ch. 2, V(J)(2)(a).

[3] See UCC § 2-207, Comment 6. If the conflict is between a term in one confirmation and the oral agreement, the orally-agreed-upon term will survive. As to gap fillers, examples include price, place/time of delivery or payment, and warranty; gap fillers can be found in §§ 2-305 to 315.

[4] For the term to be an "additional term," it must be both: (1) missing from the other confirmation and; (2) not one that would be supplied by a UCC gap filler. (If the same term would be supplied by a gap filler and the other confirmation is silent on the subject, then the two confirmations in effect agree on the term.)

[5] In other words, if you get to this circle, you should only have to worry about "different" (conflicting) terms that are added by a confirmation, and such terms never become part of the contract. See footnote 3 supra.

[6] In other words, an additional term added by a confirmation is treated as a proposal for addition to the contract, and under the general rules of § 2-207, additional terms don't enter the contract if they would materially alter it, or the other party objects within a reasonable time. Ch.2, V(J)(1), V(J)(4).

[7] A "different" term is one that directly contradicts a term in the oral agreement or a term supplied by a UCC gap filler (e.g., delivery on April 1 vs. April 15).

[8] This is true even if the party receiving the confirmation fails to object.

[9] An "additional term" is one about which the oral agreement was silent and which would not be supplied by a UCC gap filler.

Figure 2-5
The Mailbox Rule: Determining When an Acceptance Becomes Effective[1]

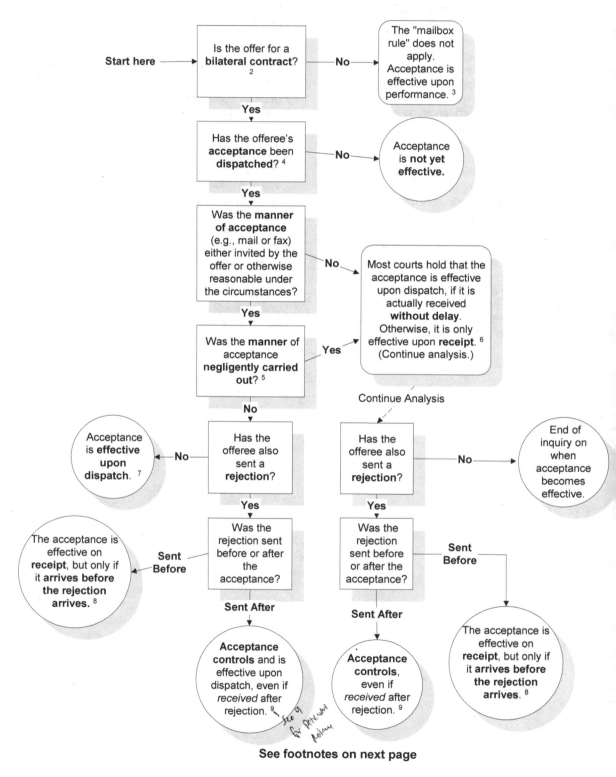

See footnotes on next page

Notes to
Figure 2-5 (The Mailbox Rule)

[1] This analysis does not apply to option contracts. Option contracts are the exception to the rule in that acceptance of an option contact is effective only upon receipt of acceptance by the offeror.

[2] An offer for a bilateral contract can be accepted by a promise to perform. A unilateral contract offer can be accepted only by performance. If the offer can be accepted by either performance or promise, and the offeree purports to accept by promise, treat this question as having a "yes" answer.

[3] Remember, however, that under Rest. 2d, §45, if the offeree to a unilateral contract begins to perform, this creates an option contract. In other words, the offer becomes temporarily irrevocable. See Ch. 2, VI(K)(1). Be sure to distinguish between the actual start of performance and the making of mere preparations to perform. See Ch. 2, VI(K)(1)(b)(ii).

[4] "Dispatch" includes physically dropping a letter into the mailbox, transmitting the acceptance electronically via fax or e-mail, and communicating the acceptance verbally by phone or in person.

[5] For example, was the letter misaddressed?

[6] See Ch. 2, VII(C)(1).

[7] However, the offer itself can always override this result by clearly stating a different rule (i.e., that acceptance will be effective only upon receipt).

[8] In other words, if the acceptance arrives before the rejection, it's effective upon receipt. If it arrives after the rejection, the acceptance is completely ineffective. See Ch. 2, VII(E)(1),

[9] See Ch. 2, VII(E)(2). However, if the rejection is received first even though sent second, and the offeror relies on it, the offeree may be estopped from trying to enforce the contract; see Ch. 2, VII(E)(2)(b).

Detrimental
reliance

Figure 3-1
Consideration -- An Overview

This chart will help you determine whether there is consideration for the promise made by the promis*or* (who is usually the defendant). In other words, it helps you decide whether the promis*ee* (the person to whom the promisor has made the promise) has given consideration in return for the promisor's promise. Except for promises binding without consideration (discussed in the next chapter), the promisor's promise will not be binding unless the promisee has given consideration in return for that promise.

You will find this chart most useful in bilateral contracts (i.e., contracts in which the parties have made an exchange of promises), though it's also usable in unilateral-contract situations. In bilateral situations, you should test each party as both promisor and promisee (though if one party is clearly a potential defendant and the other isn't, you should concentrate on the defendant as promisor and the plaintiff as promisee.)

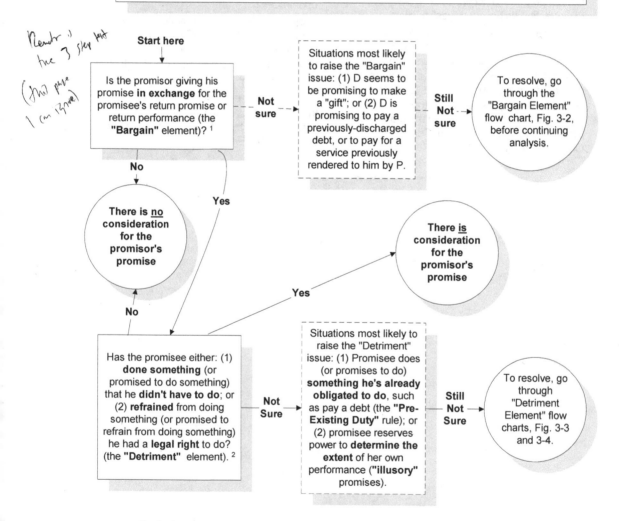

Footnotes:

[1] For a general discussion of the "bargain element" of consideration, see secs. II and III, *infra*.

[2] For a general discussion of the "detriment element" of consideration, see the text beginning *infra*, sec. IV, and running to the end of the Chapter.

Figure 3-2
The Bargain Element of Consideration

Part A
Use this part for fact patterns that may involve an
unenforceable <u>promise to make a gift</u>

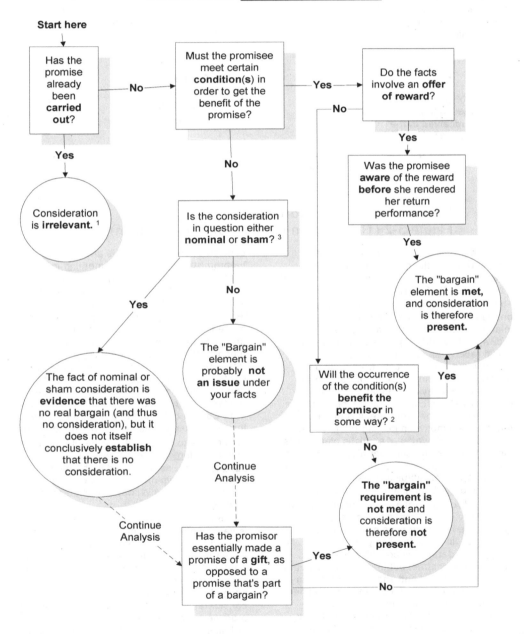

See Part B and footnotes,
both on next page

Part B
Use this part for fact patterns that may involve
"past consideration" [4]

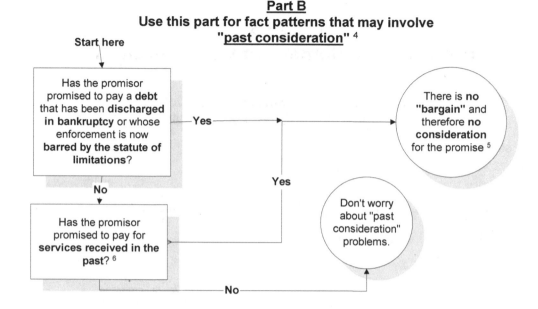

Notes to
Figure 3-2 (The Bargain Element of Consideration)

[1] Only the promise to make a gift requires consideration. If the gift has already been given, the giver cannot "rescind" and try to get it back. See Ch. 3, II(H).

[2] The benefit does not have to be an economic one to be consideration -- it can be an intangible one. See, for example, *Hamer v. Sidway*, Ch. 3, II(C)(2), where the uncle (D) would receive an intangible benefit (constituting consideration) from having his nephew (P) not smoke, drink or gamble. As long as there is evidence that the promisor bargained at least slightly for the benefit he is to receive from the promisee, it is irrelevant that his main motive in making the promise was altruism. However, if altruistic pleasure is the only motive, the consideration in question will fail the Bargain element because a person who seeks purely altruistic pleasure is not deemed to be "bargaining" for that benefit.

3 "Nominal" consideration is consideration that is relatively insignificant when measured against the return promise opr performance. (*Example:* "In consideration of $1.00 paid...") Sham consideration is consideration that is stated in the contract but that is never actually paid. Both nominal and sham consideration are evidence of lack of a bargain, but neither the fact that the value received by the promisor was nominal nor the fact that that value was recited in the contract but never paid automatically means that there was no

consideration -- the issue is always, Did thepromisor "bargain" for something in return for his promise? That's why you must continue your analysis even after answering yes to the "nominal or sham" question.

[4] "Past consideration" involves a promise that is made in return for a detriment that the promisee has already suffered, or in return for a benefit that the promisee has already conferred. See Ch. 3, III. Promises to pay debts that are no longer legally enforceable, and promises to pay for services that were rendered under circumstances that made the promisor not obligated to pay for them, are the prime illustrations, as shown in the chart.

[5] But be sure to check out whether the promise may be enforceable even without consideration, as described in the next chapter. For help on this issue, go to the "Promises Binding Without Consideration" flowchart, Fig. 4-1.

[6] The only time a "yes" answer to this question is very significant is if the promisor was not obliged to pay for the services at the time they were rendered. (*Example:* The services were rendered to a friend of the promisor, not to the promisor herself, so the promisor was not obliged to pay -- here, there is no consideration for the promisor's after-the-fact promise to pay for the services [but the promise might be enforceable even without consideration].)

Figure 3-3
The Detriment Element of Consideration[1]

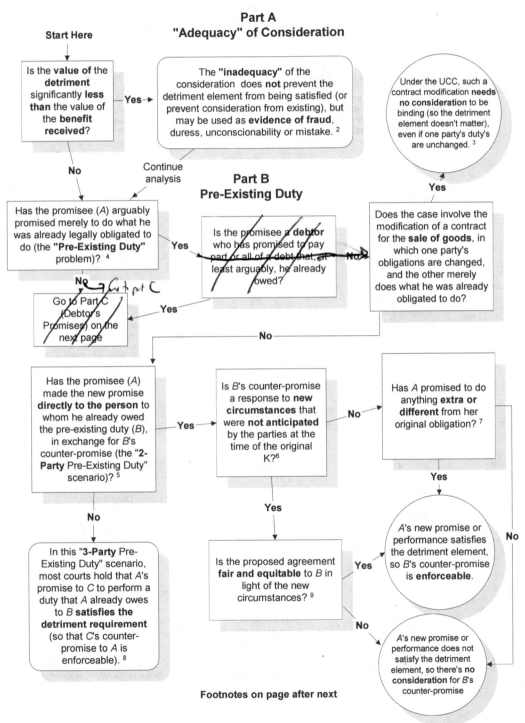

Part A
"Adequacy" of Consideration

Start Here

Is the **value of** the **detriment** significantly **less than** the value of the **benefit received**?

—**Yes**→ The **"inadequacy"** of the consideration does **not** prevent the detriment element from being satisfied (or prevent consideration from existing), but may be used as **evidence of fraud**, duress, unconscionability or mistake. [2]

Under the UCC, such a contract modification **needs no consideration** to be binding (so the detriment element doesn't matter), even if one party's duty's are unchanged. [3]

No / **Continue analysis**

Part B
Pre-Existing Duty

Has the promisee (*A*) arguably promised merely to do what he was already legally obligated to do (the **"Pre-Existing Duty"** problem)? [4]

—**Yes**→ Is the promisee a **debtor** who has promised to pay part or all of a debt that, at least arguably, he already owed?

No ~~Go to pt C~~

—**No**→ Does the case involve the modification of a contract for the **sale of goods**, in which one party's obligations are changed, and the other merely does what he was already obligated to do?

Yes ↑

Go to Part C (Debtor's Promises) on the next page

—**Yes**→

No

Has the promisee (*A*) made the new promise **directly to the person** to whom he already owed the pre-existing duty (*B*), in exchange for *B*'s counter-promise (the **"2-Party** Pre-Existing Duty" scenario)? [5]

—**Yes**→ Is *B*'s counter-promise a response to **new circumstances** that were **not anticipated** by the parties at the time of the original K? [6]

—**No**→ Has *A* promised to do anything **extra or different** from her original obligation? [7]

No

Yes ↓

In this **"3-Party** Pre-Existing Duty" scenario, most courts hold that *A*'s promise to *C* to perform a duty that *A* already owes to *B* **satisfies the detriment requirement** (so that *C*'s counter-promise to *A* is enforceable). [8]

Yes ↓

Is the proposed agreement **fair and equitable** to *B* in light of the new circumstances? [9]

—**Yes**→ *A*'s new promise or performance satisfies the detriment element, so *B*'s counter-promise is **enforceable**.

No →

No ↓

A's new promise or performance does not satisfy the detriment element, so there's **no consideration** for *B*'s counter-promise

Footnotes on page after next

Figure 3-3
The Detriment Element of Consideration
(Cont.)

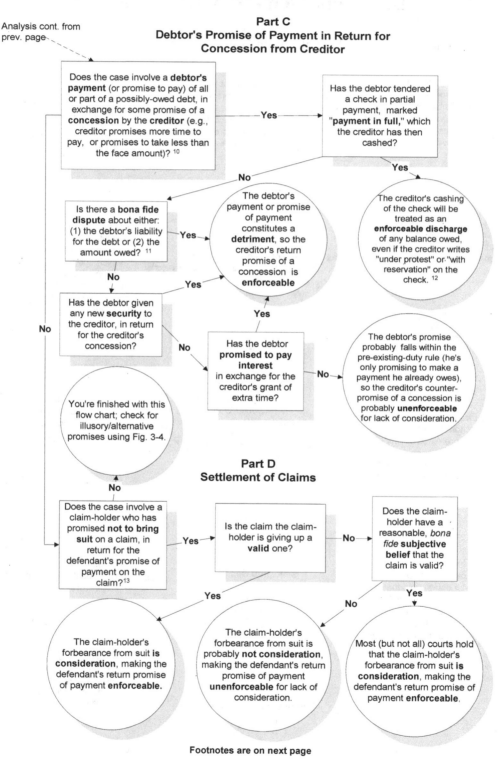

Part C
Debtor's Promise of Payment in Return for
Concession from Creditor

Analysis cont. from prev. page

Does the case involve a **debtor's payment** (or promise to pay) of all or part of a possibly-owed debt, in exchange for some promise of a **concession** by the creditor (e.g., creditor promises more time to pay, or promises to take less than the face amount)? [10]

— **Yes** → Has the debtor tendered a check in partial payment, marked **"payment in full,"** which the creditor has then cashed?

— **No** →

Yes → The creditor's cashing of the check will be treated as an **enforceable discharge** of any balance owed, even if the creditor writes "under protest" or "with reservation" on the check. [12]

Is there a **bona fide dispute** about either: (1) the debtor's liability for the debt or (2) the amount owed? [11]

— **Yes** → The debtor's payment or promise of payment constitutes a **detriment**, so the creditor's return promise of a concession is **enforceable**

No

Has the debtor given any new **security** to the creditor, in return for the creditor's concession?

— **Yes** →

— **No** → Has the debtor **promised to pay interest** in exchange for the creditor's grant of extra time?

— **Yes** →

— **No** → The debtor's promise probably falls within the pre-existing-duty rule (he's only promising to make a payment he already owes), so the creditor's counter-promise of a concession is probably **unenforceable** for lack of consideration.

You're finished with this flow chart; check for illusory/alternative promises using Fig. 3-4.

No

Part D
Settlement of Claims

Does the case involve a claim-holder who has promised **not to bring suit** on a claim, in return for the defendant's promise of payment on the claim? [13]

— **Yes** → Is the claim the claim-holder is giving up a **valid** one?

— **No** → Does the claim-holder have a reasonable, *bona fide* **subjective belief** that the claim is valid?

Yes → The claim-holder's forbearance from suit **is consideration**, making the defendant's return promise of payment **enforceable**.

No → The claim-holder's forbearance from suit is probably **not consideration**, making the defendant's return promise of payment **unenforceable** for lack of consideration.

Yes → Most (but not all) courts hold that the claim-holder's forbearance from suit **is consideration**, making the defendant's return promise of payment **enforceable**.

Footnotes are on next page

Notes to
Figure 3-3 (The Detriment Element of Consideration)

[1] This chart covers most, but not all, aspects of the Detriment element. It covers: (1) "adequacy" of the consideration (in Part A), (2) the Pre-Existing Duty Rule (Part B); (3) Debtor-Creditor agreements (Part C); and (4) Settlement of Claims (Part D). It does not cover Illusory and Alternative Promises (as to which, see Ch. 3, VII and Fig. 3-4), Implied Promises (Ch. 3, VII), or Requirement and Output Contracts (Ch. 3, VIII).

[2] See Ch. 3, IV(E)(2).

[3] See UCC § 2-209(1). The modification must be made in good faith and it must not violate any express terms of the contract, such as a "no oral modifications" clause.

[4] See Ch. 3, V(A).

[5] The most common examples of this are: (1) construction cases in which the contractor tries to get more money for completing the work already contracted for; and (2) cases involving rewards or bonuses for work already required of the promisee (e.g., a police officer cannot enforce a promise to pay a reward for catching a criminal the officer was already required to try to catch).

[6] *Example:* Contractor agrees to drill a water well on O's property for $1,000. Contractor unexpectedly hits solid rock, and doesn't want to continue for the original fee; O agrees to pay $2,000 instead of $1,000 if Contractor will complete the work. As shown in next two boxes, if the revised K is fair to O, it will be enforced against O.

[7] In order to answer "yes," the change in obligation must be more than a mere pretense. You should answer "no" if the new obligation is less than the original (e.g., an agreement to accept partial payment of a debt in satisfaction of the whole debt).

[8] See Ch. 3, V(F). Example: Sub-Contractor (A in the chart) originally contracts with Contractor (B) to do work for Owner (C). Owner worries that Sub won't perform; Sub promises Owner that he'll do what he promised Contractor he'd do. Owner can enforce this promise, even though Sub was only promising Owner that he'd do what he was already obligated to do by the Contractor-Sub contract.

[9] See Rest. 2d, § 89(a).

[10] A debtor's promise to pay the arguably-owed debt is really just a special case of the Pre-Existing Duty Rule. However, we present the debtor's-promise scenario separately in this chart (rather than as part of Part B on the Pre-Existing Duty Rule), because of the special rules that have evolved to handle it.

[11] In the situation described in (2) (amount of debt is in question), the debt is called an "unliquidated" debt.

[12] See UCC § 3-311 and Ch. 3, V(C)(5)(b). However, the discharge occurs only if: (1) the debtor acts in "good faith" (i.e., he really believes that he owes less than the full amount, or he is not financially able to pay the full amount); and (2) the words "payment in full" or the equivalent are written by the debtor conspicuously on the check, or in a letter accompanying the check.

[13] This "Settlement of Claims" discussion applies mainly to non-contract claims, such as tort claims.

Figure 3-4
Illusory and Alternative Promises

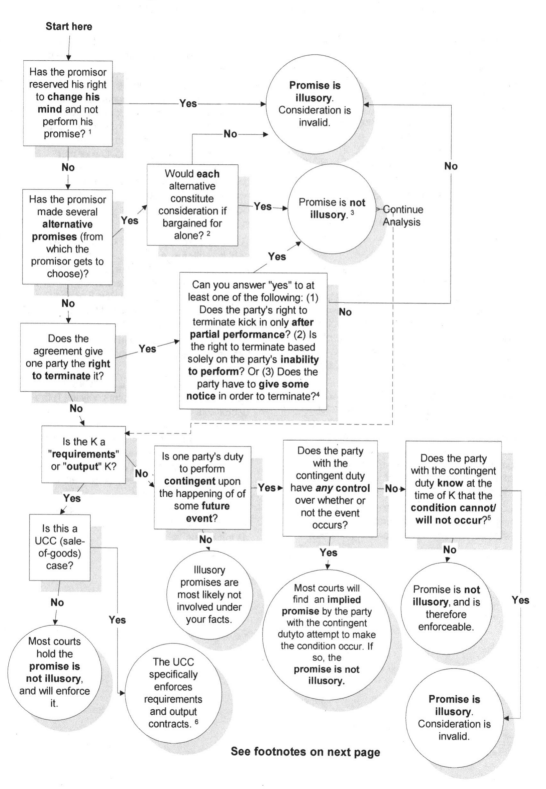

See footnotes on next page

Notes to
Figure 3-4 (Illusory and Alternative Promises)

[1] But distinguish this "change of mind" situation from the case where the promisor merely has a right to "terminate the contract" (dealt with in the box that includes footnote 4 below). The true "change of mind" promise is always illusory, whereas a promise that's subject to termination of the contract may or may not be illusory, depending on the facts.

[2] See Rest. 2d, §77 and Ch. 3, VII(C).

[3] Arrival at this circle merely means that the termination right or the existence of alternatives does not <u>automatically</u> make the promise illusory; the promise may be illusory for other reasons. Therefore, you should continue your analysis by advancing to the "requirements or output contracts" box, below.

[4] See Ch. 3, VII(D) for a discussion of the right to terminate.

[5] See Rest. 2d, § 76(1).

[6] See UCC § 2-306. Good faith is implied in the determination of the output or requirements quantity.

Figure 4-1

Promises Binding Without Consideration

In general, a contract requires consideration in order to be binding. There are several exceptions to this rule, however. If your fact pattern failed the consideration test found in Figures 3-1 through 3-4, use the chart below to see if the facts fall within one of the exceptions to the consideration requirement.

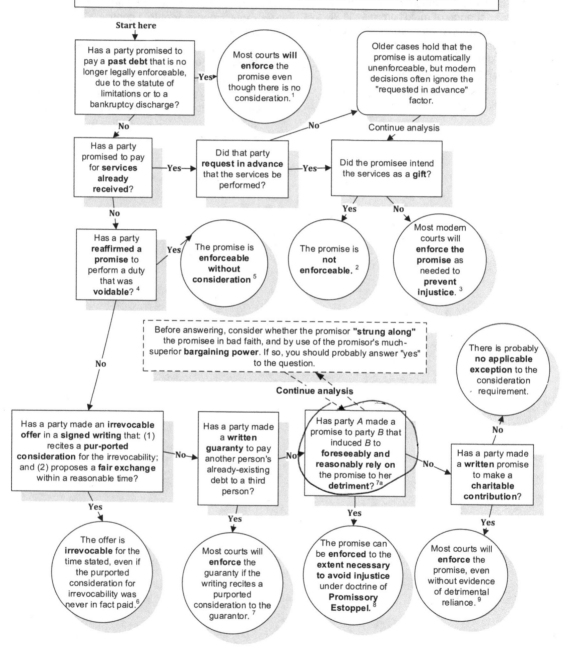

Start here

Has a party promised to pay a **past debt** that is no longer legally enforceable, due to the statute of limitations or to a bankruptcy discharge?

—Yes→ Most courts **will enforce** the promise even though there is no consideration.[1]

Older cases hold that the promise is automatically unenforceable, but modern decisions often ignore the "requested in advance" factor.

Continue analysis

No

Has a party promised to pay for **services already received**?

—Yes→ Did that party **request in advance** that the services be performed?

—Yes→ Did the promisee intend the services as a **gift**?

Yes → The promise is **not enforceable.**[2]

No → Most modern courts will **enforce the promise** as needed to **prevent injustice.**[3]

No

Has a party **reaffirmed a promise** to perform a duty that was **voidable?**[4]

—Yes→ The promise is **enforceable without consideration**[5]

No

Before answering, consider whether the promisor **"strung along"** the promisee in bad faith, and by use of the promisor's much-superior **bargaining power**. If so, you should probably answer "yes" to the question.

Continue analysis

There is probably **no applicable exception** to the consideration requirement.

No

Has a party made an **irrevocable offer** in a **signed writing** that: (1) recites a **pur-ported consideration** for the irrevocability; and (2) proposes a **fair exchange** within a reasonable time?

—No→ Has a party made a **written guaranty** to pay another person's already-existing debt to a third person?

—No→ Has party *A* made a promise to party *B* that induced *B* to **foreseeably and reasonably rely on** the promise to her **detriment?**[7a]

—No→ Has a party made a **written** promise to make a **charitable contribution?**

Yes → The offer is **irrevocable** for the time stated, even if the purported consideration for irrevocability was never in fact paid.[6]

Yes → Most courts will **enforce** the guaranty if the writing recites a purported consideration to the guarantor.[7]

Yes → The promise can be **enforced** to the **extent necessary to avoid injustice** under doctrine of **Promissory Estoppel.**[8]

Yes → Most courts will **enforce** the promise, even without evidence of detrimental reliance.[9]

See footnotes on next page

Notes to
Figure 4-1 (Promises Binding Without Consideration)

[1] See Rest. 2d, §§ 82, 83. Note that if a party promises to pay an amount less than that originally due, the other party can only enforce the payment of the new amount promised. See Ch. 4, I(C).

[2] See Rest. 2d, § 86(2)(a) (fact that promisee intended a gift is dispositive).

[3] The Second Restatement/emerging modern view is that the promise is enforceable to the "extent necessary to prevent injustice." Rest. 2d, § 86(1). Enforcement is especially likely if the benefit of the services, and the cost of rendering them, are both <u>substantial.</u>

[4] Examples include promises to perform duties that were originally promised through fraud or duress, and promises made during infancy.

[5] See Rest. 2d, § 85.

[6] See Rest. 2d, § 87(1)(a). See also Ch. 4, IV(C).

[7] See Rest. 2d § 88(a); Ch. 4, IV(D). The guarantee will be enforced even if the recited consideration was never in fact paid.

[7a] A "yes" answer makes it likely that the court will uphold a claim for promissory estoppel, as detailed in the box containing note 8. (But "stringing along" is not a *necessary* component of successful a p.e. claim; for instance, in note 8 below, Examples (1) and (2) would not generally involve a stringing along of the promisee by a promisor having greater bargaining power.)

<u>Example 1 of "stringing along"</u>: *O*, a home owner, has a mortage with *B*, a bank. The mortgage is not now in default, but *O* is short of money. *O* asks for a reduction of payments. *B* responds, "We can't consider any mortgage relief until you are actually in default. Once you're in default, if you submit detailed financial information, we will seriously consider reducing your monthly payments." *O* lets a default occur (which O could

have avoided, though with sacrifice), and submits detailed financial information to justify the payment-reduction request. *B* never seriously considers reducing the required payments, and attempts to foreclose on the mortgage. On these facts, a court might well conclude that *B* used the promise of considering a reduction, plus *B*'s superior bargaining power, to "string along" *O* and to induce the default. If so, the court might well recognize *O*'s action for promissory estoppel, and require *B* to offer *O* a modification. (For more illustrations of p.e., see note 6 below.)

<u>Example 2 of "stringing along"</u>: See the "promise of franchise or license" scenario summarized in note 8, Example (3), below. Typically, the party promising the franchise or license will have much greater bargaining power than the promisee (the would-be franchisee or licensee), and the promisor will drag out the negotiations for a long time before the promisor decides not to grant the promised status.

[8] See Rest. 2d, §90(1) and Ch. 4, V. The full contractual measure of damages is not usually available under these circumstances. Most courts will award reliance or restitution damages instead.

<u>Examples where p.e. will apply</u>: (1) a promise to make a monetary gift, which reasonably induces the promisee to spend (or commit to spend) the money; (2) a sub-contractor's bid, which reasonably induces the general contractor to rely on the bid in submitting his own binding (and successful) bid; and (3) a company's promise to award the promisee a franchise, license or other major contract, which induces the promisee to quit another job, invest, or otherwise foreseeably rely on the promise.

[9] See Rest. 2d, § 90(2); also Ch. 4, V(E)(2).

Figure 6-1
The Parol Evidence Rule [1]

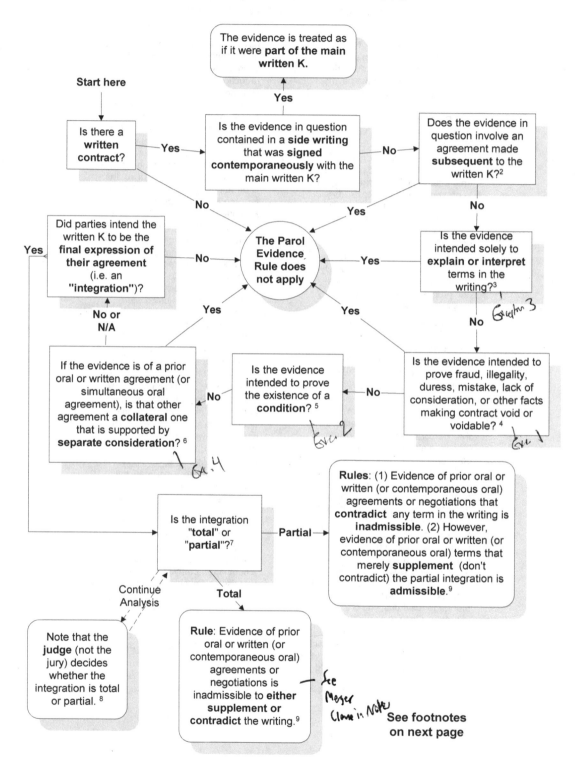

See footnotes
on next page

Notes to
Figure 6-1 (Parol Evidence Rule)

[1] Use this chart to see whether evidence can be introduced to *supplement* or *contradict* a written contract. To determine whether evidence can be introduced to *interpret* the meaning of terms contained in the writing, see Ch. 6, V.

[2] Remember that evidence of subsequent agreements is never barred by the parol evidence rule. This is true even if the subsequent agreement is oral (but the oral agreement won't be allowed in evidence if there's a valid "no oral modifications" clause in the original written agreement.)

[3] See Ch. 6, V.

[4] The parol evidence rule never prevents the introduction of evidence to prove that no valid contract exists or that the contract is voidable.

[5] This rule is usually held to apply to two different types of conditions: (1) conditions to the contract's very existence; and (2) conditions to a party's duty of performance.

[6] See Ch. 6, IV(C).

[7] A "total integration" is a document intended by the parties to include all details of their agreement. A "partial integration" is a document intended by the parties to include some — but not all — details of their agreement.

The more elaborate and/or formal the contract, the more likely it is to be a total integration. Also, where an oral agreement is shown to have been reached contemporaneously with a written one, some courts treat the oral agreement as evidence that the writing was not intended to be a total integration (thus allowing evidence of supplemental terms from the oral agreement to be admitted).

[8] The judge (not jury) also decides: (1) whether the writing is an integration (final expression of agreement) at all; and (2) whether a given piece of evidence would contradict, supplement, or merely interpret the writing.

[9] These rules apply under the UCC as well as at common law; see UCC § 2-202.

Figure 7-1
Breach under the UCC,
Where a Seller Ships
Nonconforming Goods

Use this chart to analyze the parties' rights when a seller ships non-conforming goods. A key theme of this chart is that the common-law "perfect tender" rule -- under which a seller could permanently reject goods and cancel the contract, even if the non-conformity was minor -- has been effectively abolished by the UCC.

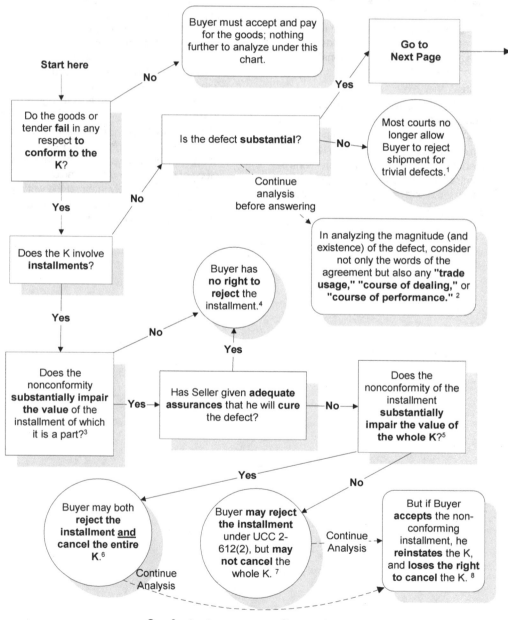

See footnotes on page after next

Figure 7-1 (Cont.)
Breach under the UCC, Where a Seller
Ships Nonconforming Goods

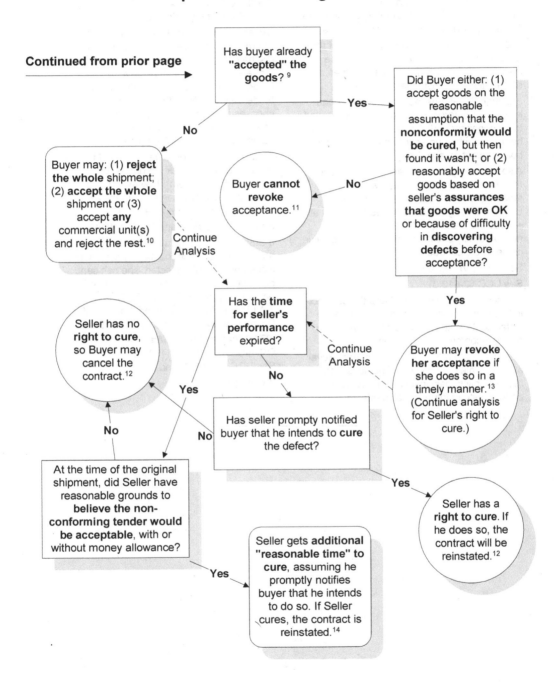

See footnotes on next page

Notes to
Figure 7-1 (Breach by Seller)

[1] See Ch. 7, VI(D)(2)(a) and (b).

[2] See UCC §1-303; Ch. 7, VI(D)(2)(b). See also Ch. 6, VI(B)(1), for definitions of the terms.

[3] That is, does the defect deprive Buyer of the benefit she reasonably expected from the installment? See Ch. 7, VI(C), for further explanation of "substantially impair."

[4] Although Buyer must accept the goods and keep the K in force, Buyer may still be entitled to damages for partial breach, to compensate her for the minor non-conformity. Be sure to point this out on any essay exam.

Also, if Seller gives assurances of cure and then fails to carry out the cure within a reasonable time, treat this the same as if Seller had not given assurances of cure at all — proceed to the question of whether the nonconformity substantially impaired the value of the whole contract.

[5] See Ch. 7, VI(D)(3).

[6] See UCC §2-612(3).

[7] In other words, Buyer must keep the contract in force, and must accept future conforming installments, just as if there had never been any non-conforming installment.

[8] See UCC §2-612(3), second sentence. Buyer also reinstates the contract if he sues with respect only to past installments, or demands performance of future installments. Id.

[9] See UCC §2-606(a) and Ch. 7, VI(D)(4)(b) for definitions of "acceptance."

[10] "Reject" in this context means Buyer can return goods to seller and be completely discharged from the contract. In order for the rejection to be valid, however, it must be done within a reasonable time after tender/delivery. Note that even if Buyer chooses to reject, she may be entitled to other remedies as well, such as a suit for damages. See Ch. 7, VI(D)(8).

[11] Thus it is too late for Buyer to cancel the contract and give back the goods (or refuse to pay for them). However, Buyer may still recover damages, perhaps as an offset against the purchase price.

[12] See UCC §2-508(1) and Ch. 7, VI(D)(6).

[13] If Buyer successfully revokes the acceptance, she's in the same position as if she had properly rejected: she can send back the goods, cancel the contract, and pay nothing. See UCC §2-608(2), and Ch. 7, VI(D)(5). But keep in mind that even if Buyer may revoke the acceptance, Seller may have the right to cure, just as in the ordinary rejection scenario.

[14] See UCC §2-508(2) and Ch. 7, VI(D)(6)(b).

Figure 9-1
The Statute of Frauds

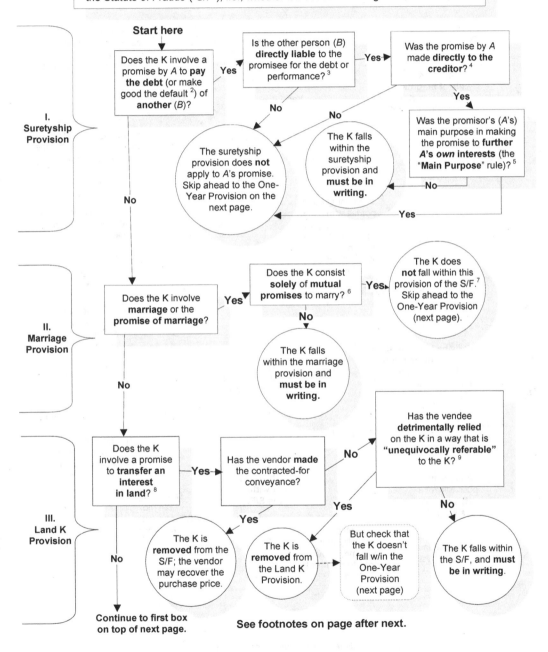

See footnotes on page after next.

Figure 9-1
The Statute of Frauds (Cont.)

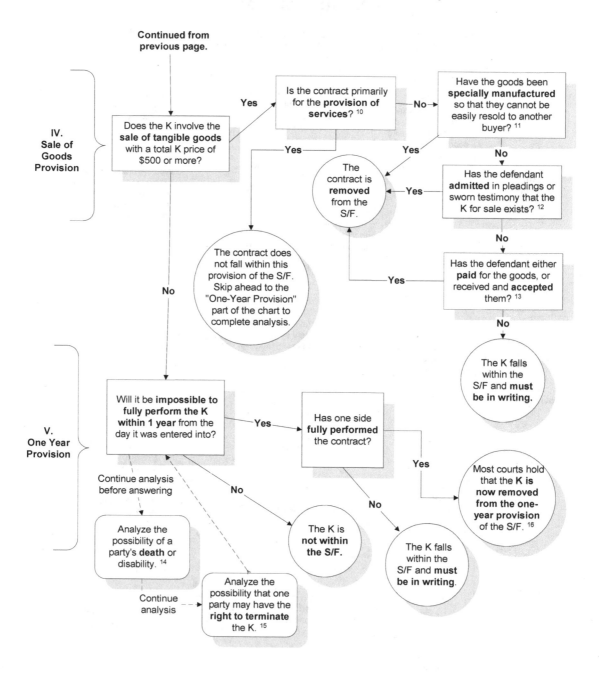

See footnotes on next page

Notes to
Figure 9-1 (Statute of Frauds)

[1] You can skim the five main "parts" on the left and jump into the chart wherever your facts apply. However, keep in mind that your contract can fall within more than one provision (e.g., a contract for the sale of goods can also fall within the one-year provision), so check each of the 5 parts.

[2] A "default" is any contractual obligation that the obligor fails to perform. The obligation can be something other than the mere payment of money, from painting a house to providing shipping services. The surety's obligation may be to pay, or it may be to perform if the person with the obligation fails to perform.

[3] The answer will be "no" where it's only the "surety" who's liable. Example: *A* telephones *B*, and says, "Send merchandise to *C*; I'll pay." Since *C* never ordered the merchandise, *C* isn't liable to *B*. Therefore, *A*'s promise isn't a true promise of surety, and isn't within the Statute of Frauds.

[4] The term "creditor" here means either the person to whom the debt is owed or the person to whom the obligor owes a contractual performance. See footnote 2.

[5] Under the Main Purpose Rule, if the surety's principal purpose in making the guaranty was to further his own interests, the promise is not within the Statute of Frauds. Example: Owner engages Contractor to do work on Owner's property. Contractor needs supplies, and Supplier refuses to give Contractor credit without a guarantee. Owner guarantees Supplier that if Contractor doesn't pay, Owner will pay. Owner's main purpose is to benefit himself (by getting the work done), so Owner's promise falls within the Main Purpose Rule and doesn't have to be in writing.

[6] The answer will be "no" if any other interests are involved, such as a corresponding promise to transfer property.

[7] In other words, an ordinary engagement, with no side promises (e.g., promises about property transfers) is enforceable even though oral.

[8] "Interests in land" include the following: (1) fee simple; (2) leases (although most state statutes allow oral contracts if the term of the lease is one year or less); (3) easements; (4) promises to give a mortgage on real property as security for a loan; and (5) contracts under which the buyer will have extraction rights to oil, gas, or minerals on the land. See Ch. 9, IV(B).

[9] The action must be one that by its nature wouldn't have been taken had the alleged oral contract not occurred. Most common example: Vendee moves onto the property and makes improvements. Insufficient: Vendee pays all or part of the purchase price.

[10] The classic example is a construction contract: although the contract may involve thousands of dollars in materials, it is considered primarily a service contract and therefore not within this provision. See Ch. 9, VI(B)(2).

[11] Your answer to this question should be "yes" even if the goods have not been completed at the time of breach, provided that the seller/manufacturer has made a substantial beginning on their production or commitments for their procurement. § 2-201(3)(a).

[12] However, a "yes" answer will entitle plaintiff to enforce the contract only up to the quantity of goods admitted. § 2-201(3)(b).

[13] See § 2-201(3)(c).

[14] Remember that it is always possible that the person who is to perform under the contract may die (or become disabled) within one year. Depending on interpretation, a party's death/disability would either make performance "complete" within the year (in which case the contract would not be within the Statute) or it would simply "discharge" the contract (in which case the contract would still be within the Statute). To decide which interpretation is correct, ask yourself whether the principal purpose of the contract would be fulfilled even if one of the parties died or became disabled within the year. If so, complete performance is possible within one year.

Examples where death/disability means full performance rather than discharge (so the promise is not within the S/F and need not be in writing): (1) *A* promises to employ *B* for *B*'s lifetime; (2) *A*, a seller of a business, promises not to compete with *B*, the buyer, for a period longer than one year (because even if dead, *A* will be fulfilling her promise not to compete). Example where death means discharge (so the promise is within the S/F and must be in writing): *A* employs *B* for a term of 4 years.

[15] Whether a party's exercise of the right to terminate the contract within the first year should be viewed as a form of "performance" (in which case the contract is not within the 1-year provision and need not be in writing) or as a form of "discharge" (with the opposite result) is to be determined by looking to whether the contract has fulfilled its principal purpose. See Ch. 9, V(B)(2)(b).

[16] Therefore, the party who hasn't fully performed yet must carry out the performance that he orally agreed to make. Note that this is the case even if the fully-performing party's performance actually took more than one year to complete.

Figure 10-1
Damages in Sales Contracts Under
UCC: Buyer's Remedies[1]

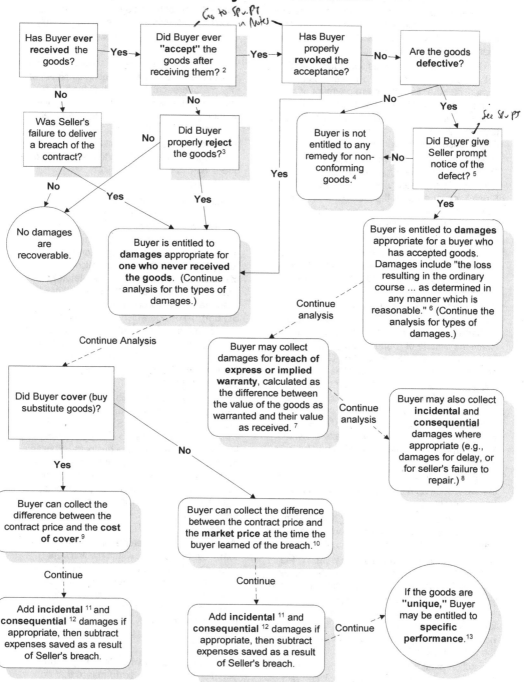

See footnotes on next page

Notes to
Figure 10-1 (Damages in Sales contracts under UCC: Buyer's Remedies)

[1] There are two flowcharts on remedies in sales cases: Buyer's Remedies (this chart) and Seller's Remedies (Fig. 10-2). In any fact pattern where it is possible that both parties breached, you should go through both charts. because both parties may be entitled to damages. When this is the case, the award to one party will be offset by the amount that party owes to the other.

[2] See Ch. 7, VI(D)(4)(b) for a discussion of when a buyer is deemed to have "accepted" goods.

[3] Before answering yes, check whether seller has a right to cure the defective performance (which she will have if the time for performance has not yet expired, or in a few other circumstances.) If there is a right to cure, treat the answer to this box as yes only if seller has failed to make a prompt cure.

[4] However, buyer may be entitled to damages for reasons other than the goods' non-conformity (e.g., late delivery).

[5] See UCC § 2-607(3)(a) (buyer must notify seller promptly of breach or be barred from all remedy).

[6] See UCC § 2-714(1).

7 See UCC § 2-714(2). Most courts use the contract price to determine the value the goods would have had if they had been tendered as warranted. See Ch. 10, XIII(D)(2)(c)(i), for a discussion of how courts determine the value of the goods as received.

[8] For a discussion of incidental and consequential damages, see Ch. 10, XIII(B)(3).

[9] See UCC § 2-712(1). Note that a buyer who actually covers probably cannot elect to receive the "contract price minus market price" measure of damages (shown in box at right). See supra, XIII(B)(2)(b).

[10] See UCC § 2-713(1). See also Ch. 10, XIII(B)(2).

[11] See UCC § 2-715(1) and Ch. 10, XIII(B)(3)(b).

[12] See UCC § 2-715(2) and Ch. 10, XIII(B)(3)(a). These can include profits Buyer could have made by reselling the goods. Consequential damages must be proved with reasonable certainty, and their occurrence must have been reasonably foreseeable to one in the seller's position. See Ch. 10, IX.

[13] Specific performance is rare in sale of goods cases, but will be granted where "goods are unique or in other proper circumstances." UCC § 2-716(1).

Figure 10-2
Damages in Sales Contracts Under UCC: Seller's Remedies[1]

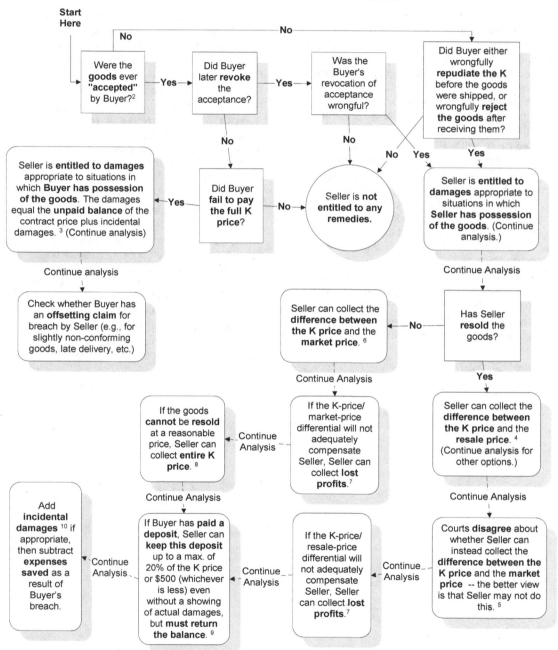

See footnotes on next page

Notes to
Figure 10-2 (Damages in Sales contracts under
UCC: Seller's Remedies)

[1] This is the second of two charts on Remedies. See also Fig. 10-1, dealing with Buyer's Remedies.

[2] See Ch. 7, VI(D)(4)(b) for a discussion of when a buyer is deemed to have "accepted" goods.

[3] See UCC § 2-709(1)(a). For a discussion of incidental damages, see UCC § 2-715(1) and Ch. 10, XIII(B)(3)(b).

[4] See UCC § 2-706(1). Resale must be made in good faith and in a commercially reasonable manner. Id. See UCC § 2-706(4) and Ch. 10, XIII(C)(1)(a), for public vs. private sales and the notice requirements for each.

[5] See Ch. 10, XIII(C)(2)(a).

[6] See UCC §2-708(1). Market price is determined as of the time and place for tender.

[7] See UCC § 2-708(2) and Ch. 10, XIII(C)(3).

This "lost profits" measure of damages will apply most often in these 2 situations: (1) Seller is a "lost volume" seller, i.e., one who has more supply than customers; (2) Seller is a "jobber," i.e. a middleman. "Lost profits" may include "reasonable overhead." § 2-708(2).

[8] See UCC § 2-709(1)(b). This remedy will apply where the goods were custom-made for Buyer, or where the market for the goods has virtually disappeared for some reason.

[9] See UCC § 2-718(2)(b). However, the amount kept by Seller may be greater or lesser than this, if there is a valid liquidated-damages clause in the contract. Id. See generally Ch. 10, XIII(C)(7).

[10] See UCC § 2-710 and Ch. 10, XIII(C)(5).

CAPSULE SUMMARY

SUMMARY OF CONTENTS
OF CAPSULE SUMMARY

CAPSULE SUMMARY

CHAPTER 1
INTRODUCTION

I. MEANING OF "CONTRACT"

A. Definition: A "contract" is an agreement that the law will enforce.

    1. Written v. oral contracts: Although the word "contract" often refers to a written document, a writing is not always necessary to create a contract. An agreement may be binding on both parties even though it is oral. Some contracts, however, must be in writing under the Statute of Frauds.

II. SOURCES OF CONTRACT LAW

A. The UCC: Contract law is essentially common law, i.e. judge-made, not statutory. However, in every state but Louisiana, sales of **goods** are governed by a statute, Article 2 of the Uniform Commercial Code.

    1. State enactments: A national drafting body, the National Conference of Commissioners of Uniform State Laws (NCCUSL) proposes revisions to various UCC Articles from time to time. Each state legislature then makes its own decision about whether and when to adopt the proposed revision.

        a. 2003 Revision: The NCCUSL drafted a **revision** of Article 2 in **2003**. That revision made some significant changes, especially in the area of electronic commerce. However, **no state adopted it**. Therefore, the NCCUSL withdrew the 2003 revision in 2011. Consequently, the version of Article 2 in force virtually everywhere in the U.S. as of this writing (mid-2016) is the **1990 text**.

        b. Our text: Therefore, when this book refers to an Article 2 provision, the reference is to the **1990 version** of Article 2, which is essentially unchanged since the original promulgation of Article 2 in 1957.

    2. Common law: If the UCC is silent on a particular question, the common law of the state will control. See UCC §1-103.

CHAPTER 2
OFFER AND ACCEPTANCE

I. INTENT TO CONTRACT

A. Objective theory of contracts: Contract law follows the **objective theory of contracts**. That is, a party's intent is deemed to be what a **reasonable person** in the position of the other party would think that the first party's objective manifestation of intent meant. For instance, in deciding whether *A* intended to make an offer to *B*, the issue is whether *A*'s conduct reasonably indicated to one in *B*'s position that *A* was making an offer.

> **Example:** *A* says to *B*, "I'll sell you my house for $1,000." If one in *B*'s position would reasonably have believed that *A* was serious, *A* will be held to have made an enforceable offer, even if subjectively *A* was only joking.

B. Legal enforceability: The parties' intention regarding whether a contract is to be *legally enforceable* will normally be effective. Thus if both parties intend and desire that their "agreement" not be legally enforceable, it will not be. Conversely, if both desire that it be legally enforceable, it will be even if the parties mistakenly believe that it is not.

> **Example:** Both parties would like to be bound by their oral understanding, but mistakenly believe that an oral contract cannot be enforceable. This arrangement will be enforceable, assuming that it does not fall within the Statute of Frauds.

1. Presumptions: Where the evidence is ambiguous about whether the parties intended to be bound, the court will follow these rules: (1) In a *"business"* context, the court will presume that the parties intended their agreement to be legally enforceable; (2) but in a *social* or *domestic* situation, the presumption will be that legal relations were *not* intended.

> > **Example:** Husband promises to pay a monthly allowance to Wife, with whom he is living amicably. In the absence of evidence otherwise, this agreement will be presumed not to be intended as legally binding, since it arises in a domestic situation.

C. Intent to put in writing later: If two parties agree (either orally or in a brief writing) on all points, but decide that they will subsequently put their entire agreement into a more formal written document later, the preliminary agreement may or may not be binding. In general, the parties' *intention* controls. (*Example*: If the parties intend to be bound right away based on their oral agreement, they will be bound even though they expressly provide for a later formal written document.)

1. Where no intent manifested: Where the evidence of intent is ambiguous, the court will generally treat a contract as existing as soon as the mutual assent is reached, even if no formal document is ever drawn up later. But for very large deals (e.g., billion dollar acquisitions), the court will probably find no intent to be bound until the formal document is signed.

II. OFFER AND ACCEPTANCE GENERALLY

A. Definitions:

1. "Offer" defined: An *offer* is "the manifestation of willingness to enter into a bargain," which justifies another person in understanding that his assent can conclude the bargain. In other words, an offer is something that creates a power of acceptance.

2. **"Acceptance" defined:** An *acceptance* of an offer is "a manifestation of assent to the terms thereof made by the offeree in a manner invited or required by the offer."

> **Example:** *A* says to *B*, "I'll sell you my house for $100,000, if you give me a check right now for $10,000 and promise to pay the rest within 30 days." This is an offer. If *B* says, "Here is my $10,000 check, and I'll have the balance to you next week," this is an acceptance. After the acceptance occurs, the parties have an enforceable contract (assuming that there is no requirement of a writing, as there probably would be in this situation).

B. **Unilateral vs. bilateral contracts:** An offer may propose either a bilateral or a unilateral contract.

   1. **Bilateral contract:** A *bilateral* contract is a contract in which *both* sides make *promises*.

   > **Example:** *A* says to *B*, "I promise to pay you $1,000 on April 15 if you promise now that you will walk across the Brooklyn Bridge on April 1." This is an offer for a bilateral contract, since *A* is proposing to exchange his promise for *B*'s promise.

   2. **Unilateral contract:** A *unilateral* contract is one which involves an exchange of the *offeror's promise* for the *offeree's act*. That is, in a unilateral contract *the offeree does not make a promise*, but instead simply acts.

   > **Example:** *A* says to *B*, "If you walk across the Brooklyn Bridge, I promise to pay you $1,000 as soon as you finish." *A* has proposed to exchange his promise for *B*'s *act* of walking across the bridge. Therefore, *A* has proposed a unilateral contract.

III. VALIDITY OF PARTICULAR KINDS OF OFFERS

A. **Offer made in jest:** An offer which the offeree knows or should know is made *in jest* is not a valid offer. Thus even if it is "accepted," no contract is created.

B. **Offer must indicate that other party can seal the bargain:** For an expression to be an "offer," the other person must be justified in thinking that the would-be offeror has intended to give the other person the ability to *"seal the deal" immediately, without further assent from the offeror.*

   1. **More details to work out:** Therefore, if a statement by one party, call her *A*, to *B* indicates that *A* believes that *further details must be worked out* between *A* and *B* before a deal is completed — details that *A* must approve — *A*'s statement is almost certainly *not* an offer, but merely an invitation to continue discussions or negotiations.

   2. **"Let's discuss":** Thus if *A* and *B* have had discussions about a deal, and *A* then makes a statement or proposal accompanied by words like *"Let's discuss,"* those words probably put *B* on notice that *A* has not just made an offer, but has merely invited continuing negotiations. In that event, there is nothing for *B* to "accept," and *B* cannot unilaterally bind *A* to a contract by *B*'s response.

C. Preliminary negotiations: If a party who desires to contract *solicits bids*, this solicitation is not an offer, and cannot be accepted. Instead, it merely serves as a basis for preliminary negotiations.

> **Example:** *A* says, "I would like to sell my house if I can get at least $100,000." This is almost certainly a solicitation of bids, rather than an offer, so *B* cannot "accept" by saying, "Here's my check for $100,000."

D. Advertisements: Most *advertisements* appearing in newspapers, store windows, etc., are *not* offers to sell. This is because they do not contain sufficient words of commitment to sell. (*Example*: A circular stating, "Men's jackets, $26 each," would not be an offer to sell jackets at that price, because it is too vague regarding quantity, duration, etc.)

1. **Specific terms:** But if the advertisement contains specific words of commitment, especially a promise to sell a *particular number* of units, then it may be an offer. (*Example*: "100 men's jackets at $26 apiece, first come first served starting Saturday," is so specific that it probably is an offer.)

2. **Words of commitment:** Look for words of *commitment* — these suggest an offer. (*Example*: "Send three box tops plus $1.95 for your free cotton T-shirt," is an offer even though it is also an advertisement; this is because the advertiser is committing himself to take certain action in response to the consumer's action.)

E. Auctions: When an item is put up for *auction*, this is usually *not* an offer, but is rather a solicitation of offers (bids) from the audience. So unless the sale is expressly said to be "without reserve," the auctioneer may withdraw the goods from the sale even after the start of bidding. See UCC §2-328(3).

IV. THE ACCEPTANCE

A. Who may accept: An offer may be accepted *only by a person in whom the offeror intended to create a power of acceptance*.

> **Example:** O says to *A*, "I offer to sell you my house for $100,000." *B* overhears, and says, "I accept." Assuming that O's offer was reasonably viewed as being limited to *A*, *B* cannot accept even though the consideration he is willing to give is what O said he wanted.

B. Must be in response to an offer: An acceptance must be *in response to an offer,* not in response to something other than an offer such as a *solicitation* of offers.

> **Example:** An uncle mails a letter to his adult nephew that says: "I am thinking of selling my pickup truck. I would consider taking $7,000 for it." The nephew writes back, "I will buy the truck for $7,000 cash." Because the uncle's letter is a solicitation of offers, not an offer, the nephew's response "I will buy" is *not an acceptance* (but is instead itself an offer).

C. Offeree must know of offer: An acceptance is usually valid only if the offeree *knows of the offer* at the time of his alleged acceptance.

1. **Rewards:** Thus if a *reward* is offered for a particular act, a person who does the act without knowing about the reward cannot claim it.

D. Method of acceptance: The offeror is the *"master of his offer."* That is, the offeror may prescribe the *method* by which the offer may be accepted (e.g., by telegram, by letter, by mailing a check, etc.).

1. **Can suspend mailbox rule:** The offeror's right to prescribe the method of acceptance means that the offeror can *suspend* the usual *"mailbox"* rule, under which an acceptance is effective upon dispatch. (See *infra*, p. 59.) The offeror can do this by saying, "No acceptance shall be effective until received by offeror" — such a provision will be *enforced*.

2. **Where method not specified:** If the offer does not specify the mode of acceptance, the acceptance may be given in *any reasonable* method.

3. **Acceptance of unilateral contract:** An offer for a unilateral contract is accepted by *full performance* of the requested act.

   Example: *A* says to *B*, "I'll pay you $1,000 if you cross the Brooklyn Bridge." This can only be accepted by *A*'s act of completely crossing the bridge. (However, the offer will be rendered temporarily irrevocable once *B* starts to perform, as discussed below.)

4. **Offer invites either promise or performance:** If the offer does not make clear whether acceptance is to occur through a promise or performance, the offeree may accept by *either* a promise or performance.

   a. **Shipment of goods:** For instance, if a buyer of goods places a "purchase order" that does not state how acceptance is to occur, the seller may accept by either promising to ship the goods, or by in fact shipping the goods. UCC §2-206(1)(b).

   b. **Accommodation shipment:** If the seller is "accommodating" the buyer by shipping what the seller knows and says are *non-conforming goods*, this does *not* act as an acceptance. In this *"accommodation shipment"* situation, the seller is making a counter-offer, which the buyer can then either accept or reject. If the buyer accepts, there is a contract for the quantity and type of goods actually sent by the seller, not for those originally ordered by the buyer. If the buyer rejects, he can send back the goods. In any event, seller will not be found to be in breach. UCC §2-206(1)(b).

      Example: Buyer sends Seller an order for "100 red gizmos, at $5.75 each, for immediate shipment." Seller sends 100 blue gizmos, with a note reading "I'm all out of red gizmos. I've taken the liberty of shipping you 100 blue ones instead, at the same price, hoping that they'll do for you."

      Seller's shipment of the blue gizmos is an accommodation shipment under §2-206(1)(b). Therefore, Seller's shipment does not constitute an acceptance. Instead, it is a counter-offer of blue gizmos. Buyer can accept the counter-offer (by keeping them, in which case he owes the $5.75 for each with no discount for the non-conformity) or reject the counter-offer (by sending them back). If Buyer rejects the counter-offer by sending the blue gizmos back, Seller has not breached (because there was never any accepted order), so Seller does not owe Buyer any compensation.

5. **Acceptance by silence:** Generally, an offer cannot be accepted by *silence*. But there are a few exceptions:

    a. **Reason to understand:** Silence can constitute acceptance if the offeror has given the offeree *reason to understand* that silence will constitute acceptance, and the offeree subjectively intends to be bound.

    b. **Benefit of services:** An offeree who silently receives the benefit of *services* (but not goods) will be held to have accepted a contract for them if he: (1) had a reasonable opportunity to reject them; and (2) knew or should have known that the provider of the services expected to be compensated.

    c. **Prior conduct:** The *prior course of dealing* may make it reasonable for the offeree's silence to be construed as consent.

        Example: Each time in the past, Seller has responded to purchase orders from Buyer either by shipping, or by saying, "We don't have the item." If Seller now remains silent in the face of an order by Buyer for a particular item, Seller's silence will constitute an acceptance of the order.

    d. **Acceptance by dominion:** Where the offeree receives *goods*, and *keeps them*, this exercise of "dominion" is likely to be held to be an acceptance.

    e. **"Implied-in-fact" contracts:** The above scenarios in which the parties do not expressly exchange an offer and acceptance, but in which they *indicate by their silence (or non-verbal conduct)* their understanding that a contract is being formed, are sometimes said to involve *"implied-in-fact"* contracts.

        i. **Distinction:** Be sure to distinguish the true implied-in-fact contract situation (in which each party, by his conduct, knowingly leads the other to believe that they have an agreement) from a situation in which at least one party *fails to take any action* that would justify the other in believing that a contract is intended.

        ii. **Intra-familial transactions:** For example, when one party performs small-scale services for another and the two are *close relatives*, if neither party expressly brings home to the other that payment is expected, the court is likely to conclude that the services were a *gift* rather than a commercial transaction.

6. **Notice of acceptance of unilateral contract:** Where an offer looks to a unilateral contract, most courts now hold that the offeree must give *notice* of his acceptance after he has done the requested act. If he does not, the contract that was formed by the act is discharged.

    Example: *A* says to *B*, "I'll pay you $1,000 if you cross the Brooklyn Bridge by April 1." *B* crosses the bridge on time. As soon as *B* crosses, a contract is formed. But if *B* does not notify *A* within a reasonable time thereafter that he has done so, *A*'s obligation will be discharged.

V. ACCEPTANCE VARYING FROM OFFER

A. Common law "mirror image" rule: Under the common law, the offeree's response operates as an acceptance only if it is the ***precise mirror image*** of the offer. If the response conflicts at all with the terms of the offer, or adds new terms, the purported acceptance is in fact a rejection and counter-offer, not an acceptance.

> **Example:** *A* writes to *B*, "I'll sell you my house for $100,000, closing to take place April 1." *B* writes back, "That's fine; let's close April 2, however." At common law, *B*'s response is not an acceptance because it diverges slightly from the offer, so there is no contract.

B. UCC view on "battle of the forms": The UCC ***rejects the "mirror image" rule***, and will often lead to a contract being formed even though the acceptance diverges from the offer. Wherever possible, the UCC tries to find a contract, so as to keep the parties from weaseling out (as they often try to do when the market changes). This entire ***"battle of the forms"*** is dealt with in UCC §2-207, probably the most important UCC provision for the Contracts student.

   1. **General:** At the most general level, §2-207(1) provides that any ***"expression of acceptance"*** or ***"written confirmation"*** will ***act as an acceptance*** even though it states terms that are "additional to or different from" those contained in the offer.

   > **Example:** Buyer sends a "purchase order" containing a warranty. Seller responds with an "acknowledgment," containing a disclaimer of warranty. There will be a contract under the UCC, even though there would not have been one at common law.

   2. **Acceptance expressly conditional on assent to changes:** An "expression of acceptance" does ***not*** form a contact if it is ***"expressly made conditional on assent to...additional or different terms."*** §2-207(1). So if the purported "acceptance" contains additional or different terms from the offer, and also states something like, "This acceptance of your offer is effective only if you agree to all of the terms listed on the reverse side of this acceptance form," ***there is no contract*** formed by the exchange of documents.

      a. **Limited:** Courts are reluctant to find that this section applies. Only if the second party's form makes it clear that that party is ***unwilling to proceed with the transaction*** unless the first party agrees to the second party's changes, will the clause be applied so as to prevent a contract from forming.

   3. **"Additional" term in acceptance:** Where the offeree's response contains an ***"additional"*** term (i.e., a clause taking a certain position on an issue with which the offer does not deal at all), the consequences depend on whether both parties are merchants.

      a. **At least one party not merchant:** If at least one party is ***not a merchant***, the additional term does not prevent the offeree's response from giving rise to a contract, but the additional term becomes part of the contract only if the offeror ***explicitly*** assents to it.

Example: Consumer sends a purchase order to Seller, which does not mention how disputes are to be resolved. Seller sends an acknowledgment form back to Consumer, which correctly recites the basic terms of the deal (price, quantity, etc.), and then says, "All disputes are to be arbitrated."

Even though the acknowledgment (the "acceptance") differed from the purchase order by introducing the arbitration term, the acknowledgment formed a contract. However, since at least one party (Consumer) was not a merchant, this additional term will only become part of the contract if Consumer explicitly assents to that term (e.g., by initialing the arbitration clause on the acknowledgment form).

  b. **Both merchants:** But if *both parties* to the transaction are *"merchants,"* then the additional term *automatically becomes part of the contract*, as a general rule. (*Example:* On facts of prior example, if Buyer was a merchant, the arbitration clause would become part of the contract.) However, there are two important exceptions to this "additional term becomes part of the contract" rule:

  i. **Materiality:** The addition will not become part of the contract if it is one which *"materially alters"* the contract. For instance, a *disclaimer of warranty* will always be found to materially alter the contract, so if the seller includes such a disclaimer in his acknowledgment form after receiving the buyer's purchase order, the disclaimer will not become part of the contract.

  ii. **Objection:** If the offeror *objects* to having the additional term become part of the contract, it will not so become.

4. **Acceptance silent:** If an issue is handled in the first document (the offer), but *not in the second* (the acceptance), the acceptance will be treated as covering *all* terms of the offer, not just those on which the writings agree.

   Example: Buyer's purchase order says that disputes will be arbitrated; Seller's acknowledgment is silent on the issue of arbitration. Seller's form will be found to be an acceptance, and disputes will be arbitrated.

5. **Conflicting terms in documents:** If an issue is covered one way in the offering document and another (*conflicting*) way in the acceptance, most courts apply the *"knock out" rule*. That is, the conflicting clauses "knock each other out" of the contract, so that *neither enters the contract*. Instead, a UCC "gap-filler" provision is used if one is relevant; otherwise, the common law controls.

   Example: Buyer's purchase order states that disputes will be litigated in New York state court. Seller's acknowledgment form states that disputes will be arbitrated. Most courts would apply the "knock out" rule, whereby neither the "New York courts" nor "arbitration" clauses would take effect. Instead, the common law — allowing an ordinary civil suit to be brought in any state that has jurisdiction — would apply.

6. Response diverges too much to be acceptance: If a purported acceptance *diverges greatly* from the terms of the offer, it will not serve as an acceptance at all, so *no contract is formed*.

7. Contract by parties' conduct: If the divergence referred to in the prior paragraph occurs (so that the exchange of documents does not create a contract), the parties' *conduct* later on can still cause a contract to occur. Section 2-207(3) provides that "conduct by both parties which recognizes the existence of a contract is sufficient to establish a contract for sale although the writings of the parties do not otherwise establish a contract."

> **Example:** Buyer's purchase order is for 100 widgets at $5 each. Seller's acknowledgment form is for 200 widgets at $7 each. Buyer does not say anything in response to the acknowledgment form. Seller ships the 200 widgets, and Buyer keeps them. Even though the exchange of documents did not create a contract, the parties' conduct gave rise to a contract by performance.

    a. Terms: Where a contract by conduct is formed, the terms "consist of those terms in which the writings of the parties agree, together with any supplementary terms incorporated under any other provisions of this Act." §2-207(3). For instance, the price term would be a "reasonable price at the time for delivery," as imposed by §2-305's price "gap filler."

8. Confirmation of oral contract: If the parties initially reach an *oral agreement*, a document later sent by one of them memorializing the agreement is called a *"confirmation."*

    a. Additional terms in confirmation: If the confirmation contains a term that is *additional* to the oral agreement, that additional term becomes part of the contract unless either: (1) the additional term *materially alters* the oral agreement; or (2) the party receiving the confirmation *objects* to the additional terms.

    b. "Different" term in confirmation: If a clause contained in the confirmation is *"different"* from a term on the same issue reached in the oral agreement, the new clause probably does *not* become part of the agreement.

    c. Request that confirmation be signed: Suppose that, after an oral agreement, one party sends a confirmation, and *requests that the other party sign and return that confirmation*. In this kind of scenario, there will be *no consequence* if the recipient doesn't sign or return the confirmation — the deal is complete when the confirmation is received.

9. "Terms to follow" contracts (a/k/a "rolling" contracts): Goods are sometimes sold under what is sometimes called a *"terms to follow"* or *"rolling" contract*. In such a contract, the buyer, usually a consumer, orders and pays for the goods *without seeing most of the contract terms*. The detailed terms are then contained *on or in the box* containing the goods. The buyer is told that if she does not agree with the detailed terms, she has a certain time within which to return the goods for a full credit. Courts are split on how to analyze such rolling contracts.

a.   **The "not formed until receipt" approach:** Some courts say that §2-207 doesn't apply, and that *no contract is formed until the buyer has received the goods and has kept them* for beyond the prescribed return period. This approach tends to yield a contract that includes *all of the seller's terms,* on the theory that the action of the buyer in keeping the goods rather than returning them should be interpreted as an *acceptance by performance,* an acceptance that includes the buyer's assent to all of the seller's proposed terms.

> **Example:** P orders a personal computer from D (the manufacturer) by phone. No forms are exchanged at the time. The box arrives, containing the computer and a document of "Standard Terms," which include an arbitration clause. The Standard Terms say that P can return the computer for a full refund anytime within 30 days of receipt; thereafter, the computer is no longer returnable, and P will be deemed to have accepted the Standard Terms. P doesn't return, then sues, and D contends that the arbitration clause became part of the contract.

> Some courts would hold for D, on the theory that (1) §2-207 doesn't apply because it's not a "battle of the forms" (only D has used a form); and (2) no contract was formed until P kept the computer for 30 days, at which point P was deemed to have accepted the Standard Terms, including the arbitration clause. Therefore, the arbitration clause would be held to have become part of the contract. Cf. *Hill v. Gateway 2000,* so holding.

b.   **Contract formed under §2-207 at time of order:** But other courts hold that §2-207 *does* apply to the rolling-contract scenario, and that *a contract is therefore formed at the time of the order.* Under this approach, the buyer is usually considered to be the offeror, the seller is an offeree who is proposing additional or different terms, and at least where the buyer is a consumer those terms *never become part of the contract* unless the buyer expressly agrees to them (which she usually doesn't). This is probably the better approach.

> **Example:** Same facts as above Example. Probably the better view is that §2-207 applies (even though the only form ever used is D's Standard Terms document, which acts as a confirmation of the parties' earlier oral deal). P is an offeror, and D is an offeree who is proposing the arbitration clause as an additional term. Because P is a consumer, the arbitration clause doesn't become part of the contract under §2-207(2) unless P agrees to it, which P didn't do. Therefore, there is no arbitration clause in the contract. Cf. *Klocek v. Gateway, Inc.,* so holding.

VI. DURATION OF THE POWER OF ACCEPTANCE

A. **General strategy:** For an acceptance to be valid, it must become effective while the power of acceptance is still in effect. So where there is doubt about whether the acceptance is timely: (1) pinpoint the moment at which the "acceptance" became effective; and (2) ask whether the power of acceptance was still in effect at that moment. If the answer to part (2) is "yes," the acceptance was timely.

B. Ways of terminating power of acceptance: The offeree's power of acceptance may be *terminated* in five main ways: (1) *rejection* by the offeree; (2) *counter-offer* by the offeree; (3) *lapse* of time; (4) *revocation* by the offeror; and (5) *death or incapacity* of the offeror or offeree.

1. Rejection by offeree: Normally, if the offeree *rejects* the offer, this will terminate her power of acceptance.

    a. Exceptions: But rejection will not terminate the power of acceptance if either: (1) the offeror indicates that the offer still stands despite the rejections; or (2) the offeree states that although she is not now accepting, she wishes to consider the offer further later.

2. Counter-offer: If the offeree makes a *counter-offer*, her power to accept the original offer is terminated just as if she had flatly rejected the offer.

    Example: On July 1, *A* offers to sell *B* 100 widgets at $5 each, the offer to be left open indefinitely. On July 2, *B* responds, "I'll buy 50 at $4." *A* declines. On July 3, the market price of widgets skyrockets. On July 4, *B* tells *A*, "I'll accept your July 1 offer." No contract is formed, because *B*'s power of acceptance was terminated as soon as *B* made her counter-offer on July 2.

    a. Contrary statement: But as with a rejection, a counter-offer does not terminate the power of acceptance if either offeror or offeree indicates otherwise. (*Example*: On facts of above example, if *B* said on July 2, "I'll buy 50 from you right now for $4; otherwise, I'd like to keep considering your original offer," *A*'s offer would have remained in force.)

    b. Distinguish counter-offer from exploration: Be careful to distinguish a counter-offer from a response by the offeree that is too *equivocal* or *uncertain* to be a counter-offer, and that instead merely *explores the possibility of some other arrangement* while keeping the original offer alive. Statements like *"Would you consider...?"* or "I might be interested instead in ..." will typically have this non-counter-offer effect (so that the original offer remains in place).

3. Lapse of time: The offeror, as "master of his offer," can set a *time limit* for acceptance. At the end of this time limit, the offeree's power of acceptance automatically terminates.

    a. End of reasonable time: If the offeror does not set a time limit for acceptance, the power of acceptance terminates at the end of a *reasonable* time period.

        i. Face-to-face conversation: If the parties are bargaining face-to-face or over the phone, the power of acceptance continues *only during the conversation*, unless there is evidence of a contrary intent.

4. Revocation: The offeror is free to *revoke* his offer *at any time* before it is accepted (except in the case of option contracts).

    a. Effective upon receipt: A revocation by the offeror does not become effective until it is *received by the offeree*.

Example: On June 15, *A* mails an offer to B. On July 1, *A* mails a revocation to B. On July 3, *B* has a letter of acceptance hand delivered to A. On July 5, *A*'s revocation is received by B. *B*'s acceptance is valid, because *A*'s revocation did not take effect until its receipt by *B*, which was later than the July 3 date on which *B*'s acceptance took effect.

    i. **Lost revocation:** If the letter or telegram revoking the offer is *lost* through misdelivery, the revocation *never becomes effective*.

  b. **Indirect communication of revocation:** If the offeror behaves in a way *inconsistent with an intention to enter the contract* she has proposed and the offeree *learns* (even *indirectly*) that the offeror has taken such an action, there is a revocation, even though the offeror never intended to communicate directly with the offeree.

    Example: *A* offers to sell Blackacre to *B* at a stated price, and gives *B* a week in which to respond. Within the week, *A* contracts to sell the land to *C*, and *B* learns of this through a tenant of Blackacre. *B* nonetheless sends a formal acceptance, which is received by *A* within the week. There is no contract between *A* and *B*, because *A*'s offer to *B* was revoked at the time that *B* learned that *A* had made the contract with *C*.

    i. **Negotiations or offer not enough:** But the mere fact that the offeror has entered into *negotiations* with a third person, or even that she has made an *offer* to a third person, is generally *not* sufficient to constitute a revocation when the original offeree learns of it.

5. **Death or incapacity of offeror or offeree:** If either the offeror or offeree *dies* or loses the *legal capacity* to enter into the contract, the power to accept is terminated. This is so even if the offeree does not learn of the offeror's death or incapacity until after he has dispatched the "acceptance."

    Example: On July 1, *A* sends an offer. On July 2, *A* dies. On July 3, *B* telegraphs her "acceptance." On July 4, *B* learns of *A*'s death. There is no contract.

C. Irrevocable offers: The ordinary offer is *revocable* at the will of the offeror. (This is true even if it states something like, "This offer will remain open for two weeks.") However, there are some exceptions to this general rule of revocability:

1. **Standard option contract:** First, the offeror may grant the offeree an *"option"* to enter into the contract. The offer itself is then referred to as an "option contract."

  a. **Common law requires consideration:** The traditional common-law view is that an option contract can be formed only if the offeree gives the offeror *consideration* for the offer.

  b. **Modern (Restatement) approach:** But the modern approach, as shown in the Restatement, is that a *signed* option contract that *recites* the payment of consideration will be irrevocable, even if the consideration was never paid.

2. **"Firm offers" under the UCC:** The UCC is even more liberal in some cases: it allows formation of an irrevocable offer even if no recital of the payment of consideration is made. By §2-205, an offer to buy or sell goods is irrevocable if it:

[1] is by a ***merchant*** (i.e., one who "deals in goods of the kind or otherwise by his occupation holds himself out as having knowledge or skill peculiar to the practices or goods involved in the transaction");

[2] is in a ***signed writing***; and

[3] gives ***explicit assurance*** that the offer will be ***held open***.

Such an offer is irrevocable even though it is without consideration or even a recital of consideration.

> **Example:** Jeweler gives Consumer a signed document stating, "For the next 60 days, I agree to buy your two-carat diamond antique engagement ring for $4,000." Even though Consumer has not paid consideration for the irrevocability, and even though there is no recital of consideration in the signed offer, Jeweler's offer is in fact irrevocable for 60 days, because it is by a merchant (Jeweler deals in goods of the kind involved in the transaction), is in a signed writing, and explicitly assures that the offer will be held open.

a. **Three month limit:** No offer can be made irrevocable for any longer than ***three months***, unless consideration is given. §2-205. If the offer lists a period longer than three months, the offer ***becomes revocable*** after three months.

> **Example:** On July 1, Dealer, a car dealer, sends a signed email to Consumer offering to sell Consumer a Model X car with certain specs for $20,000; the email says that the offer "will remain open until the end of the year." On Nov. 1, Dealer phones Consumer to say, "The offer is withdrawn." Consumer immediately purports to accept, citing the "open until the end of the year" language.
>
> No matter what the offer said, it was not irrevocable under §2-205 past September 30 (three months). Therefore, Dealer's revocation was effective, and Consumer's acceptance was not effective. (But if Dealer had purported to revoke on *August 1* and Consumer purported to accept on August 2, then the revocation would have been ineffective and the acceptance would have been effective.)

  i. **Can still be a valid offer:** Even after an offer becomes revocable because the three months have passed, that doesn't mean it can't still be a valid, outstanding offer. Thus in the above Example, on Oct. 1, Consumer could still have accepted, since nothing had occurred by then to actually revoke the offer.

b. **Forms supplied by offeree:** If the firm offer is on a form drafted by the *offeree*, it is irrevocable only if the particular "firm offer" clause is ***separately signed*** by the offeror.

c. **Effect if not by a merchant:** Be on the lookout for a purported firm offer that relates to a sales contract, but that is ***made by a non-merchant*** (i.e., a consumer) — such an offer is ***not firm***, and will therefore be ***revocable***.

Example: Consumer sends a letter to Furniture Co. offering to sell it some used office shelving presently on the walls of Consumer's house. The letter says that the offer "will remain open for the next 60 days." After 40 days, Consumer sends another letter, saying "I sold the shelving to someone else."

This revocation letter is effective, because Consumer is not a "merchant," and only "merchants" can make firm offers. (For purposes of firm offers, virtually any person who is making an offer during the course of her business is a "merchant," but Consumer does not meet this definition.) Consequently, the offer was revocable even though it recited that it wasn't.

3. **Part performance or detrimental reliance:** The offeree's part performance or detrimental reliance (e.g., preparations to perform) may transform an otherwise-revocable offer into a temporarily irrevocable one.

    a. **Offer for unilateral contract:** Where the offer is for a *unilateral* contract, the *beginning of performance* by the offeree makes the offer *temporarily irrevocable*. As long as the offeree continues diligently to perform, the offer remains irrevocable until he has finished.

        Example: *A* says to *B*, "I'll pay you $1,000 if you cross the Brooklyn Bridge anytime in the next three hours." Before *B* starts to cross the bridge, *A* may revoke. But once *B* starts to cross the bridge, *A*'s offer becomes temporarily irrevocable. If *B* crosses the bridge within three hours, a contract is formed and *A* owes *B* the money. If *B* starts to cross, then changes his mind, neither party will be bound.

        i. **Preparations:** This doctrine applies only to the beginning of *actual performance*, not the making of *preparations* to perform. (*Example*: On facts of above example, if *B* went out and bought expensive walking shoes in preparation for crossing, this act would not cause his offer to be irrevocable.)

    b. **Preparations by offeree:** If the offer is for a *bilateral* contract (i.e., a contract which is to be accepted by a return promise), the offeree's making of *preparations* will cause the offer to be temporarily irrevocable if justice requires. "An offer which the offeror should reasonably expect to induce action or forbearance of substantial character on the part of the offeree before acceptance and which does induce such action or forbearance is binding as an option contract *to the extent necessary to avoid injustice*." Rest.2d, §87(2).

        i. **Offers by sub-contractors:** Most importantly, an offer by a *sub-contractor* to a general contractor will often become temporarily irrevocable under this rule.

            Example: *A*, sub-contractor, offers to supply steel to *B* on a job where *B* is bidding to become the general contractor. *B* calculates his bid in reliance on the figure quoted by A. *B* gets the job. Before *B* can accept, *A* tries to revoke.

If *B* can show that he bid a lower price because of *A*'s sub-bid, the court will probably hold *A* to the contract, or at least award *B* damages equal to the difference between *A*'s bid and the next-lowest available bid. But observe that *B*, the offeree, is *not* bound, so *B* could accept somebody else's sub-bid.

VII. WHEN ACCEPTANCE BECOMES EFFECTIVE

A. Mailbox rule: In most courts, the acceptance is ***effective upon proper dispatch***. This is called the ***"mailbox"*** rule.

> **Example:** On July 1, *A* offers to sell 100 widgets to *B* at $5 apiece. On July 2, *B* deposits a properly-addressed acceptance in the mail. On July 10, *A* finally receives the letter, several days later than would ordinarily be expected from first-class mail. A contract was formed on July 2. Any attempt at revocation by *A* on, say, July 5 would have been ineffective.

1. Offer provides otherwise: The "mailbox" rule does not apply if the offer provides otherwise (e.g., "This offer will be accepted when and if your letter of acceptance is personally received by me").

2. Lost in transmission: If the acceptance is ***lost in transmission*** or ***delayed***, the applicability of the mailbox rule depends on whether the communication was properly addressed.

a. Properly addressed: If the acceptance is ***properly addressed***, it is effective at the time of dispatch even if it is lost and ***never received*** by the offeror at all. (But a court might "discharge" the offeror in this circumstance, for instance if he had sold the goods to someone else.)

b. Not properly addressed: If the acceptance is ***not*** properly addressed, or not properly dispatched (e.g., sent by an unreasonably slow means), it will be effective upon dispatch only if it is received within the time in which a properly dispatched acceptance would normally have arrived. If it comes later than this "normal" time, it will not be effective until receipt.

> **Example:** On July 1, *A* sends an offer letter to *B*, and says that *B* should "give me your answer in writing by July 10." On July 8, *B* mails an acceptance letter, but uses a slightly wrong address for *A*. Assume that a properly addressed letter would have been delivered on July 10. *B*'s letter arrives on July 11. Meanwhile, *A* revokes by phone on the evening of July 10.
>
> *B*'s letter is not effective upon dispatch, because it did not arrive within the same time in which a properly addressed letter would have arrived. (But if the misaddressed letter had arrived on July 10, at the same time as a properly-addressed letter, it would have been retroactively deemed effective upon dispatch, and a revocation by *A* on July 9 would have been too late.)

B. Both acceptance and rejection sent by offeree: If the offeree sends *both* an acceptance and rejection, the rule depends on which is dispatched first.

    1. Rejection sent first: If the *rejection* is sent first, then the acceptance will be effective if (and only if) the offeror receives it before he receives the rejection.

    2. Acceptance dispatched first: If the acceptance is sent before the rejection, the acceptance is effective upon dispatch, and the subsequently-dispatched "rejection" (really a "revocation of acceptance") does not undo the acceptance, whether that rejection is received by the offeror before or after he receives the acceptance.

C. Option contracts: The acceptance of an *option contract* is effective upon *receipt* by the offeror, *not upon dispatch*.

VIII. INDEFINITENESS

A. Generally: No contract will be found if the terms of the parties' "agreement" are unduly *indefinite*. (*Example*: *A* and *B* agree that *B* will buy widgets from *A* from time to time. The parties do not decide anything about quantity, price, delivery, etc. A court would probably find that even though *A* and *B* may have meant to conclude a binding agreement, the absence of terms makes their agreement void for indefiniteness.)

    1. Court supplies missing term: But if the court believes that the parties intended to contract, and the court believes that it can supply a *"reasonable"* value for the missing term, it will generally do so.

        a. UCC: The UCC expressly allows the court to fill in terms for price, place for delivery, time for shipment, time for payment, etc., as long as the parties have intended to make a contract. See §2-204(3). The UCC also implies a term requiring *good faith* in every contract for the sale of goods. §1-203.

        b. Non-UCC: In non-UCC cases, most modern courts follow this "supply the missing term on a reasonable basis" approach, as long as the parties have shown an intent to create a binding contract.

        c. Too indefinite: But there may be situations where even though the parties intended to create a binding contract, they have fleshed out the terms of their deal so little that the court simply cannot meaningfully supply all of the missing terms. In that case, the court will find the agreement void for indefiniteness. (But this is rare.)

    2. Implied obligation of good faith: In both UCC and non-UCC contracts, an important type of term the court will supply is an obligation of *good faith* and *fair dealing*. See, e.g., UCC §1-304, which says that "every contract or duty within this Act imposes an obligation of good faith in its performance or enforcement." (§1-201(19) then defines good faith as "*honesty* in fact and the observance of *reasonable commercial standards of fair dealing*.")

        a. Consistency with other party's expectations: An important aspect of this duty of good faith is that a party is required to behave in a way that is consistent with the other party's *reasonable expectations* about how the contract will work.

Example: Insurer writes a homeowner's policy on Owner's home. The policy says that in the event Owner suffers a loss, Owner must report the loss "in detail" and in writing to Insurer within 30 days. 28 days after Owner's home is burglarized, he submits a one-sentence description of the loss to Insurer. Insurer says merely, "Your description is not specific enough," but refuses to tell Owner what type of detail must be added. (Assume that Insurer's evasiveness is an intentional attempt to prevent Owner from submitting a claim meeting the requirements of the policy.) The deadline passes without Owner's rewriting the description, and Insurer refuses to pay to the claim.

A court would probably find that Insurer's intentionally evasive behavior violated its implied duty of good faith, because the behavior was an attempt to deprive Owner of his reasonable expectation that his loss would be covered by the policy.

3. **Agreement to agree:** The court will generally supply a missing term if the parties intentionally leave that term to be *agreed upon later*, and they then don't agree. See, e.g., UCC §2-305(1)(b), which allows the court to supply a reasonable *price* term if "the price is left to be agreed by the parties and they fail to agree...."

4. **Part performance:** Even if an agreement is too indefinite for enforcement at the time it is made, the *subsequent performance* of the parties may cure this indefiniteness.

   Example: *A* contracts to make a suit for *B*, without specifying the type or color of material to be used. This is probably unenforceable for indefiniteness when made. But if *A* begins to make the suit with gray cotton cloth, and *B* knows this and raises no objection, the indefiniteness will be cured by this part performance.

IX. MISUNDERSTANDING

A. **General rule:** If the parties have a *misunderstanding* about what they are agreeing to, this may prevent them from having the required "meeting of the minds," and thus prevent a contract from existing. No contract will be formed if: (1) the parties each have a different subjective belief about a term of the contract; (2) that term is a material one; and (3) neither party knows or has reason to know of the misunderstanding.

   Example: *A* offers to ship goods to *B* on the steamer "Peerless." *B* accepts. Unknown to both, there are in fact two steamships by this name. *A* intends to use the later one; *B* subjectively intends to get shipment on the earlier one. Because both are in subjective disagreement about the meaning of a material term, and neither has reason to know of the disagreement, there is no contract. [*Raffles v. Wichelhaus*]

1. **Fault:** Conversely, if one party *knows* or *should know* that he has a different understanding as to the meaning of an ambiguous term than the other, a contract will be formed on the term as understood by the other (innocent) party.

Example: Same facts as above example. This time, *A* knows or should know that there are two Peerlesses, and knows or should know that *B* means the earlier one. *B* doesn't and shouldn't know know that there are two. *A* contract is formed for shipment on the earlier (the one understood by *B*, the "innocent" party).

B. Offeree doesn't understand offer: Where the offeree fails to **understand** or **read** the offer, a similar "fault" system applies:

1. **Offeree is negligent:** If the offeree's failure to read or understand the offer is due to his own negligence, he is bound by the terms of the contract as stated in the offer.

2. **Misrepresentation:** But if the offeree's misunderstanding is due to the offeror's **misrepresentation** of the terms of the offer, and the offeror knows this, there is a contract on the terms as understood by the offeree.

CHAPTER 3
CONSIDERATION

I. INTRODUCTION

A. Definition of consideration: As a general rule, a contract will not be enforceable unless it is supported by "consideration." (The few exceptions are treated in "Promises binding without consideration" below.) A promise is supported by consideration if:

1. **Detriment:** The promisee **gives up something of value**, or circumscribes his liberty in some way (i.e., he suffers a **"legal detriment"**); *and*

2. **Exchange:** The promise is given as part of a **"bargain"**; that is, the promisor makes his promise **in exchange** for the promisee's giving of value or circumscription of liberty.

B. More about "legal detriment": The **"legal detriment"** (the "something of value or circumscription of liberty") that the promisee must exchange for the promisor's promise, can consist of **any of the following** kinds of things:

❏ an **act** by the promisee.

> **Example:** Promisor promises to pay $100 if Promisee actually walks across the Brooklyn Bridge. Promisee does the walk. The act of walking is consideration for Promisor's promise to pay $100.

❏ a **forbearance** by the promisee.

> **Example:** Promisor promises to pay $100 if Promisee refrains from smoking for the next month. Promisee in fact refrains. Promisee's forbearance from smoking is consideration for Promisor's promise to pay $100.

❏ a **return promise** by the promisee.

Example: Promisor promises to pay $100 if Promisee promises now to walk across the Brooklyn Bridge next Saturday. Promisee makes this promise. Promisee's making of the promise to walk is consideration for Promisor's promise to pay $100.

❏ an act, forbearance or return promise *by a third person* (someone other than the promisee).

Example: Promisor promises Promisee that if Promisee's sister Sue paints Promisor's house, Promisor will pay Promisee $100. Even though Sue is not the promisee, her act of painting will be consideration for Promisor's promise to pay Promisee the $100.

❏ a promise or act by the promisee, *delivered to a third person*, rather than to the promisor.

Example: Promisor promises $100 to Merchant if Merchant delivers $100 in groceries to Promisor's son. Merchant delivers. The fact that the bargained-for performance is rendered to one other than Promisor does *not* prevent Merchant's delivery to the son from being consideration for Promisor's promise to pay $100.

See generally Rest. 2d, §71.

C. Uses of doctrine: The requirement of consideration renders unenforceable two main types of transactions:

[1] Promises to *make gifts* (which are promises that do not satisfy the "*bargain*" element); and

[2] Business situations in which one party has *not really promised to do something* or given anything up, even though he may appear to have done so (scenarios that do not satisfy the "*detriment*" element). The main situations falling into this category are cases where the parties to an existing contract *modify* it to the sole benefit of one of the parties (the "pre-existing duty" scenario).

II. THE BARGAIN ELEMENT

A. Promises to make gifts: A *promise to make a gift* is generally *unenforceable*, because it lacks the "bargain" element of consideration.

Example: *A* says to *B*, his daughter, "When you turn 21 in four years, I will give you a car worth $10,000." The four years pass, *A* refuses to perform, and *B* sues for breach of contract. *B* will lose, because there was no consideration for *A*'s promise. In particular, *A*'s promise was not "bargained for."

1. Existence of condition: Even if the person promising to make a gift requires the promisee to meet certain *conditions* in order to receive the gift, there will still be no consideration (and the promise will thus be unenforceable) if the meeting of the conditions is not really "bargained for" by the promisor.

Example: *A* promises his widowed sister-in-law *B* a place to live "if you will come down and see me." In response, *B* travels to see *A*, thereby incurring expenses. Even though *B* has suffered a "detriment" (the expenses), the "bargain" element is lacking — *A* was not promising *B* a place to live because he wanted to see her, but was merely imposing a necessary pre-condition for her to get the gift. Therefore, his promise is unenforceable for lack of consideration. [*Kirksey v. Kirksey*]

a. **Occurrence of condition is of benefit to promisor:** But if the promisor imposes a condition, and the occurrence of this condition is of *benefit* to him, then the bargain element probably *will* be present.

> **Example:** *A* promises his nephew *B* $5,000 if *B* will refrain from smoking, drinking and gambling until age 21. *B* so abstains. Here, *A*'s promise was "bargained for" (and thus supported by consideration), because *A* was attempting to obtain something he regarded as desirable. [*Hamer v. Sidway*]

> i. **Altruistic pleasure not sufficient:** But the fact that one who promises to make a gift expects to derive *altruistic pleasure*, or love and affection, from making the gift is *not* sufficient to constitute a "bargain."

b. **Mixture of bargain and gift:** Where a transaction is a *mixture of a bargain and a gift,* the consideration requirement is nonetheless *satisfied.* For instance, if one party promises to sell the other an item at a price that both parties recognize is a *large discount* to its market value, that promise is supported by consideration (in the form of the buyer's promise to pay, or actual payment of, the discounted price).

> **Example:** *A* is a close friend of *B*. *B* has long admired *A*'s painting "Irises" by Picasso, which as both parties know has a market value of $200,000. *A* promises to sell "Irises" to *B* for $20,000, and *B* promises to buy it for that price. The contract is enforceable because each promise is supported by consideration, notwithstanding the presence of a significant "gift" element to the exchange.

2. **Executed gifts:** It is only the *promise* to make a gift, not the actual making of a gift, that is unenforceable for lack of consideration. Once the promisor makes the gift, he cannot rescind it for lack of consideration.

B. **Sham and nominal consideration:** Even though a deal looks on its face as if it is supported by consideration, the court may conclude that the purported consideration is *sham* or *nominal*, and is thus not consideration at all.

1. **Nominal amount:** Thus where the "consideration" that has been paid is so small as to be *nominal*, the court may conclude as a factual matter that there is no real "bargain" present at all. If so, the promise will not be enforced, due to lack of consideration.

> **Example:** *A* says to *B*, his son, "In consideration for $1 paid and received, I promise to give you a car worth $10,000 four years from now." Even if the $1 is actually paid, the court will probably conclude that *A* did not "bargain" for the $1, and that there is thus no consideration; *A*'s promise will therefore be unenforceable.

       a. **"Adequacy" irrelevant:**   But if the consideration is big enough to suggest that there was a bargain, the fact that it is "inadequate" is irrelevant. (See *infra.*)

    2. **Payment not in fact made:**   If a non-trivial payment is recited, but the payment was *not in fact made*, most courts will take this as evidence that no bargain was present. Always, the question is whether there was in fact a bargain, and payment or non-payment is merely non-dispositive evidence of whether there was a bargain.

C. Promisee unaware: Generally, the promisee must be *aware* of the promise, for the act performed by him to be consideration for the promise. This means that if a *reward* is promised for a certain act, and the act is performed without the actor's being aware of the reward, he cannot recover.

D. Promise exchanged for previous detriment: If the promise is made in return for detriment *previously* suffered by the promisee, there is no bargain, and thus no consideration.

    1. **"Past consideration is no consideration":** As the idea is often put, *"past consideration is no consideration."* This statement is essentially correct.

    2. **Illustrations:** Thus promises to *pay a pre-existing debt,* and promises to *pay for services already received*, usually lack the "bargain" element, so there is no consideration to support them. (But these two types of promises may be binding even without consideration, as discussed below.)

III. THE "DETRIMENT" ELEMENT

A. Generally: For consideration to be present, the promisee must suffer a *"detriment."* That is, she must do something she does not have to do, or refrain from doing something that she has a right to do. (*Example*: After P has already retired from working for D, D promises P a lifetime pension, for which P need not do anything. At common law, this promise would probably be unenforceable, because P has not suffered any detriment in return for it.)

    1. **Non-economic detriment:**   Even a *non-economic* detriment will suffice. (*Example*: If *A* promises *B* $5,000 in return for *B*'s abstaining from alcohol and tobacco, *B*'s refraining will be a "detriment" that will serve as consideration for *A*'s promise. Thus *A*'s promise will be enforceable.)

    2. **Adequacy not considered:**   The court will *not* inquire into the *"adequacy"* of the consideration. As long as the promisee suffers some detriment, no matter how small, the court will not find consideration lacking merely because what the promisee gave up was of much less value than what he received.

        Example: D is desperate for funds during WWII, and promises to pay P $2,000 after the war in return for $25 now. Held, there is consideration for D's promise, so P may collect. Mere "inadequacy of consideration" is no defense. [*Batsakis v. Demotsis*].

a. **Minor effort or other thing of non-monetary value:** The principle that courts will not acquire into the adequacy of the consideration means that consideration can consist of the promisee's doing something that requires *only a tiny bit of effort and has no financial value.* For instance, the promisee's effort in *clipping a coupon* or *filling out a contest entry form* will typically be *enough* to constitute consideration for the other side's promise.

> **Example:** D, an auto manufacturer, runs an online contest that says, "Fill out this form, and if your entry is drawn, you'll get a brand new car." P spends 30 seconds filling out the form online, and is lucky enough to have his entry selected. D then refuses to deliver the car, raising a lack-of-consideration defense. P would almost certainly win — the court would hold that P's act of spending 30 seconds filling out the form constituted consideration sufficient to support D's promise of a car to the winner.

b. **Lack of bargain:** But remember that extreme disparity in value between what the promisee gives up and receives may suggest that there is not in fact a "bargain," in which case there will be no consideration even though the detriment requirement is satisfied.

B. **Pre-existing duty rule:** If a party does or promises to do what he is *already legally obligated* to do, or if he forbears or promises to forbear from doing something which he is *not legally entitled to do,* he has not incurred a "detriment" for purposes of consideration. This is the *pre-existing duty* rule.

1. **Modification:** This general rule means that if parties to an existing contract agree to *modify* the contract for the sole benefit for one of them, the modification will usually be unenforceable at common law, for lack of consideration. Be on the lookout for this scenario especially in *construction* cases.

> **Example:** Contractor agrees to pave Owner's driveway for $5,000, the job to be completed by May 1. Halfway through the project, Contractor tells Owner, "I've gotten very busy. Increase the price to $6,000, or I'll have to finish 6 weeks late." Owner says, "OK, I agree to pay you $6,000, now just finish on time." Contractor finishes on time, but Owner refuses to pay more than $5,000. Contractor sues for the extra $1,000.
>
> Owner's promise to pay the extra $1,000 (a modification of the contract) will *not be enforceable* — the contract was modified to the sole benefit of Contractor, who was merely promising to do what he was already legally obligated to do. Therefore, he did not furnish consideration to support Owner's promise of the extra $1,000.

a. **Restatement:** The Second Restatement, and most modern courts, follow this general rule.

2. **Exception for unanticipated circumstances:** But modern courts (and the Restatement) make an *exception* to the pre-existing duty rule where the modification is *"fair and equitable* in view of circumstances *not anticipated* by the parties when the contract was made."

Example: Contractor makes a six-year contract, for $50,000 per year, to annually repaint a bridge owned by City, using specified paint to be furnished by Contractor. Before the fourth year, Contractor tells City (truthfully) that the cost of the particular paint specified in the contract has doubled in the last year, due to new safety legislation. City agrees to adjust the contract price to $55,000, which would restore Contractor to the same level of profit as both parties anticipated when the contract was originally signed. When the time comes for payment, City refuses to pay the extra $5,000, citing the pre-existing duty rule.

Even though, in return for the promise of extra money, Contractor merely promised to do what he was always required to do (paint the bridge and supply the specified paint), the modification is "fair and equitable in view of circumstances not anticipated by the parties when the contract was made." So City's promise to modify will not be invalid for lack of consideration, and Contractor can require City to pay the extra $5,000.

3. **Extra duties:** Even under the traditional pre-existing duty rule, if the party who promises to do what he is already bound to do assumes the *slightest additional duties* (or even *different* duties), his undertaking of these new duties *does* constitute the required "detriment."

Example: Contractor agrees to build a house for Owner for $30,000. Midway through the job, Contractor realizes he's losing money, and threatens to walk off the job if Owner does not increase the price to $40,000. In return for this price increase, Contractor is willing to change the kind of fittings in the windows, as requested by Owner; this change will actually save Contractor money.

Most courts would hold that the change of specifications, even though actually less burdensome to Contractor, constituted consideration for Owner's promise to pay more for the house.

a. **Where change is mere pretense:** The "additional" or "different" duties promised by the person already legally bound must not, however, be merely a *pretense* for avoiding the pre-existing duty rule.

4. **Rewards and bonuses:** Outside of the modification context, a promise to pay a *reward* or *bonus* will be unenforceable under the pre-existing duty rule, if the promisee is *already under a legal obligation* to perform the act being rewarded.

Example: Officer, employed by City, has the duty to investigate crimes and arrest the guilty. He learns of a reward offered by City for "information leading to the arrest and conviction of..." the person responsible for a particular robbery. Officer arrests a suspect, who is convicted. Officer won't be entitled to the reward, because there is no consideration for his act of making the arrest — he was only doing what his job already required him to do.

5. **UCC:** For contracts for the sale of goods, the UCC *abolishes the pre-existing duty rule*. Section 2-209(1) provides that "an agreement modifying a contract...needs no consideration to be binding." But there must be good faith, and any no-oral-modification clause must be complied with.

6. **Agreement to accept part payment of debt:** Some courts apply the pre-existing duty rule to render unenforceable a creditor's promise *not to require payment* by his debtor *of the full debt*. These courts also treat as unenforceable a creditor's promise to allow the debtor *extra time* to pay. These courts reason that the debtor already owes the money, and is therefore not promising to do something he was not already required to do. This is known as the rule of *Foakes v. Beer*.

   a. **Modern trend:** But the modern trend is to abolish or limit the rule of *Foakes v. Beer*. For instance, the UCC, in §2-209(1), says that "an agreement modifying a contract within this article needs no consideration to be binding...." This seems to overrule *Foakes v. Beer*, and to make a seller's promise to take partial payment in return for goods enforceable.

   b. **Disputed debt:** Also, the rule of *Foakes v. Beer* applies only to debts where the parties are in agreement about amount and liability, called *"liquidated"* debts. If the debtor in good faith and reasonably *disputes* his liability, or the *amount* of that liability, then a settlement by which the creditor agrees to take less than *he* thinks is due is *enforceable* (even in courts following the traditional *Foakes v. Beer* rule).

   c. **Cashing of check tendered as settlement:** Debtors sometimes send a check for less that the amount due, and mark it "in full settlement." Even if the creditor writes "In protest" on the check, but cashes it, the UCC holds that the cashing normally constitutes an acceptance by the creditor of the proposed settlement, and the creditor cannot sue for the balance. §3-311.

      i. **Requirements:** But §3-311 allows the debtor to be discharged by the creditor's cashing of the check only if *three conditions* are met:

         ❑ the check or accompanying written communication contained a *"conspicuous statement* to the effect that the instrument was tendered as full satisfaction of the claim," and

         ❑ the claim was either *"unliquidated"* or was "subjected to a *bona fide dispute*," and

         ❑ the debtor acted in *good faith.*

      ii. **Right to return payment:** There's an important exception that can hurt the debtor, though: the creditor has the right, within 90 days after cashing the check, to reverse the transaction by *paying the debtor back* the amount of the check; the creditor is thereby restored to the rights it had before cashing the check. §3-311(c)(2).

7. **Other settlements (e.g., tort suits):** Settlements of other kinds of suits (e.g., tort suits) may similarly raise consideration problems. If the plaintiff is surrendering a claim that is in fact invalid, has he given consideration to support the defendant's promise to pay a settlement? To facilitate settlements, courts today generally take a relaxed view of what's needed to constitute consideration by the plaintiff in return for the settlement promise:

a.   **Valid claim surrendered:**   If a plaintiff promises to waive a *valid claim*, all courts are in agreement that this promise is a "detriment" to the plaintiff, and constitutes consideration for the defendant's promise to pay a settlement.

b.   **Surrender of invalid claim:**   If, on the other hand, the claim that the plaintiff promises to forbear from suing on is *invalid* (or of uncertain validity), things are trickier. But even here, the modern view (represented by the Second Restatement) is that the forbearing plaintiff gives consideration if *either:*

❑   the plaintiff's forborne claim is one *whose validity is uncertain, or*

❑   the plaintiff *subjectively believes* that the forborne claim has possible merit (even if it doesn't in fact have any possible merit).

i.   **Execution of release:**   Furthermore, even if the would-be plaintiff who is forbearing from asserting her claim *does not subjectively believe* that the claim is valid, if the plaintiff *executes a written instrument settling the claim,* and the prospective defendant *bargained* for that instrument, the instrument itself will be sufficient consideration for the defendant's counter-promise, in most states.

IV. ILLUSORY, ALTERNATIVE AND IMPLIED PROMISES

A. Illusory promises: An *"illusory"* promise is not supported by consideration, and is therefore not enforceable. An illusory promise is a statement which appears to be promising something, but which in fact does not *commit* the promisor to do anything at all.

> **Example:** *A* says to *B*, "I'll sell you as many widgets at $4 apiece, up to 1,000, as you choose to order in the next 4 weeks." *B* answers, "Fine, we've got a deal." *B* then gives *A* an order for 100 widgets, and *A* refuses to sell at the stated price because the market has gone up. *B*'s promise is illusory, since she has not committed herself to do anything. Therefore, *A*'s promise is not supported by consideration, and is not binding on him.

1.   **Right to terminate:**   If the contract allows one or both parties to *terminate* the agreement at his option, this right of termination might make the promise illusory and the contract therefore unenforceable.

a.   **Unfettered right:**   If the agreement allows one party to terminate simply by giving *notice at any time*, the traditional common-law view is that the party with the termination right has not furnished consideration. But the modern trend is to hold that as long as the terminating party has the obligation to *give notice* (even if this obligation is an *implied* one), this duty of notice itself furnishes consideration.

B. Implied promises: Courts try to avoid striking down agreements for lack of consideration. One way they do this is by finding that the promisee has made an *implied promise* in return.

Example: D, a fashion designer, gives P the exclusive right to sell products made from D's designs. P promises to pay royalties on any product sold, but the agreement does not expressly require P to make sales. D violates the agreement by letting someone else sell her designs. P sues D, who defends on the grounds that P did not really promise to do anything, and that there is thus no consideration for D's promise of exclusivity.

> *Held,* for P — P can be impliedly found to have promised to use reasonable efforts to market D's designs, thus furnishing consideration for D's counter-promise. [*Wood v. Lucy, Lady Duff Gordon*].

V. REQUIREMENTS AND OUTPUT CONTRACTS

A. Requirements and output contracts generally: In a *requirements* contract, the parties agree that the seller will be the exclusive source of all the buyer's requirements for a particular type of item for a particular time. In an *output* contract, the buyer agrees to take all of the seller's output of a particular type of item.

   1. Enforceable today: Under traditional consideration rules, requirements and output contracts were sometimes found lacking in consideration. But today, requirements contracts are generally *enforced*, assuming (as is usually the case) that the buyer is found to have *implicitly promised to use his best efforts to generate a need for the goods.* Similarly, output contracts are generally enforced, as long as the seller has implicitly promised to attempt to maintain his production at a reasonable level.

   2. UCC approach: The *UCC explicitly validates requirements and output contracts.* UCC § 2-306 provides that "a term which measures the quantity by the output of the seller or the requirements of the buyer means such actual output or requirements as may occur in *good faith*, except that no quantity *unreasonably disproportionate* to any stated estimate or in the absence of a stated estimate to any normal or otherwise comparable prior output or requirements may be tendered or demanded."

   a. Best efforts imposed on buyers and sellers: There is a special type of good-faith obligation imposed by §2-306 on buyers and sellers under requirements contracts. §2-306(2) says that "A lawful agreement by either the seller or the buyer for exclusive dealing in the kind of goods concerned *imposes* unless otherwise agreed an obligation by the *seller to use best efforts to supply the goods* and by the *buyer to use best efforts to promote their sale.*"

   i. Significance: Therefore, under a requirements contract the buyer must make best efforts to promote the sale of the goods, and *cannot simply decide that the entire product line is not worth carrying*. Conversely, under an output contract the seller cannot simply decide to *stop selling or manufacturing* the item, and must instead make best efforts to supply the goods.

Chapter 4

PROMISES BINDING WITHOUT CONSIDERATION

I. PROMISES TO PAY PAST DEBTS

A. General rule: Most states enforce a ***promise to pay a past debt***, even though no consideration for the promise is given. Thus promises to pay debts that have been discharged by bankruptcy, or that are no longer collectible because of the statute of limitations, are enforceable in most states.

    1. Writing required: Most states require a ***signed writing***, at least where the promise is to pay a debt barred by the statute of limitations.

II. PROMISE TO PAY FOR BENEFITS RECEIVED

A. Generally: A promise to pay for ***benefits*** or ***services*** one has previously received will generally be enforceable even without consideration. This is especially likely where the services were ***requested***, or where the services were furnished without request in an ***emergency***.

III. OTHER CONTRACTS BINDING WITHOUT CONSIDERATION

A. Modification of sales contracts: Under the UCC, a ***modification*** of a contract for the sale of goods is binding without consideration. See §2-209. (*Example*: *A* contracts to supply 100 widgets to *B* at $4 a piece. Before shipment, *A* says, "My costs have gone up; I'll have to charge you $5." *B* agrees. Under UCC §2-209, this modification is enforceable, even though *B* received no consideration for promising to pay the higher price.)

    1. No-oral-modification clauses: But a "no oral modifications" clause in a sales contract will normally be enforced. (*Example*: On the facts of the above example, if the original contract between *A* and *B* said that any modification must be in writing, *B*'s promise to pay the higher price would be enforceable only if in writing.)

B. Option contracts: Recall that ***option contracts*** are sometimes enforceable without consideration. Thus an offer that purports to be enforceable, and that falsely recites that consideration was paid for the irrevocability, will be enforced in most courts. Also, remember that UCC §2-205 renders enforceable "firm offers" under certain circumstances.

C. Guaranties: In most states, a ***guaranty*** (that is, a promise to pay the debts of another) will be enforced without consideration. Generally, the guarantee must be in writing, and must state that consideration has been paid (though the consideration does not in fact have to have been paid).

IV. PROMISSORY ESTOPPEL

A. General approach: Promises which foreseeably induce *reliance* on the part of the promisee will often be enforceable without consideration, under the doctrine of *promissory estoppel ("P.E.")*. Rest.2d, §90's definition of the doctrine is as follows: "A promise which the promisor *should reasonably expect to induce action or forbearance* on the part of the promisee or a third person and which does induce such action or forbearance *is binding if injustice can be avoided only by enforcement of the promise*."

> **Example:** *A* promises to pay for *B*'s college education if *B* will attend school full time. *A* intends this to be a gift. *B* gives up a good job and enrolls in college, incurring a liability of $5,000 for the first year. *A* then refuses to pay the bill. Under the doctrine of P.E., *B* would be able to recover at least the value of the lost job and first-year tuition from *A*, even though *A*'s promise was a promise to make a gift and was thus not supported by consideration.

1. Actual reliance: The promisee must *actually rely* on the promise. (*Example*: On the facts of the above example, *B* must show that without *A*'s promise, *B* would not have quit his job and attended college.)

2. Foreseeable reliance: The promisee's reliance must also have been *reasonably foreseeable* to the promisor.

B. Possible applications:

1. Promise to make a gift: The P.E. doctrine is most often applied to enforce promises to *make gifts*, where the promisee relies on the gift to his detriment.

    a. Intra-family promises: The doctrine may be applied where the promise is made by one member of a *family* to another. (*Example*: Mother promises to pay for Son's college education, and Son quits his job. Probably the court will award just the damages Son suffers from losing the job, not the full cost of a college education.)

2. Charitable subscriptions: A written promise to make a *charitable contribution* will generally be binding without consideration, under the P.E. doctrine. Here, the doctrine is watered down: usually the charity does not need to show detrimental reliance. (But *oral* promises to make charitable contributions usually will not be enforceable unless the charity relies on the promise to its detriment.)

3. Gratuitous bailments and agencies: If a person promises to *take care of* another's property (a "gratuitous bailment") or promises to carry out an act as another person's *agent* (gratuitous agency), the promisor may be held liable under P.E. if he does not perform at all. (However, courts are hesitant to apply P.E. to promises to *procure insurance* for another.)

4. Offers by sub-contractors: Where a *sub-contractor* makes a *bid* to a general contractor, and the latter uses the bid in computing his own master bid on the job, the P.E. doctrine is often used to make the sub-bid temporarily irrevocable.

    a. Reliance by general contractor: In the sub-contractor-bid scenario, be sure to *check for reliance by the general contractor (GC)*. If there is no real (and justifiable) reliance by the GC on the sub-contractor's bid, the GC will **not be permitted to use P.E.** to make the sub-contractor's bid temporarily irrevocable.

> **Example:** Suppose the sub-contractor discovers its bid is too low and tells the GC about this *before* the GC's own bid has been opened by the owner. In this scenario, the GC might be able to avoid the problem by revising or withdrawing its master bid. If the GC has this opportunity and doesn't use it, then the GC has not reasonably relied, and will not qualify for promissory estoppel.

5. **Promise of job:** If an employer promises an ***at-will job*** to an employee, and then revokes the promise before the employee shows up for work, P.E. may apply.

> **Example:** *A* offers a job to *B*, terminable by either at any time. *B* quits his established job. Before *B* shows up for work, *A* cancels the job offer. A court might hold that even though *B* could have been fired at any time once he showed up, *B* should be able to collect the value of the job he quit from *A*, under a P.E. theory.

6. **Negotiations in good faith:** A person who ***negotiates*** with another may be found to have a duty to ***bargain in good faith***; if bad faith is found, the court may use P.E. to furnish a remedy.

> **Example:** *A*, owner of a shopping mall, promises that it will negotiate a lease for particular space with *B*, a tenant. *B* rejects an offer of space from another landlord. *A* then leases the space to one of *B*'s competitors for a higher rent. A court might apply P.E., by holding that *A* implicitly promised to use good faith in the negotiations and breached that promise.

   a. **Promises of franchise:** The use of P.E. to protect negotiating parties is especially likely where the promise is a promise by a national corporation to award a ***franchise*** to the other party.

   > **Example:** P, a national company that runs a fast food chain, promises B a franchise. B quits his job and undergoes expensive training in the restaurant business. If A then refuses to award the franchise, a court might use P.E. to enforce the promise, at least to the extent of reimbursing B for his lost job and training expenses.

   b. **Unequal bargaining power:** Beyond the promise-of-a-franchise situation, the court may apply P.E. in any scenario like this: two parties (call them *A* and *B*) engage in a lengthy business negotiation, where *A* is a powerful company that seems to be ***"stringing along"*** the relatively powerless *B* by holding out the likelihood that if *B* does certain acts, *A* will likely enter into some sort of business arrangement with *B* to *B*'s benefit. If the court believes that *A* has acted in bad faith for the purpose of gaining the ***"upper hand"*** over *B*, the court may apply P.E. to protect at least *B*'s reliance interest, ***even if there was no reasonably-definite "contract" that the parties were negotiating.***

   > **Example:** Bank, a large money-center bank, holds a mortgage on a home owned by O. O loses her job. At a time when O has not yet fallen behind

on her mortgage, O calls Bank to find out whether Bank would be willing to give her any relief. Bank responds, "We can and will negotiate with you to see if your mortgage can be modified to make it easier for you to pay. However, we can do that only if you first furnish certain financial information, and only if your mortgage is in default at the time you furnish the info." O, in response, stops paying the mortgage and immediately furnishes the required information. Bank refuses to enter into modification negotiations, and instead immediately starts a foreclosure proceeding.

There is a respectable chance that the court will find that O can successfully assert the promissory estoppel defense. There is a large disparity of bargaining power between Bank and O, and there is evidence that Bank has "strung O along," by foreseeably causing O to fall into default, thereby enabling Bank to bring a foreclosure that it could not otherwise have brought. And the court might well apply P.E. even though Bank never promised to actually enter into a loan modification, merely to negotiate towards one. (That is, the court would in effect be enforcing the *promise to negotiate*, not enforcing any actual modification.) [Cf. *Dixon v. Wells Fargo, N.A.*]

C. Amount of recovery: Where P.E. is used, the damages awarded are generally limited to those necessary to ***"prevent injustice."*** Usually, this will mean that the plaintiff receives ***reliance*** damages, rather than the greater expectation measure. In other words, P is placed in the position he would have been in had the promise never been made.

Example 1: If *A* promises *B* a franchise, and *B* quits his job in reliance, the court will probably award *B* the value of the lost job, not the greater sum equaling profits that *B* would have made from the franchise.

Example 2: On facts like the mortgage-modification example *supra*, the court will probably restore O's mortgage to its pre-default status, not impose an actual mortgage modification of the sort that Bank promised to negotiate towards. Then, if O can't resume making timely mortgage payments in the original amount, Bank would be permitted to resume the foreclosure.

CHAPTER 5

MISTAKE

I.   MISTAKE GENERALLY

A. Definition: A "mistake" is a ***"belief that is not in accord with the facts."***

1. **Mutual mistake:** If both parties have the same mistaken belief, the mistake is said to be ***"mutual."***

2. **Unilateral:** By contrast, if only one party has the mistaken belief, the mistake is ***"unilateral."***

3. **Existing fact:** The doctrines applicable to mistake apply only to a mistaken belief about an ***existing fact***, ***not*** an erroneous belief about ***what will happen in the future***.

> **Example:** If Buyer and Seller both think that a stone is an emerald when it is in fact a topaz, this is a mistake. But if Buyer and Seller both think that the price of oil will remain relatively stable over the next five years, and in fact it goes up by 50% per year, this is not a mistake, since it does not relate to existing fact.

4. **Mistake of law:** A mistake about a ***legal principle***, according to most courts today, can be a mistake.

II. MUTUAL MISTAKE

A. **Three requirements for avoidance:** Three requirements must be satisfied before the adversely-affected party may ***avoid the contract*** on account of ***mutual mistake***:

1. **Basic assumption:** The mistake must concern a ***basic assumption*** on which the contract was made. (*Examples*: The belief that a violin is a Stradavarius when it is in fact a worthless 20th century imitation is a "basic" mistake. But the seller's belief that a buyer to whom he is selling on credit is credit-worthy is probably a "collateral" rather than a "basic" mistake.)

2. **Material effect:** The mistake must have a ***material effect*** on the "agreed exchange of performance." (*Example*: If both Buyer and Seller thinks that a violin is a Stradavarius, but it is in fact a Guarnarius worth almost the same amount, the mistake would not have a "material effect" on the agreed exchange.)

3. **Risk:** The adversely-affected party (the one seeking to avoid the contract) must not be the one on whom the contract has implicitly ***imposed the risk*** of the mistake. Often, the contract does not make it clear which party is to bear the risk of a certain type of mistake, so the court allocates this risk in the manner that it finds to be ***"reasonable"*** in the circumstances.

B. **Special contexts:**

1. **Market conditions:** Mistakes as to ***market conditions*** will generally ***not*** be "basic" ones, so the mistaken party will not be able to avoid the contract. (*Example*: Seller agrees to sell Blackacre to Buyer. Both parties believe that comparable land is worth $5,000 per acre. Buyer can't avoid the contract if comparable land is really worth $2,000 per acre.)

2. **Existence of subject matter:** The ***existence*** of the subject matter of the contract is usually a "basic" assumption.

> **Example:** Seller agrees to sell land containing timber to Buyer. Both parties believe that there are 100,000 board feet on the property. In fact, fire has destroyed much of the timber, so that only 20,000 feet remain. This will be a basic assumption, so Buyer can avoid the contract when the facts emerge, whether this is before or after closing.

3. **Quality of subject matter:** A major mistake as to the *quality* of the contract's subject matter is often a "basic" assumption, so the disadvantaged party can avoid the contract. (*Example*: If both parties believe a violin is a Stradavarius when in fact it is an almost worthless imitation, this will be a mistake on a basic assumption, and Buyer can avoid the contract.)

4. **Minerals in land:** In land-sale contracts, the Seller will almost always bear the risk that valuable *oil and gas* deposits will be found on the land (i.e., Seller cannot avoid the contract when such a discovery is made).

5. **Building conditions:** When a builder contracts to **construct a building** on land owned by the other party, the builder will almost always be found to bear the risk of a mistake about soil or other unexpected conditions, so he cannot avoid the contract if construction proves much more difficult than expected.

6. **Used paintings and other collectibles:** Suppose the owner of a painting or other *used "collectible"* sells it in a private sale, and the object turns out to be of a fundamentally different — and more valuable — nature than either side believed. Courts generally have allocated this risk to the *owner/seller*, on the theory that seller had the opportunity to ascertain the true value and can't ride on the coattails of a buyer who does so.

III. UNILATERAL MISTAKE

A. **Modern view:** Where the mistake is *unilateral*, it is more difficult for the mistaken party to avoid the contract than in the mutual mistake situation. The mistaken party must make the same three showings as for mutual mistake (basic assumption, material effect, and risk on the other party), *plus* must show *either* that:

> [1] **Unconscionability:** The mistake is such that enforcement of the contract would be *unconscionable*; or

> [2] **Reason to know:** The other party had *reason to know* of the mistake, or the other party's *fault* caused the mistake.

1. **An offer too good to be true:** As indicated in [2] above, a person who wants to avoid a contract on account of unilateral mistake will often try to show that the *other party had reason to know of the mistake.* In the case of a mistake reflected in an *offer* that the offeree accepted, and that the offeror now wants to rescind for mistake, the offeror will try to show that the *offeree knew or should have known* that the offer (with the mistake embedded in it) was *"too good to be true."*

    a. **"Snapping up" the offer:** If the offeror can make this "too good to be true" showing, she will have a good chance of meeting all the elements for rescission on grounds of unilateral mistake. As the idea is usually put, "[a]n offeree *may not snap up an offer* that is on its face *manifestly too good to be true."* [*Lange v. U.S.*]

    b. **Mechanical errors and "mental blunders":** Most often, what makes an offer "too good to be true" is that the circumstances would suggest to any reasonable offeree that the offer is probably the result of a *"mechanical error"* or a *"mental blunder."*

Example: Two parties, *A* and *B*, have been negotiating a contract under which *A* will pay *B* about $2 million for certain services by *B*; *A* indicates a willingness to pay up to $2.51 million, and *B* insists on receiving at least $2.53 million. Then, *A* emails *B*, "I'll meet you halfway — I hereby offer to pay $2.55 million." *B* emails back, "I accept — $2.55."

In view of the prior discussions (where *B* indicated that he would take $2.53 million) and *A*'s current "meet you halfway" remark, *B* should know that *A*'s "$2.55 million" offer was likely a computational error or some other sort of basic blunder, not a thought-out concession. Therefore, *B* was not entitled to "snap up" the offer, and *A* will likely succeed in using the unilateral-mistake doctrine to have the contract either thrown out entirely, or reformed to $2.52 million (halfway between the $2.51 and $2.53 numbers previously discussed). [Cf. *Sumerel v. Goodyear Tire & Rubber Co.*]

B. Construction bids: One common type of unilateral mistake occurs where a ***contractor*** or sub-contractor makes an error on a ***bid*** for a construction job.

   1. Unconscionability: The mistaken contractor will succeed in showing unconscionability (one of the two alternate special showings needed for unilateral mistake) only if he shows that not only will he be ***severely harmed*** if forced to perform, but also that the other party ***has not relied*** on the bid.

   Example: Sub-contractor gives contractor a bid of $50,000 for electrical work. Contractor relies on this bid to prepare her own master bid for the entire project. Contractor gets the contract, enters into a sub-contract with Sub-contractor, and Sub-contractor then discovers that his $50,000 bid should have been $75,000, due to a clerical error. The court would probably not find it unconscionable to hold Sub-contractor to the contract, because Contractor has relied on the $50,000 sub-bid.

   2. "Snapping up" of offer: Alternatively, the mistaken bidder can win on unilateral mistake if she can show that the other party either ***knew*** or had ***reason to know*** of the error, and ***"snapped up"*** this offer that was "too good to be true." (See Par. 1(a) and 1(b) above.)

   Example: In the above example, if Sub-contractor can show that Contractor should have known that there probably was a mistake, because Sub-contractor's bid was 50% lower than all other sub-bids, the court is likely to let Sub-contractor avoid the contract based on unilateral mistake.

IV. DEFENSES AND REMEDIES

A. Negligence: Where a party seeks to avoid the contract because of his own (or both parties') mistake, the fact that the mistake was due to his ***negligence*** will ordinarily ***not prevent relief***.

   1. Failure to read writing: But if the mistake stems from a party's ***failure to read the contract***, he will ***not*** normally be entitled to rescind.

B. Remedies: There are two main *remedies* that may be appropriate for mistake:

   1. Avoidance: The most common remedy is *avoidance* of the contract (sometimes called *"rescission"*). Here, the court treats the contract as if it has never been made, and attempts to return each party to the position he was in just before the contract was signed. Generally, *restitution* will be ordered — each party will return the benefits he has received from the other.

   > **Example:** Seller agrees to sell its interest in a particular parcel of vacant land to Buyer, under an installment contract. Buyer makes it clear to Seller that Buyer's only intended use for the property is to grow a particular shrub on it, something which requires adequate water supplies. After the purchase, wells drilled by Buyer show that there is no adequate water beneath the property. Buyer sues Seller for rescission on grounds of mutual mistake.

   > A court would hold that Buyer is entitled to return of its down payment. However, the court would also probably require Buyer to pay Seller for the fair rental value of the property during the time Buyer had possession of it. Conversely, Seller would be required to compensate Buyer for any increase in the value of the property brought about by Buyer's drilling of test wells. (But Buyer wouldn't get the cost of the drilling of the test wells, except to the extent those wells increased the value of the property.)

   2. Reliance: Alternatively, the court may award *reliance* damages, especially where restitution/avoidance would not work because one party has suffered loses but the other has not received benefits.

V. REFORMATION AS REMEDY FOR ERROR IN EXPRESSION

A. Generally: If the parties orally agree on a deal, but mistakenly prepare and execute a document which *incorrectly reflects* the oral agreement, either party may obtain a court order for *reformation* (i.e., a re-writing of the document).

   > **Example:** Seller orally agrees to sell Blackacre to Buyer for $100,000. Their oral deal includes a provision that Buyer will also assume an existing mortgage of $50,000. The written agreement neglects the assumption provision. At either party's request, the court will reform the document so that it includes the assumption provision.

CHAPTER 6

PAROL EVIDENCE AND INTERPRETATION

I. PAROL EVIDENCE RULE GENERALLY

A. What the rule does: The parol evidence rule limits the extent to which a party may establish that discussions or writings prior to the signed written contract should be taken as part of the agreement. In some circumstances, the rule bars the fact-finder from considering any evidence of certain preliminary agreements that are not contained in the final writing, even though this evidence might show that the preliminary agreement did in fact take place and that the parties intended it to remain part of their deal despite its absence from the writing.

II. TOTAL AND PARTIAL INTEGRATIONS

A. Definitions:

1. **"Integration":** A document is said to be an *"integration"* of the parties' agreement if it is intended as the *final expression* of the agreement. (The parol evidence rule applies *only to documents which are "integrations,"* i.e., final expressions of agreement.)

2. **Partial integration:** A *"partial"* integration is a document that is intended to be final, but that is *not* intended to include *all details* of the parties' agreement.

3. **Total integration:** A *"total"* integration is a document that is not only a final expression of agreement, but that is also intended to include *all details* of the agreement.

B. Statement of rule: The "parol evidence rule" is in fact two sub-rules:

1. **Partial integration:** When a writing is a *partial integration*, no evidence of prior or contemporaneous agreements or negotiations (oral or written) may be admitted if this evidence would *contradict* a term of the writing.

2. **Total integration:** When a document is a *total integration*, no evidence of prior or contemporaneous agreements or negotiations may be admitted which would *either contradict* or *add* to the writing.

3. **Summary:** Putting the two sub-parts together, the parol evidence rule provides that evidence of a prior agreement may never be admitted to *contradict an integrated writing*, and may furthermore not even *supplement* an integration which is intended to be *complete*.

4. **Prior writings and oral agreements:** The parol evidence rule applies to *oral agreements and discussions* that occur *prior* to a signing of an integration. It also applies to *writings* created prior to an integration (e.g., draft agreements that were not intended to be final expressions of agreement).

5. **Contemporaneous writing:** If an *ancillary writing* is signed at the *same time* a formal document is signed, the ancillary document is treated as *part of the writing*, and will not be subject to the parol evidence rule.

6. **Subsequent agreements:** The parol evidence rule *never bars consideration of subsequent oral agreements*. That is, *a written contract may always be modified after its execution*, by an oral agreement.

   a. **"No oral modifications" clause:** However, if the written document contains a *"no oral modification"* clause, that clause will usually be enforced by the court, unless the court finds that the defendant *waived* the benefits of that clause.

C. UCC: Section 2-202 of the *UCC* essentially follows the common-law parol evidence rule as summarized above.

III. ROLES OF JUDGE AND JURY

A. Preliminary determinations made by judge: Nearly all courts hold that the *judge*, not the jury, decides: (1) whether the writing was intended as an integration; (2) if so, whether the integration is "partial" or "total"; and (3) whether particular evidence would supplement the terms of a complete integration.

    1. Conflicting views: Courts disagree about how the judge should make these decisions. Two extreme positions are: (1) the *"four corners"* rule, by which the judge decides whether there is an integration, and whether it is total or partial, by looking *solely at the document*; and (2) the "Corbin" view, by which these questions are to be answered by looking at *all available evidence*, including testimony, to determine the *actual intention* of the parties.

    2. Merger clause: Most contracts contain a *"merger" clause*, i.e., a clause stating that the writing constitutes the sole agreement between the parties. The presence of such a clause makes it more likely that the court will find the writing to have been intended as a total integration (in which case not even consistent additional prior oral or written terms may be shown).

IV. SITUATIONS WHERE PAROL EVIDENCE RULE DOES NOT APPLY

A. Fraud, mistake or other voidability: Even if a writing is a total integration, a party may always introduce evidence of earlier oral agreements to show *illegality, fraud, duress, mistake, lack of consideration*, or any other fact that would make the contract void or voidable. In other words, the parol evidence rule never prevents the introduction of evidence that would show that *no valid contract exists* or that the contract is voidable.

    Example: In order to induce Buyer to buy a rental property, Seller lies about the profitability of the property. The parties then sign a sale contract that contains a standard "merger" clause, reciting that the contract constitutes the sole agreement between the parties. The parol evidence rule will not prevent Buyer from showing that Seller made fraudulent misrepresentations to induce him to enter into the contract.

    1. Particular disclaimer: But if the contract contains a very specific statement that no representations of a *particular sort* have been made, some courts prevent a party from showing that the disclaimer is false.

        Example: On the facts of the above example, suppose that the contract stated, "Seller has made no representations or warranties regarding the profitability of the property, and Buyer has relied solely on his own investigation as to profitability." Some courts — though probably a minority — would prohibit Buyer from showing that Seller in fact made fraudulent misrepresentations about profitability.

B. Existence of a condition: If the parties orally agree on a *condition* to the enforce-ability of the contract, or to the duty of one of them, but this condition is then not included in the writing, courts generally *allow proof* of this condition despite the parol evidence rule.

> **Example:** *A* and *B* agree that *A* will sell a patent to *B* for $10,000 if C, an engineer advising *B*, approves. *A* and *B* sign a written agreement that seems to be complete, except that the contract does not mention C's approval. Nearly all courts would allow *B* to prove that the oral agreement regarding approval was in fact made.

C. Collateral agreements: An oral agreement that is supported by *separate consider-ation* may be demonstrated, even though it occurred prior to what seems to be a total integration.

> **Example:** In a written agreement that seems to be a complete expression of the parties' intent, *A* promises to sell *B* a particular automobile. As part of the transac-tion, the parties orally agree that *B* may keep the car in *A*'s garage for one year for $15 per month. Because the alleged oral agreement is supported by separate con-sideration — the $15 per month — *B* may prove that the oral agreement occurred even though there is an integrated writing that does not include that agreement.

   1. Not inconsistent with total integration: However, if the writing is a total inte-gration, the separate agreement must not be *directly inconsistent* with the writing.

   > **Example:** Same facts as above example. Assume the writing has a merger clause, saying that there are no other agreements between the parties regard-ing the automobile transaction. Suppose further that the writing says, "*B* shall have no right to keep the car in *A*'s garage at any time." *B* will not be allowed to prove the alleged oral collateral agreement, since that agreement is directly inconsistent with the writing, and the writing is a total integration.

D. Subsequent transactions: Recall that the parol evidence rule never bars evidence that *after the signing of the writing*, the parties orally or in writing agreed to modify or rescind the writing.

E. Interpretation: The parol evidence rule does not bar extrinsic evidence when offered to aid in the *interpretation* to be given to an *ambiguous term* of the contract. This rule is discussed extensively in the next section, "Interpretation," immediately below.

V. INTERPRETATION

A. Modern view: Most courts today allow parties to introduce extrinsic evidence to aid in the *interpretation* of a contract, even if the writing is an integration. However, courts vary on the details of how and when extrinsic evidence is allowed in connection with a question of interpretation.

   1. Extrinsic evidence in the case of ambiguous terms: *All courts agree* that if a term is found by the trial court to be *ambiguous* — capable of more than one meaning — *extrinsic evidence must be allowed*.

   a. Evaluated by jury: Furthermore, courts are in near-universal agreement that this extrinsic evidence is to be *evaluated by the jury*, not by the judge.

    b. Evidence of parties' own pre-contract negotiations: Finally, courts are in unanimous agreement that the types of extrinsic evidence that are to be allowed to help resolve the meaning of the ambiguous term are *extremely broad*. In particular, courts agree that evidence about what the parties' own *pre-contract negotiations* indicated to be the meaning of the ambiguous term is to be *admitted*, and heard by the jury.

        Example: Seller sells a business to Buyer. Part of the purchase price is a delayed payment equal to 10% of the "Gross Profit" of the business in the first year after sale. The parties have a dispute about what "Gross Profit" means. If the trial court finds that the term is ambiguous, the judge will then let the jury hear testimony from each side about any statements either party made during the negotiations that might bear on what the term means.

  2. Unambiguous terms: Now, let's suppose that the trial judge decides that the term in question is completely *unambiguous*. Here, too, courts are in virtual unanimity about what happens next. Since the term is unambiguous, it is *for the judge*, not the jury, to *say what the term means*. Consequently, the jury will be instructed by the judge on the term's meaning, and the jury will never hear any sort of extrinsic evidence about what the term means.

  3. How judge determines existence of ambiguity: The area of main disagreement among courts is *how the judge should decide whether the term is ambiguous*. There are three main approaches: (1) the *"four corners"* rule; (2) the *"plain meaning"* rule; and (3) the *"liberal"* rule.

    a. The "four corners" rule: The *"four corners"* rule is the most stringent of the three. Under this approach, when the judge decides whether the term is ambiguous, the judge *may not consult any extrinsic evidence whatsoever.* That is, the existence of ambiguity is to be determined *solely by looking within the "four corners" of the contract itself.* Thus not only will the court not consider evidence about the parties' negotiations, it will not even consider evidence about the context surrounding the making of the agreement. This hyper-strict rule is followed by relatively few courts.

    b. The "plain meaning" rule: The *"plain meaning"* rule is in the *middle* of the three approaches in terms of strictness. The most significant aspect of the plain meaning rule is that when the court goes to decide whether a term used in the agreement is ambiguous, the court *will not hear evidence about the parties' preliminary negotiations.* (However, the court *will* hear evidence about the circumstances, or *"context,"* surrounding the making of the agreement.)

        Example: On the facts of the above example, suppose the judge is deciding whether the term "Gross Profit" is ambiguous. A court following the "plain meaning" rule would probably hear testimony about what the term usually means in contracts of this sort (just to help the judge determine whether the term is or isn't ambiguous), but would *not* hear testimony about what the parties said during their negotiations (e.g., testimony by

Seller that "Buyer told me that 'everybody knows that Gross Profit means [thus-and-such]' ").

    c. **The "liberal" rule:** Finally, what might be called the *"liberal"* rule rejects — or at least significantly weakens — the plain meaning approach. Under the liberal view, *evidence of the parties' statements during their pre-contract negotiations* is *admissible* for the limited purpose of letting the trial judge determine whether the term is ambiguous.

        Example: On the facts of the above example, a court following the liberal approach would, when trying to decide whether the term Gross Profit is ambiguous, hear Seller's testimony about what Buyer told him during the pre-contract negotiations about the meaning of the term.

B. Maxims of interpretation: There are a number of "maxims" that courts use in deciding which of two conflicting interpretations of a clause should be followed:

    1. **Primary purpose:** If the *"primary purpose"* of the parties in making the contract can be ascertained, that purpose is given great weight.

    2. **All terms made reasonable, lawful and effective:** All terms will be interpreted, where possible, so that they will have a *reasonable, lawful* and *effective* meaning.

    3. **Construed against drafter:** An ambiguous term will be *construed against the person who drafted the contract*.

    4. **Negotiated terms control standard terms:** A term that has been *negotiated* between the parties will control over one that is part of a standardized portion of the agreement (i.e., the fine print "boilerplate"). (*Example*: A clause that has been typewritten in as a "rider" to a pre-printed form contract, or a clause that has been handwritten onto a typewritten, agreement, will have priority.)

C. One party knows or should know of the other's meaning: Where the parties *attach different meanings to a particular term,* some special rules of interpretation apply:

    ❏ If one party *knows* (or has *reason to know*) that the two parties attach different meanings to the term, and the other *does not know or have reason to know* this, then the meaning given by the latter *("innocent") party controls*;

    ❏ If *neither* party *knows or should know* that the two parties attach different meanings to the term, then *neither party is bound* by the other's meaning. In that case, the court will *supply a reasonable value* for the unagreed-upon term.

VI. TRADE USAGE, COURSE OF PERFORMANCE, AND COURSE OF DEALING

A. Definitions: There are three special sources which are used in interpreting the terms of a contract. These are especially important in sales contracts, since the UCC gives these sources specific treatment:

1. **Course of performance:** A *"course of performance"* refers to the way the parties have previously conducted themselves in performing the ***particular contract at hand***.

    Example: The contract calls for repeated deliveries of "highest grade oil." Evidence as to the quality of oil delivered and accepted in the first installments would be admissible as a course of performance to help determine whether oil delivered in a later installment met the contract standard.

2. **Course of dealing:** A *"course of dealing"* refers to how the parties have acted with respect to ***past contracts***.

3. **Usage of trade:** A *"usage of trade"* is "any practice or method of dealing having such regularity of observance in a place, vocation or trade as to justify an expectation that it will be observed with respect to the transaction in question." UCC §1-303(c). Thus the meaning attached to a particular term in a certain region, or in a certain industry, would be admissible.

B. **Used to interpret even a complete integration:** Course of dealing, course of performance, and usage of trade may be introduced to help interpret the meaning of a writing ***even if the writing is a complete integration***. That is, these sources are not affected by the parol evidence rule — even though a writing is found to be the final and exclusive embodiment of the agreement, it may still be explained by evidence from these three sources.

    Example: Customer orders 1,000 letterheads from Printer. Assume that it is a custom in the printing industry that where a particular quantity is ordered, any variation by the printer from that quantity is acceptable as long as it is not greater than 5% above or below it. Printer delivers 960 letterheads, and Customer rejects the shipment as non-conforming.

    Notwithstanding the parol evidence rule, Printer will likely be able to introduce this 5%-variation custom as a "trade usage." To do so, Printer will have to show that the custom is so regularly observed in the industry as to *"justify an expectation that it will be observed* with respect to the transaction in question" — §1-303(c). But Printer doesn't have to show that Customer *actually* knew of the trade usage, merely that Customer *should* have known of it, due to its regular observation in the industry.

    1. **Contradiction of express terms:** But these customs may not be used to ***contradict*** the express terms of a contract. See UCC §1-303(e). However, if these customs can reasonably be harmonized with the writing, then the customs may be shown and may become part of the contract.

C. **Priorities:** Where more than one of these types of customs is present, the ***most specific pattern controls***. Thus an express contractual provision controls over a course of performance, which controls over a course of dealing, which controls over a trade usage. UCC §§1-303(e)(1)-(3).

VII. OMITTED TERMS SUPPLIED BY COURT

A. Generally: Courts will generally *supply a missing term* (that is, a term as to which the contract documents are silent) if it is apparent that the parties wanted to bind themselves, and there is a reasonable way for the court to go about formulating the missing term. Here are some examples:

1. **Good faith:**   The court will normally supply a term imposing on each party a *"duty of good faith."* (*Example*: Where *A* agrees to have exclusive marketing rights to a design or invention produced by *B*, *A* will be found to have an implied duty to make good-faith efforts to promote *B*'s product.) See *supra*, p. C-60, for more about this obligation of good faith.

2. **Duty to continue business:**   In requirement and output contracts, generally there will ***not*** be a duty to *continue the business* (assuming the owner acted in good faith when she closed it down.)

3. **Termination of dealership or franchise:**   Some but not all courts will supply a term to prevent one party from arbitrarily terminating a *franchise* or *dealership* arrangement. Sometimes, the court will refuse to allow termination except for cause. More commonly, courts will find an implied requirement of a *reasonable notice* prior to termination.

4. **Termination of employment contract:**   A strong minority of courts now find that an *at-will employment contract* contains an implied term prohibiting the employer from terminating the arrangement in *bad faith*. In these courts, an employer may not terminate an at-will arrangement in order to deprive the employee of a pension, to retaliate for the employee's refusal to commit wrongdoing at the employer's urging, or for other bad faith reasons.

CHAPTER 7

CONDITIONS, BREACH AND OTHER ASPECTS OF PERFORMANCE

I. CONDITIONS GENERALLY

A. Definition of "condition":   An event which must occur before a particular performance is due is called a *"condition"* of that performance.

Example: Seller promises to ship Buyer 100 widgets. Buyer promises to pay for the widgets within 30 days of receipt. The parties agree that if the widgets don't meet Buyer's specs, he may return them and he will not have to pay for them. It is a condition of Buyer's duty of payment that the widgets be shipped, and that they meet his specifications. Buyer's duty is said to be conditional on the shipment of satisfactory widgets.

1. **Concurrent:**   A *concurrent* condition is a particular kind of condition precedent which exists only when the parties to a contract are to exchange performances at the *same time*. (*Example*: *A* promises to deliver his car to *B* on a certain date, at which time *B* is to pay for the car. Delivery and payment are "concurrent condi-

tions," since performance by both is to be rendered simultaneously.) Concurrent conditions are found most frequently in contracts for the sale of goods and contracts for the conveyance of land.

2. **Express and constructive conditions:** If the parties explicitly agree that a duty is conditional upon the happening of some event, that event is an *"express"* condition. If, instead, the happening of an event is made a condition of a duty because a court so determines, the condition is a *"constructive"* one (or a condition "implied in law").

> **Example of express condition:** *A* is to ship widgets to *B*, and *B* agrees to either return them if they don't satisfy her, or pay for them. The contract states, "*B*'s duty to pay for the widgets shall be conditional upon her being satisfied with them." This is an express condition.

> **Example of constructive condition:** Same facts as above example — *A* contracts to ship widgets to *B*, and *B* agrees to either return the widgets as unsatisfactory, or pay for them. No language of condition is used in the agreement. As a matter of common law (or the UCC), the court will impose a constructive condition: *B*'s duty to pay for the widgets will be constructively conditioned upon her receiving them and being satisfied with them.

   a. **Significance of distinction:** The reason we distinguish between express and constructive conditions is that *strict compliance* with express conditions is ordinarily necessary, but merely *substantial compliance* is usually required to satisfy a constructive condition.

B. **Distinction between conditions and promises:** The fact that an act is a condition does not by itself make it also a promise. If the act is a condition on the other party's duty, and the act fails to occur, the other party won't have to perform. If the act is a promise, and it doesn't occur, the other party can sue for damages. But the two don't automatically go together.

> **Example:** Landlord promises Tenant that Landlord will make any necessary repairs on the leased premises, provided that Tenant gives him notice of the need for such repairs. Tenant's giving notice of the needed repairs is an express condition to Landlord's duty to perform the repairs. But such notice is not a promise by Tenant.

> Therefore, if Tenant does not give the notice, he has not committed any breach of contract, but a condition to Landlord's duty has failed to occur. Landlord is relieved from having to make the repairs, but cannot sue Tenant for breach.

1. **Distinguishing:** To determine whether a particular act is a condition, a promise, or both, the main factor is the *intent of the parties*. Words like "upon condition that" indicate an intent that the act be a condition; words like "I promise" or "I warrant" indicate a promise (though as described below, failure to keep the promise will also generally constitute the failure of a constructive condition).

II. EXPRESS CONDITIONS

A. Strict compliance: *Strict compliance* with an express condition is ordinarily required.

> **Example:** *A* contracts to sell his house to *B* for $100,000. The contract provides that *B*'s duty to consummate the purchase is "conditional upon *B*'s receiving a mortgage for at least $80,000 at an interest rate no higher than 9%." If the best mortgage *B* is able to obtain, after reasonable effort, is at 9.25%, the court will probably hold that *B* is not obligated to close, since the condition is an express one, and strict compliance with express conditions is ordinarily required.

1. **Avoidance of forfeiture:**   However, courts often avoid applying the "strict compliance" rule where a *forfeiture* would result. A forfeiture occurs when one party has *relied* on the bargain (e.g., by preparing to perform or by making part performance), and insistence on strict compliance with the condition would cause him to fail to receive the expected benefits from the deal.

    > **Example:** *A* contracts to build a house for *B* on land owned by *B*, for a price of $100,000. The contract provides that "*B*'s duty to pay for the house is expressly conditional upon the finished house exactly matching the specifications of *B*'s architect." *A* builds the house in general accordance with the specifications, but the living room is six inches shorter than shown on the plans, a deviation which does not noticeably affect the market value of the house.
    >
    > Despite the rule that strict compliance with an express condition is ordinarily required, the court would probably hold that strict enforcement here would amount to a forfeiture, and would therefore hold that the condition was satisfied despite the trivial defect.

    a. **Excuse of condition:**   Alternatively, a court may find that the fulfillment of the express condition is *"excused"* where extreme forfeiture would occur. This will only be done, however, if the damage to the other party's expectations from non-occurrence of the condition is relatively *minor*. (*Example*: On the facts of the above example, the damage to *B*'s expectations from the short living room is very small, so the court would probably excuse the non-occurrence of the condition.)

B. Satisfaction of a party: If a contract makes one party's duty to perform expressly conditional on that party's being *satisfied* with the other's performance, the court will usually presume that an *objective* standard of *"reasonable"* satisfaction was meant.

1. **Subjective:**   But it is the *intent* of the parties that controls here: If the parties clearly intend that one party's *subjective* satisfaction should control, the court will honor that intent. This is likely to be true, for instance, where the bargain clearly involves the *tastes* of a person. Here, dissatisfaction that is in good faith but unreasonable will still count as the non-occurrence of the condition.

C. Satisfaction of third person: If the duty of performance is expressly conditioned on the satisfaction of some *independent third party* (e.g., an architect or other professional), the third party's subjective judgment usually controls. But this judgment must be made in good faith.

1. **Good faith:** But this third-party judgment must be made in *good faith*.

    a. **Lack of careful consideration:** If there is an indication that the third party did not even *give careful consideration* to the issue requiring satisfaction, this will be powerful evidence that the third party did not act in good faith. In that case, the court will treat the satisfaction condition as being waived.

    > **Example:** Owner's duty to make progress payments to Builder for construction of a house is made conditional upon approval of each phase of the work by Architect, Owner's architect, and the payments are due five days after such approval. Builder submits to Architect a description of the work done up to a particular point, and requests the progress payment. Architect goes out of town for two months, does not inspect the work, and sends an email from abroad saying "I don't approve the work." Builder waits a month, then cancels the contract and sues Owner.
    >
    > A court would almost certainly hold that Architect's failure to inspect the work means that his lack of satisfaction was not determined in good faith, and that the non-occurrence of the condition of satisfaction should therefore be deemed waived by Owner. Consequently, when Owner didn't pay, that non-payment was itself a breach justifying Builder in canceling the contract.

III.　CONSTRUCTIVE CONDITIONS

A. **Use in bilateral conditions:** Remember that a *constructive condition* is a condition which is not agreed upon by the parties, but which is supplied by the court for fairness. The principal use of constructive conditions is in bilateral contracts (where each party makes a promise to the other).

    1. **General rule:** Where each party makes one or more promises to the other, *each party's substantial performance of his promise is generally a constructive condition to the performance of any subsequent duties by the other party*.

    > **Example:** Contractor agrees to build a house for Owner for $100,000. The contract provides that Owner will pay $10,000 upon completion of the foundation, and provides a schedule on which the work is to proceed. No language of condition is used anywhere in the document. Contractor builds the foundation on schedule, but Owner without cause refuses to pay the $10,000 charge.
    >
    > Owner's fulfillment of his promise — to pay $10,000 — is a constructive condition of Contractor's duty to continue with the work. Therefore, Contractor does not have to continue with the work until Owner pays the $10,000, even though the contract does not expressly make Contractor's duty of continuation conditional upon Owner's making the first payment. The court simply supplies this "constructive condition" for fairness, reasoning that Contractor shouldn't have to keep doing work if Owner hasn't been keeping his part of the bargain.

B. **Order of performance:** Be careful to interpret the contract to determine the *order* in which the parties' performances are to occur.

1. **Intent:**　The parties' *intent* always controls. Where the intent is not clear, the court supplies certain presumptions, as discussed below.

2. **Periodic alternating:**　The parties may agree that their performances shall *alternate*. This is true of most *installment* contracts. Here, a series of alternating constructive conditions arises: each party's obligation to perform his duty is constructively conditioned on the other's having performed the prior duty. It's therefore important to decide who was the *first* to fail to substantially perform, since that failure of substantial performance is the non-occurrence of a constructive condition of the other party's subsequent duty.

3. **No order of performance agreed upon:**　If the parties do not agree upon the order of performance, there are several general presumptions courts use:

   a. **Only one party's work requires time:**　Where the performance of one party requires a *period of time*, and the other's does not, the performance requiring time must ordinarily occur first, and its performance is a constructive condition to the other party's performance. This applies to contracts for *services* — a party who is to perform work must usually *substantially complete* the work before he may *receive payment* if the parties do not otherwise agree.

   b. **Sales of goods and land:**　If each party's promised performance can occur at the *same time* as the other's, the court will normally require that the two occur *simultaneously*, in which case the two performances are "concurrent conditions." This applies to *sales of goods and land*.

      i. **Tender of performance:**　Courts express this by saying that where the two performances are concurrent, each party must *"tender"* (i.e., *conditionally offer*) performance to the other. See UCC §§2-507(1) and 2-511(1).

         Example: Seller contracts to sell Blackacre to Buyer. The closing is to take place on July 1, at which time Seller will deliver a deed to the property free and clear of liens, and Buyer will deliver a certified check for $100,000. Since each performance can occur simultaneously, the court will presume that simultaneity is what the parties intended.

         Therefore, on July 1, Seller's duty to deliver the deed will be conditional upon Buyer's coming forward with the certified check, and Buyer's duty to come forward with the check will be conditional upon Seller's tendering the deed. If Seller fails to show up with a proper deed, Buyer will not be able to sue Seller for breach unless Buyer shows that he tendered the certified check, i.e., had the check in his possession and arrived at the place of closing with it.

C. Independent or dependent promises:　In the normal bilateral contract, the court will presume that the promises are *in exchange for each other*. That is, the court will treat the promises as being *mutually dependent*, so that each party's duty is constructively conditional upon the other's substantial performance of all previous duties.

1. **Independent promises:** But in a few situations, circumstances may indicate that the promises are intended to be *independent* of each other. Here, the court will *not* apply the theory of constructive conditions.

   a. **Real estate leases:** For instance, promises in the typical *real estate lease* are generally construed as being *independent* of each other. Thus a tenant's promise to pay rent, and a landlord's return-promise to make repairs, are treated as independent, so if the landlord does not make the repairs, the tenant cannot refuse to pay the rent (though he can of course sue for damages). But a growing minority of courts have rejected this rule of independence.

D. Divisible contracts: A *divisible* contract is one in which both parties have divided up their performance into units or installments, in such a way that each part performance is roughly the compensation for a corresponding part performance by the other party. If a contract is found to be divisible, it will for purposes of constructive conditions be treated as a series of *separate contracts*.

   1. **Significance:** If the contract is found to be divisible, here's the significance: if one party partly performs, the other will have to make *part payment*. If the contract is not divisible, then the non-breaching party won't have to pay anything at all (at least under the contract).

      Example: In a single document, Contractor agrees to build a deck for Owner and renovate Owner's kitchen. The contract lists a price of $30,000 for the renovation and $20,000 for the deck. Payment on the entire contract is due when all work is done. Contractor completes the deck but never even starts on the kitchen.

      If the contract is found to be divisible into two parts, Owner will be required to pay $20,000 for the deck even though he never gets the kitchen. If the contract is not divisible, Contractor will be found to not have substantially performed the whole, and he will not be able to recover on the contract for the work on the deck (though he will be able to recover the fair value of what he has done on a quasi-contract or restitution theory).

   2. **Test for divisibility:** A contract is divisible if it can be "apportioned into corresponding pairs of part performances so that the parts of each pair are properly regarded as *agreed equivalents*...." (*Example*: On the facts of the above example, a court would probably find that the parties implicitly agreed that $20,000 would be an agreed equivalent for the deck and $30,000 for the kitchen. Therefore, the court would probably find that the contract was divisible.)

      a. **Employment contracts:** Most *employment* contracts are looked on as being divisible. Usually, the contract will be divided into lengths of time equal to the *time between payments*. Thus if the employee is paid by the week, the contract will be divided into one-week "sub-contracts"; payment for a particular week will be constructively conditioned only on the employee's having worked that week, not on his having fulfilled the entire contract.

      b. **Fairness:** The court will not find a contract to be divisible if this would be *unfair* to the non-breaching party. For instance, even though the contract recites separate prices for different part performances, requiring the non-breaching party to pay the full stated price for the part performance received may deprive him of fair value.

> **Example:** A construction contract requires Owner to pay one-tenth of the contract price for each of 10 weeks of estimated work. The first week, Contractor does everything scheduled for that week, but the scheduling is very light, consisting mainly of site preparation. If Contractor breaches after the first week, the court will probably not find the contract divisible, since a finding of divisibility would require Owner to pay one-tenth of the contract price for performance that represents less than one-tenth of the full job.

IV. SUBSTANTIAL PERFORMANCE

A. Doctrine generally: Recall that it is a constructive condition to a party's duty of performance that the other party have made a *"substantial performance"* of the latter's previous obligations. In other words, if one party fails to substantially perform, the other party's remaining duties do not fall due.

B. Suspension followed by discharge: If a party fails to substantially perform, but the defects could be fairly easily cured, the other party's duty to give a return performance is merely *suspended*; the defaulter then has a chance to *cure* his defective performance. If, on the other hand, the defect is so substantial that it cannot be cured within a reasonable time, or if the defaulter fails to take advantage of a chance to cure, the other party is then completely *discharged*, and may also sue for breach.

C. Factors regarding materiality: Here are some factors that help determine whether a breach is material (i.e., whether the breaching party has nonetheless substantially performed):

1. Deprivation of expected benefit: The more the non-breaching party is deprived of the *benefit which he reasonably expected*, the more likely it is that the breach was material.

2. Part performance: The *greater the part of the performance* which has been rendered, the less likely it is that a breach will be deemed material. Thus a breach occurring at the very *beginning* of the contract is more likely to be deemed material than the same "size" breach coming near the end.

3. Likeliness of cure: If the breaching party seems likely to be able and willing to *cure*, the breach is less likely to be material than where cure seems impossible.

4. Willfulness: A *willful* (i.e., *intentional*) breach is more likely to be regarded as material than a breach caused by negligence or other factors.

5. Delay: A delay, even a substantial one, will not necessarily constitute a lack of substantial performance. The presumption is that *time* is *not "of the essence"* unless the contract so states, or other circumstances make the need for promptness apparent. (Even if the contract *does* contain a "time is of the essence" clause, a short delay will not be deemed "material" unless the circumstances show that the delay seriously damaged the other party.)

D. Material breach in contracts for the sale of goods: The UCC imposes special rules governing what constitutes substantial performance by a seller of goods (and thus when a buyer can reject the goods).

1. **"Perfect tender" rule:** UCC §2-601 says that as long as the contract does not involve installments (i.e., multiple deliveries), "Unless otherwise agreed...if the goods or tender of delivery fail *in any respect* to conform to the contract, the buyer may (a) reject the whole; or (b) accept the whole; or (c) accept any commercial unit or units and reject the rest." On its face, this section seems to impose the *"perfect tender"* rule — that is, it seems to give the buyer the right to cancel the contract, and refuse to pay, if the goods deviate from the contract terms in any respect, no matter how slight.

    a. **Not so strict:** But in reality, there are loopholes in this "perfect tender" rule. Courts usually only allow buyers to reject the seller's delivery if the defect is a substantial one. Also, the buyer must follow strict procedures for rejecting the delivery, and the seller generally has the right to "cure" the defect. See below.

2. **Mechanics of rejection:** The buyer may *"reject"* any non-conforming delivery from the seller. As noted, in theory this right exists if the goods deviate *in any respect* from what is required under the contract. But the buyer's right of rejection is subject to some fairly strict procedural rules:

    a. **Time:** Rejection must occur within a *"reasonable time"* after the goods are delivered. The buyer must give prompt *notice* to the seller that buyer is rejecting. §2-602(1).

    b. **Must not be preceded by acceptance:** The buyer can only reject if he has not previously "accepted" the goods. He will be deemed to have "accepted" them if either: (1) after a reasonable opportunity to *inspect*, buyer has indicated to the seller that the goods are conforming or that he will keep them despite non-conformity; or (2) buyer fails to make a timely rejection (though this cannot happen until buyer has had a reasonable inspection opportunity); or (3) buyer does "any act inconsistent with the seller's ownership" (e.g., using the goods as part of a manufacturing process). See §2-606(1).

3. **Revocation of acceptance:** Even if the buyer has "accepted" the goods, if he then discovers a defect he may be able to *revoke* his acceptance. If he revokes, the result is the same as if he had never accepted — he can throw the goods back on the seller and refuse to pay.

    a. **Revocation vs. rejection:** The buyer who wants to revoke an acceptance must make a *stronger showing of non-conformity* than the buyer who rejects — the revoker must show that the non-conformity "substantially impairs" the value of the goods, whereas the rejecter must merely show that the goods fail to conform "in any respect." On the other hand, a buyer probably gets more time to revoke than to reject.

4. **Cure:** Both the buyer's right to reject and his right to revoke an acceptance are subject to the seller's right to *cure* the non-conformity. See §2-508(1).

a. Beyond contract: Even *after* the time for performance under the contract has passed, the seller has a limited right to cure: he gets additional time to cure once the time for delivery under the contract has passed, if he *reasonably thought* that either: (1) the goods, though non-conforming, would be *acceptable* to the buyer; or (2) the buyer would be satisfied with a *money allowance*. See UCC §2-508(2).

5. **Installment contracts:** The Code is more lenient to sellers under *installment* contracts (i.e., contracts calling for several deliveries) than in single delivery contracts. In the case of an installment contract, "the buyer may reject any installment which is non-conforming if the non-conformity *substantially impairs the value* of that installment and *cannot be cured....*" §2-612(2).

   a. Slight non-conformity not enough: So a *slight* non-conformity in one installment does *not* allow the buyer to reject it, as he could in a single-delivery contract.

   > **Example:** Cotton, Inc. contracts to deliver 100 blue towels each month to Hotel for one calendar year. This monthly delivery is intended to replenish Hotel's existing stock of towels as they wear out. In July, Cotton delivers only 97 blue towels, and indicates that it will make up for this shortage by delivering 103 towels in August. Assume that there's no reason to believe that Hotel can't simply keep 3 of its pre-July towels in service for one extra month.
   >
   > The non-conformity (the 3-towel shortage) hasn't "substantially impaired the value" of the July installment. Therefore, Hotel can't reject the 97 towels (as it could in a one-shot deal for 100 towels, assuming that the shortage was not curable).

   i. Right to cure: Even where the non-conformity is major, the buyer can't reject the installment without giving the seller a *chance to cure* if circumstances permit. (This rule is the same as in the non-installment "one-shot" scenario.)

   > **Example:** Seller contracts to deliver a computer on May 1, as well as a printer on June 1 customized to work only with that computer. Buyer's application requires both parts to work successfully. Seller delivers a defective computer on May 1, fails in its first attempt to cure, and says that it won't make any further attempts to do so.
   >
   > Buyer can cancel the whole contract, since the defect in the computer substantially impairs the value to him of the whole contract, including the customized printer.

   ii. Reasonable fears of later non-conformities: Another way the defective installment might impair the value of the whole contract is if the defect in the early installment gives the buyer *reasonable fears* that the seller will not adequately perform on the later installments, and the seller fails to give satisfactory assurances that this will not be the case.

V.   EXCUSE OF CONDITIONS

A. Introduction: In some instances, the non-occurrence of a condition is *"excused,"* so that the other party nonetheless must perform.

B. Hindrance: Where one party's duty is conditional on an event, and that same party's wrongful conduct *prevents* the occurrence of the condition, the non-occurrence of the condition is excused, and the party must perform despite the non-occurrence.

    1.   Implied promise of cooperation: Courts sometimes express this concept by saying that each party makes the other an "implied promise of cooperation." One consequence of a breach of this implied promise is that the non-occurrence of the condition to that party's duty is excused.

        Example: P agrees to live with D, his grandmother, and to care for her for the rest of her life, in return for D's promise to leave P $100,000 in D's will. P lives with D for seven years, at the end of which D unreasonably forces P to leave the house. Five years later, D dies. P will be able to recover the $100,000, even though he did not live with D for the rest of her life. The reason is that the non-occurrence of the condition — caring for D for the rest of her life — was excused by D's failure to cooperate.

        a.   Causality issue: But even if the beneficiary of a condition failed to use reasonable efforts to cause the condition to be satisfied, the condition won't be deemed excused unless the beneficiary's failure to make reasonable efforts *substantially contributed* to the non-occurrence of the condition. That is, if the condition *wouldn't have been satisfied even if the beneficiary had made all reasonable efforts to make it be satisfied*, no constructive waiver will be found.

            Example: Seller contracts to sell Blackacre to Buyer. Buyer's duty to close is made conditional on Buyer's obtaining a mortgage of at least $200,000 at no more than 7% from First Bank. Buyer never submits any application to First Bank. However, in a breach action brought by Seller, Buyer shows that even if Buyer *had* submitted a complete and truthful application to First Bank, First Bank would not have given a loan of at least $200,000 at an interest rate of 7% or lower.

            In this scenario, Buyer's failure to make the reasonable efforts to satisfy the condition (i.e., failure to make an application) did not change the outcome — the condition wouldn't have been satisfied anyway — so Buyer will be entitled to rely on the non-occurrence of the condition.

C. Waiver: A party who owes a conditional duty may indicate that he will *not insist* upon the occurrence of the condition before performing. A court will often take the party at his word, and enforce that party's willingness to forego the benefit of the condition. In this event, the party is said to have *waived* the condition.

    1.   Minor conditions: Generally, the court is much more likely to find that the condition is waived if it is a *minor* one, such as a procedural or technical one.

2. **Continuation of performance:** If a promisor *continues his own performance* after learning that a condition of duty has failed to occur, his conduct is likely to be found to operate as a waiver of the condition.

> **Example:** Insurer insures Owner's house for fire; Insurer's duty to pay a claim is expressly conditional upon notice by Owner within seven days of any fire. Owner gives notice three weeks after a fire. Insurer sends an adjuster, attempts to make a settlement, and otherwise behaves as if it is not insisting on strict compliance with the notice provision. This continuation of performance will probably be found to be a waiver of the timely-notice condition.

   a. **Right to damages not lost:** When a party continues his own performance after breach, or otherwise waives a condition, he has *not* necessarily lost his right to recover *damages,* if the non-occurrence of the condition was also a *breach* of a promise.

   b. **Waiver of subsequent conditions:** If a contract contains a series of similar conditions, will waiver of one condition (e.g., by the acceptance of a defective performance) excuse the later conditions? Generally, the answer is "no." However, *if a party accepts several similarly defective performances without objecting, his conduct may lead the other party to justifiably conclude that all conditions were intended to be excused.* If so, these later conditions are *waived*.

> **Example:** P contracts to build a movie theater for D. The contract price is to be paid in installments, and an architect's certificate is a condition to D's duty to make each installment. However, D makes six or seven payments without insisting on such a certificate. When P does not receive the final portion of the contract price, he sues. D defends on the grounds that no architect's certificate for the last payment was ever procured.
>
> *Held,* for P. D, by his continued failure to enforce the requirement of a certificate, has waived his right to assert that condition as to the final payment. [*McKenna v. Vernon*].

   c. **Retraction of waiver:** If there has been no consideration given for the waiver, and the party receiving the benefit of the waiver *has not detrimentally relied* on it, the person who waived may at any time *retract* the waiver, thereby *reinstating* the condition.

> **Example:** On February 1, Sehl agrees to sell his house to Bye. Bye makes a $5,000 deposit. The contract provides that closing will occur on April 1, with time to be of the essence, so that if Bye is not ready to close by exactly April 1, Sehl may retain the deposit. On February 15, Sehl tells Bye that Sehl will not insist on the April 1 date, and that Sehl will convey as long as Bye is ready to close by May 1. On February 20 (before Bye has relied in any way on the later closing date), Sehl tells Bye, "I've changed my mind. I'm insisting that you close by April 1, or I'll keep your deposit."
>
> Since Bye has not yet detrimentally relied on Sehl's waiver of the condition that Bye close by April 1, Sehl's reinstatement of the condition was

proper. Therefore, if Bye isn't ready to close on April 1, and tries to close on April 9, Sehl can refuse to do so, and can keep Bye's deposit.

But now suppose that Bye *relied* on the Feb. 15 waiver, by waiting until March 20 to apply for a mortgage (a date that would still have been enough in advance of the new May 1 closing date to allow Bye to get an appropriate mortgage). Suppose further that on March 28, Sehl attempted to reinstate the April 1 closing date. Bye's material change of position would make it unjust for Sehl to reinstate the condition, so Sehl will not be permitted to do so, and the waiver of closing until May 1 will stand.

VI. REPUDIATION AND PROSPECTIVE INABILITY TO PERFORM

A. General effect of prospective breach: If a party indicates that he will *subsequently* be unable or unwilling to perform, this will act as the non-occurrence of a constructive condition, in the same way as a present material breach does. In other words, the other party has the right to *suspend his own performance*.

   1. Distinction: Where the party indicates that he will *refuse* to perform, this is called an *"anticipatory repudiation"* of the contract. If he indicates that he would like to perform but will be unable to do so, this is an indication of *"prospective inability to perform"* but not repudiation; however, the consequence is still that the other party may suspend performance.

B. Insolvency or financial inability: If a party is *insolvent* or otherwise financially incapable of performing, this will entitle the other party to stop performance.

C. Cancellation: If the prospective inability or unwillingness to perform is *certain* or almost certain, the other party can not only suspend her performance, but can actually *cancel* the contract. But where it is not so clear whether the first party will be unable or unwilling to perform, the other party may only *suspend* performance.

D. Right to adequate assurances of performance: If a party's conduct or words don't constitute an outright repudiation, but merely suggest that that party may not perform, the other party may *demand assurances* that the first party will perform. If the first party fails to provide these assurances, this failure will itself be considered a repudiation, entitling the innocent party to cancel.

   1. UCC § 2-609: Thus UCC § 2-609(1) provides that "when reasonable grounds for insecurity arise with respect to the performance of either party the other may in writing demand adequate assurance of due performance and until he receives such assurance may, if commercially reasonable, suspend any performance for which he has not already received the agreed return."

   Example: Buyer places two orders (separate contracts) with Seller, one for shipment on July 1 and the other for shipment on September 1. Each shipment is to be paid for within 30 days. Seller ships the first order promptly, and by August 28 the bill is almost one month past due.

Seller may in writing demand assurances that Buyer will pay for both the first order and the second order in a timely fashion. If Buyer fails to respond, Seller may cancel the second contract, and sue for breach of both. But if Buyer furnishes reasonable assurances — as by demonstrating that non-payment of the first invoice was a clerical omission, and immediately rectifying it — Seller must reinstate the second contract.

2. **Repudiation:** Once the party who has reasonable grounds for insecurity makes a written demand for adequate assurance, the other party *must furnish the requested assurance within a reasonable time*. If the receiving party *doesn't* do this, the party who made the demand for assurance may *treat the failure to give it as a repudiation*, and may cancel the contract even though the time for performance has not yet arrived. See UCC § 2-609(4): "After receipt of a justified demand[,] failure to provide within a reasonable time not exceeding thirty days such assurance of due performance as is adequate under the circumstances of the particular case *is a repudiation of the contract.*"

3. **What qualifies as "demand for assurance":** Notice that the party who is worried that the other may default gets rights under § 2-609(1) only if the worrier "in writing *demand[s] adequate assurance* of due performance[.]" What words constitute a "demand for assurances"? Courts are generally pretty *easy to satisfy* on this point: they usually hold that the writing *does not need to expressly use the words "demand" or "assurances."*

    a. **A general insistence on performance suffices:** Rather, it's usually enough if the worried party (call her *A*) gets across in writing to the possibly-about-to-default party (*B*) the more general message that *A has reason to fear that B may default,* and that if *B* doesn't promptly show she intends to perform, *A intends to assert all her legal rights*.

    Example: Buyer writes (accurately) to Seller, "You've been consistently late on delivery under our other recent contracts with you. As to the present contract, if you don't satisfy us immediately that you will make next week's delivery on time, we will cancel the contract now, and pursue our legal remedies." This probably qualifies as a "demand for assurances" under § 2-609, even though it doesn't use the words "demand" or "assurances." Therefore, if Seller doesn't furnish the requested assurance of timely delivery reasonably soon, Buyer will have the right to cancel the contract (and procure substitute goods) even before the contracted-for delivery date arrives. [Cf. *Rocheux Int'l of N.J. v. U.S. Merchants Fin. Group*]

CHAPTER **8**

ANTICIPATORY REPUDIATION AND OTHER ASPECTS OF BREACH

I. ANTICIPATORY REPUDIATION

A. General rule: If a party makes it clear, even before his performance is due, that he cannot or will not perform, he is said to have *anticipatorily repudiated* the contract.

All states except Massachusetts allow the victim of such an anticipatory repudiation to *sue before the repudiator's time for performance has arrived*. This is sometimes called the rule of *Hochster v. De La Tour.*

> **Example:** Star promises Movie Co. that Star will act in Movie Co.'s movie, shooting for which is scheduled to commence in the U.S. on July 1. On June 1, Star announces to the press that he is going to live abroad for a year beginning the next day and will not do the movie. Under the rule of *Hochster v. De La Tour*, in force is nearly all states, Movie Co. can sue Star for breach as soon as he issues his press statement; Movie Co. need not wait until July 1, the time at which Star's performance is due.

B. What constitutes repudiation: An anticipatory repudiation occurs whenever a party clearly indicates that he cannot or will not perform his contractual duty.

1. **Statement:** Sometimes, the repudiation takes the form of a *statement* by the promisor that he intends not to perform. (The above example illustrates this.)

   a. **Vague doubts not enough:** But the fact that the promisor states *vague doubts* about his willingness or ability to perform is *not enough*.

   > **Example:** On the basic facts of the above example, suppose Star says, "I'm feeling pretty exhausted, so I don't know if I'll be able to perform the role, but let's hope I'll feel well enough." This would probably not be an anticipatory repudiation, because it is equivocal.

   > **Note:** But even the expression of vague doubts may entitle the promisee to request *assurances of performance*, and the promisor's failure to give such assurances would be a repudiation. See *supra*, p. 96.

   b. **Grudging willingness to perform:** Similarly, if the promisor merely indicates *unhappiness* about the deal, or a feeling that it is "unfair," or a wish to get out of it, this will not be a repudiation as long as the promisor either (1) indicates that if legally obligated to do so, he will perform or (2) refrains from any clear indication that he intends *not* to perform.

2. **Voluntary actions:** The repudiation may occur by means of an *act* by the promisor that makes his performance impossible.

   > **Example:** Seller contracts to convey Blackacre to Buyer, the closing to take place on July 1. On June 15, Seller conveys Blackacre to X. This is an anticipatory repudiation by action, and Buyer may sue immediately, rather than waiting until July 1.

3. **Prospective inability to perform:** Something analogous to anticipatory repudiation occurs when it becomes evident that the promisor will be *unable* to perform, even though he desires to do so. When this occurs, all courts agree that the promisee may *suspend her performance*. But courts are split on whether the promisee may bring an immediate suit for breach, as she is allowed to do where the repudiation is a statement or a voluntary act.

   a. **Insolvency:** The promisor's *insolvency* usually is *not* considered to be the type of anticipatory repudiation that allows the other party to sue immediately for breach. But the promisee may request assurances of performance, and if the promisor can't give these (e.g., he can't show that he will become sufficiently solvent to perform), then an immediate suit for breach is allowed.

II. OTHER ASPECTS OF REPUDIATION

A. Repudiation after performance is due: Similar rules apply where a party's time for performance becomes due, and the party then repudiates (i.e., he indicates by word or deed that he cannot or will not perform). Here, even though the repudiation is not "anticipatory," the other party may cancel the contract and bring an immediate suit for breach, just as in the anticipatory situation.

B. Retraction of repudiation: A repudiation (whether anticipatory or occurring after the time for performance) may normally be *retracted* until some event occurs to make the repudiation final.

   1. Final acts: In most courts, the repudiator's time to retract *ends* as soon as the other party: (1) *sues* for breach; (2) *changes her position* materially in *reliance* on the repudiation; or (3) states that she *regards the repudiation as final*. See UCC §2-611(1).

   2. Cancellation and new contract with someone else: These retraction rules mean that if the repudiatee cancels the contract and *makes an alternative contract* with someone else, the repudiation can no longer be retracted.

      a. UCC illustrations: So, for instance, in a UCC context, the following events would *end* the repudiator's time to retract:

         ❑   The *buyer* repudiates, and the seller *sells the goods in question* to someone else (even if the repudiator didn't yet know of this sale);

         ❑   The *seller* repudiates, and the buyer instead *buys comparable goods* from someone else.

C. Mitigation required: After a repudiation occurs, the repudiatee may *not* simply ignore the repudiation and continue the contract, if this would aggravate her damages. That is, the repudiatee must *mitigate her damages* by securing an alternative contract, if one is reasonably available. If she does not do this, she cannot recover the damages that could have been avoided.

   1. UCC: The UCC, in §2-610(a), expresses this mitigation requirement by saying that the repudiatee may "for a *commercially reasonable time* await performance by the repudiating party...." Comment 1 to this section then says that "If [the repudiatee] awaits performance *beyond* a commercially reasonable time he cannot recover resulting damages which he *should have avoided*."

D. Repudiation ignored, then sued on: Most courts hold that the repudiatee may *insist on performance*, at least for a while, rather than cancelling the contract. Then, if the repudiator fails to retract the repudiation, the repudiatee may sue without being held to have waived any rights.

   1. UCC in accord: The UCC similarly takes the view that the repudiatee's insistence on performance *does not constitute a waiver of his right to sue* for breach.

a. Party has choice of remedies: Whether it is the buyer or seller who anticipatorily repudiates, UCC §2-610 gives the repudiatee a choice of remedies if the lost performance "will *substantially impair the value of the contract*" to him. The repudiatee gets the choice between:

❏ "*await[ing] performance* by the repudiating party" for a "commercially reasonable time"; or

❏ "*resort[ing] to any remedy for breach* ..., even though [the repudiatee] has notified the repudiating party that he would await the latter's performance and has urged retraction."

Example: On Oct. 1, Buyer orders a new Vista automobile from Seller, delivery to occur Dec. 1. On Nov. 1, Seller repudiates by saying that he won't be able to ship the car for a full year. A full-year delay would certainly "substantially impair the value of the contract" to Buyer.

Therefore, on Nov. 1, Buyer can choose: (1) he can wait to see whether Seller changes his mind and performs (and, if Buyer wishes, Buyer can urge Seller to change his mind); or (2) he can immediately "resort to any remedy for breach." Choice (2) means that he can *cover* (i.e., buy the goods from a different seller) and immediately sue for the contract-cover differential, or alternatively *not cover* and sue for the contract-market differential. If Buyer elects course (1) (waiting and hoping), he can at any time switch to course (2).

E. Repudiatee owes no remaining duties: If the repudiatee *does not owe any remaining performances* as of the time of the repudiation, he is generally *not* permitted to bring an immediate suit for anticipatory repudiation; instead, he must wait until the time for the other party's performance is due. The reason is that the ordinary rule allowing immediate suit is designed to give the innocent party a chance to avoid having to render his own performance; where the innocent party does not owe any performance, the rationale does not apply.

1. Payment of money: This exception means that an anticipatory repudiation of an unconditional unilateral obligation to *pay money* at a fixed time does not give rise to a claim for breach until that time has arrived.

Example: The tycoon Donald Tramp contracts to repay to Bank a $100 million loan, repayment to occur July 1. On June 1, Tramp declares publicly, "I won't be paying Bank back on July 1. Let 'em sue me." Because Bank does not owe any further performance under the contract (it's already made the loan), Bank may *not* sue Tramp until July 1 arrives and the payment is not made.

2. Installments: This also means that if a debtor fails to pay a particular *installment* of a debt, and says that he will not make later payments, the creditor cannot bring suit for those later installments until they fall due. But lenders ordinarily avoid this problem by inserting an *"acceleration clause"* into the loan agreement, by which failure to pay one installment in a timely manner causes all later installments to become immediately due; such acceleration clauses are enforceable.

F. UCC damages for repudiation: Pay special attention to damages suffered by a *buyer* under a contract for the sale of goods, where the seller has anticipatorily repudiated the contract. UCC §2-713(1) says that "the measure of damages for...repudiation by the seller is the difference between the market price *at the time when the buyer learned of the breach* and the contract price, together with any incidental and consequential damages."

     1. Meaning: The phrase "time when the buyer learned of the breach" is ambiguous. Most courts hold that this phrase means "time when the buyer *learned of the repudiation."*

Chapter 9

STATUTE OF FRAUDS

I. INTRODUCTION

A. Nature of Statute of Frauds: Most contracts are valid despite the fact that they are only oral. A few types of contracts, however, are *unenforceable* unless they are *in writing*. Contracts that are unenforceable unless in writing are said to fall "within the Statute of Frauds." The Statute of Frauds is pretty much identical from state to state.

B. Five categories: There are five categories of contracts which, in almost every state, fall with the Statute of Frauds and must therefore be in writing:

     1. Suretyship: A contract to answer for the *debt* or duty of *another.*

     2. Marriage: A contract made upon *consideration of marriage.*

     3. Land contract: A contract for the *sale of an interest in land.*

     4. One year: A contract that cannot be performed within *one year* from its making.

     5. UCC: Under the UCC, a contract for the sale of *goods* for a price of *$500* or more.

II. SURETYSHIP

A. General rule: A promise to pay the *debt* or duty of *another* is within the Statute of Frauds, and is therefore unenforceable unless in writing.

B. Main purpose rule: If the promisor's chief purpose in making his promise of suretyship is to further *his own interest*, his promise does *not* fall within the Statute of Frauds. This is called the *"main purpose"* rule.

> **Example:** Contractor contracts to build a house for Owner. In order to obtain the necessary supplies, Contractor seeks to procure them on credit from Supplier. Supplier is unwilling to look solely to Contractor's credit. Owner, in order to get the house built, orally promises Supplier that if Contractor does not pay the bill, Owner will make good on it. Because Owner's main purpose in giving the guarantee is to further his own economic interest — getting the house built — his promise does *not* fall within the suretyship provision, and is therefore not required to meet the Statute of Frauds. So it is enforceable even though oral.

C. Memorandum requirement: A document signed by the surety will meet the requirement of a writing even if it is *not addressed to the obligee*, even if it is not created until *long after the oral promise* of guarantee, and even if it is *never seen* by the obligee. (See p. 107 for more about what type of document satisfies the memorandum requirement.)

> **Example:** *A* orally promises *B* that if *B* will extend credit to *C*, *A* will guarantee repayment. *B* extends credit to *C*. Two months later, *A* writes a letter to *C*, saying "I'm not sure you knew this, but I guaranteed *B* that I would repay your debt if you do not." The promise by *A* falls within the suretyship provision: *C* is the primary obligor, and *A* is the surety. However, the letter to *C* satisfies the writing requirement — even though this writing was not addressed to *B*, or ever sent to him, it is a sufficient memorandum. Therefore, *A*'s oral guarantee is enforceable against him.

III. THE MARRIAGE PROVISION

A. Contract made upon consideration of marriage: A promise for which the consideration is *marriage* or a promise of marriage is within the Statute.

> **Example:** Tycoon says to Starlet, his girlfriend, "If you will promise to marry me, I'll transfer to you title to my Malibu beach home even before our marriage." Starlet replies, "It's a deal." No document is signed. If Tycoon changes his mind, Starlet cannot sue to enforce either the promise of marriage or the promise to convey the beach house, since the consideration for both of these promises was her return promise to marry Tycoon. Conversely, if Starlet changes her mind, Tycoon cannot sue for breach either.

1. Exception for mutual promises to marry: But if an oral contract consists *solely of mutual promises to marry* (with no ancillary promises regarding property transfers), the contract is *not* within the Statute of Frauds, and is enforceable even though oral. That is, *an ordinary oral engagement is an enforceable contract*.

IV. THE LAND CONTRACT PROVISION

A. Generally: A promise to transfer or buy *any interest in land* is within the Statute. The Statute does not apply to the conveyance itself (which is governed by separate statutes everywhere) but rather to a *contract providing for* the subsequent conveyance of land.

> **Example:** O, the owner of Blackacre, orally promises to convey it to *A* in return for *A*'s payment of $100,000. If *A* fails to come up with the $100,000 by closing date, O cannot sue for breach. Conversely, if O refuses to make the conveyance even though *A* tenders the money, *A* cannot sue O for breach.

1. Interests in land: The Statute applies to promises to transfer not only a fee simple interest in land, but to transfer most other kinds of interests in land.

> **a. Leases:** For instance, a *lease* is generally an "interest in land," so that a promise to make a lease will generally be unenforceable if not in writing.

     i. **One year or less:** But most states have statutes making oral leases enforceable if their duration is *one year or less*.

  b. **Mortgages:** A promise to give a *mortgage* on real property as security for a loan also usually comes within the Statute.

  c. **Contracts incidentally related to land:** But contracts that relate only *incidentally* to land are not within the Statute. Thus a contract to *build a building* is not within the Statute, nor is a promise to lend money with which the borrower will buy land.

B. Part performance: Even if an oral contract for the transfer of an interest in land is not enforceable at the time it is made, subsequent *acts* by either party may make it enforceable.

  1. **Conveyance by vendor:** First, if the vendor under an oral land contract makes the contracted-for conveyance, he may recover the contract price.

C. Part performance: Even if an oral contract for the transfer of an interest in land is not enforceable at the time it is made, subsequent *acts* by either party may make it enforceable.

  1. **Conveyance by vendor:** First, if the vendor under an oral land contract makes the contracted-for conveyance, he may recover the contract price.

  2. **Part performance of the alleged contract by the vendee:** Second, the court will often grant specific performance of an oral land contract at the vendee's request if the vendee has *committed acts* (apart from payment to the vendor) that seem to have been made in reliance on the alleged contract. However, the acts must be of a sort that the vendee is *very unlikely to have committed* had the alleged oral contract not existed. Generally, the acts by the vendee that are most likely to be found to have been made in reliance on the contract consist of his having taken possession of the property and *making improvements on it.*

    Example: O owns Whiteacre, a vacant 1/4 acre parcel. P buys a mobile home; then, with O's permission, P pays for the pouring of a concrete foundation on Whiteacre. P has the home installed on the foundation and moves into the home without objection by O. Soon after, P asserts that O orally promised P that O would sell P the property for its market value, and that P bought the home and built the foundation in what O knew was reliance on this promise. O asserts that he made no such promise, and merely let P buy the home and pay for the foundation in lieu of paying rent to O for the first year of occupancy.

    Let's assume that the court believes that O really made the alleged promise of sale. If so, the court would likely conclude that P's improvements (especially his paying for the foundation, something that a mere tenant would probably not have done) constituted part performance of that oral contract of sale. If the court made that conclusion, the part performance would be deemed to take the contract out of the Statute of Frauds, making it enforceable against O by specific performance.

a. **The "unequivocally referable to the contract" standard:** There's an obvious danger that a purported "vendee" will *falsely claim* that she made improvements or otherwise relied on the promise of a conveyance. To fight this danger, many courts apply a tough standard: the would-be vendee has to show that her actions were *"unequivocally referable"* to the asserted oral agreement of sale, and not explainable by some other motive that's plausible under the known circumstances.

> **Example:** P claims that D orally promised to sell P Blackacre, which contains a house, for $100,000. The only acts that P points to as her conduct in reliance on D's oral promise of sale are that she (1) moved onto Blackacre; and (2) made four $2,000 payments to D, one in each of four consecutive months, after which D refused any further payments and tried to evict P. P says that these were initial payments under an oral installment-sale agreement, and that at the end of all agreed-upon payments D was to transfer title to P. D claims that these payments were made pursuant not to a sale agreement but rather, to an oral lease cancellable by either party on one month's notice. D also shows that $2,000 would be a reasonable monthly lease payment for Blackacre.

> A court applying the tough "unequivocally referable" standard is likely to hold that P has *not met* standard here. That's because the payments here are just as consistent with being *lease payments* as with being installment-purchase payments. Therefore, it can't be said that the payments were unequivocally referable to the alleged oral installment-sale contract. The Statute of Frauds will apply, and the court will deny P an order of specific performance.

V. THE ONE-YEAR PROVISION

A. **General rule:** If a promise contained in a contract is *incapable of being fully performed within one year* after the making of the contract, the contract must be in writing.

1. **Time runs from making:** The one-year period is measured from the *time of execution of the contract*, not the time it will take the parties to perform.

> **Example:** On July 1, 2011, Star promises Network that Star will appear on a one-hour show that will take place in September, 2012. This contract will be unenforceable if oral, because it cannot be performed within one year of the day it was made. The fact that actual performance will take only one hour is irrelevant.

B. **Impossibility:** The one-year provision applies only if complete performance is *impossible* within one year after the making of the contract. The fact that performance within one year is highly unlikely is not enough.

1. **Judge from time of contract's execution:** The possibility of performing the contract within one year must be judged *as of the time the contract is made*, not by benefit of hindsight.

Example: O orally promises *A* that O will pay *A* $10,000 if and when *A*'s husband dies. *A*'s husband does not die until four years after the promise. The promise is nonetheless enforceable, because viewed as of the moment the promise was made, it was possible that it could be completed within one year — the fact that it ended up not being performed within one year is irrelevant.

C. Possibility of performance, not possibility of discharge: It is only the possibility of *"performance,"* not the possibility of *"discharge,"* that takes a contract out of the one-year provision. Thus the fact that the contract might be discharged by *impossibility*, *frustration*, or some other excuse for non-performance will not take the contract out of the Statute.

1. **Fulfillment of principal purpose:** It will often be hard to tell whether a certain kind of possible termination is by performance or by discharge. The test is whether, if the termination in question occurs, the contract has *fulfilled its principal purpose*. If it has fulfilled this purpose, there has been performance; if it has not, there has not been performance. Using this rule gives these results:

    a. **Personal service contract for multiple years:** A *personal services contract* for more than one year of employment falls within the one-year rule (and is thus unenforceable unless in writing) even though the contract would terminate if the employee died. The reason is that when the employee dies, the contract has merely been "discharged," not performed.

        Example: Boss and Worker orally agree that Worker will work for Boss for 5 years. Even though the contract would end at the moment of Worker's death or disability (which might happen in the first year), that possibility doesn't prevent the one-year provision of the Statute from applying. (Such an event would be a discharge, not a "full performance.") Therefore, the agreement is unenforceable against either party, because it's not in writing.

    b. **Lifetime employment:** By contrast, a promise to employ someone for his *lifetime* is probably *not* within the one-year provision, since if the employee dies, the essential purpose of guaranteeing him a job forever has been satisfied. So an oral promise of a lifetime job is probably enforceable.

    c. **Non-compete:** A promise by a seller of a business *not to compete* with the buyer for a period longer than a year is *not* within the one-year provision, since if the seller dies within a year, the buyer has received the equivalent of full performance (he knows the seller won't be competing with him).

D. Termination: Courts are *split* about whether the existence of a *termination clause* that permits termination in less than a year will remove a more-than-one-year contract from the one-year provision.

Example: Boss orally hires Worker to work for three years. Their oral agreement allows either party to cancel on 60 days notice. Courts are split on whether this contract is within the one-year agreement and must therefore be in writing. The Second Restatement seems to say that the giving of 60 days notice would be a form of "performance," so that this contract will be enforceable even though oral

— Worker might give notice after one month on the job, in which case the contract would have been "performed" within three months of its making, less than one year.

E. Full performance on one side: Most courts hold that *full performance* by *one party* removes the contract from the one-year provision. This is true even if it actually takes that party more than one year to perform.

> **Example:** On Jan. 1, 2011, Producer and Star orally agree that Star will perform in Producer's Broadway show 6 nights a week for 18 months, beginning on July 1, 2012. Star's fee for the entire run is set at a total of $200,000. Because Star develops cash needs, Producer prepays the entire $200,000 on May 1, 2012. Star then refuses to perform.
>
> Star's promise to perform is not within the one-year provision, because Producer has fully performed. That's true even though Producer's performance didn't occur until more than one year after the making of the contract.

F. Applies to all contracts: The rule that a contract incapable of performance within one year must satisfy the Statute applies to *all* contracts (including those that just miss falling within some other Statute of Frauds provision). For instance, even though the special UCC sale-of-goods statute (discussed below) requires a writing only where goods are to be sold for more than $500, a contract to sell goods for $300, to be delivered 18 months after the contract is made, must be in writing.

VI. CONTRACTS FOR THE SALE OF GOODS

A. General rule: UCC §2-201(1) says that "a contract for the sale of goods for the price of *$500 or more* is not enforceable…unless there is some writing sufficient to indicate that a contract for sale has been made…." So an oral contract for goods at a price of $500 or more is unenforceable under the UCC.

B. Exceptions: Even if a sales contract is for more than $500, it is *exempted* from the Statute of Frauds requirement in three situations:

1. **Specially manufactured goods:** No writing is required if the goods are to be *specially manufactured* for the buyer, are not suitable for sale to others, and the seller has made "either a substantial beginning of their manufacture or commitments for their procurement." §2-201(3)(a).

2. **Estoppel:** A writing is also not required "if the party against whom enforcement is sought *admits* in his pleading, testimony or otherwise in court that a *contract for sale was made*, but the contract is not enforceable under this provision beyond the quantity of goods admitted." §2-201(3)(b).

3. **Goods accepted or paid for:** Finally, no writing is required "with respect to goods for which *payment has been made* and accepted or which have been *received and accepted*." §2-201(3)(c).

> **Example:** Buyer orally orders three pairs of shoes from Seller for a total of $600. Buyer then sends a check for this amount in advance payment. Once

Seller takes the check and deposits it in the bank, Seller loses his Statute of Frauds defense.

VII. SATISFACTION BY A MEMORANDUM

A. General requirements for: Even if there is no signed "contract," a signed *"memorandum"* summarizing the agreement may be enough to meet the Statute of Frauds. A memorandum satisfies the Statute if it meets all these requirements:

- ❏ it reasonably *identifies the subject* of the contract,

- ❏ it indicates that a *contract has been made* between the parties,

- ❏ it states with reasonable certainty the *essential terms* of the contract, and

- ❏ it is *signed* "by or on behalf of *the party to be charged."*

B. Signature: Because of the requirement of a signature "by the *party to be charged,"* some contracts will be enforceable against one party, but not against the other.

> **Example:** Buyer orally agrees to buy Owner's house for $200,000. Buyer then sends a document marked "confirmation," which states, "This confirms our agreement whereby I will buy your house for $200,000. [signed, Buyer]" Owner can enforce the agreement against Buyer, but Buyer cannot enforce it against Owner, since only Buyer has signed the memorandum.

C. UCC: Under the UCC, a writing satisfies the Statute if it is "sufficient to indicate that a contract for sale has been made between the parties and [is] signed by the party against whom enforcement is sought...." §2-201(2).

1. Omissions: Even if the writing contains a *mistake* as to a term, there will often be enough to satisfy the Statute, under the UCC. For instance, a mistake on *price* or quantity, or even description of the item, will not be fatal (but plaintiff may only recover for the quantity actually stated in the memorandum). Contrast this with non-UCC cases, where a major mistake is likely to invalidate the memorandum.

2. Confirmation: Under the UCC, there is one situation in which a memorandum will be enforceable even against a party who does *not* sign it: if the deal is *between merchants*, one merchant who receives a signed *confirmation* from the other party will generally be bound, unless the recipient *objects* within 10 days after receiving the confirmation.

> **Example:** Buyer and Seller are both merchants (i.e., they deal in goods of the kind in question). Buyer telephones Seller to order 1,000 widgets at $10 apiece. Immediately after receiving the order, Seller sends a written confirmation, correctly listing the quantity and price. Assume that this confirmation constitutes a memorandum which would be enforceable by Buyer against Seller. Unless Buyer objects in writing within 10 days after receiving the memo, he will be bound by it, just as if he had signed it.

VIII. ORAL RESCISSION AND MODIFICATION

A. Oral rescission: Where a contract is in writing, it can be ***orally rescinded*** (i.e., orally cancelled) even though the original was required to be in writing because of the Statute. That is, ***a rescission does not have to satisfy the Statute of Frauds***.

B. Modification: Application of the Statute of Frauds to oral ***modifications*** is trickier.

   1. General rule: Generally, to determine whether an oral modification of an existing contract is effective, ***the contract as modified must be treated as if it were an original contract***. This is true whether the original contract is oral or written.

      a. Consequence: If the modifications are unenforceable under this test, ***the original contract is left standing***. That is, the modification is treated as if it never occurred.

   2. Reliance on oral modification: But if either party ***materially changes his position*** in ***reliance*** on an oral modification, the court may enforce the modification despite the Statute.

   3. Modification of contracts under UCC : Contracts under the UCC work pretty much the same way: if the contract ***as modified*** would (if it were an original contract) have to meet the Statute of Frauds, any modification of a ***key term*** (e.g., price or quantity) must probably be in writing.

      a. Original left standing: So if the modification of a key term is unenforceable under this rule, then the original contract is probably left standing (though this is not certain).

         Example: Seller agrees in writing to sell Buyer 100 widgets for a total of $1,000. The parties then orally agree to change the quantity to 150, for $1,500. The modification is probably not binding because it is not in writing. In that event, the original contract would probably be left in force.

      i. Minor term: But probably a ***minor term*** *may* be modified orally, as long as the major terms (description, price and quantity) remain unchanged. For instance, on the above example, suppose that the oral modification consists of a 2-week change in the delivery date. It's likely that a court would find that this change is effective even though oral, because it's on a minor point. (This is the "passing through" theory — the original writing "passes through" to the revised deal.)

C. No-oral-rescission-or-modification clauses: The parties are always free to ***agree***, in the original writing, that the contract may not be rescinded or modified except via a writing signed by both. Such a clause will be ***enforced***.

   1. Sale of goods: In the case of contracts for the sale of goods, the UCC expressly provides for the enforcement of such no-oral-rescission-or-modification clauses: "a signed agreement which ***excludes modification or rescission*** except by a signed writing ***cannot be otherwise modified or rescinded....***" (§2-209(2).)

      a. Invalid change as waiver: If an oral rescission or modification of a contract for the sale of goods is ineffective because it violates a no-oral-rescission-or-modification clause in the original contract, the rescission or modification may nonetheless "operate as a *waiver*." (§2-209(4).) This means that if, following such an ineffective rescission or modification, one party *changes his position* (as by buying the contracted-for goods elsewhere), the other party will have waived his rights to insist upon enforcement of the original contract.

  i. **Retraction:** However, such a waiver may be *retracted* "unless the retraction would be unjust in view of a material *change of position* in reliance on the waiver." (§2-209(5).)

> **Example:** Buyer and seller agree in writing that Seller will ship certain goods to Buyer to arrive by Dec. 1. The total contract price is $10,000 (bringing the contract within the Statute of Frauds). The contract says that no oral modifications will be effective. On Nov. 15, Seller phones Buyer and says, "Our shipping department is running a little behind; can we have until Dec. 10?" Buyer says, "Yes." One hour later, Buyer realizes that the later shipment will cause him problems, so he phones back and says to Seller, "I must now insist on the original Dec. 1 date."
>
> Assuming that during the intervening hour, Seller has not changed his position in reliance on the extra time, Buyer's retraction of the waiver will be effective, and the due date is now restored to the original Dec. 1 date.

IX. RESTITUTION, RELIANCE AND ESTOPPEL

A. Quasi-contractual recovery: A plaintiff who has rendered *part performance* under an oral agreement falling within the Statute of Frauds may recover in *quasi-contract* for the *value of benefits* he has conferred upon the defendant.

> **Example:** Landlord orally agrees to rent Blackacre to Tenant for two years, at a rent of $1,000 per month. After Tenant has occupied the premises for two months, Tenant moves out. Even though the agreement is unenforceable because it is for an interest in land and must therefore be in writing, Landlord can recover the reasonable value of Tenant's two-month occupancy.

  1. **Not limited by contract price:** The plaintiff's quasi-contract recovery is *not limited* to the *pro-rata contract price*, in most courts. (*Example*: On the facts of the above example, if Landlord can show that the fair market value of a lease for Blackacre is $2,000 a month, he may recover this amount times two months, even though the pro-rata lease amount is only $1,000 per month.)

B. Promissory estoppel: Instead of a quasi-contract suit (which will generally protect only the plaintiff's restitution or reliance interest), a plaintiff who has relied on a contract that is unenforceable due to non-compliance with the Statute of Frauds may instead use the doctrine of *promissory estoppel*. Where one party to an oral agreement foreseeably and reasonably *relies to his detriment* on the existence of the agreement, the court may enforce the agreement notwithstanding the Statute, if this is the only way to avoid injustice.

Example: P works for an established company, and has good job security. He orally accepts a two-year oral employment agreement with D, another company. By leaving his present employer, P loses valuable pension and other rights. Once P leaves the old employer to take the job with D, a court may well apply promissory estoppel to hold that the P-D agreement is fully enforceable notwithstanding non-compliance with the Statute of Frauds, since injustice cannot be otherwise prevented (it would be hard to protect just P's reliance interest).

1. **Misrepresentation regarding Statute:** Courts are especially likely to apply promissory estoppel where the defendant has intentionally and falsely told the plaintiff that the contract is *not* within the Statute, or that a writing will subsequently be executed, or that the defense of the Statute will not be used.

2. **UCC:** Courts are split about whether promissory estoppel may be a substitute for the Statute of Frauds in a *UCC context*.

3. **Degree of injury and unjust enrichment:** The more grievously the plaintiff is injured (or the more extensively the defendant is unjustly enriched) by application of the Statute, the more likely the court is to allow promissory estoppel to be a substitute for compliance with the Statute.

CHAPTER 10
REMEDIES

I. INTRODUCTION

A. **Distinction:** Distinguish between a suit brought *on the contract*, and a suit brought off the contract, i.e., in *quasi-contract*.

1. **Suit on the contract:** Where the parties have formed a legally enforceable contract, and the defendant (but not the plaintiff) has breached the contract, the plaintiff will normally sue *"on the contract."* That is, he will bring a suit for breach of contract, and the court will look to the contract to determine whether there has indeed been a breach, and for help in calculating damages.

2. **Quasi-contract:** But in other circumstances, the plaintiff will bring a suit in *"quasi-contract."* Here, the plaintiff is not really asking for enforcement of the contract; instead, she is usually asking for damages based on the actual value of his performance, irrespective of any price set out in the contract. Situations where a quasi-contract recovery may be available include:

   a. Where the contract is unenforceably *vague*;

   b. Where the contract is *illegal*;

   c. Where the parties are discharged because of *impossibility* or frustration of purpose;

   d. Where plaintiff has herself *materially breached* the contract.

II. EQUITABLE REMEDIES

A. Two types: Sometimes the court will award *"equitable remedies"* instead of the usual remedy of money damages. There are two types of equitable relief relevant to contract cases: (1) *specific performance*; and (2) *injunctions*.

  1. **Specific performance:**   A decree for *specific performance* orders the promisor to *render the promised performance*. (*Example*: *A* contracts to sell Blackacre to *B* on a stated date for a stated price. *A* then wrongfully refuses to make the conveyance. A court will probably award specific performance. That is, it will order *A* to make the conveyance.)

  2. **Injunction:**   An *injunction* directs a party to *refrain* from doing a particular act. It is especially common in cases where the defendant is sued by his former employer and charged with breaching an employment contract by working for a competitor.

     Example: D signs a contract with P, his employer, providing that D will not work for any competitor in the same city for one year after termination. D then quits and immediately goes to work for a competitor. If P sues on the non-compete, a court will probably enjoin D from working for the competitor for the year.

B. Limitations on equitable remedies: There are three important limits on the willingness of the court to issue either a decree of specific performance or an injunction:

  1. **Inadequacy of damages:**   Equitable relief for breach of contract will not be granted unless *damages are not adequate to protect the injured party*. Two reasons why damages might not be adequate in a contracts case are: (1) because the injury cannot be estimated with sufficient certainty; or (2) because money cannot purchase a substitute for the contracted-for performance. (*Example* of (2): Each piece of land is deemed "unique", so an award of damages for breach by the vendor in a land sale contract will not be adequate, and specific performance will be decreed.)

  2. **Definiteness:**   The court will not give equitable relief unless the contract's terms are *definite enough* to enable the court to frame an adequate order.

  3. **Difficulty of enforcement:**   Finally, the court will not grant equitable relief where there are likely to be significant difficulties in *enforcing* and *supervising* the order. (*Example*: Courts usually will not grant specific performance of a personal service contract, because the court thinks it will not be able to supervise defendant's performance to determine whether it satisfies the contract.)

C. Land-sale contracts: The most common situation for specific performance is where defendant breaches a contract under which he is to convey a particular *piece of land* to the plaintiff.

  1. **Breach by buyer:**   Courts also often grant specific performance of a land-sale contract where the seller has not yet conveyed, and it is the *buyer who breaches*. (*Example*: *A* contracts to sell Blackacre to B. If *A* fails to convey, a court will order him to do so in return for the purchase price. If *B* fails to come up with the

purchase price, the court will order him to pay that price and will then give him title.)

D. Personal services contracts:

1. **No specific performance:** Courts almost ***never*** order specific performance of a contract for ***personal services***. This is true on both sides: the court will not order the employer to resume the employment, nor will it order the employee to perform the services.

2. **Injunction:** But where the employee under an employment contract breaches, the court may be willing to grant an ***injunction*** preventing him from working for a competitor. The employer must show that: (1) the employee's services are ***unique*** or ***extraordinary***; and (2) the likely result will not be to leave the employee without other ***reasonable means of making a living***.

E. Sale of goods:
Specific performance will sometimes be granted in contracts involving the ***sale of goods***. This is especially likely in the case of ***output*** and ***requirements*** contracts, where the item is not in ready supply.

> **Example:** P, a utility, contracts with D, a pipeline company, for D to supply all of P's requirements for natural gas for 10 years at a stated price. In a time of tight energy supplies, a court is likely to find that damages are not adequate to redress D's breach, because no other vendor will enter a similar fixed-price, long-term contract; therefore, the court will probably grant a decree of specific performance ordering D to continue with the contract.

III. VARIOUS DAMAGE MEASURES

A. Three types:
There are three distinct kinds of interests on the part of a disappointed contracting party which may be protected by courts:

1. **Expectation:** In most breach of contract cases, the plaintiff will seek, and receive, protection for her ***"expectation interest."*** Here, the court attempts to ***put the plaintiff in the position he would have been in had the contract been performed***. In other words, the plaintiff is given the ***"benefit of her bargain,"*** including any ***profits*** she would have made from the contract.

2. **Reliance:** Sometimes the plaintiff receives protection for his ***reliance interest***. Here, the court puts the plaintiff in ***as good a position as he was in before the contract was made***. To do this, the court usually awards the plaintiff his ***out-of-pocket*** costs incurred in the performance he has already rendered (including preparation to perform). When reliance is protected, the plaintiff does not recover any part of the profits he would have made on the contract had it been completed.

   a. **When used:** The reliance interest is used mainly: (1) when it is impossible to ***measure*** the plaintiff's expectation interest accurately (e.g., when profits from a new business which the plaintiff would have been able to operate cannot be computed accurately); and (2) when the plaintiff recovers on a ***promissory estoppel*** theory.

3. Restitution: Finally, courts sometimes protect the plaintiff's *"restitution interest."* That is, the court forces the defendant to pay the plaintiff an amount equal to the *benefit which the defendant has received* from the plaintiff's performance. Restitution is designed to prevent unjust enrichment.

   a. When used: The restitution measure is most commonly used where: (1) a non-breaching plaintiff has partly performed, and the restitution measure is greater than the contract price; and (2) a breaching plaintiff has not substantially performed, but is allowed to recover the benefit of what he has conferred on the defendant.

   > **Note:** In contract actions, all three of these measures are used at least some of the time. In quasi-contract actions, expectation damages are almost never awarded, but reliance and restitution damages frequently are. (For instance, reliance damages are often used in promissory estoppel cases where the suit is really in quasi-contract, and restitution is used by materially-breaching plaintiffs who are in effect suing in quasi-contract.)

IV. EXPECTATION DAMAGES

A. Defined: Expectation damages are the usual measure of damages for breach of contract. The court tries to *put the plaintiff in the position he would have been in had the contract been performed by the defendant*. The plaintiff should end up with a sum equal to the *profit* he would have made had the contract been completed.

   > **Example 1:** On March 1, D, the owner of Blackacre, contracts to sell it to P on July 1 for $500,000. Real estate prices rise, and D reneges. On July 1, D sells the property for $700,000 (which is the highest price any likely buyer would have paid). P will be permitted to recover $200,000 from D, the difference between the contract price and the market price at the time of breach, since that amount will put P in the position he would have been in (making a $200,000 profit) had the contract been performed.

B. Formula for calculating:

Here's a good general formula for computing a plaintiff's expectation damages:

---

[1] *the amount by which the value of the defendant's **actual performance** was less than the **value of the promised performance***

minus

[2] *whatever **benefits**, if any, the plaintiff received from **not having to complete his own performance**.*

Generally, the benefits in [2] are *expenditures* which the plaintiff would have had to make to complete his performance under the contract, but which he didn't have to make because the defendant breached first.

   > **Example of formula:** Contractor contracts with Owner to renovate an office building owned by Owner. The contract requires that the renovation be completed

in time for Tenant, the sole tenant, to take possession by August 1. Tenant is scheduled to pay Owner August rent of $10,000. It would cost Owner $2,000 in utilities to operate the building for August if Tenant is there, but $0 if Tenant has not moved in yet. Contractor breaches by not completing the work until August 30, so that Tenant moves in on September 1. The only consequence to Owner from the delay is the loss of August's rent.

Owner's expectation damages are: (1) the value to Owner of the August rent that he didn't receive because of the delay ($10,000) less (2) the $2,000 that Owner saved in utilities by virtue of the delay. So Owner can recover only $8,000.

C. Construction contracts: Many problems involving the computation of damages involve *construction contracts*. We'll call the person doing the construction the "builder," and the person receiving the benefit of the work the "owner."

1. Builder breaches: First, let's look at how the owner's damages are computed if the *builder breaches*, and the owner has the work completed by a second builder. A good formula for computing the owner's damages is:

[1] The value the building *would have had* if it had been completed as agreed upon ...

[2] Less the value of the building *as completed* by the second builder ...

[3] Plus the amount by which (a) the *totals paid* by the owner to the first and second builders together *exceed (b) the contract price* ...

[4] Plus any consequential damages from the *delay*.

Example: Builder 1 contracts to build a house on Owner's land for $500,000. Builder 1 does the initial work defectively, then abandons the job in the middle of construction. At the time of abandonment, Owner has paid Builder 1 $200,000. If the house had been completed as contracted for, it would have been worth $600,000 (i.e., Owner made a favorable contract). Owner hires Builder 2 to complete the job for $400,000. Because the defective work done by Builder 1 before abandonment can't be readily remedied, the house as completed is worth only $550,000. Due to the delays caused by the breach, Owner loses $50,000 in rental income.

Owner can recover from Builder 1:

(1) $600,000 (value if completed as per the original contract) ....

(2) Less $550,000 (value as actually completed, due to Builder 1's poor work) ...

(3) Plus the difference between $600,000 (the sum of the $200,000 Owner paid to Builder 1 and the $400,000 he paid to Builder 2) and $500,000 (the contract price), or $100,000 ...

(4) Plus $50,000 lost rental as delay damages.

So Owner recovers:

$600,000 - $550,000 + 100,000 + $50,000, or

$200,000

2. **Owner breaches:** Now, let's look at how the *builder's* damages are computed if the *owner breaches* when the work has *not yet been completed.*[1] A good formula for computing the builder's damages is:

> [1] The money the builder has *spent so far* in fulfilling the contract (the builder's "*reliance*" cost; see *infra*, p. 117 , for more about reliance) ...
>
> [2] Less any *salvage value* to the builder from the partial performance, such as materials purchased that can be used on another project ("*loss avoided*") ...
>
> [3] Plus the *profit* the builder *would have made* had the contract been completed ...
>
> [4] Less any *progress payments* already made by the owner.

Example: Builder contracts to build a house on Owner's land for $500,000. At a time when Owner has paid Builder $60,000 and Builder has spent $200,000, Owner repudiates. Builder cancels and sues. The $200,000 spent by Builder includes $20,000 of lumber that he can use on another job. If the contract had been completed, Builder would have made a profit of $100,000. Builder can recover:

(1) The $200,000 he has spent in "reliance";

(2) Less the $20,000 he can get for the lumber ("loss avoided");

(3) Plus the $100,000 profit he would have made had the project been completed on both sides;

(4) Less the $60,000 already paid by Owner.

So Builder recovers:

$200,000 - $20,000 + 100,000 - $60,000, or

$220,000

D. **Overhead:** The plaintiff's cost of completion (the amount he has saved by not having to finish) does *not* include any part of his *overhead*.

E. **Cost of completion or decrease in value:** Where defendant has defectively performed, plaintiff normally can recover the *cost of remedying* defendant's defective performance. But if the cost of remedying defects is *clearly disproportionate* to the *loss in market value* from the defective performance, plaintiff will only recover the loss in market value.

1. **Economic waste:** This principle is often applied where the defect is minor, and remedying it would involve *"economic waste,"* such as the *destruction of what has already been done*.

---

1. If the work has been completed, the builder will simply recover the contract price less any prior payments made by the owner.

Example: Contractor contracts to build a house for Owner, with Reading pipe to be used. After the house is completely built, it is discovered that Contractor used Cohoes pipe rather than Reading pipe; the two are of virtually the same quality. Owner will be allowed to recover (or to subtract from the unpaid contract balance) only the difference in value between the two pipes (a negligible sum), not the much greater cost of ripping out the walls and all of the existing piping to make the replacement. [*Jacob & Youngs v. Kent*]

2. **Overhead:** The plaintiff's cost of completion (the amount he has saved by not having to finish) does ***not*** include any part of his ***overhead***.

3. **Cost of completion or decrease in value:** Where defendant has defectively performed, plaintiff normally can recover the ***cost of remedying*** defendant's defective performance. But if the cost of remedying defects is ***clearly disproportionate*** to the ***loss in market value*** from the defective performance, plaintiff will only recover the loss in market value.

   a. **Economic waste:** This principle is often applied where the defect is minor, and remedying it would involve *"economic waste,"* such as the ***destruction of what has already been done***.

      Example: Contractor contracts to build a house for Owner, with Reading pipe to be used. After the house is completely built, it is discovered that Contractor used Cohoes pipe rather than Reading pipe; the two are of virtually the same quality. Owner will be allowed to recover (or to subtract from the unpaid contract balance) only the difference in value between the two pipes (a negligible sum), not the much greater cost of ripping out the walls and all of the existing piping to make the replacement. [*Jacob & Youngs v. Kent*]

F. **"Reasonable certainty":** The plaintiff may only recover for losses which he establishes with *"reasonable certainty."* Mainly, this means that a plaintiff who claims that he would have ***made profits*** had the defendant not breached must show not only that there would have been profits, but also the likely ***amount*** of those profits.

   1. **Profits from a new business:** Courts are especially reluctant to award lost profits from a ***new business***, that is, a business which at the time of breach was not yet in actual operation.

   2. **Cost of completion unknown:** Also, the "reasonable certainty" requirement may fail to be met where the plaintiff cannot show accurately enough what his ***cost of completion*** would have been.

      Example: Contractor contracts to build a house for Owner for $100,000. After Contractor has done about half the work, Owner repudiates. If Contractor cannot demonstrate what his cost of completion would have been, he will be unable to recover expectation damages, and will have to be content with either reliance or restitution damages.

V. RELIANCE DAMAGES

A. Generally: *Reliance* damages are the damages needed to put the plaintiff in the *position he would have been in had the contract never been made*. Therefore, these damages usually equal the amount the plaintiff has *spent* in performing or in preparing to perform. They are used either where there is a contract but expectation damages cannot be accurately calculated, or where there is no contract but some relief is justifiable. The main situations where reliance damages are awarded are:

1. **Profit too speculative:** Where expectation damages cannot be computed because plaintiff's *lost profits* are too speculative or uncertain. (For instance, where defendant's breach prevents plaintiff from developing a new business, profits are probably too speculative to be computed.)

2. **Promissory estoppel:** Where plaintiff successfully brings an action based on *promissory estoppel*. Here, the suit is usually not truly on the contract, but is rather in quasi-contract. The court is trying to reduce injustice, so it gives plaintiff a "half-way" measure, less than expectation damages, but better than nothing.

B. Limits on amount of reliance recovery: The plaintiff's reliance damages are sometimes *limited* to a sum smaller than the actual expenditures:

1. **Contract price as limit:** Where D's only obligation under the contract is to pay a sum of money (the contract price), reliance damages will almost always be *limited to this contract price*.

2. **Recovery limited to profits:** Also, most courts do *not* allow reliance damages to *exceed expectation damages*. However, the defendant has to bear the *burden of proving* what plaintiff's profit or loss would have been.

   a. **Subtract amount of loss:** Another way to express this idea is that there will be *subtracted* from plaintiff's reliance recovery the amount of the *loss* which defendant shows plaintiff would have suffered had the contract been performed.

3. **Expenditures prior to signing:** The plaintiff will not normally be permitted to recover as reliance damages expenditures made *before the contract was signed*, since these expenditures were not made "in reliance on" the contract.

C. Cost to plaintiff, not value to defendant: When reliance damages are awarded, they are usually calculated according to the *cost to the plaintiff* of his performance, not the value to the defendant.

VI. RESTITUTION

A. Generally: The plaintiff's restitution interest is defined as the *value to the defendant of the plaintiff's performance*. Restitution's goal is to *prevent unjust enrichment*.

1. **When used:** The main uses of the restitution measure are as follows: (1) a non-breaching plaintiff who has partly performed before the other party breached may bring suit on the contract, and not be limited by the contract price (as she would be for the expectation and reliance measures); and (2) a breaching plaintiff who has

not substantially performed may bring a quasi-contract suit and recover the value that she has conferred upon the defendant.

2. **Market value:** Restitution is based on the *value rendered to the defendant*, regardless of how much the conferring of that value costs the plaintiff and regardless of how much the plaintiff was injured by the defendant's breach. This value is usually the sum which the defendant would *have to pay to acquire the plaintiff's performance*, not the subjective value to the defendant.

B. **Not limited to the contract price:** The main use of the restitution measure is that, in most courts, *it is not limited by the contract price*. If the work done by P prior to D's breach has already enriched D in an amount greater than the contract price, this entire enrichment may be recovered by P. This makes restitution sometimes very attractive, compared with both reliance and expectation measures.

> **Example:** Contractor agrees to build a house for Owner for $100,000. After Contractor has done 90% of the work, Owner repudiates. At trial, Contractor shows that Owner can now resell the mostly-built house for $120,000, not counting land. Contractor will be permitted to recover the whole $120,000 on a restitution theory, even though this sum is greater than the contract price (and thus greater than the expectation damages would be), and greater than the reliance measure (actual expenditures by Contractor).

1. **Not available where plaintiff has fully performed:** If at the time of D's breach, P has *fully performed* the contract (and D only owes money, not some other kind of performance) most courts do *not allow P to recover restitution damages*.

C. **Losing contract:** Restitution may even be awarded where P has partly performed, and *would have lost money* had the contract been completed. (*Example*: On the facts of the above example, assume that Contractor would have lost $10,000 had the contract been fulfilled. Contractor may use the restitution measure to collect $120,000, thus turning a $10,000 loss into a $10,000 profit.)

VII. SUBSTANTIAL PERFORMANCE AS A BASIS FOR SUIT ON THE CONTRACT

A. **Substantial performance generally:** Where one party *substantially performs* (i.e., does not materially breach), the other is not relieved of his duties. If the latter refuses to perform, the substantially performing party has an action for breach of contract.

1. **Expectation damages:** Putting it more simply, *a party who substantially performs may sue for ordinary (expectation) damages for breach of contract, if the other party fails to perform*. The other party has a set-off or counterclaim for the damages he has suffered from the plaintiff's failure to completely perform.

> **Example:** Contractor contracts to paint Owner's house for $10,000, with performance to be complete by April 1. There is no "time of the essence" clause, and no reason to believe that April 1 completion is especially important. Contractor finishes work on April 3. Owner refuses to pay. Contractor will be able to bring suit on the contract, and to recover expectation damages (the profit he

would have made). Owner is not entitled to refuse to pay, and must simply be content with a counterclaim for damages (probably nominal ones) due to the late completion.

B. Divisible contracts: If the contract is *divisible* into separate pairs of "agreed equivalents," a party who has substantially performed *one of the parts* may recover on the contract for that part. That's true even though he has materially breached with respect to the other portions.

VIII. SUITS IN QUASI-CONTRACT

A. Where allowed: There are a number of situations where recovery "on the contract" is not possible or allowed: (1) situations where there was no attempt even to form a contract, but the plaintiff deserves some measure of recovery anyway; (2) cases where there was an attempt to form a contract, but the contract is unenforceable because of Statute of Frauds, impossibility, illegality, etc.; (3) cases where there is an enforceable contract, but the plaintiff has materially breached, and therefore may not recover on the contract; and (4) cases where the defendant has breached but the plaintiff is not entitled to damages on the contract. In all of these situations, the plaintiff will often be allowed to recover in *"quasi-contract."*

   1. Measure of damages: Courts almost never award expectation damages in quasi-contract suits. Both reliance damages and restitution damages are frequently awarded in quasi-contract suits (with courts deciding which of these two to use based on the equities of the particular case.).

B. No contract attempted: The courts sometimes award P a quasi-contractual recovery where *no contract was even attempted*.

   1. Rationale: Courts do this on the theory that a person who has been *unjustly enriched* at the expense of another should be required to *make restitution*. A person (P) may recover on such a theory if she meets the following requirements:

   [1] P *rendered a benefit* to another (D), who would be *unjustly enriched* if he were not required to pay for that benefit; and

   [2] P did *not* confer the benefit on D *"officiously,"* that is, she did not thrust the benefit upon D *against his will* or in circumstances where she should have known that D would not want the benefit; and

   [3] P did *not* confer the benefit on D *"gratuitously,"* i.e., *without expectation of compensation*.

   2. Emergency services: The most common example is where P supplies *emergency services* to D, without first forming a contract to do so.

   Example: P, a doctor, sees D lying unconscious in the street, and gives D CPR. The court will probably allow P to recover the fair market value of her services, in an action in quasi-contract.

C. No contract attempted: The courts sometimes award P a recovery where *no contract was even attempted*. The most common example is where P supplies *emergency services* to D, without first forming a contract to do so. (*Example*: P, a doctor, sees D lying unconscious in the street, and gives D CPR. The court will probably allow P to recover the fair market value of her services, in an action in quasi-contract.)

D. Unenforceable contracts: The parties may attempt to form a binding contract which turns out to be *unenforceable* or avoidable. This may happen because of the Statute of Frauds, mistake, illegality, impossibility, or frustration of purpose. In any of these cases, the court will usually let P sue in quasi-contract, and recover either the value of the services performed (restitution) or P's reasonable expenditures (reliance).

E. Breaching plaintiff: A plaintiff who has *materially breached* may normally bring a quasi-contract suit, and recover his *restitution interest*, less the defendant's damages for the breach. This is sometimes called a recovery in *"quantum meruit"* ("as much as he deserves").

> **Example:** P agrees to work for D for one year, payment of the $20,000 salary to be made at the end. P works for six months, then unjustifiably quits. P cannot recover "on the contract," because he has not substantially performed. But he will probably be allowed to recover in quasi-contract, for the fair value of the benefits he has conferred on D. The court will estimate these benefits (which will probably be one-half of the $20,000 annual salary), and will subtract the damage to D of P's not performing the second six months.

1. Construction cases: Quasi-contract recovery by a breaching plaintiff is most often found in *construction* cases. Here, the builder gets to recover the value to the owner of the work done, even where the work does not constitute substantial performance of the contract.

2. Limited to pro-rata contract price: When a defaulting plaintiff sues in quasi-contract for his restitution interest, recovery is almost always limited to the *pro-rata contract price*, less the defendant's damages for breach.

3. Willful default: In many states, a defaulting plaintiff may not recover in quasi-contract if his breach is *"willful."*

> **Example:** Contractor agrees to build a house for Owner for $100,000. The contract expressly provides that all walls will be insulated with non-asbestos-based insulation. Contractor instead knowingly installs asbestos-based insulation, in order to save $2,000 in material costs. Even though the resulting house has substantial value, many courts will not permit Contractor to recover anything at all, on the grounds that his breach was not only material but "willful," i.e., intentional and done for Contractor's financial advantage.

4. UCC gives partial restitution to breaching buyer: The UCC gives a *breaching buyer* a right to partial restitution with respect to any *deposit* made to the seller before the buyer breached. Under §2-718(2), the seller can only keep *20% of the total contract price* or *$500*, whichever amount is smaller — the balance must be refunded to the breaching buyer.

> **Example:** Seller contracts to sell to Buyer 1,000 widgets at $2 each. The contract does not contain a liquidated damages clause. Buyer sends in a $700 deposit. Buyer cancels the order just before Seller is to ship. Seller suffers no

damages, because he has a limited supply of the widgets, and sells the ones he had earmarked for Buyer to X instead, at the same price.

Even though Buyer has breached, Seller may not keep the entire $700 deposit. Instead, Seller is entitled to keep only the lesser of: (i) 20% of the contract price ($400) and (ii) $500. Therefore, Seller may keep only $400, and must refund the other $300.

a. **Seller's counterclaim:** But where the buyer establishes such a right to restitution, the seller may *offset* the buyer's claim by any *actual damages* which he sustained as a result of the buyer's breach (computed by using Article 2's regular damages measures). §2-718(3). So the seller owes the buyer a refund of the deposit in excess of the lesser of 20% of the contract price and $500, but can subtract from this refund seller's actual damages.

IX. FORESEEABILITY

A. **General rule:** The "rule of *Hadley v. Baxendale*" limits the damages which courts will award for breach of contract. The "rule" says that courts will not award consequential damages for breach unless the damages fall into one of two classes:

1. **Arise naturally:** The damages were *foreseeable* by any reasonable person, regardless of whether the defendant actually foresaw them; or

2. **Remote or unusual consequences:** The damages were *remote or unusual*, but only if the defendant had *actual notice* of the possibility of these consequences.

> **Example:** P operates a mill, which has suspended operations because of a broken shaft. He brings the shaft to D, a carrier, to have it brought to another city for repairs. D knows that the item to be carried is a shaft of P's mill, but does not know that the mill is closed because of the broken shaft. D negligently delays delivery, causing the mill to stay closed for extra days. P sues for the profits lost during these extra days.
>
> *Held*, P cannot recover for these lost profits. The lost profits were not foreseeable to a reasonable person in D's position, nor was D on notice of the special fact that the mill was closed due to the broken shaft. [*Hadley v. Baxendale*]

B. **Parties may allocate risks themselves:** The rule of *Hadley* may always be *modified* by express agreement of the parties. For instance, if P puts D on notice of the special facts, this may cause damages to be awardable which would not otherwise be. Alternatively, the parties can simply agree that even unforeseen consequential damages shall be compensable.

X. AVOIDABLE DAMAGES

A. **General rule:** Where P *might have avoided* a particular item of damage by reasonable effort, he *may not recover* for that item if he fails to make such an effort. This is sometimes called the *"duty to mitigate"* rule. (But it's a "duty" only in the sense that if P fails to do it, he'll lose the right to collect damages, not in the sense that P has breached some obligation.)

Example: P agrees to work as an employee of D for a two-year period, at an annual salary of $50,000. After two weeks on the job, P is wrongfully fired. P must make reasonable efforts to get another job. If he does not, the court will subtract from his recovery the amount which it believes P could have earned at an alternative job with reasonable effort. Thus if the court believes that P could have lined up a $40,000-a-year job, P will only be allowed to recover at the rate of $10,000 per year for the remainder of the contract.

1. **Reasonableness:** The "duty to mitigate" only requires the plaintiff to make *reasonable efforts* to mitigate damages. For instance, P does not have to incur substantial expense or inconvenience, damage his reputation, or break any other contracts, in order to mitigate.

B. **Sales contracts:** Here's what the UCC says about an aggrieved buyer or seller's obligation to mitigate:

1. **Buyer:** If the seller either fails to deliver, or delivers defective goods which the buyer rejects, the *buyer* must *"cover"* for the goods if he can reasonably do so — he may not recover for those damages (e.g., lost profits) which could have been prevented had he covered. See UCC §2-715(2)(a) (defining "consequential damages" to include only those losses "which could not reasonably be prevented by cover or otherwise…"). (If buyer does not cover when he could have done so, he will still be entitled to the difference between the market price at the time of the breach and the contract price, but he'll lose the ability to collect consequential damages that he might otherwise have gotten.)

2. **Seller:** The *seller* has much less of a duty to mitigate, when it is the buyer who breaches by wrongfully rejecting the goods or repudiating before delivery. The seller can choose between reselling the goods (and collecting the difference between resale price and contract price), or not reselling them (and recovering the difference between market price and unpaid contract price); seller may also be able to recover lost profits.

3. **Summary:** So in UCC cases, it is really only the buyer who has a practical duty to mitigate.

C. **Losses incurred in avoiding damages:** If the aggrieved party tries to mitigate his damages, and incurs *losses* or *expenses* in doing so, he may recover damages for these losses or expenses. As long as plaintiff acted *reasonably* in trying to mitigate, it does not matter whether his attempt was successful.

XI. NOMINAL AND PUNITIVE DAMAGES

A. **Nominal damages:** Where a right of action for breach exists, but no harm has been done or is provable, P may get a judgment for *nominal damages*. That is, he may recover a small sum that is fixed without regard to the amount of harm he has suffered.

B. **Punitive damages:** Punitive damages are rarely awarded in breach of contract cases.

1. **Tort:** But if the breach of contract also *constitutes a tort*, punitive damages *are* recoverable. (*Example*: D, a car dealer, sets back the odometer on a used car before selling it to P. D then falsely claims that the car is "new." P will probably be

able to recover punitive damages, because seller's act, although it was part of a contract, also constitutes the independent tort of fraud.)

a. **Bad faith as tort:** Many courts now regard a party's ***bad faith*** conduct in connection with a contract as ***being*** itself a tort, for which punitive damages may be awarded. For instance, if a party breaches voluntarily, in order to make a better deal elsewhere, the court may find that this conduct constitutes bad faith punishable by punitive damages.

   i. **Insurance company refusal to settle:** If an ***insurance company*** refuses in bad faith to ***settle a claim*** that is covered by a policy it wrote, courts are quite likely to hold that the insured has suffered a tort, and can recover punitive damages against the insurer.

XII. LIQUIDATED DAMAGES

A. Definition: A *"liquidated damages clause"* is a provision, placed in the contract itself, specifying the ***consequences of breach***. (*Example*: Contractor contracts to paint Owner's house for $10,000. In the basic contract, the parties agree that for every day after the deadline that Contractor finishes, the price charged by him will be reduced by $100. This provision is a liquidated damages clause.)

B. General rule: Courts will enforce liquidated damages provisions, but only if the court is satisfied that the provision is not a *"penalty."* That is, the court wants to be satisfied that the clause really is an attempt to estimate actual damages, rather than to penalize the party for breach by awarding "damages" that are far in excess of the ones actually suffered. Therefore, in order to be enforceable, the liquidated damage clause must always meet one, and sometimes two, requirements:

1. **Reasonable forecast:** The amount fixed must be ***reasonable*** relative to the anticipated or actual loss for breach; and

2. **Difficult calculation:** In some courts, the harm caused by the breach must be ***uncertain or very difficult to calculate accurately***, even after the fact.

C. Reasonableness of amount: All courts refuse to enforce liquidated damages clauses that do not provide for a *"reasonable"* amount.

1. **Modern view:** Courts disagree about the ***time*** as of which the amount must appear to be reasonable. Most courts today will enforce the clause if ***either***: (1) the clause is a reasonable forecast when viewed ***as of the time of contracting***; or (2) the clause is reasonable in light of the ***actual*** damages which have occurred.

   a. **Unexpectedly high damages:** This means that a clause which is an unreasonable forecast (viewed as of the time of contracting) can still be saved if it turns out that P's damages are unexpectedly high, and therefore in line with the clause.

2. **No loss at all:** Courts are split about whether to enforce a liquidated damages clause where P has sustained ***no actual losses at all***. The Restatement does ***not*** enforce the clause if it turns out that no actual damage has been sustained.

3. **Blunderbuss clause:** A *"blunderbuss"* clause stipulates the same sum of money as liquidated damages for breach of *any* covenant, whether trivial or important. Where the actual damage turns out to be *trivial*, most courts will not enforce a blunderbuss clause (or will interpret the clause as not applying to trivial breaches).

    Example: Contractor contracts to renovate Owner's office building by June 1, to get it ready for occupancy by Tenant beginning on August 1. The contract provides that if Contractor is late in completing work, he will forfeit $100,000, whether the delay is one day or 90 days. In the actual event, Contractor is two days late, and Owner deducts the full $100,000.

    Since the clause produces the same damage amount regardless of how much actual damage is sustained by Owner (a one-day delay wouldn't prevent Tenant's on-time occupancy, but a 70-day delay would), and since the actual damage has turned out to be trivial, the clause will be struck down as a blunderbuss clause.

    a. **Major loss:** But if the breach turns out to be a *major* one (so that the liquidated amount is reasonable in light of the actual loss), courts are split on whether the blunderbuss should be enforced. The modern view is to *enforce* the blunderbuss where the actual loss is roughly equal to the damages provided in the clause.

D. **UCC rules:** The UCC basically follows the common-law rule on when a liquidated damages clause should be awarded. The UCC follows the modern view, by which the party seeking enforcement of the clause will succeed if the sum is reasonable viewed *either* as of the time the contract is made or viewed in light of the actual breach and actual damages. See UCC §2-718(1) (clause enforceable if "reasonable in the light of the anticipated or actual harm caused by the breach…").

XIII. DAMAGES IN SALES CONTRACTS

A. **Where goods not accepted:** If the buyer has *not accepted* the goods (either because they weren't delivered, or were delivered defective, or because the buyer repudiated), the UCC gives well-defined rights to the injured party:

1. **Buyer's rights:** If the seller fails to deliver at all, or delivers defective goods which the buyer rightfully rejects, the buyer has a choice of remedies.

    a. **Cover:** The most important is her right to *"cover,"* i.e., to buy the goods from another seller, and to recover the *difference between the contract price and the cover price* from the seller. §2-712(2). The buyer's purchase of substitute goods must be *"reasonable,"* and must be made "in good faith and *without unreasonable delay.*" §2-712(1).

    b. **Contract/market differential:** If the buyer does *not* cover (either because she can't, or decides she doesn't want to), she can instead recover the *contract/market differential*, i.e., the difference between the contract price and the market price "at the time when the buyer learned of the breach…." §2-713(1).

i. **Time of breach:** Typically, the buyer "learns of the breach" (setting the time for measuring the market price) at the time the breach in fact occurs (either through non-delivery or through receipt of defective goods). But if the breach takes the form of a ***repudiation*** in advance of the time for performance, most courts hold that the market price is to be measured as of the time the buyer learns of the repudiation. (See p. C-101.)

ii. **Buyer contracts to resell at fixed margin:** Notice that the contract/market differential may not correctly compensate the buyer where the market is rising and the buyer has ***already made a fixed-price or fixed-margin contract to resell*** the goods. If the market-price increase times the quantity is greater than the profit margin on the buyer's resale contract, giving the buyer the contract/market differential will put the buyer in a ***better position*** than she would have been in had the contract been fulfilled.

   [1] **Minority view limits buyer to lost profits:** Therefore, a few courts *limit the buyer to the profits the buyer would have* made under the resale arrangement.

   [2] **Majority view doesn't limit buyer:** But *most* courts hold that the buyer is *entitled to the full contract/market differential even where this would put her in a better position* than had the contract been fulfilled, because limiting damages to the buyer's lost profits would *incentivize the seller to breach.*

   > **Example:** Seller contracts to sell to Buyer 10,000 widgets (not yet manufactured) at $1 per widget, delivery to occur 90 days later. Buyer immediately contracts to resell the widgets, when produced, to Thirdco, a third party, for $1.30. (Assume that the contract with Thirdco says that if Buyer's source of supply fails to deliver, Thirdco can't sue Buyer.) By the delivery date, the market price of widgets has soared to $2.
   >
   > If Buyer is given the contract/market differential, Buyer will collect damages of $10,000, even though had Seller delivered Buyer would have made only $3,000. Yet most courts will give Buyer the contract/market differential anyway, since limiting Buyer to the $3,000 "profits it would have made" would give Seller an incentive to breach: Seller pockets an extra $10,000, pays out $3,000 in damages, and is ahead of the game for having breached.

iii. **Probably not available to covering buyer:** Probably the buyer may recover the contract/market differential *only where she did not cover.* This means that if the market price declines between the time the buyer learns of the breach and the time he covers by buying substitute goods, the buyer can't get a windfall — limiting him to the contract/market differential puts him in the same position he would have been in had the contract been fulfilled, not a better one.

    c. **Consequential and incidental damages:** The buyer, regardless of whether he covers, may recover for *"incidental"* and *"consequential"* damages.

        i. **Consequential:** *Consequential* damages include the *profits* which the buyer could have made by reselling the contracted-for goods had they been delivered. But remember that these profits must be proved with appropriate certainty, and must be shown to have been reasonably foreseeable at the time of the contract.

        ii. **Incidental damages:** *"Incidental"* damages include such items as transportation expenses, storage expenses, and other small but direct expenses associated with the breach and buyer's attempts to cover for it.

    d. **Rejection:** All of the above are judicial remedies. But the buyer who receives non-conforming goods can also exercise the self-help remedy of *rejecting the goods*. The buyer thus throws the goods back on the seller and cancels the contract. (Observe that where the buyer has actually made a losing contract, rejection lets him escape his bad bargain.)

2. **Seller's damages for breach:** Where it is the buyer who breaches, by wrongfully refusing to accept the goods (or by repudiating the contract before shipment is even made), the seller has several possible remedies:

    a. **Contract/resale differential:** Normally, the seller will *resell the goods* to a third party. Assuming that the resale is made in good faith and in a "commercially reasonable" manner, seller may recover the difference between the *resale price* and the *contract price*, together with incidental damages.

    b. **Contract/market differential:** If the seller does *not* resell the goods, he may recover from the breaching buyer the difference between the *market price* at the time and place for delivery, and the *unpaid contract price*, together with incidental damages. §2-708(1). (Probably a seller who has resold the goods may *not* use this contract/market differential, but must use the contract/resale differential.)

    c. **Lost profits:** The contract/resale differential (for a reselling seller) and the contract/market differential (for a non-reselling seller) may not make the seller whole. Where this is the case, §2-708(2) lets the seller recover his *lost profits* instead of using either of these differentials.

        i. **"Lost volume" seller:** Most importantly, this means that the *"lost volume"* seller may recover the profit he has lost by reason of the breach. In the usual case of a seller who has resold the item, a "lost volume" seller is one who (1) had a big enough supply that he could have made both the contracted-for sale and the resale; (2) probably would have made the resale anyway as well as the original sale had there been no breach; and (3) would have made a profit on both sales.

            Example: Auto Dealer sells cars made by Smith Motors. Auto Dealer can get as much inventory from Smith as Auto Dealer can sell. Auto Dealer contracts to sell a particular 1999 Thunder Wagon to Consumer for $10,000. Consumer repudiates just before delivery. Auto

Dealer resells the car for the same $10,000 price to X, a walk-in customer.

The traditional contract/resale differential (here, $0) would not make Auto Dealer whole, since he could have sold cars to both consumer and X and made a profit on each. Therefore, Auto Dealer can recover from Consumer the profit he would have made had the contract with Consumer been fulfilled. Auto Dealer is on these facts a "lost volume" seller.

d. **Action for contract price:** In a few situations, the UCC allows the seller to sue for the *entire contract price*:

  i. **Accepted goods:** First, if the buyer has *"accepted"* the goods, the seller may sue for the entire contract price (though the buyer has a counterclaim for damages for non-conformity). (*Example*: Buyer orders 10 widgets at $50 each from Seller. Seller ships the goods late, but Buyer keeps the goods for 30 days without saying anything. Buyer will be held to have "accepted" the goods, and Seller can therefore sue for the entire contract price, $500. But Buyer may counterclaim for the damages he has actually suffered due to the late delivery.)

  ii. **Risk of loss:** Second, if the *risk of loss* has passed to the buyer, and the goods are lost in transit, the seller may sue for the entire contract price. (*Example*: As per the contract, Seller ships goods "F.O.B. Seller's plant." The goods are destroyed while on the trucking company's truck. Seller can sue for the whole price; Buyer's remedy is against the trucker.)

  iii. **Unresaleable goods:** Lastly, if the seller has already *earmarked* particular goods as being ones to be supplied under the contract, and the buyer rejects them or repudiates before delivery, seller may recover the entire contract price if he is *unable to resell them* on some reasonable basis. Most commonly, this applies to *perishable* goods and *custom-made* goods.

e. **Incidental damages:** A seller who pursues and achieves one of the four above remedies (resale, contract/market differential, lost profits, action for price) may *also* recover *"incidental damages."* These include such items as transportation charges, storage charges, and other charges relating to the seller's attempt to deal with the goods after the buyer's breach. See §2-710.

f. **Consequential damages:** Nearly all courts hold that the seller may *not* recover *"consequential damages."* This is a big difference from how buyers are treated.

B. **Accepted goods:** If the buyer has *accepted* the goods (and has not rightfully revoked this acceptance), then the remedies given to buyer and seller are different:

  1. **Seller's action for price:** If the buyer has accepted the goods, the seller may recover the *full contract price*. (But if the goods are non-conforming, Buyer may counterclaim for breach of warranty.)

2. **Buyer's claim:**   If the buyer has accepted the goods, and they turn out to be defective, buyer's remedy is to sue for breach of contract.

    a. **Breach of warranty:**   Most importantly, buyer may sue for ***breach of warranty***. These may be either express warranties or warranties implied by the UCC. The measure of damages for breach of warranty is "the difference at the time and place of acceptance between the value of the goods accepted and the value they would have had if they had been as warranted, unless special circumstances show proximate damages of a different amount." §2-714(2).

    b. **Non-warranty damages:**   Buyer may also be able to recover for non-warranty damages. For instance, damages resulting from seller's ***delay*** in shipping the goods, or his breach of an express promise to ***repair*** defective goods, may be recovered on top of or instead of breach-of-warranty damages.

CHAPTER 11

CONTRACTS INVOLVING MORE THAN TWO PARTIES

I.   ASSIGNMENT AND DELEGATION GENERALLY

A. **Assignment distinguished from delegation:**   Be sure to distinguish ***assignment*** from ***delegation***:

1. **Assignment:**   When a party to an existing contract transfers to a third person her ***rights*** under the contract, she has made an ***assignment***.

2. **Delegation:**   When an existing party appoints a third person to perform her ***duties*** under the contract, she has made a ***delegation***.

3. **Combination:**   Frequently, an existing party will both assign and delegate. That is, she will both transfer her rights to a third person, and appoint the latter to perform her duties. But don't presume that where there is an assignment, there is necessarily a delegation, or vice versa — there will often be just an assignment, or just a delegation.

II. ASSIGNMENT

A. **Present transfer:**   An assignment is a ***present*** transfer of one's rights under a contract. Thus a ***promise*** to transfer one's rights in the future is not an assignment, even though it may be a contract.

1. **No consideration:**   Because an assignment is a present transfer, ***no consideration is required*** for it (just as no consideration is required for a present gift).

B. **Terminology:**   An assignment is a ***three-part*** transaction. The ***"assignor"*** assigns to the ***"assignee"*** the performance due the assignor from the ***"obligor."*** (*Example*: Contractor contracts to paint Owner's house for $10,000. Contractor then assigns to Bank Contractor's right to receive the $10,000 when due. Contractor is the assignor, Bank is the assignee, and Owner is the obligor.)

C. UCC rules: The *UCC* applies to many assignments, even ones not involving contracts for the sale of goods. In general, if a party assigns his *right to receive payment* under a contract as security *financing*, *Article 9* of the UCC applies to the terms of the assignment.

> **Example:** Contractor contracts to paint Owner's house for $10,000. Contractor assigns his right to receive payment to Bank, in return for a present payment of $9,500. Even though there is no contract for the sale of goods, Article 9 of the UCC applies to this assignment, and governs such items as whether the assignment must be in writing, the rights of Bank against Owner if Owner does not pay, etc.

D. Writing: At common law, an assignment of contract rights does *not have to be in writing*. However, many states have statutes requiring certain types of assignments to be in writing.

1. **Article 9:** In particular, where a party assigns to a third person his *right to receive payment*, in a financing-type transaction covered by Article 9 of the UCC, the assignment is not enforceable against either the assignor or the obligor unless the assignor has signed a document called a *"security interest."* See §9-203.

E. Gratuitous assignments: A *"gratuitous assignment"* is an assignment that is in the nature of a gift, i.e., one in which the assignor receives nothing of value in return. Gratuitous assignments are generally *enforceable*, just like ones given for value.

1. **Revocability:** But gratuitous assignments, unlike ones given for value, are automatically *revoked* if the assignor does any of the following three things:

   [1] The assignor *dies*;

   [2] The assignor makes a *subsequent assignment* of the same right to a different person; or

   [3] The assignor gives *notice* to *either the assignee or the obligor* that the assignment has been revoked.

   a. **Becomes irrevocable:** But a gratuitous assignment may become *irrevocable* in some circumstances:

      i. **Delivery of symbolic document:** This can happen if the contract right being assigned is evidenced by a *document* that commonly *symbolizes* the right, and that document is delivered to the assignee.

         > **Example:** Insured, who owns an insurance policy on his own life, delivers the policy to Friend, with the words, "I am assigning you this policy." At that moment, the assignment becomes irrevocable, even though it was gratuitous.

      ii. **Writing:** If the assignor puts the assignment *in writing*, most courts treat it as irrevocable if the writing is delivered to the assignee.

      iii. **Reliance:** If the assignee *relies to his detriment* on the assignment, and the reliance is reasonably foreseeable by the assignor, the assignment is irrevocable.

      iv. Obligor's performance: If the obligor gives the assignee the *payment* or performance, the assignment becomes irrevocable.

F. What rights may be assigned: All contract rights are assignable, unless they fall within a small number of exceptions, most of which are noted below:

    1. Materially alter the obligor's duty: If the obligor's duty would be *materially changed* by the assignment, the assignment will be disallowed.

        a. Personal services contract: This happens most commonly in certain *personal services* contracts. If there is a special relationship of *trust* or *confidence* between the parties, for instance, assignment will usually not be allowed.

> **Example:** Star, a movie star, hires Secretary for a below-market wage, which Secretary agrees to take because she wants to work closely with Star. Star probably cannot assign the contract to Friend, thus requiring Secretary to work for Friend for the same wages, because the assignment would materially alter Secretary's duties.

    2. Materially vary the risk: Assignment will also not be allowed if it will materially *vary the risk* assumed by the obligor. This is most commonly true of *insurance* policies.

    3. Impairment of obligor's chance to obtain return performance: An assignment may not be made if it would materially impair the obligor's chances of obtaining *return performance*.

> **Example:** Brenda, a famous fashion designer, contracts to have Manco custom-manufacture certain dresses that Brenda says she will sell under her own name for $2,000 apiece. Brenda has agreed to pay Manco $500 each for the dresses. The contract is silent about assignability. Manco has agreed to a relatively low price because it wants to be able to advertise in the trade that it makes dresses for the famous and prestigious Brenda. Brenda then assigns her rights under the contract to Schlock, a mass-market designer of goods that are widely regarded as of low quality.
>
> A court might well hold that this assignment is void, on the grounds that it would materially impair Manco's chance of obtaining return performance. That's because, even though Brenda remains liable for payment, a meaningful part of the "return performance" anticipated by Manco — being able to say that Brenda sells clothes Manco makes — has been taken from it.

G. Contract terms prohibiting assignment: Normally, if the contract itself contains a *clause prohibiting assignment*, the courts will *enforce* the clause. But there are a number of important exceptions.

    1. Restatement: Under the Restatement, an anti-assignment clause is generally enforceable, but subject to the following rules:

        a. Fully performed: Assignment is allowed if the assignor has already *fully performed*. (In other words, an assignor who has already earned the *right to* *payment* by doing the contracted-for work may always assign the payment right.)

b. **Total breach:** The right to *sue for damages* for breach of contract may always be assigned.

c. **Ban on assigning "the contract":** If the anti-assignment clause states that *"the contract"* may not be assigned (as opposed to stating that "rights under the contract may not be assigned"), the contract will be interpreted to bar only *delegation*, not assignment.

d. **Damages:** An assignment made in violation of an anti-assignment clause generally does *not* render the assignment ineffective. All it does is to give the obligor a right to *damages* against the assignor for breach.

e. **Rules of construction:** In any event, these rules are merely *rules of construction*. If the parties clearly manifest a different intent, that intent will be honored.

2. **UCC:** Where a party assigns his *right to payment* (or creates a *"security interest"* in his right to payment, as collateral for a loan), an anti-assignment clause is automatically *invalid*. That's because the UCC has two special provisions (§§ 2-210(3) and 9-406) that have this effect, whether the underlying contract that gave rise to the right to payment was for the sale of goods or not.

> **Example:** Painter agrees to paint Owner's house for $10,000. The contract says that Painter can't assign his right to payment. Before doing the work, Painter assigns his right to payment to Bank, to which he owes money. The anti-assignment clause won't be effective, because of the UCC provisions barring such clauses. Therefore (1) Owner can't cancel the contract if he finds out that Painter has assigned; and (2) Owner has to pay Bank, not Painter, once Owner gets notice of the assignment (under the rule explained in (H)(1) below).

H. **Assignee vs. obligor:** As a general rule, the assignee *"stands in the shoes of his assignor."* That is, with a few exceptions, he takes *subject to all defenses, set-offs and counterclaims which the obligor could have asserted against the assignor.* This is the most important single rule to remember about assignment.

> **Example:** Contractor contracts to paint Owner's house for $10,000. Contractor assigns his right to payment to Wife, to satisfy an alimony obligation. If Owner fails to make payment, Owner may raise against Wife any defense, counterclaim or set-off that Owner could have raised against Contractor. Thus if the work was not done in a merchantable manner, Owner may raise this defense against Wife just as he could have raised it against Contractor.

1. **Effect if obligor gives performance to assignor:** Once the obligor has received *notice* of the assignment (from either the assignor or assignee), *she cannot thereafter pay* (or otherwise give her performance to) *the assignor.* If she does, she won't be able to use the defense of payment against the assignee. But if the obligor pays the assignor or otherwise gives him the required performance *before* she

has received notice of the assignment, she may use this as a defense against the assignee.

2. **Modification of contract:** The right of the obligor and assignor to *modify* the original contract depends mainly on whether the modification takes place before the obligor has notice of the assignment:

   a. **Before notice:** *Before* the obligor has received notice of the assignment, he and the assignor are *completely free* to modify the contract. (See UCC §9-405(a), (b).)

      Example: Contractor contracts to paint Owner's house for $10,000, does the work, then assigns his right to payment to Bank. Before Owner receives notice of the assignment, Owner and Contractor can together agree to modify the contract, and this will be binding on Bank. For instance, they may agree to reduce the contract price.

   b. **After notice of assignment:** But *after* notice of assignment has been given to the obligor, he and the assignor may modify the contract *only if the assignor has not yet fully performed*.

      Example: Same facts as above example. Now, assume that Contractor has already finished painting the house, and that Bank has notified Owner of the assignment. At this juncture, any attempt by Owner and Contractor to lower the contract price will not be binding on Bank.

      i. **Assignee gets benefits under modified contract:** Where modification *is* allowed, the assignee gets the benefit of whatever new rights are given to the assignor by the modification.

3. **"Waiver of defenses" clause:** Many contracts contain *"waiver of defenses"* clauses, by which one party agrees that if the other assigns the contract, the former will not raise against the assignee defenses which he could have raised against the assignor. Most commonly, the buyer of goods on credit agrees that the seller may assign the installment contract, and that the buyer will not assert against the assignee (usually a bank or finance company) defenses which the buyer might have against the seller. The enforceability of such "waiver of defenses" clauses depends mostly on whether the transaction is a consumer one.

   a. **"Real" defenses:** A waiver-of-defenses clause is *never* effective as to so-called *"real"* defenses. "Real" defenses include: (1) infancy, incapacity, or duress; (2) illegality of the original contract; and (3) misrepresentation that induced the buyer to sign the contract without knowledge of its essential terms ("fraud in the essence"). See UCC §9-403(c).

   b. **Consumer goods:** Very importantly, waiver-of-defenses clauses in *consumer transactions* are basically *unenforceable*. This stems mainly from an FTC regulation.

      i. **Commercial contracts:** By contrast, the FTC regulation does *not* apply to *commercial* contracts. So a businessperson who, say, buys goods on installment may not raise defenses such as breach of the implied warranty of merchantability against the assignee, typically a financing institution.

4. Counterclaims, set-offs, and recoupment by the obligor: Most states (and the UCC) follow these rules for determining when the obligor may assert a *counterclaim*, *set-off* or *recoupment* in a suit brought against him by the assignee:

    a. Claim relates to assigned contract: If the obligor's claim against the assignor is related to the *same contract* that has been assigned to the assignee, the obligor may use this claim whether it arose *prior to* or *subsequent* to the obligor's receipt of notice of the assignment. See UCC §9-404(a)(1). This is called a "recoupment." It may only be used to reduce the assignee's claim, *not to yield an affirmative recovery* for the obligor.

> **Example:** Contractor agrees to paint Owner's house for $10,000. Contractor assigns to Bank on July 1, and Bank notifies Owner of the assignment on July 2. If Contractor has done the work in a slightly improper or late way (whether the defect occurred before or after the July 2 notice), Owner may assert this as a defense in any suit brought by Bank for the money, and Bank's recovery will be diminished by this amount. (But no affirmative recovery by Owner will be allowed even if the damages aggregate more than $10,000.)

    b. Claim unrelated to assigned contract: If the obligor's claim against the assignor is *not related to the contract* which has been assigned, the obligor may assert this claim against the assignee *only if the claim accrued before the obligor received notice of the assignment*. §9-404(a)(2). This is called a *"set-off."* Like recoupment, a set-off may not yield affirmative recovery.

    c. Counterclaims: The obligor may obtain an *affirmative recovery* against the assignee only if the claim relates to a transaction *directly between the obligor and the assignee*. This is called a *counterclaim*.

> **Example:** Same facts as above two examples. Assume that Owner also has a claim against Bank for lending him money at a rate in violation of state usury laws. Assuming that the claim is allowed to be part of the same suit under state practice rules, this claim can not only wipe out any recovery by Bank as assignee of the Contractor-Owner contract, but also may yield an affirmative recovery for Owner. But no claim by Owner relating to the Owner-Contractor contract may yield an affirmative recovery, since only dealings directly between the obligor (Owner) and the assignee/plaintiff (Bank) may yield such a recovery.

I. Rights of successive assignees of the same claim: Where there are *two assignees* of the same claim, and assuming that both assignees gave value and the later one did not know about the first, here is the way most states treat their relative rights:

    1. Restatement rule: In transactions not governed by Article 9 of the UCC, the Restatement *"four horsemen"* rule is applied by most states. The subsequent assignee loses to the earlier assignee, unless the subsequent one did one of four things: (1) he received *payment* or other satisfaction of the obligation; (2) he obtained a *judgment* against the obligor; (3) he obtained a *new contract* from the obligor by novation; or (4) he *possessed* a *writing* of a type customarily accepted as a symbol or evidence of the right assigned (e.g., a bank book or insurance policy).

2. **UCC:** In transactions governed by Article 9 of the UCC (most assignments of the right to receive money in return for financing), rights of successive assignees are governed by a *filing system*. In general, the assignee who *files first* has priority, regardless of whether he received his assignment first, and regardless of whether he gave notice of the assignment to the obligor first.

J. Rights of assignee against assignor: If the obligor is *unable to perform*, or in some other way the assignee doesn't obtain the value he expected from the contract, the *assignee* may be able to recover *against the assignor*.

1. **Gratuitous assignments:** If the assignment was a *gratuitous* one, the assignee probably will *not* be able to recover against his assignor. Exceptions exist where the assignor interferes with the assignee's ability to collect the performance, or where the assignor makes a subsequent assignment. But in the more common case where the obligor simply *fails to perform*, the assignee has no *claim* against the assignor under a gratuitous assignment.

2. **Assignments made for value:** But it is quite different if the assignment was made *for value*. Every assignor for value is held to have made a series of *implied warranties* to the assignee. If these warranties turn out not to be accurate, the assignee may sue the assignor for damages. These warranties are:

    a. **No impairment:** That the assignor will do nothing which will *interfere* with the assignee's enforcement of the obligation.

       Example: Assignor implicitly promises that he will not try to collect the obligation himself, and that he will not assign it to some third party.

    b. **Claim is valid and unencumbered:** That the assigned claim is a *valid* one, not subject to any *limitations or defenses* other than those that have been disclosed.

       Example: Contractor agrees to paint Owner's house for $10,000. Contractor performs the work sloppily, giving Owner a partial defense. Contractor then assigns to Bank his right to be paid. Regardless of whether Contractor knows, at the time of assignment, that Owner has a defense, Contractor breaches his implied warranty to Bank if he does not disclose to Bank Owner's defense of non-performance.

    c. **Documents valid:** That any documents which are delivered to the assignee that purport to evidence the right are *genuine*.

    d. **No warranty of solvency or willingness to perform:** But the assignor does *not* warrant that the obligor is *solvent*, or that he will be *willing or able to perform*. Thus if the obligor turns out to be unwilling or unable to perform, the assignee has *no recourse* against the assignor.

       Example: Same facts as above example. If Contractor does the work properly, but Owner goes broke, or simply refuses to pay, Bank cannot sue Contractor.

      i.   **Free to agree otherwise:** But the assignor may explicitly *agree* to guarantee the obligor's performance, in which case the assignee can sue if the obligor fails to perform.

   e.   **Sub-assignees not covered:** Unless the assignor indicates otherwise, his warranties do not extend to any *sub-assignee*, i.e., one who receives the assignment from the assignee.

   f.   **Rules of construction:** All of the above rules on warranties are generally *common law*, rather than statutory. Most states treat them as *rules of construction*, which may be varied by showing that the parties intended a different result.

III. DELEGATION OF DUTIES

A. Definition: Recall that "delegation" refers to *duties* under a contract, not to rights. If a party to a contract wishes to have another person perform his duties, he delegates them.

B. Continued liability of delegator: When the performance of a duty is delegated, *the delegator remains liable*.

> **Example:** Owner contracts with Contractor for Contractor to paint Owner's house for $10,000. Contractor delegates his duties to Painter. If Painter fails to perform in the manner required by the original Owner-Contractor contract, Owner may sue Contractor for breach, just as if Contractor had improperly performed the work herself.

   1.   **Novation:** But the obligee may expressly agree to accept the delegate's performance in place of that of the delegator. If he does so, he has given what is called a *novation*.

C. Non-delegable duties: In general, a duty or performance is *delegable*, unless the obligee has a *substantial interest in having the delegator perform*.

   1.   **Particular skills:** Contracts which call for the promisor's use of his *own particular skills* are normally *not* delegable. Thus contracts involving *artistic performances*, the *professional services* of a lawyer or doctor, etc., are not delegable.

> **Example:** Client is charged with murder. He signs an engagement letter (a contract) with Lawyer, a solo practitioner who specializes in white-collar criminal defense work, under which Lawyer will represent him at the trial for a fixed fee of $30,000. The contract says nothing about assignment or delegation. One month before trial, Lawyer sends Client an e-mail that Lawyer is delegating his duties to his friend Barrister. Barrister is in fact much more suited than Lawyer to represent Client, because Barrister specializes in murder cases whereas Lawyer has never done one before.
>
>   Client need not accept performance from Barrister — the contract calls for personal professional services, and Lawyer's duties under it were therefore not delegable without Client's consent. If Lawyer insists on making the delegation, Client can refuse and hire someone else (and sue Lawyer for

breach). Alternatively, Client can accept the proposed delegation, in which case Lawyer will remain liable if Barrister fails to deliver a defense of the quality called for in the contract.

    a. Close supervision: Similarly, contracts in which there are duties of *close personal supervision* may not be delegated.

  2. Construction and repair contracts: *Construction* contracts, and contracts for the repair of buildings or machinery, are normally delegable.

  3. Agreement of parties: The parties have complete freedom to determine whether duties may be delegated. This cuts both ways: they may agree that duties which would otherwise be delegable may not be delegated, or conversely that duties normally thought to be too personal may in fact be delegated.

D. Delegate's liability:

  1. Two forms: A delegation agreement between delegator and delegate may be in one of two forms: (1) the delegator may simply give the delegate the *option* to perform, with the delegate making no promise that she will perform; or (2) the delegate may *promise* that she will perform.

    a. Option: If the delegate is given the *option* to perform, the delegate is *not liable* to *either* the delegator or the obligee.

    b. Promise: If the delegate has promised to perform, the delegate may or may not be liable to the *obligee*. That is, the obligee may or may not be a *third party beneficiary* of the delegate's promise. This is normally a question of intent of the parties — if delegator and delegate intend that the obligee get the benefit of the delegate's promise, then the obligee may sue the delegate.

> **Example:** Contractor promises Owner that Contractor will paint Owner's house for $10,000. Contractor gets too busy to perform, but wants to make sure that Owner is not inconvenienced by a bad or tardy performance. Contractor therefore delegates performance to Painter, under terms that permit Painter to keep the $10,000 fee when earned. Painter expressly promises to perform the work. A court would probably hold that Owner was an intended third party beneficiary of Painter's promise, so that Owner may sue Painter (not just Contractor) if Painter fails to perform.

  2. "Assumption": If a delegate is held to have undertaken liability to the obligee as well as to the delegator, he is said to have *assumed* the delegator's liability.

  3. Assignment of "the contract": If a party purports to "assign the contract" to a third person, this language will normally be interpreted to constitute a *promise* by the assignee to perform, and the obligee will normally be interpreted to be an *intended beneficiary* of this promise.

    a. Obligee can sue both: In other words, the assignee/delegate under such a general assignment clause will normally be held *liable to both parties* to the original contract if she fails to perform.

Example: Owner contracts with Contractor for Contractor to paint Owner's house for $10,000. Contractor then signs a document saying he "assigns to Painter my contract to paint Owner's house." Painter accepts the assignment. Under the standard view, there are three consequences:

(1) Contractor is deemed to have *delegated* his duties to Painter (not just assigned his rights, such as the right to payment);

(2) Painter, by accepting the assignment, is deemed to have *promised* Contractor that Painter will perform the duties owed by Contractor; and

(3) Owner is an *intended beneficiary* of this promise by Painter to Contractor, so if Painter doesn't perform, Owner can sue Painter (as well as Contractor).

b. Exception for land sales: But an assignment of "the contract" made by a *vendee* under a *land contract* will *not* usually be found to follow this rule. That is, the assignee under a land sale contract usually does *not* incur liability to the original seller.

c. UCC: The UCC, in §2-210(4), follows the common-law rule: "An assignment of 'the contract' or of 'all my rights under the contract'…is an assignment of rights and unless the languages or circumstances…indicate the contrary, it is a *delegation of performance* of the duties of the assignor and its acceptance by the assignee constitutes a *promise by him* to perform those duties. This promise is enforceable by *either* the assignor or the other party to the original contract."

i. Security: But if a general assignment is made for the purpose of giving *collateral* to the assignee in return for a *loan*, the lender will *not* normally be deemed to have undertaken to perform the assignor's duties.

> **Example:** Owner contracts with Contractor for Contractor to paint Owner's house for $10,000. Contractor then assigns "the contract" to Bank as security for a loan of $9,000. Bank will not be deemed to have promised to paint the house, and may not be sued by Owner if the house does not get painted.

IV. THIRD PARTY BENEFICIARIES

A. Introduction: A *third party beneficiary* is a person whom the promisee in a contract intends to benefit.

> **Example:** Contractor agrees to paint Owner's house for $10,000. Contractor wants to pay off a debt he owes Creditor, so he provides that upon completion, payment should be made not to Contractor but to Creditor. Creditor is a third party beneficiary of the Owner-Contractor contract.

B. When beneficiary may sue: The most important question about third party beneficiaries is: When may the third party beneficiary sue the promisor on the contract? The modern rule, exemplified by the Second Restatement, is that *"intended"* beneficiaries may sue, but *"incidental"* beneficiaries may not sue.

1. **Intended beneficiaries may sue:** "Intended beneficiaries" fall into two categories:

   a. **Payment of money:** First, a person is an intended beneficiary if the performance of the promise will satisfy an obligation of the promisee to *pay money* to the beneficiary. This is sometimes called a *"creditor beneficiary."*

      Example: Contractor agrees to paint Owner's house for $10,000. The contract provides that payment should be made to Creditor, to satisfy a debt previously owed by Contractor to Creditor. Since Owner's fulfillment of his side of the contract will cause money to be paid to Creditor, Creditor is an intended beneficiary, of the "creditor beneficiary" variety.

   b. **Intent to give benefit:** Second, a person will be an intended beneficiary if the circumstances indicate that the promisee *intends to give the beneficiary the benefit* of the promised performance. A person may fall into this class even if the purpose of the promisee is to give a gift to the beneficiary (in which case the beneficiary is sometimes called a *"donee* beneficiary"). But intent to make a gift is not necessary — a beneficiary may fall into this "intended beneficiary" class even if the promisee's purpose is not to make a gift, but rather to fulfill some other business objective.

      Example: Tycoon contracts with Painter for Painter to paint a portrait of Magnate, a businessman friend of Tycoon, and to deliver the portrait to Magnate. Since Tycoon intends for Magnate to get the benefit of Painter's performance, Magnate is an intended beneficiary who may sue Painter for non-performance; this is true even though Tycoon's motive is to butter up Magnate so that Magnate will do business with Tycoon.

      i. **Promisee's intent versus promisor's intent:** Most courts hold that a person will be an intended beneficiary if the promis*ee* (alone) intended to benefit the beneficiary. But a minority hold that the person is an intended beneficiary *only* if *both* promisee *and promisor* intend to benefit her. (So in such a court, Magnate couldn't sue Painter unless Magnate showed that Painter, as well as Tycoon, intended to benefit Magnate.)

2. **Incidental beneficiaries:** A beneficiary who does not fall into the above two classes is called an *"incidental"* beneficiary. An incidental beneficiary may *not* sue the promisor.

   Example: Developer contracts with Contractor to have Contractor put up an expensive building on developer's land. Neighbor, who owns the adjoining parcel, would benefit enormously because her land would increase in value if the building were built. However, since the parties don't intend to benefit Neighbor, and aren't paying money to her, Neighbor is an incidental beneficiary, not an intended one. Therefore, Neighbor cannot sue Contractor if Contractor fails to perform as agreed.

3. **Public contracts:** When *government* makes a contract with a private company for the performance of a service, a *member of the public* who is injured by the contractor's non-performance generally may *not* sue.

Example: City contracts with Water Co. to supply water for fire hydrants. P's house burns down when Water Co. does not give adequate hydrant pressure. *Held*, P is not an intended beneficiary of the City-Water Co. contract, and therefore may not recover. [*H.R. Moch & Co. v. Rensselaer*]

   a. Exceptions: But there are two exceptions — a member of the public may sue: (1) if the party contracting with the government has *explicitly promised* to undertake liability to members of the public for breach of the contract; or (2) if the government has a *duty of its own* to provide the service which it has contracted for. (*Example*: City contracts to have its street-repair duty picked up by Contractor. A member of the public who is injured when the street is improperly maintained may sue Contractor).

4. Mortgage assumptions: In a fact pattern involving one party taking over another's *mortgage payments*, distinguish between two situations: (1) the mortgagor sells the property *"subject to"* the mortgage, in which case the purchaser does not promise to pay off the mortgage, though he bears the risk of losing the property if the mortgage payments are not made; and (2) the purchaser *"assumes"* the mortgage, in which case he makes himself personally liable for repayment (so that the mortgagee may not only foreclose but also obtain a deficiency judgment against the purchaser). These two scenarios have different third party beneficiary consequences:

   a. Assumption: If the purchaser has *assumed* the mortgage, the mortgagee (i.e., the lender) is a *creditor beneficiary* of the assumption agreement between seller and buyer. The mortgagee may therefore sue the purchaser to compel him to make the mortgage payments. If the purchaser then sells to a sub-purchaser who also assumes, the lender may sue either the purchaser or the sub-purchaser if payments are not made.

   b. Subject to: Where the mortgagor sells to a purchaser who takes *"subject to"* the mortgage, the mortgagee cannot sue that purchaser, since the purchaser has incurred no liability. But if this non-assuming purchaser sells to a sub-purchaser who *does* assume, courts are *split* on whether the mortgagee can recover personally against the assuming sub-purchaser.

C. Discharge or modification by the original parties: The modern view is that the original parties' power to *modify* the contract *terminates* if the beneficiary, before he *receives notification* of the discharge or modification, does any of three things:

   [1] materially *changes his position* in justifiable *reliance* on the promise;

   [2] *brings suit* on it; or

   [3] *manifests assent* to it at the request of either of the original parties.

1. Original parties maintain right to modify or discharge: This rule means that until one of the three events listed above occurs, the original parties *maintain the power to modify or discharge* the beneficiary's rights. But if any of the three events occurs before the beneficiary gets notice of a modification or discharge, the beneficiary's rights *"vest,"* and can no longer be altered by the original parties.

Example: Uncle and Landowner, the owner of Blackacre, sign an agreement under which Uncle promises to deposit $100,000 in Landowner's bank account by April 1, and in return Landowner promises that on April 2, he will convey Blackacre to Uncle's nephew Nick. (Assume that Nick is an intended beneficiary of this agreement.) Uncle sends a copy of the agreement to Nick, and says, "Let me know whether you agree to receive title to Blackacre as provided in this document." On March 26, Nick responds, "That's great, yes, I agree. Thanks, Unc." On March 30, Uncle and Landowner sign an amendment to the agreement, purporting to discharge Uncle's obligation to pay the $100,000 and Landowner's obligation to transfer title to Nick.

When Nick "manifested assent" to the agreement at the request of one of the original parties, this assent took away Uncle's and Landowner's power to modify the agreement as it concerned Nick. Therefore, Nick can sue both Uncle and Landowner for breach on account of their purported modification. The same would be true if Nick, instead of manifesting assent, had changed his position in reliance (e.g., by giving up the chance to buy some alternative property because he knew he could count on receiving Blackacre).

2. **Clause preventing modification:** The original parties may themselves agree at the time of contracting that no subsequent modification may occur without the beneficiary's consent. Such a clause will be honored.

D. **Defenses against the beneficiary:** The promisor-defendant may assert against the beneficiary *any defenses which he could have asserted had he been sued by the promisee*. The beneficiary is said to *"step into the shoes of the promisee."*

1. **Defense based on promisee's breach:** Most importantly, this means that the promisor-defendant may defend on the ground that the promisee never rendered the performance which he promised under the contract, i.e., that the *promisee breached*.

Example: Contractor agrees to paint Owner's house for $10,000, with payment to be made to Friend, in repayment of a debt owed by Contractor to Friend. If Owner does not make payment and Friend sues Owner as a third party beneficiary, Owner may defend on the grounds that Contractor did not perform the painting work as promised.

2. **Set-offs not allowed:** But this principle that the beneficiary "stands in the shoes" of the promisee is limited — only defenses *relating to the main contract* may be asserted by the promisor-defendant. The promisor-defendant may *not* assert against the beneficiary defenses or claims from *unrelated transactions* with the promisee.

Example: Same facts as above example. Contractor performs the painting work correctly. However, Contractor also owes Owner $2,000 in damages from work previously done incorrectly by Contractor for Owner on a different contract involving Owner's office. If Friend sues Owner for the $10,000 fee, Owner may not reduce the payment by the $2,000 owed on the office contract.

E. **Other suits in beneficiary contracts:**

1. **Beneficiary v. promisee:** When the beneficiary sues the promisor, the beneficiary does *not* waive his right to later sue the promisee.

   Example: Same facts as above example. Friend sues Owner, but recovers only $4,000 because Owner shows that Contractor did not perform the house-painting work correctly. Friend may now sue Contractor for the remaining $4,000 due.

2. **Promisee vs. promisor:** Most courts allow the promisee to bring her own suit against the promisor, if the promisor breaches.

   a. **Third party is creditor beneficiary:** This is most important where the third party is a *creditor* beneficiary. Here, most courts let the promisee-debtor recover from the promisor the amount which the promisor promised that he would pay the creditor (at least where the promisee has already paid the debt to the creditor).

      Example: Contractor agrees to paint Owner's house for $10,000, with payment to be made to Friend, in repayment of a $10,000 debt owed by Contractor to Friend. Contractor does the work correctly, but Owner does not make any payment to Friend. At least if Contractor pays his debt to Friend first, Contractor may sue Owner to recover the $10,000. (Some courts would let Contractor bring the suit even if he *hadn't* yet paid off Friend.)

CHAPTER 12

IMPOSSIBILITY, IMPRACTICABILITY, AND FRUSTRATION

I. INTRODUCTION

A. Nature of the problem: The parties may be *discharged* from performing the contract if: (1) performance is *impossible*; (2) because of new events, the fundamental *purpose* of one of the parties has been *frustrated*; or (3) performance is not impossible but is much more *burdensome* than was originally expected (*"impracticable"*). If a party is "discharged" from performing for such a reason, he is *not liable* for breach of contract.

B. Risk allocation: The doctrines of impossibility, impracticability and frustration apply only where the parties themselves *did not allocate the risk* of the events which have rendered performance impossible, impracticable or frustrated. Thus the parties are always free to agree explicitly that certain contingencies will or will not render the contract impossible, etc., and these understandings will be honored by the courts.

1. **Question to ask:** Therefore, in evaluating a problem that seems to involve impossibility, frustration, etc., always ask, "Did the parties expressly allocate the risk?" If they did, this allocation controls regardless of the general doctrines discussed here.

II. IMPOSSIBILITY OF PERFORMANCE

A. Generally: If a court concludes that performance of the contract has been rendered *"impossible"* by events occurring after the contract was performed, the court will generally *discharge* both parties.

> **Example:** Contractor agrees to paint Owner's house for $10,000. Just before painting starts, the house burns down. A court will almost certainly conclude that performance has become impossible, and will therefore discharge both parties. Contractor does not have to do the painting, and Owner does not have to pay anything.

B. Three classes: There are three main types of impossibility: (1) destruction of the subject matter; (2) failure of the agreed-upon means of performance; and (3) death or incapacity of a party.

   1. Destruction of subject matter: If performance involves particular goods, a particular building, or some other tangible item, which through the fault of neither party is *destroyed* or otherwise made unavailable, the contract is discharged. The discharge will occur only where the particular subject matter is *essential* to the performance of the contract.

      a. Specifically referred to: If property which the performing party expected to use is destroyed, that party is discharged only if the destroyed property was *specifically referred to* in the contract, or at least understood by *both* parties to be the property that would be used. It is not enough that the party who seeks discharge intended to use the destroyed property.

> **Example:** Contractor agrees to paint Owner's house for $10,000. Unknown to Owner, Contractor intends to use 100 gallons of paint which Contractor has left over from another job. After the signing, this paint is destroyed in a fire. Contractor will not be discharged by impossibility, because the specific left-over paint is not referred to in the contract, and is not understood by both parties to be the particular paint to be used in the contract.

      b. Construction contracts: If a building contractor contracts to *construct* a building from scratch on particular land, and the building is destroyed by fire when it is partially completed, most courts hold that the contractor may *not* use the defense of impossibility.

      c. Repair of buildings: But when a party contracts to *repair* an *existing* building, she usually *will* be discharged if the building is destroyed.

      d. Sale of goods: Contracts for the sale of goods may or may not be discharged when there is destruction of the "subject matter" of the contract.

         i. General rule: The general UCC section applicable here is §2-615(a), which provides that unless otherwise agreed, "delay in delivery or non-delivery...is not a breach of [seller's] duty under a contract for sale if performance as agreed has been made impracticable by the occurrence of a contingency the non-occurrence of which was a *basic assumption on which the contract was made....*"

    ii. **Destruction of identified goods:** If a contract calls for the delivery of a particular *identified* unique good, and that good is destroyed before the "risk of loss" has passed to the buyer, the contract will be discharged. (*Example*: *A* contracts to sell to *B* a painting hanging on *A*'s wall. If the painting is destroyed before the delivery process starts, this will normally be before "risk of loss" has passed to *B*, and both parties will be discharged.)

    iii. **Goods not identified at time of contracting:** Usually, sale contracts call for goods to be taken from the seller's *general inventory*, not for particular identified goods. Where such unidentified goods are to be *shipped* by seller, and are destroyed *in transit*, the result depends on whether the contract is a "shipment" contract or a "destination" contract.

        [1] **"Shipment" contract:** In a "shipment" contract, where the seller's only obligation is to deliver the goods to the carrier (the contract usually says, "F.O.B. seller's plant" in this case), the *risk of loss passes to the buyer as soon as the seller delivers the goods to the carrier*; if the carrier loses the goods, the buyer bears the loss and must pay the purchase price, and sue the carrier.

        [2] **"Destination" contract:** But if the contract is a *"destination"* contract ("F.O.B. buyer's place of business"), the risk of loss does not pass to the buyer until the carrier actually delivers; here, the seller cannot use the impossibility defense if the goods are destroyed while in transit.

2. **Impossibility of intangible but essential mode of performance:** If an *essential* but *intangible* aspect of the contract becomes impossible, the contract may be discharged, just as where the "subject matter" is destroyed.

    Example: Seller contracts to deliver 100 widgets to Buyer at a stated price; both parties understand that Seller will get the widgets from Widget Co., with whom Seller has a long-term supply contract. If Widget Co. breaches or goes bankrupt, a court might hold that an essential intangible aspect of Seller's ability to perform has been nullified, and might let Seller use the impossibility defense.

    a. **Impossibility due to failure of third persons:** Where a *middleman* contracts to supply goods that he will be procuring from some third party, and the third party cannot or will not supply the goods to the middleman, the middleman's ability to use the impossibility defense depends on the precise situation:

        i. **Source not specified in contact:** If the contract does *not specify* the source from which the seller is to obtain the goods, then the seller whose source does not pan out will almost surely *not* be allowed to use the impossibility defense.

    ii. **Seller unable to make contract:** Similarly, if the seller-buyer contract contemplates that the seller will procure the goods from a given supplier, and that supplier is ***unwilling to contract*** to sell the items to the seller, the seller generally may ***not*** use impossibility.

    iii. **Where seller's supply contract is breached:** But if the contract contemplates that seller will make a particular supply contract, and seller does make a contract with this supplier, many courts will allow the impossibility defense if the ***supplier breaches***.

3. **Non-essential mode of performance:** If ***non-essential*** aspects of the contract — such as ones dealing with the ***means of delivery*** or the means of payment — become impossible, usually the contract will ***not*** be discharged. Instead, a ***commercially reasonable substitute*** must be used. (*Example*: If *A* agrees to ship goods by post office to *B*, and the post office goes on strike, *A* must use a truck, UPS, or other commercially reasonable substitute.)

4. **Death or illness:** If a contract specifically provides that performance shall be made by a ***particular person***, that person's ***death or incapacity*** will discharge both parties.

    a. **Death or illness of a third party:** A contract may similarly be discharged by virtue of the death or illness of some ***third person***, who is necessary to performance of the contract even though he is not himself a party to it. (*Example*: Impresario contracts with Arena Co. to have Singer appear in a concert at Arena Co. If Singer develops laryngitis the day of the concert, the Arena-Impresario contract will be discharged by reason of impossibility, even though Singer is not directly a party.)

    b. **Temporary impossibility:** If events render performance of the contract only ***temporarily*** impossible, this will normally merely ***suspend*** the duty of performing until the impossibility ends. But if after the temporary impossibility is over, performance would be much more burdensome, then suspension will turn into discharge.

III. IMPRACTICABILITY

A. **Modern view of impracticability:** Modern courts generally equate *"extreme impracticability"* with "impossibility." In other words, if due to changed circumstances, performance would be ***infeasible*** from a commercial viewpoint, the promisor may be excused just as he would be if performance were literally impossible.

1. **UCC:** The UCC deals with impracticability this way: §2-615(a) provides that the seller's non-delivery is excused "if performance as agreed has been made impracticable by the occurrence of a contingency the non-occurrence of which was a basic assumption on which the contract was made...." Complete cutoffs of supplies (e.g., because of war, crop failure due to drought, strike, etc.) will often be found to be covered by 2-615, thus relieving the seller.

2. **Cost increases:** Most impracticability cases relate to ***extreme cost increases*** suffered by sellers who have signed ***fixed-price contracts***. Here, while it is theoretically possible for the seller of goods or services to escape the contracts on the grounds of impracticability, sellers generally *lose*. The reason is that such sellers are generally found to have implicitly *assumed the risk* of cost increases, when they signed a fixed-price contract. This is true both in services contracts and in sales contracts governed by the UCC. It is especially likely that the seller will lose where the cost increase was *foreseeable*.

> **Example:** Oil Co. contracts to sell to Utility oil for 10 years at a price of $10 per barrel. Due to increased price discipline by OPEC, Oil Co.'s cost per barrel jumps from $9 to $29. A court will probably hold that Oil Co. cannot escape the contract on grounds of impracticability, because: (1) Oil Co. implicitly assumed the risk of price increases by agreeing to a fixed-price contract; and (2) disturbances in the supply of oil, with consequent price increases, were reasonably foreseeable to Oil Co. at the time it signed.

3. **Allocation of risk by parties:** In both UCC and non-UCC cases, the parties are always free to *make their own allocation of the risk of impracticability,* and the courts will *enforce* that allocation. So, for instance, if the parties decide that the seller should not have the right to raise the impracticability defense in the event that all potential suppliers to the seller fail, the court will refuse to allow the defense in that scenario even though the requirements for impracticability might otherwise be met.

    a. **Implicit allocation:** This type of re-allocation by the parties of the risk of impracticability can be either explicit or *implicit*. Thus the UCC commentary to §2-615 says that the impracticability defense "[does] not apply when the contingency in question is *sufficiently foreshadowed* at the time of contracting to be *included among the business risks which are fairly to be regarded as part of the dickered terms,* either consciously or as a matter of *reasonable, commercial interpretation from the circumstances.*"

        i. **Risk of technological breakthrough:** For instance, suppose that Seller and Buyer agree that Seller will develop a not-yet-existing product to meet certain specifications, and both parties are aware that a *technological breakthrough* will be required in order for Seller to perform. A court would probably conclude, as a matter of "reasonable, commercial interpretation from the circumstances," that the risk of non-occurrence of the breakthrough was to rest upon Seller (the party with greater insight into the looming obstacles), in which case Seller would *not* be excused by impracticability if the breakthrough did not develop despite Seller's best efforts.

IV. FRUSTRATION OF PURPOSE

A. **Frustration generally:** Where a party's *purpose* in entering into the contract is destroyed by supervening events, most courts will discharge him from performing. This is the doctrine of *"frustration of purpose."*

1. **Distinguish from impossibility:** Be sure to distinguish frustration of purpose from impossibility. In frustration cases, the person seeking discharge is not claim-

ing that he "cannot" perform, in the sense of inability. Rather, she is claiming that it makes no sense for her to perform, because what she will get in return does not have the value she expected at the time she entered into the contract.

> **Example:** P rents his apartment to D for a two-day period, at a very high rate. As known to P, D's purpose is to view the coronation of the new king. The coronation is cancelled because of the king's illness. *Held*, D is discharged from performing because his purpose in entering the contract has been frustrated. [*Krell v. Henry*]

2. **Usually used by buyers of goods and services:** You also need to understand the *difference* between the defenses of *impracticability* and *frustration*. The two defenses are similar, in that each gives a party a chance to escape from a bargain that has turned out to be unfavorable because an event occurred whose non-occurrence was a basic assumption on which the contract was made. The main practical difference between the two is that:

   [1] where it is the *seller or supplier* of goods, land or services who wishes to escape the bargain, that party typically claims *impracticability*; whereas

   [2] where it is a *buyer or recipient* of goods, land or services who wishes to escape the bargain, that party typically claims *frustration*.

B. **Factors to be considered:** Here are the two main factors courts look to in deciding whether to apply the doctrine of frustration:

1. **Foreseeability:** The less *foreseeable* the event which thwarts the promisor's purpose, the more likely the court is to allow the frustration defense. (*Example*: In *Krell*, it was quite unlikely, at the time of the contract, that the king would be too sick to be crowned.)

2. **Totality:** The more *totally* frustrated the party is in achieving the benefits he anticipated from the transaction, the more likely he is to be allowed to use the defense.

C. **Extreme economic dislocation:** Sometimes a party who has agreed to buy or pay for goods, land or services relies on *extreme economic dislocation* as the reason she should be allowed to escape from the bargain by use of the frustration defense. For instance, suppose that due to some macro-economic event, the good or service for which the plaintiff has agreed to pay a fixed price suddenly becomes *vastly less valuable* than indicated by the contract price. The plaintiff argues that requiring her to pay will *cause her serious economic loss* of a sort that neither party had reason to anticipate.

1. **Usually unsuccessful:** Such claims by buyers based on a plunge in the market value of the contracted-for good or service typically *fail*. The court is likely to rule that in the circumstances, a market-price plunge — no matter how great — was *not the sort of event the non-occurrence of which was a basic assumption* on which the contract was based. In other words, the court is likely to take the position that where buyer and seller agree on a *fixed price* or fee for some good or service, allocating the *risk of a plunge* in market prices to the buyer (and the risk of a sharp *rise* in market prices to the *seller*) is the *very purpose* of the contract.

Example: P takes out a home mortgage loan on her home from D, a bank. The Great Recession occurs, causing the market value of P's home to drop to less than 50% of the amount then owed by P on the mortgage. P falls behind in her payments, and D begins a foreclosure proceeding. P asserts that she should be permitted to use the frustration doctrine to be relieved from her loan obligations; she argues that the non-occurrence of an extreme real estate depression, and the consequent drastic loss of value of the property, were basic assumptions made by the parties under the loan contract.

The court is highly unlikely to allow the frustration defense, probably on the grounds that the parties implicitly allocated the not-unforeseeable risk of a real estate crash on the borrower. [Cf. *Bean v. BAC Home Loans Servicing, L.P.*]

V. RESTITUTION AND RELIANCE WHERE THE PARTIES ARE DISCHARGED

A. Generally: Where the contract is discharged because of impossibility, impracticability or frustration, the courts generally try to adjust the equities of the situation by allowing either party to *recover the value* he has rendered to the other, and sometimes even the expenditures made in preparation.

B. Restitution: Courts generally allow one who has been discharged by impossibility or frustration to recover in quasi-contract for *restitution*, i.e., for the value of the *benefit* conferred on the other party.

    1. Time for measuring benefit: Usually, the benefit is measured *just before the event* causing the discharge. (*Example*: Contractor contracts to paint Owner's house for $10,000. After half the work is done, the house burns down. A court will first discharge both parties from the contract. It will then probably measure the benefit conferred by Contractor on Owner as of the moment just before the fire; if it concludes that $5,000 "worth" of work had been done as of that moment, it will award this amount to Contractor.)

    2. Pro-rata contract price: Where the performance has been partly made, recovery will normally be limited to the *pro-rata contract price*, if such a pro-rating can be sensibly done. But if the reasonable value to the other party is *less* than the pro-rata contract price, this lesser value will be awarded.

    3. Down payment: If one party has made a *down payment* to the other prior to discharge, he will generally be allowed to recover this down payment.

C. Reliance: Occasionally, if restitution will not "avoid injustice," the court will protect the parties' *reliance* interests instead. This might allow a party to recover his *expenditures* made in *preparation* for performance.

    1. Rare: Courts only *rarely* give reliance damages — if the performance does not actually render a benefit to the other party before discharge, the partly performing plaintiff is usually out of luck.

CHAPTER 13
MISCELLANEOUS DEFENSES

I. ILLEGALITY

A. Generally: In general, if a contract is found to be *"illegal,"* the court will *refuse to enforce it*.

B. Kinds of illegal contracts: Here are some of the kinds of contracts frequently found to be illegal and thus unenforceable: (1) *"gambling"* or "wagering" contracts; (2) lending contracts that violate *usury* statutes; and (3) contracts to *perform services* where the provider lacks a required *license* or *permit*.

1. **Non-compete covenants:** A very important type of possibly illegal contract is a *covenant not to compete*. In general, if a non-compete agreement is *unreasonably broad*, it will be held to be illegal and not enforced.

   a. **Sale of business:** If the *seller of a business* is selling its "good will," his ancillary promise that he will not compete in the same business as the purchaser will be *upheld*, provided that it is not unreasonably broad either *geographically*, in *duration*, or in the *definition of the industry* in which competition is prohibited.

   b. **Employment contracts:** *Employment agreements* often include a clause by which the employee agrees not to compete with his employer if he leaves the latter's employ. Such covenants are closely scrutinized by courts, and will be enforced only if they are designed to safeguard either the employer's *trade secrets* or his *customer list*. Even where these objectives are being pursued, the non-compete will be struck down if it is unreasonably broad as to either *geography* or *duration*.

      i. **Divisibility and the "blue pencil" rule:** If a non-compete is overly broad, most courts today will enforce it *up to reasonable limits*. Some courts apply the *"blue pencil"* rule, by which the clause will be enforced only if it can be narrowed by striking out certain portions (so that a ban on competing in "Ohio and Pennsylvania" could be modified by striking out "and Pennsylvania," but a ban lasting for "20 years" could not be modified by reducing it to "five years," since this would require redrafting, not merely striking). Most courts today, however, do not follow the blue pencil rule, and will "redraft" the non-compete to bring it back to within reasonable limits.

2. **Agreements concerning family relations:** Questions often arise about the enforceability of contracts regarding *family relations*, such as pre-nuptial agreements and agreements regarding cohabitation.

   a. **Pre-nuptial agreements:** A *prenuptial agreement* is one in which the "non-moneyed" spouse, typically the wife, agrees that in the event of divorce or separation, that spouse will receive lesser alimony, or a smaller property division, than the standard legal rules of the jurisdiction would impose.

> > > **i.   Modern approach tends to enforce:** Most courts today are willing to *enforce* prenuptial agreements, especially where basic conditions of procedural fairness are observed before signing. For instance, about half the states have enacted the ***Uniform Premarital Agreement Act***, under which voluntarily-signed prenuptial agreements are enforceable if *either*:
> > >
> > > > [1] the agreement was ***not unconscionable*** when signed; or
> > > >
> > > > [2] even though the agreement *was* unconscionable when signed, the signer was either ***provided a fair and reasonable disclosure*** of the other party's financial condition, ***knew or reasonably could have known*** of that financial condition, or voluntarily and expressly ***waived*** in writing any right to such disclosure.

> > **b.   Cohabitation:** Many courts refuse to enforce *cohabitation* agreements, i.e., agreements regarding property division entered into by couples who are living together without marriage. But a growing minority of courts now enforce such living-together arrangements, at least where they do not explicitly trade sex for money.

> **C. Enforceability:** As a general rule, ***neither party to an illegal contract may enforce it***. This is not an ironclad rule. In general, contracts that are still ***wholly executory*** are less likely to be enforced by the court than those that have been at least partly performed.

> > **1.   Wholly executory:** If the contract is ***completely executory*** (i.e., neither party has rendered any performance), there are only a few situations where the court will allow one party to recover damages for breach:

> > > **a.   Ignorance of facts:** Where one of the parties is justifiably ***unaware*** of the facts which make the contract illegal, and the other is not, the former may usually recover. (*Example*: Owner hires Electrician to perform electrical work; Owner does not know that Electrician is unlicensed. Owner may enforce the contract, even if he discovers the illegality before any work is done or payments made.)

> > > **b.   Wrongful purpose:** Where only one party has a ***wrongful purpose***, the other may recover for breach, at least if the wrongful purpose does not involve a crime of serious moral turpitude. (*Example*: *A* sells diamonds to *B* knowing that *B* plans to smuggle them into an Eastern Bloc country, where such importation is not allowed. *A* may recover for breach before money or goods changes hands, even if *A* knew of the proposed smuggling at the time of signing.)

> > > **c.   Statute directed at one party:** If the statute is designed to ***protect one party***, the person for whose protection the statute is designed may enforce the contract or sue for its breach. (*Example*: *A* agrees to sell stock to *B*, in violation of Blue Sky laws. *B*, as an investor whom the statute is designed to protect, may enforce the contract.)

> > **2.   Partly- or fully-performed illegal contracts:** Where one or both parties have ***partly or fully performed***, the courts are more willing to enforce the contract or at

least grant a quasi-contractual remedy. The three above situations will generally lead to enforcement as in the wholly-executory situation. Also:

    a. **Malum prohibitum:** If the conduct is illegal even though it does ***not involve moral turpitude*** (a contract involving *"malum prohibitum"* rather than *"malum in se"*), the court may allow the partly-performing party to recover at least the restitutionary value of his services.

        Example: Where a contractor fails to obtain a permit or license, and the permit or license is merely a revenue-raising rather than public-protection mechanism, the contractor may be able to recover the value of the work he has done.

    b. **Pari delicto:** If one party, although blameworthy, is ***much less guilty*** than the other party, he may use the doctrine of ***"pari delicto"*** to gain enforcement. This may only be used where the plaintiff is not guilty of serious moral turpitude (but may be used even by a plaintiff who knew of the illegality).

        Example: If Bank lends money to Contractor for Contractor to build a house, even though Bank knows that Contractor is not licenced, there is a good chance that Bank will be held not to be "in *pari delicto*," and will thus be permitted to recover on the loan. But if Bank financed a cocaine deal, Bank's conduct would be found to be of serious moral turpitude, so the *pari delicto* doctrine would not apply, and Bank could not recover.

    c. **Divisibility:** Finally, if a ***divisible part*** of the contract can be performed on both sides without violating public policy, the court will enforce that divisible portion.

        Example: Owner contracts to have Plumber supply a bathtub, and to install the bathtub. Plumber does not have a license. A court might hold that Plumber cannot recover that portion of the contract attributable to services, but might still allow Plumber to recover for the value of the tub he supplied.

II. DURESS

A. Generally: The defense of ***duress*** is available if D can show that he was ***unfairly coerced*** into entering into the contract, or into modifying it. Duress consists of "any wrongful act or threat which ***overcomes the free will*** of a party."

    1. **Subjective standard:** A *subjective standard* is used to determine whether the party's free will has been overcome. Thus even though the will of a person of "ordinary firmness" might not have been overborne, if D can show that he was unusually timid, and was in fact coerced, he may use the defense.

B. Ways of committing: Here are some of the acts or threats that may constitute duress: (1) ***violence*** or threats of it; (2) ***imprisonment*** or threats of it; (3) wrongful ***taking*** or ***keeping*** of a party's ***property***, or threats to do so; and (4) threats to ***breach*** a contract or commit other wrongful acts.

1. **Abusive or oppressive acts:** If one party *threatens another* with a certain act, it is *irrelevant* that the former would have had the *legal right* to perform that act — if the threat, or the ensuing bargain, are *abusive* or *oppressive*, the contract will be void for duress.

   > **Example:** Client hires Lawyer to prepare Client's defense against criminal charges, for a flat $10,000 fee. The night before the trial is to begin, Lawyer tells Client, "Double the fee, or I'm resigning from the case." Client agrees. A court will probably hold that given the timing of Lawyer's threat, the threat and/or the ensuing bargain were abusive or oppressive, in which case the court will not enforce the modification.

C. **Threat to breach contract:** Most commonly, duress arises in contract cases because one party *threatens to breach the contract* unless it is *modified* in his favor; the other party reluctantly agrees, and the question is whether the modification is binding. In general, courts apply a *"good faith"* and *"fair dealing"* standard here: if the party seeking modification is using the other's vulnerability to extract an unfair advantage, the duress defense is likely to succeed. If, by contrast, the request for modification is due to unforeseen difficulties, the duress defense will probably fail.

III. MISREPRESENTATION

A. **Generally:** If a party can show that the other made a *misrepresentation* to him prior to signing, he may be able to use this in either of two ways: (1) he may use this as a *defense* in a breach of contract action brought by the other; or (2) he may use it as the grounds for *rescission* or damages in a suit in which he is the plaintiff.

B. **Elements of proof:**

1. **Other party's state of mind:** P does *not* generally have to prove that the misrepresentation was *intentionally* made. A *negligent* or even *innocent* misrepresentation will usually be sufficient to avoid the contract, if it is made as to a *material fact*.

2. **Justifiable reliance:** The party asserting misrepresentation must show that he *justifiably relied* on the misstatement.

3. **Fact, not opinion:** The misrepresentation must be one of *fact*, rather than of *opinion*.

   > **Example:** A salesman's statement, "This is a very reliable little car," is probably so clearly opinion, or "puffing," that the buyer cannot rescind for misrepresentation by showing that the car in fact breaks down a lot. But, "This car gets 30 miles per gallon in city driving," is an assertion of fact, so it can serve as the basis for a misrepresentation claim.

C. **Non-disclosure:** As a general rule, only *affirmative statements* can serve as the basis for a misrepresentation action. A party's *failure to disclose* will generally *not* justify the other party in obtaining rescission or damages for misrepresentation. But there are some exceptions, situations where non-disclosure *will* support an action:

1. **Half truth:** If *part of the truth* is told, but another part is not, so as to create an overall misleading impression, this may constitute misrepresentation.

2. **Positive concealment:** If a party takes *positive action* to *conceal* the truth, this will be actionable even though it is not verbal. (*Example*: To conceal termite damage, Seller plasters over wooden beams in the house he is selling.)

3. **Failure to correct past statement:** If the party knows that disclosure of a fact is needed to prevent some *previous assertion* from being misleading, and doesn't disclose it, this will be actionable.

4. **Fiduciary relationship:** If the parties have some kind of *fiduciary relationship*, so that one believes that the other is looking out for her interests, there will be a duty to disclose material facts.

5. **Failure to correct mistake:** If one party knows that the other is *making a mistake* as to a *basic assumption*, the former's failure to correct that misunderstanding will be actionable if the non-disclosure amounts to a "failure to act in *good faith*." (*Example*: Jeweler lets Consumer buy a stone, knowing that Consumer falsely believes that the stone is an emerald when it is in fact a topaz worth much less. This would probably be such bad faith that it would constitute misrepresentation.)

IV. UNCONSCIONABILITY AND ADHESION CONTRACTS

A. **Adhesion contracts:** *"Adhesion contract"* is an imprecise term used to describe a document containing non-bargained clauses that are in fine print, complicated, and/or exceptionally favorable to the drafter. Generally, adhesion contracts are found in situations where the non-drafter has very little bargaining power, because all potential parties on the other side have similar terms that they offer on a non-negotiable "take it or leave it" basis.

1. **Steps for avoiding contract:** A litigant who wants to avoid enforcement of a contractual term on the grounds that it is part of an adhesion contract usually has to make *two showings*:

   [1] that the contract itself is an *adhesion contract*; and

   [2] that the contract (or the clause complained of) either (i) violates his *reasonable expectations* or (ii) is *unconscionable*.

   a. **Reasonable expectations:** When the court decides whether the plaintiff's *"reasonable expectations"* were thwarted, this determination is based mostly upon whether a *reasonable person in P's position* would have *expected* that the clause in question was *present in the contract*. So a very *unusual and burdensome clause* stuck into the *fine print* on the back of a standard form contract might flunk this "reasonable expectations" test, and entitle the plaintiff to avoid the contract.

      Example: RentalCo, a car rental agency, sticks a clause in the fine print that says the renter is liable for four times the actual cost of any damage to the car, even if the renter is completely without fault. A court would probably say that this clause is so unusual and burdensome that its presence would thwart the renter's "reasonable expectations." In that event, the clause would probably be held unenforceable, even without the renter's having to show that it was "unconscionable."

2. **Tickets and other "pseudo contracts":** Refusal to enforce what the court finds to be a "adhesion contract" is especially likely where the transaction is one in which the non-drafter does not even *realize that he is entering into a contract at all*. Parking-garage tickets, tickets for trains or planes, and tickets to sporting events, are examples: there is often contractual language in fine print on the back of the ticket, but the purchaser does not understand that by buying the ticket she is agreeing to the printed contractual terms.

   a. **Refusal to enforce:** The language printed on the ticket will generally be enforced only if: (1) the purchaser signs or somehow *manifests assent* to the terms of the ticket; and (2) the purchaser has *reason to believe* that such tickets are regularly used to contain contractual terms like those in fact on the ticket. Even if the ticket is found to be generally enforceable, the court will strike *unreasonable terms*.

B. **Unconscionability:** If a court finds that a contract or clause is so unfair as to be *"unconscionable,"* the court may decline to enforce that contract or clause. See UCC §2-302(1).

   1. **No definition:** There is no accepted definition of unconscionability. The issue is whether the clause is so *one-sided*, so unfair, that a court should as a matter of judicial policy refuse to enforce it.

   2. **Consumers:** Courts have very rarely allowed *businesspeople* to claim unconscionability; only *consumers* are generally successful with an unconscionability defense.

   3. **Varieties:** Clauses can be divided into two categories for unconscionability analysis: (1) "procedural" unconscionability; and (2) "substantive" unconscionability.

      a. **Procedural:** The *"procedural"* sort occurs where one party is induced to enter the contract without having any *meaningful choice*. Here are some possible types: (1) burdensome clauses tucked away in the fine-print boilerplate; (2) high-pressure salespeople who mislead the uneducated consumer; and (3) industries with few players, all of whom offer the same unfair "adhesion contracts" to defeat bargaining (e.g., indoor parking lots in a downtown area, all disclaiming liability even for gross negligence).

      b. **Substantive:** The *"substantive"* sort of unconscionability occurs where the clause or contract itself (rather than the process used to arrive at the contract) is unduly unfair and one-sided.

         i. **Excessive price:** An important example of substantive unconscionability is where the seller charges an *excessive price*. Usually, an excessive price clause only comes about when there is also some sort of procedural unconscionability (e.g., an uneducated consumer who doesn't understand what he is agreeing to), since otherwise the consumer will usually simply find a cheaper supplier.

ii. **Remedy-meddling:** Also, a term may be substantively unfair because it unfairly limits the buyer's *remedies* for breach by the seller. Types of remedy-meddling that might be found to be unconscionable in a particular case include: (1) disclaimer or limitation of *warranty*, especially prohibiting consequential damages for personal injury; (2) limiting the remedy to repair or replacement, where this would be a valueless remedy; (3) unfairly broad rights of *repossession* by the seller on credit; (4) waiver of defenses by the buyer as against the seller's *assignee*; and (5) a *cross-collateralization* clause by which a secured seller who has sold multiple items to a buyer on credit has the right to repossess all items until the last penny of total debt is paid.

4. **Arbitration clauses:** A large number of unconscionability claims are attempts to strike down so-called *"mandatory arbitration"* clauses. By such a clause, both parties to the contract agree that any dispute between them *must be subject to arbitration* rather than resolved by a *lawsuit. Consumers* and *small businesses* that are required to sign such clauses as part of a large market-leading company's "take it or leave it" adhesion contract are usually the ones who, after signing, claim that the arbitration clause is unconscionable.

a. **Class-action waivers combined with arbitration clauses:** A claim that a mandatory-arbitration clause is unconscionable is especially powerful when the clause *combines* a mandatory arbitration provision with a *waiver* of the *right to bring a "class" arbitration.*

i. **Ban on class arbitration:** The issue arises because large corporations often specify, in the mandatory-arbitration clause, that any arbitration must be *"one on one" (or "bilateral")*, i.e., must involve *only a single plaintiff*. (The big company hopes that where each contract and claim tends to be for a small amount, no lawyer is likely to find it worthwhile to take a one-on-one arbitration case on contingent fee, since only a small recovery, and thus a small attorney fee award, is likely.)

ii. **Struck down by state courts:** State courts have often been *sympathetic* to the claims of plaintiffs — especially consumers — that a combined mandatory-arbitration and no-class-arbitrations clause is unconscionable because it tends to leave plaintiffs in small-dollar-amount contract cases *without an effective remedy.* [Cf. *Scott v. Cingular Wireless*]

b. **The U.S. Supreme Court steps in (the *AT&T Mobility* case):** But   the U.S. Supreme Court *has taken away* a large portion of the right of courts to find that mandatory-arbitration clauses — including ones that prohibit class arbitrations — are unconscionable under state law. In *AT&T Mobility v. Concepcion* (2011), the Court held that a federal statute intended to encourage arbitration (the "FAA") will often *pre-empt* the right of state court to strike down on state-law unconscionability grounds a mandatory-arbitration clause that forbids class arbitrations and class actions.

i. Effect of *Mobility* case: At the least, *AT&T Mobility* seems to mean that state law is preempted if that law (whether judge-made or statutory) makes class litigation unconscionable merely because there is ***no other effective remedy***.

> **Example:** Multiple Ps sign service contracts with D, a cellular telephone company. Each P's contract involves a small amount of money. The contracts state that each P waives the right to sue in court for breach; instead, each agrees that any dispute will be subject to mandatory arbitration, and that each arbitration will involve only one claimant. The Ps now want to bring a class action lawsuit against D claiming fraud in D's marketing; the Ps want the class to consist of the hundreds of thousands of customers who have signed identical contracts. The Ps argue that the arbitration clause, insofar as it bans any kind of collective proceeding, is unconscionable and thus unenforceable.
>
> Before *AT&T Mobility*, the state court would have been free to rely heavily on the fact that the contracts' ban on class arbitrations and class action lawsuits would leave small-dollar plaintiffs like the proposed class members without any effective remedy. The court could therefore hold (as one did on essentially these facts, in *Scott v. Cingular Wireless, supra*), that because of the "lack of effective remedy" problem alone, the individual-arbitrations-only clause is unconscionable and thus unenforceable under state law, so that the Ps can bring their class action lawsuit.
>
> But *Mobility* seems to mean that such a state-law-based holding of unconscionability on these facts is now ***pre-empted*** by the federal FAA statute. The Supreme Court held in *Mobility* that Congress's purpose in enacting the FAA was to enforce arbitration clauses as written. Letting consumers use the state-law doctrine of unconscionability to force corporate defendants into class-based rather than individual arbitrations would (the Court said in *Mobility*) make arbitration so much less attractive to corporate defendants that it would defeat the pro-arbitration purposes of the FAA. Therefore, the FAA as interpreted in *Mobility* probably pre-empts state courts from making widespread use of unconscionability to block anti-class-arbitration clauses. There may be an exception if the particular arbitration clause is hugely unfair or one-sided (e.g., it provides that a consumer claimant must not only bring an individual arbitration, but must, if she loses, pay triple the corporate winner's actual attorneys fees); a holding that such a rare and patently one-sided clause is unconscionable might have such a small effect on the general attractiveness of arbitration as not to be pre-empted by the FAA. But if the state court merely wants to find a generic no-class-arbitrations clause unconscionable because small-dollar plaintiffs wouldn't be able to attract a lawyer to take the case, that's the sort of broad state-law holding about unconscionability that is probably no longer allowed post-*Mobility*.

5. Remedies for unconscionability: Here are some of the things a court might do to remedy a clause or contract which it finds to be unconscionable:

   a. Refusal to enforce clause: Most likely, the court will simply **strike the offending clause**, but enforce the rest of the contract;

   b. Reformation: Alternatively, the court may **"reform"** the offending clause (e.g., by modifying an excessive price to make it a reasonable price);

   c. Refusal to enforce whole contract: Very occasionally, the court may simply refuse to enforce the **entire contract**, denying P any recovery at all.

V. CAPACITY

A. Generally: Certain classes of persons have only a limited power to contract. Most important are **infants** and the **mentally infirm**. For these people, any contract they enter into is **voidable** at their option — they can enforce the contract or escape from it.

B. Infants: Until a person reaches majority, any contract which he enters into is **voidable** at his option. That is, the minor has the power to **"avoid"** or **"disaffirm"** the contract.The age of majority is a matter of statute, and in most states is now 18.

   Example: *A*, a 16 year old, agrees to sell Greenacre to B. *A* later changes his mind and refuses to go through with the sale. *B* may not enforce the agreement against A. But *A*, if he wishes, may enforce it against *B*, e.g., by suing *B* for damages for failure to go through with the purchase.

1. Time for disaffirmance: In nearly every state, an infant may avoid the contract even **before** he reaches majority. He may do this orally, by his conduct (e.g., refusing to go through with the deal), or by a defense when sued for breach.

   a. Land conveyances: But where the contract is for a conveyance of **land**, most states do not allow the infant to disaffirm the contract until he has reached majority.

2. Ratification: A contract made by an infant is not void, but merely voidable, so the infant can choose to **enforce it** if he wishes. If he does this, he is said to have **ratified** the contract.

   a. Must reach adulthood: The most important thing to remember about ratification is that the minor **may not ratify until she has reached adulthood**. Ratification may occur in three ways:

      i. Failure to disaffirm: By **inaction** — if the infant does not disaffirm within a reasonable time after reaching majority, she will be held to have implicitly ratified.

      ii. Express: **Expressly** — the contract may be ratified by words, either written or (in most states) oral.

      iii. By conduct: By **conduct** — if the former infant actively induces the other party to perform, this conduct may constitute a ratification (e.g., both parties begin to exchange performances after the infant's majority).

But mere part payment or part performance by the former infant is probably not by itself a ratification.

3. **Economic adjustment:** After disaffirmance, courts will try to make an economic adjustment to unwind the contract.

    a. **Where infant is defendant:** If the infant is a *defendant* to a breach-of-contract suit brought by the non-infant, the latter will not be allowed to recover profits he would have made, or any other contract damages. But he will have a limited right of *restitution*, the right to require the defendant infant to *return the goods* or other value *if he still has them*.

    b. **Where infant is plaintiff:** If the infant is a *plaintiff* who is suing to recover money already paid by him, the court will require the infant to return any value which he has, and will in fact subtract from the infant's recovery any value obtained and dissipated.

    > **Example:** Infant buys a car for $4,000 in cash from D. Infant then disaffirms and sues to recover his $4,000. To recover the $4,000, Infant will have to return the car. If Infant has wrecked the car, or sold it for money which he has then spent, the value of the car will be subtracted from any recovery by Infant. So if the car was in fact worth $4,000, Infant will recover nothing if he no longer has the car.

    c. **Necessaries:** Virtually all jurisdictions allow a person who supplies *"necessaries"* to an infant to recover in *quasi-contract* (not on the contract) for the *reasonable value* of those necessaries. The minor cannot avoid such a recovery by disaffirmance. What constitutes "necessaries" varies from state to state, but needed *food, clothing, shelter, medical care* and *legal services* are among the items that are likely to be covered.

    > **Example:** Minor shows up at the emergency room of Hospital with appendicitis. Minor agrees to pay the bill. Hospital treats him. Hospital will be entitled to recover the reasonable value of the services directly from Minor — since the services were "necessaries," Minor does not have the right to disaffirm.

4. **Lies about age:** If the infant *lies about his age*, all courts let the other party *avoid the contract* on grounds of fraud. In other words, the infant who falsely claims adulthood loses his power to ratify the contract.

C. **Mental incompetents:** A *mental incompetent* is governed by the same basic rules as an infant — he may either disaffirm the contract or ratify it. A person lacks capacity to contract because of mental incompetence if either: (1) he doesn't understand the contract; or (2) he understands it, but acts irrationally, and the other person knows he is acting irrationally.

D. **Intoxication:** *Intoxication* will give a party the power of avoidance only if: (1) he is so intoxicated that he cannot *understand* the nature of his transaction; *and* (2) the other party has a *reason to know* that this is the case.

CHAPTER 14
WARRANTIES

I. WARRANTIES GENERALLY

A. Types: Under the UCC, a seller may make several warranties that are of importance: (1) an *express* warranty; (2) an implied warranty of *merchantability*; and (3) a warranty of *fitness for a particular purpose*. If the seller breaches any of these warranties, the buyer may bring a damage action for breach of warranty, which can be viewed as a special type of breach-of-contract action.

II. EXPRESS WARRANTIES

A. Definition: An express warranty is an *explicit* (not just implied) promise or guarantee by the seller that the goods will have certain qualities. See UCC §2-313(1)(a): "Any *affirmation of fact or promise* made by the seller to the buyer which relates to the goods and becomes part of the *basis of the bargain* creates an express warranty that the goods shall conform to the affirmation or promise."

    1. Description: A *description* of goods can be an express warranty. (*Example*: A bill of sale issued by Jeweler to Consumer recites, "Three carat flawless white diamond ring." This constitutes an express warranty that the ring is a diamond with those characteristics.)

    2. Sample or model: If the buyer is shown a *sample* or *model*, this will normally amount to an express warranty that the rest of the goods conform to the sample or model.

    3. Puffing: If the seller is clearly *"puffing,"* or expressing an *opinion*, he will not be held to have made a warranty. (*Example*: A used-car salesperson's statement that, "This is a top-notch car," will probably be held to be mere puffing, not an express warranty of anything. But the statement, "This car will do 30 m.p.g. in city driving," is specific enough to amount to an express warranty.)

III. IMPLIED WARRANTY OF MERCHANTABILITY

A. Generally: The most important warranty given in the UCC is the implied warranty of *merchantability*. UCC §2-314(1) provides: "Unless excluded or modified…a warranty that goods shall be merchantable is *implied* in a contract for their sale if the seller is a *merchant* with respect to goods of that kind."

B. Meaning of "merchantable": There is no precise definition of "merchantable." The most important meaning is that the goods must be *"fit for the ordinary purposes for which such goods are used."* §2-314(2)(c). (*Example*: Dealer sells a new car to Buyer. Due to a manufacturing defect, the car cannot go more than 25 m.p.h. Since cars are generally sold and used for high-speed highway driving, this would be a breach of the implied warranty of merchantability, even though Dealer never expressly promised any particular speed.)

C. Always given unless disclaimed: The implied warranty of merchantability is *always* given by a merchant seller, unless it is expressly excluded by a *disclaimer* that meets stringent formal requirements imposed by the Code.

IV. WARRANTY OF FITNESS FOR PARTICULAR PURPOSE

A. Generally: Depending on the circumstances, a seller may be found to have impliedly warranted that the goods are *fit for a particular purpose*. UCC §2-315 provides that "where the seller at the time of contracting has *reason to know* any particular purpose for which the goods are required and that the buyer is *relying on the seller's judgment* to select or furnish suitable goods, there is...an implied warranty that the goods shall be fit for such purpose."

B. Elements: The buyer must prove three things to recover for breach of this implied warranty: (1) that the seller had reason to know the buyer's *purpose*; (2) that the seller had reason to know that the buyer was *relying* on the seller's skill or judgment to furnish suitable goods; and (3) that the buyer *did in fact rely* on the seller's skill or judgment.

    1. Use of trade name: If the buyer insists on a particular *brand* of goods, he is not relying on the seller's skill or judgment, so no implied warranty of fitness for a particular purpose arises.

V. PRIVITY

A. Definition: Two persons are *"in privity"* with each other if they contracted with each other.

B. When privity is necessary: UCC §2-318, stating when privity is necessary for a UCC breach-of-warranty action, actually has three separate alternatives. Each has been adopted in some states.

    1. Alternative A: Alternative A extends the seller's warranty (express or implied) only to a member of the buyer's *family* or *household*, or a house guest, and only where it is foreseeable that the person may use and be injured by the goods. A person other than the buyer thus cannot recover in states adopting Alternative A unless he is *physically injured*, and is a *relative or house guest* of the buyer.

    2. Alternative B: Alternative B covers any person, even if not a relative or house guest of the buyer, who may reasonably be expected to use or be affected by the goods. But, as with Alternative A, only *personal injury* is covered.

    3. Alternative C: Alternative C is the broadest: it extends the warranty to all persons who may be expected to use or be affected by the goods. Most importantly, it covers *property* and *economic* damage as well as personal injury, and may even cover intangible economic loss.

VI. DISCLAIMERS OF WARRANTY

A. Generally: The UCC limits the extent to which a seller may *disclaim* warranties.

B. Express warranties: The seller is basically free to disclaim *express* warranties, as long as he does so in a clear and reasonable way. However, this rarely happens — since nothing forces the seller to make an express warranty in the first place, he will usually have no reason to disclaim it after making it.

C. Implied warranties: Disclaimers of the two *implied* warranties (merchantability and fitness for particular purpose) are tightly limited by the Code:

   1. Explicit disclaimers: The seller may make an *explicit disclaimer* of these warranties, but only by complying with strict procedural rules:

      a. Merchantability: A disclaimer of the warranty of *merchantability* must *mention the word "merchantability."* §2-316(2). The disclaimer does not have to be in writing, but *if it is in writing, it must be "conspicuous."* In other words, the disclaimer cannot be buried in the *fine print* of the contract. (Usually, capital letters, bold face type, bigger type, or a different color type are used to meet the "conspicuous" requirement where the disclaimer is written.)

      b. Fitness for a particular purpose: A disclaimer of the warranty of fitness for a particular purpose *must be in writing*, and must also be *conspicuous*. (But it does not need to use any particular words, in contrast to a disclaimer of the warranty of merchantability.) (*Example*: The following language, if in writing and conspicuous, would suffice: "There are no warranties which extend beyond the description on the face hereof.")

   2. Implied limitations and disclaimers: There are also several ways in which the implied warranties may be *implicitly* limited or disclaimed:

      a. Language of sale: The *language of the sale* may implicitly disclaim the warranty. Most importantly, if the sale is made *"as is,"* this will implicitly exclude all implied warranties.

      b. Examination of sample or model: If the buyer is asked to *examine* a *sample* or *model*, or the *goods themselves*, there is no implied warranty with regard to defects which an examination ought to have revealed. UCC §2-316(3)(b). (*Example*: Buyer buys a floor sample T.V. from Dealer. If inspection of the cabinetry would have shown a dent, Buyer cannot claim that the dent is a violation of the implied warranty of merchantability.)

      c. Course of dealing: An implied warranty can be excluded or modified by *course of dealing*, *course of performance*, and *usage of trade*. (*Example*: The dealings of the parties on prior contracts might create a "course of performance" to the effect that the goods are bought "as is" in return for a lower price.)

VII. MODIFYING CONTRACT REMEDIES

A. UCC limits: Instead of disclaiming warranties, the seller may try to *limit* the buyer's *remedies* for breaches of warranty or other contract breaches. (*Example*: Seller may insert a clause that Buyer's remedies are limited to repair or replacement of defective goods or parts, with no consequential damages.) But the UCC limits the seller's right to do this "remedy meddling" in two ways.

1. **"Failure of essential purpose":** First, if the remedy as limited by seller would *"fail of its essential purpose,"* the standard UCC remedies come back into the contract.

    Example: Seller sells yarn to Buyer, knowing that Buyer will dye the yarn and use it in products. Seller limits the warranty to repair or replacement of defective yarn. Buyer then spends a great deal of labor knitting the yarn into expensive sweaters, which fall apart due to poor quality yarn. A court might hold that here, repair or replacement of yarn that has already been expensively knitted into sweaters would be a useless remedy, in which case the basic Code remedy of money damages for breach of the implied warranty of merchantability would re-enter the contract.

2. **Unconscionability:** Second, the court will refuse to enforce a damage limitation if it finds that this is *unconscionable*. According to §2-713(3): (1) barring consequential damages for *personal injury* will virtually always be unconscionable; but (2) limiting damages where the loss is *commercial* will generally not be unconscionable.

CHAPTER 15

DISCHARGE OF CONTRACTS

I. RESCISSION

A. **Mutual rescission:** As long as a contract is *executory* on both sides (i.e., neither party has fully performed), the parties may agree to *cancel* the whole contract. This is a *"mutual rescission."*

1. **No writing:** In most states, a mutual rescission does *not have to be in writing*. This is true even if the original contract fell within the Statute of Frauds.

2. **Fully performed on one side:** If the contract has been *fully performed* on one side, a mutual rescission will *not be effective*, because there is no mutual consideration.

B. **Unilateral rescission:** Where one of the parties to a contract has been the victim of fraud, duress, mistake, or breach by the other party, he will generally be allowed to cancel the contract, terminating his obligations under it. Some courts call this a *"unilateral rescission."* But it is better to say that the innocent party may *"cancel"* or "terminate."

II. EXECUTORY ACCORDS, AND "ACCORD AND SATISFACTION"

A. **Executory accord generally:** An *executory accord* is an agreement by the parties to a contract under which one promises to render a *substitute performance* in the future, and the other promises to *accept that substitute* in discharge of the existing duty.

    Example: Debtor owes Creditor $1,000 due in 30 days. Creditor promises Debtor that if Debtor will pay $1,100 in 60 days, Creditor will accept this payment in discharge; Debtor promises to make the $1,100 payment in 60 days. The new agreement is an executory accord.

B. Consequences: Executory accords are enforceable. However, an accord does ***not discharge*** the previous contractual duty as soon as the accord is made; instead, no discharge occurs until the terms of the accord are ***performed***. Once the terms of the accord are performed, there is said to have been an "accord and satisfaction."

    1. Failure to perform accord: If a party ***fails to perform*** under the terms of the executory accord, the other party may sue for breach of the ***original agreement***, or breach of the accord, at her option.

        Example: On the facts of the above example, if Debtor fails to make the $1,100 payment, Creditor may sue for either $1,000 plus damages for failure to get the money in 30 days, or $1,100 plus damages for failure to get the money in 60 days.

III. SUBSTITUTED AGREEMENT

A. Nature of substituted agreement: A *"substituted agreement"* is similar but not identical to an executory accord. Under a substituted agreement, the previous contract is ***immediately discharged***, and replaced with a new agreement.

    Example: On the facts of the above example, if the new agreement were be found to be a substituted agreement rather than an executory accord, and Debtor then failed to make the payment in 60 days, Creditor would only be able to sue on the new promise, not the old promise.

    1. Distinguishing: In determining whether a given agreement is a substitute agreement or executory accord, an important factor is whether the claim is a disputed one as to liability or amount — if the debtor in good faith ***disputes*** either the existence of the debt or its amount, the presumption is that there is a substituted agreement. If the amount and obligation are undisputed, the presumption will be that there is an executory accord.

        a. Level of formality: Another important factor in distinguishing substituted agreements from executory accords is the ***level of formality:*** the more ***deliberate and formalized*** the agreement, the more likely it is to be a substituted agreement. For instance, an ***oral*** agreement is very likely to be an ***accord***, not a substituted agreement, because of its informality.

B. Writing: If the substituted agreement would have to satisfy the Statute of Frauds were it an original contract, the substituted agreement must be in ***writing***. (Some states also require the substituted agreement to be in writing if the original is in writing, even where neither falls within the Statute of Frauds.)

IV. NOVATION

A. Definition: A *"novation"* occurs where the obligee under an original contract (the person to whom the duty is owed) agrees to relieve the obligor of all liability after the duty is *delegated* to some third party. A novation thus substitutes for the original obligor a stranger to the original contract, the delegate.

> **Example:** Contractor agrees to paint Owner's house for $10,000. Contractor does not have enough time to get the job done, so with Owner's consent he recruits Painter to do the job instead. If Owner agrees to release Contractor from liability, the result is a novation: Painter steps into the shoes of Contractor, and only Painter, not Contractor, owes a duty to Owner.

B. Consent: The obligee must *consent* to the novation. But the obligor, who is being discharged, need not consent. (*Example*: On the facts of the above example, Owner must consent to the novation, but Contractor need not consent, at least to the delegation/release aspect of it.)

V. ACCOUNT STATED

A. Generally: Where a party who has sold goods or services to another sends a *bill*, and the buyer holds the bill for an unreasonably long time *without objecting* to its contents, the seller will be able to use the bill as the basis for a suit on an *"account stated."* The invoice is not dispositive proof that that amount is owing, but the burden of proving that the invoice is wrong shifts to the buyer.

VI. RELEASES

A. Generally: Where a contract is executory only on one side, the party who has fully performed may give up his rights by virtue of a *release*, a document executed by him discharging the other party.

B. Formal requirements: In most states, a release must either be supported by *consideration*, or by a statutory substitute (e.g., a signed writing).

1. **UCC view:** Under the UCC, a signed writing can release a claim for breach of contract, even without consideration.

EXAM TIPS

TABLE OF CONTENTS
for EXAM TIPS

EXAM TIPS

***Exam Tips** on*
OFFER AND ACCEPTANCE

Offer

☛ **Identifying an offer:** Many essays require you to determine initially whether a valid offer has been made. Remember that this ***question of fact*** is analyzed from the viewpoint of a ***reasonable offeree.*** Ask yourself: Has the party ***exhibited a willingness to be bound without further action on her own part***?

☞ **Inquiries not enough:** Distinguish offers from mere ***inquiries*** or expressions of ***interest***, which are not offers because they don't indicate a willingness to be immediately bound:

Example: "Will $2,000 buy your piano?" is a mere inquiry, not an offer.

☞ *Trap:* Don't be misled by a party's own characterization of a statement as an "offer." Analyze the relevant statement yourself from the perspective of a "reasonable offeree" — something the speaker (or listener) refers to as an "offer" may not be one.

☞ **Speaker keeps right of final approval:** Look out for circumstances and words indicating that the person speaking retains the right to give final approval to the deal — these indicate that the speaker is ***not*** making an offer, because the speaker doesn't intend to give the other person the power to seal the seal by "accepting."

Example: After months of negotiation over a proposed contract, *A* sends *B* a draft, with a cover email saying, "I've put in the terms you wanted. Let's discuss this document." Since the email indicates that *A* believes a further discussion will be needed, the sending of the draft cannot be an offer, and *B* cannot cause the contract to be formed even if he emails back, "I accept the deal on exactly the terms proposed in your draft."

☞ Look out for the following special situations which frequently appear on exams:

☛ **Quotations:** A price quotation is usually construed as an invitation, but may be considered an offer if it's ***specific enough*** that the offeree is reasonable in perceiving it as an offer.

☛ **Advertisements**: These are usually considered invitations unless they include sufficient promissory language. (*Example:* "Ten pearl necklaces on sale for $300 to the first ten cash buyers" would qualify.) Language such as "while they last" probably does *not* indicate an intent to be bound.

☛ **Solicitations for bids**: These are usually mere invitations, with the responding bids considered offers.

Example: X sends a letter to A, B, C and D which states: "I need to sell my heart-shaped diamond ring by January 15 for $1,500. If interested, please contact me before January 15." On January 14, X receives a letter from A agreeing to pay $1,500. X doesn't respond. On January 17, X receives a letter from B agreeing to pay $1,700. X responds to B: "I agree to the terms of your letter." A can't sue X for breach because X's letter was not an offer (just an invitation to make an offer), so A's letter **was an offer that X never accepted.**

❑ *Exception:* ***Words of commitment.*** Watch for a solicitation that includes words indicating a commitment to sell to the highest bidder by a certain date. In this case, the solicitation becomes an offer and the solicitor is bound to the person fulfilling the stated conditions.

☞ ***Exam-writing tip***: Remember that since questions involving offers should be viewed from the perspective of the reasonable offeree (an objective standard), most questions will present gray-area fact patterns. ***Don't forget to argue both sides***. (But be sure to point out the one you think would prevail.)

Acceptance

☛ Here are things to look out for when you analyze something that might be an acceptance:

☞ Just as an offer must contain language of commitment, an acceptance must be ***unequivocal***.

    ☛ But keep in mind that acceptance may be ***implied through conduct***, such as shipment of the items, payment for the items, or the offeree's later statement (to the offeror or to a third party) that a contract exists.

☞ **Manner of acceptance:** Make sure that the ***manner*** of acceptance was one that the offer allowed (or that was reasonable if the offer didn't say what manner was acceptable).

    ☛ Remember that where the offeror is ***indifferent*** as to the ***manner*** of acceptance, the offer can be accepted ***by performance or promise.*** (*Example:* Under the UCC, the seller can usually accept *either* by shipping or promising to ship.)

☞ Also, remember that even without an explicit acceptance, the ***parties' conduct can give rise*** to an ***"implied-in-fact"*** contract. (*Example: A*, a professional music teacher, gives music lessons to *B*'s child, while *B* stands silently by, knowing that *A* expects payment. *B*'s silent acquiescence gives rise to an implied-in-fact contract to pay *A*'s standard rate.)

Unilateral Contracts

☞ Offers for unilateral contracts appear often on exams. Look for a situation where an offeror is requesting the performance of a particular action. Most common: offers of an ***award*** or ***reward***.

☞ **Offeree aware:** Remember that ***the offeree must know about the offer*** in order to accept it. Common scenario: A ***reward*** is offered for a lost possession and somebody returns it without knowing that the owner has offered a reward — not an enforceable contract.

☞ ***Trap:*** Remember that ***promises are irrelevant*** if the offer is truly for a unilateral contract. Don't get sidetracked by a party who promises to perform the act requested. The promise doesn't transform the agreement into a bilateral contract. The offer may be revoked even after such a statement has been made.

> **Example:** H announces to a group in a bar: "I'll pay $1,000 to anyone who tells me the name of the thief that stole a hand-carved stool out of my garage last night." This is an offer for a unilateral contract, which can be accepted only by supplying the name, not by promising to tell the name.

☞ **Revocation**: It's important to note when performance has occurred, because the acceptance of the offer ***prevents revocation*** by the offeror.

> **Example:** P is about to enter law school and plans to marry during winter break. His father offers him $1,000 if he postpones his wedding plans until after he has completed his first year. P postpones the wedding as requested, and shortly thereafter his father dies. The father's death does not terminate the offer because P already accepted the offer prior to the father's death by postponing the wedding. P is therefore entitled to the $1,000.

☞ Also remember that under the Restatement, an offer for a unilateral contract becomes ***temporarily irrevocable*** if the offeree has ***commenced but not yet completed performance*** (recall the "Brooklyn Bridge" hypo — If P starts to cross the Bridge, D can't revoke).

> ☞ Make sure, however, that the party has already begun the actual ***performance*** requested, not just made mere ***preparations*** to perform.

Acceptance Varying from Offer

☞ **Battle of the forms:** Be prepared for "battle of the forms" problems, such as where buyer's purchase order and seller's acknowledgment contain different or conflicting terms.

☞ **No deal:** First, make sure that the two forms agree on the basic terms (price, quantity, delivery date) well enough that they form a contract. If they don't, then there's *no agreement* unless the subsequent actions of the parties (e.g., seller ships, buyer accepts the goods) is enough to form a contract.

☞ **Material alteration:** Remember the basic rule that an additional or different term in the second form is merely a *proposal for addition* to the contract.

    ☞ That term *doesn't* become part of the contract if:

        ☞ one or both parties is *not a merchant*; or

        ☞ the term *materially alters* the deal. *Example:* Arbitration clauses, and disclaimers of warranties, are usually held to be material alterations, so they don't become part of the contract unless the other party agrees to them.

    ☞ If the term in the second form *directly conflicts* with a term in the first form, probably the two *"knock each out."* Then, any relevant Code "gap filler" can be used.

> **Example:** Buyer's p.o. says, "You warrant that the machine you're selling us is fit for use in our manufacturing operation, and that it will perform properly for 10 years." Seller's acknowledgment says, "No warranties, express or implied." Since the Seller's clause materially alters the deal, the two clauses cancel each other. But the Code's implied warranty of merchantability would "fill the gap."

Duration of the Power of Acceptance

☞ Make sure that the moment at which "acceptance" occurred was a moment at which the *offer was still open.*

    ☞ **Mailbox rule:** Remember that an acceptance is *effective upon dispatch*, provided it is communicated by a method specified in the offer (or by a reasonable method, if none is specified).

> **Example:** *B* mails a signed order to *S* that reads, "Sell me 1,000 gadgets as listed on p. 3 of your catalog at the price listed there." *S* gets the order on March 7 and that same day mails to *B* a properly signed, addressed and stamped letter stating, "We accept your order." On March 8 (before *B* has received *S*'s letter), *B* telephones *S* and says, "I revoke my order." *B* gets *S*'s letter on March 9. Because of the phone message, *S* never ships. Is

there a contract between *S* and *B* on March 10?

Yes. First, *B*'s order was an offer. Under UCC §2-206(1), an order to buy goods for immediate shipment can normally be accepted either by a promise to ship or by shipment. So *S* was entitled to accept by promising to ship, which its March 7 letter did. Under the mailbox rule, this acceptance occurred on March 7 (when *S* mailed the properly-addressed letter). So by the time *B* purported to revoke on March 8, there was already a contract, and *B*'s revocation was of no effect.

☛ **Offeror can suspend:** But also keep in mind that the offeror, as "master of the offer," can *suspend* the mailbox rule (e.g., by saying "I must receive your acceptance by 5 p.m. Tuesday").

☛ **Counter-offer**: Remember that a counter-offer effectively terminates the power to accept just as if there was an outright rejection of the offer.

☛ **Lapse of time:** Determine whether an acceptance has been communicated in time:

☞ If the offer specifies when an offer lapses, it lapses automatically on that date. *Tip:* Watch for an offer sent by mail. Unless otherwise specified, the time begins to run from the date the offer is *received*.

☞ If the offer doesn't specify when the offer lapses, it expires within a *reasonable amount of time*. Look at the nature of the contract to determine what would be considered a reasonable amount of time. In a land sale deal, for example, six days' time would probably not be considered an unreasonable amount of time in which to accept, but one month probably would.

☛ **Revocation**: Be sure that the offer wasn't revoked before it was accepted. Here are the two methods of rejection:

☞ An unequivocal statement of revocation (e.g., offeror says, "The deal is off").

☞ Revocation by an *indirect* communication. This is the most frequently tested mode of revocation. Look for an offeror who behaves in a way that is *inconsistent with the intention of entering into the proposed contract*, where the *offeree learns* of the inconsistency.

Example: X, who has offered to buy Y's garden tractor, learns from Z that Y has already sold the tractor to Y. Once X gets this knowledge, the revocation has occurred.

Firm Offers and Option Contracts

☛ When you analyze an offeror's *promise to hold an offer open*, it's key that you start with deciding whether the UCC applies:

☞ **UCC Transactions:** If the offer involves the sale of goods (i.e., it's a UCC Article 2 transaction), here's a recap of the main rules:

☞ **Merchant:** An offeror who is a *merchant* — one who deals professionally in the kind of goods in question — may extend an irrevocable *firm offer*, even without consideration, as long as the writing is *signed*.

☞ **Time limit:** A firm offer for which no consideration is given cannot be made irrevocable for a period *longer than three months*. (If the offer states it's irrevocable for longer than 3 months, the irrevocability lasts for 3 months.)

   ☞ **No-longer-firm offer can still be in force:** But even if you conclude that an offer is not firm (or was firm but is no longer so), check to see if it's *still in force* — it might be in force just because it *hasn't been revoked*, even though it's no longer firm.

   Example: On Feb. 1, Accountant gets a catalog from Stationer, with a cover letter saying "We'll sell you as many as you wish of anything in this catalog at the published prices, and we promise not to raise prices until the end of this calendar year." There is no further communication between the parties. Then, on June 1, Accountant sends in an order for "1000 monogrammed pens, your catalog #201."

   Stationer and Accountant have a binding contract for the pens. Stationer's offer was only a firm offer for the 3 months beginning Feb. 1. So beginning April 1, Stationer *could* have revoked. But it didn't do so. Therefore, Accountant's June 1 acceptance was effective even though it occurred beyond the 3-month irrevocability period.

☞ **Non-merchant:** A *non-merchant* who gratuitously (i.e., without consideration) promises to hold an offer open is *not* held to that promise.

   Example: *A*, a non-merchant, posts a message on e-bay.com saying, "I offer to sell my 1953 Barbie & Ken set to highest bidder over $100. This offer is firm, and I won't revoke it before 11:59 p.m. March 17." *B* makes a $150 offer, which is the highest as of 11 p.m. on March 17. *A* revokes at 11:45. There's no contract, because *A* could revoke any time he wanted even though he said he wouldn't, since: (1) he's a non-merchant; and (2) offers by non-merchants aren't irrevocable without consideration.

☞ **Non-UCC transactions:** For non-UCC transactions (sales of realty and services), there's just one rule:

☞ An offer that purports to be irrevocable for a certain period is *not irrevocable*, unless the offeree gives *consideration* for the irrevocability. This is true even if the offeror is a businessperson (i.e., would be a "merchant" if this were a sale of goods).

   Example: On the facts of the above e-bay example, suppose *A* were a professional developer who offered to sell Blackacre to the highest bidder, with a promise that the offer wouldn't be revoked before conclusion of the auction. *A* could revoke anyway, since no offeree is giving consideration for the promise of irrevocability.

☞ But remember that consideration can be ***non-monetary***.

> **Example:** *A* offers to sell Blackacre to *B* for $100,000. *B*, who lives 150 miles from the property, wants to inspect it but doesn't want to take the trip if *A* might sell to someone else in the interim. Therefore, *A* promises to hold the offer open for one week, in return for *B*'s promise to visit the property during that week. *A*'s offer is irrevocable for the week, because *B*'s return promise to travel is consideration.

☞ For both UCC and non-UCC contracts, remember that the acceptance of an option contract is effective not upon dispatch, but upon ***receipt by the offeror***.

Temporary Irrevocability

☛ Look for instances where an offer is ***temporarily irrevocable***, such as the following:

☞ Where a party has ***commenced performance of a unilateral contract***.

☞ Where a ***sub-contractor*** submits a bid to a general contractor. If the sub-contractor's bid is relied upon by the general contractor when he submits his overall bid to the customer, it is irrevocable for the time necessary for the general contractor to receive the job and accept the sub-contractor's bid.

> ☛ However, in this sub-contractor-bid situation, what's being applied is in effect ***promissory estoppel***, so the sub's offer is only irrevocable to the extent needed to ***avoid injustice***. (*Example:* If the general contractor still has time to amend his own bid after receiving the news that the sub has revoked his sub-bid offer, enforcement of the sub's bid won't be necessary to avoid injustice.)

Indefiniteness

☛ Agreements with indefinite terms appear quite often in fact patterns. When analyzing an agreement, look for the ***four essential elements***: Parties to the contract, subject matter, time for performance, and price. But don't automatically void an agreement for indefiniteness if one of these terms is missing.

☞ **UCC test:** Under the UCC, the agreement is not void if it expresses an intention by both parties to be bound and there is a ***reasonably certain basis for giving an appropriate remedy***. (Most courts today apply pretty much the same approach in non-UCC cases.)

Example: If the items to be supplied (e.g., name of product) or the quantity are missing, and there's no way for a court to know reliably what was intended, the contract will be void for indefiniteness.

☞ **Missing terms:** Be sure to fill in any omitted terms. Most fact patterns will present a situation where the essential terms are specified, so then the court (i.e., you, the exam writer) may supply a reasonable term. Be on the lookout for these common contexts where terms are omitted:

☛ **Real estate transactions.** The same general rules apply, even in a non-UCC context. *Examples of terms whose omission would probably **not** be fatal:* Type of deed, type of title or type of warranty, dates of tendering of down payment and completion of transaction.

Example: X agrees in writing to sell to Y a property called Farmland for $8 an acre. X later claims that the agreement is void for indefiniteness. Several details are missing from this contract: the total price (because the aggregate number of acres is unknown), the time for performance, the type of deed and condition of title Y will receive. *Solution:* Aggregate acres could be ascertained by a survey, and the total price could then be calculated by multiplying the acres times $8. The other terms could be implied from what is customary in the area.

❏ *Remember that price is an essential term in a realty contract and its absence violates the Statute of Frauds.*

☛ **Sale of goods.** The most commonly omitted terms in this type of transaction are the manner of payment (cash or credit), the place of delivery, total contract price and type of warranties.

☞ **Place of delivery; time for payment:** If the contract doesn't otherwise specify, delivery is at the *seller's place of business*, and a *cash payment* is due at that time. Also, if the contract contemplates delivery in lots, cash payment is due at the time an individual lot is delivered.

Example: Bathrooms 'R Us contracts to sell Apartments 100 identical sets of bathroom sinks and toilets (collectively, "fixtures"). 50 sets are due on May 1, and the other 50 on June 1, at a price of $300 per set. The contract is silent about the place for delivery or the time and place for payment.

Bathrooms must tender the first 50 fixtures on May 1 at Bathrooms' place of business (not Apartments' place of business). However, that duty of tender is conditioned on Apartments' tendering the price for the 50 fixtures in cash at Bathrooms' place of business, on May 1. (So if Apartments doesn't show up with cash at Bathrooms' showroom, Bathrooms doesn't have to do anything. And Apartments can't demand credit, or the right to wait until all 100 have been tendered.)

☞ **"Reasonable" price:** If there's no price specified, the court can supply a "reasonable" one, provided that the parties intended to be bound even though no price was set.

☛ **Past performance:** Watch for a situation where the parties have already been conducting business under an agreement that one party is now claiming is void because it is "indefinite." The parties' *past performance* may show that there is mutual agreement regarding the supposedly indefinite term.

☞ **Open term:** Don't worry if the contract indicates that a term will be specified by one of the parties (or agreed on by both) in the future: the contract will still be enforceable if there is a reasonable way for a court to fill the gap and to determine damages.

> **Example:** A purchase agreement reads in part: "*B* Aircraft Company agrees to sell and *A* agrees to buy 50 planes to be delivered as ordered within the next year at these prices: Gulls — $100,000 each; Terns — $200,000 each. *A* to specify shipping dates. Number of each type wanted on each shipment to be specified by *A* at least thirty days before each shipping date." After *A* places and receives an order of 10 planes, he refuses to place an order for any more. Although the quantity of each type of plane isn't specified, there is a reasonably certain basis for awarding damages by figuring that the least *A* would have bought prospectively was 40 Gulls (the least expensive plane).

Misunderstanding

☛ **Ambiguous term:** Where a contract term is ambiguous and one party should know the meaning understood by the other party, a contract is formed based on the other party's understanding.

> **Example:** In October, *C*, an art collector, telephones *A*, an artist, and says, "In February I saw your painting of Sunflowers. Is it still available, and, if so, how much do you want for it?" The contract they later sign states: "*A* hereby sells to *C A*'s sunflower painting..." *C* was referring to a painting entitled "Sunflowers." In July *A* had painted another picture of sunflowers entitled "Sunflowers II," and *A* subjectively was referring to this painting in the contract. *C* had the first "Sunflowers" in mind. Since *C* mentioned that he had seen the painting in February, *A* should have known that *C* was referring to the first "Sunflowers." Therefore, a contract exists, and for the

first Sunflowers.

On the other hand, if neither party was at fault in the misunderstanding, the lack of agreement on which painting was intended would be great enough to cause the contract to be void for misunderstanding.

Exam Tips *on* CONSIDERATION

Consideration

☞ Always check whether or not a contract is supported by consideration. Consideration is a *legal detriment suffered by the promisee in exchange for the promisor's promise.*

> *Example where there is a legal detriment:* X, the owner of a chain of dry cleaning stores, promises to give to Y, her cousin, a franchise if Y promises to move from a distant state to where X lives. Y promises to do so. It is irrelevant whether X gains any benefit from Y's move. What matters is that Y has promised to suffer a detriment in exchange for X's promise. Therefore, there's consideration for X's promise.

> *Example where there isn't a legal detriment:* University receives a pledge from X, an alumnus, for a donation of $50,000. X later withdraws the pledge. The promise lacks consideration because University hasn't suffered a legal detriment. (But the promise may still be enforceable without consideration, through promissory estoppel.)

☞ Remember that something can be consideration even though it is done by (or for) a *third person*, one who is *not a party* to the contract.

Example 1: A promises B that A will pay B $100 if B's son drives A to the airport. Even though B's son is not the promisee (B is), the son's act of driving will be consideration for A's promise to pay B.

Example 2: A promises B $100 if B promises to drive A's daughter to the airport. The fact that the performance being given in exchange for A's promise is to be rendered to someone other than A (the promisor) doesn't matter.

☞ Where the issue of consideration is prominent in an essay, it usually manifests itself in one of the following four situations:

(1) Promises to make gift: D promises to make a *gift*, usually to a relative or charity. There's no consideration supporting D's promise, so it's not enforceable (unless it falls under one of the exceptions to the consideration requirement, covered in the next chapter).

☞ **Mixture of bargain and gift:** But a transaction that's a *mixture of bargain and gift satisfies* the consideration requirement, making the generous party's promise enforceable.

Example: D promises to sell P D's antique car at a 90% discount to its market value, in return for P's promise to buy it at this low price. As long as there is some sort of a "bargain," the fact that there's a gift element doesn't prevent D's promise from being supported by consideration (P's promise of payment).

(2) Promises to pay for past services: D promises to pay for *past services* which P rendered to him. Most commonly, P is a *Good Samaritan* who saves D, an unconscious person, who later promises compensation and then reneges.

☞ **No compensation reasonably expected:** A promise to pay for past services isn't supported by consideration where the services were performed with *no reasonable expectation of compensation.* Fact patterns may trick you into thinking that under certain circumstances consideration has in fact been offered. Don't be fooled if:

❏ The unconscious person regains consciousness *immediately after* the rescue and then promises to pay the savior.

❏ The savior happens to be someone with medical expertise, such as a *retired doctor.*

❏ A *relative* of the party who was saved promises after the fact to pay the savior (still no "bargained for" exchange).

❏ The promise to pay is made *in writing* and/or is promised "in consideration" for services rendered.

In all four of the above scenarios, there is no consideration for the promise to pay for the past services. (But the promises might be binding without consideration, to the extent necessary to avoid injustice — see the next chapter.)

These examples should be distinguished from emergency medical services provided by parties who *would* reasonably expect compensation, such as an ambulance service or hospital emergency room. Here, there would be consideration for the patient's (or patient's relative's) subsequent promise to pay.

(3) Pre-existing duty: P promises to pay (or perform services) that P is already legally obligated to pay/perform — D's return promise is not supported by consideration.

☛ **Contract modifications:** The most common scenario is a *contract modification.* Here, you must distinguish between the UCC and non-UCC situation.

☞ **Non-UCC:** If P merely promises to do what P already promised to do under the contract, and there are no unanticipated circumstances, D's new promise (e.g., more money) given in return is not supported by consideration.

Example: D promises to pay $5,000 if P paints D's house by June 14. After the house is halfway painted, P threatens to walk off the job unless D raises the price to $7,500. D agrees. D's promise to pay the extra $2,500 is not supported by consideration, because P merely promised to do what he was already contractually required to do.

☞ **Substitute performance by P:** But if P *changes his own duty,* however slightly, in response to D's promised modification, then D's counter-promise *is* supported by consideration. (*Example:* In the above example, if P promised to finish the job one day earlier [or to use a different color of paint] than previously promised in return for the extra $2,500, D's counter-promise of the extra $2,500 would be supported by consideration.)

> *Common scenario:* A party who is owed money due on a later date agrees to accept a lesser amount in exchange for a promise of immediate tender of payment. The creditor has received consideration for the promise to take less.

☞ **Unanticipated circumstances:** Also, if the modification is a response to *new circumstances unanticipated by the parties* when they made their original deal (e.g., a well-driller hits rock, and asks for a higher price to finish the job), remember that most modern courts will find that the modification is binding.

☞ **UCC:** Under the UCC, the pre-existing duty rule simply doesn't apply to the contract-modification scenario — under Article 2, "An agreement modifying a contract within [Article 2] needs no consideration to be binding."

Example: On the above house-painting example, if P had promised to sell paint to D rather than perform painting services, the lack of consideration for D's promise to pay more would not prevent D's new promise from being binding.

(4) Settlement of claim: Similarly, if a party who has a contractual claim for money agrees to take less in a *"settlement,"* the promise to take less is supported by consideration, so long as the other party *disputed* in good faith the *amount* or *validity* of the claim.

> **Example:** P, a painting contractor, agrees to paint O's house for $5,000. The contract provides that P will deliver a satisfactory result. When the job is completed O tells P that he doesn't find the work satisfactory, but he's willing to call it "square" if P will accept $4,500. P agrees to take the less amount in payment. P's promise to take the lesser amount is supported by consideration (O's willingness not to dispute whether P performed), so that promise is binding, and P can't change his mind and demand full payment.

☞ **Invalid claims:** This is true *even if the claim is not valid,* so long as the holder of the claim *believes in good faith* that the claim is valid.

> **Example:** *B,* acting as a Good Samaritan without expectation of payment, saves *A*'s life. *A* promises in writing to pay *B* $1,000. *B* honestly believes that *A*'s promise is binding. *A* then reneges. *B* threatens to sue, then agrees to forebear from suing if *A* will sign a new writing promising to pay $750. *A* signs the new writing. *A* will be bound — even though *A*'s original promise to pay was not binding (it was a promise to pay for past services, rendered without expectation of payment), the new promise is supported by consideration, since it was in settlement of *B*'s good-faith claim for breach of the prior promise.

Illusory Promises

☛ **Total discretion by one party:** When you spot a contract that gives one party *total discretion on whether to perform*, that party's promise is illusory, because the party hasn't committed to anything. Therefore, the other party isn't bound, either.

> ***Example:*** Seller offers Buyer an annual contract for the sale of widgets at a stated price, with the quantity to be "whatever quantities you choose to order, up to a maximum of 10,000." Notice that Buyer isn't obligated to purchase *anything* under these terms. Therefore, Seller's promise isn't supported by consideration, and Buyer can't sue Seller for refusing to fill the orders Buyer places.

But keep in mind that contracts with apparently-illusory promises may nonetheless be wholly or partly enforceable. Some situations to watch for:

☞ **A divisible contract:** If there is a long-term agreement in which the seller's promise is illusory, but the buyer places individual orders, the seller's promise will be interpreted as an offer for a *series of unilateral contracts*, and each order will be an *acceptance of a unilateral contract* (which the seller is then bound to fill).

Example: Buyer requests an annual price quote for fuel oil from Seller. On Dec. 24, Seller writes to Buyer, "I offer to supply you with any no. 2 fuel oil ordered by you during the next year beginning January 1 under the following terms: 14 cents a gallon to be ordered only in 3,000 gallon tank cars." On Dec. 30, Buyer writes, "I accept your offer." Since there isn't any language indicating a quantity (e.g., Buyer's requirements) or exclusivity of source, the contract is illusory at this point (and either party could cancel it completely).

But now, suppose that on the following Jan. 20, Buyer writes, "My first order is for 6,000 gallons." This would probably be interpreted as an acceptance of Seller's outstanding offer to enter into a series of unilateral contracts. Therefore, Seller would have to fulfill the order. (But Seller could cancel at any time, and not have to fill any orders placed after the cancellation date.)

☞ **An implied promise by a party:** In certain circumstances a promise may be *implied*, thus making that party's duty not illusory.

  ☛ **Exclusive distributorships:** Where Buyer has exclusive rights to distribute (resell) Seller's product, Buyer has an implied duty to ***use her reasonable efforts*** to sell the product. This implied duty will furnish consideration for Seller's return duty to sell to Buyer.

  ☛ **Requirements contracts:** Similarly, in a ***requirements*** contract, Buyer's promise of exclusivity supplies consideration for Seller's return promise to supply Buyer.

    ☞ **Good-faith quantities:** Remember that the ***quantity*** in both requirements and output contracts is measured by the actual quantity that occurs ***in good faith.*** However, the quantity can't be an amount which is unreasonably disproportionate to any stated estimate or, in the absence of a stated estimate, to any normal or otherwise comparable prior output or requirements.

    Example: *S* and *B* have an exclusive five-year contract whereby *S*, a chair manufacturer, supplies a certain type of chairs to *B*, a chair distributor. (*S* is to sell this type of chair only to *B*, and *B* is to buy this chair only from *S*.) Orders for the first three years are 330, 100 and 250 chairs, respectively. *B* orders 1,000 chairs in the fourth year and *S* cannot produce that amount. *S* will probably not be liable for breach, because the amount requested is disproportionate to the prior requirements.

  ☛ **Personal satisfaction of party.** Look for a contract where a party's duty to pay arises only if he's personally satisfied with the work done by the other party. His promise to pay isn't illusory because of the requirement that dissatisfaction, if it occurs, be in *good faith.*

- ☛ **Notice of cancellation:** Lastly, if a party can *cancel* the contract at any time, but only on some period of notice, the obligation to give the notice (and to perform or be bound til them) supplies consideration for the other party's promise.

☛ Two further points to remember:

- ☞ Courts seldom care about the *"adequacy"* of consideration. So a big imbalance between the "value" of what *A* got and what *B* got won't mean a lack of consideration.

- ☞ A promise to make a gift is unenforceable, as noted. However, a gift, *once it has been completed*, can't be rescinded by the donor.

Exam Tips on
PROMISES BINDING WITHOUT CONSIDERATION

☛ *General Tip:* When a fact pattern contains a contract that you think is enforceable despite the fact that it's not supported by consideration, first discuss your conclusion that consideration is lacking, then discuss why the contract's enforceable regardless of this flaw.

Modification

- ☛ **UCC:** A modification of a contract for *goods* is enforceable even if it isn't supported by consideration.

  - ☞ Look for a *one-sided change* in the terms of a sales agreement — even though the change is benefits only one party, it's still enforceable.

    Example: W, a wholesaler of office supplies, contracts with R, a retailer, for the sale of 50 printer cartridges for $450. Two weeks later, W calls R and says that due to a shortage of materials, his costs have increased drastically and that he has to raise the price to $650. R agrees in writing to the change in price. A few days later R purchases 50 cartridges from another supplier for $500 and later rejects delivery of the cartridges from W. The contract between W and R is enforceable at the $650 price.

  - ☞ Watch for the following *traps*:

    - ☛ A modification of an agreement for *services*. Such a modification must normally be supported by consideration (see prior chapter), and a modification in which only one party's duty changes (and there are no unanticipated circumstances) does not qualify.

☛ A modified agreement that violates the **Statute of Frauds** (i.e., the sales price is greater than $500 and the modification is not in writing). The modified contract will be unenforceable, not because of consideration problems but because of the lack of a writing reflecting the change. (See Ch. 9.)

☛ A **"no oral modification"** (N.O.M.) clause. In both UCC and non-UCC cases, a N.O.M. clause will be enforced (so even consideration won't save an oral modification that violates such a clause).

    ☞ But remember, an N.O.M. clause can be **waived**. So if one party foreseeably relies to her substantial detriment on the other party's oral promise to modify the agreement, despite an N.O.M. clause, you should argue that promissory estoppel dictates that the promise be enforced to the extent needed to protect the person who relies.

    Example: Contractor agrees to paint Owner's house for a stated price, work to be completed by August 15, with time of the essence. The contract says that there may be no oral modifications. Contractor's worker gets sick, so Contractor orally asks Owner to give him til Sept. 1. Owner says ok. Contractor relies on the extension, and finishes on Sept. 1. The N.O.M. clause will be deemed waived because a waiver is needed to protect Contractor's reliance interest.

Assignment

☛ If the fact pattern involves an assignment of rights or duties, remember that **consideration isn't required** because an assignment is a present transfer of rights, not a promise.

Guaranty

☛ When you have one person guaranteeing another's debt, look at the timing of the guaranty:

    ☞ If the guaranty is given **at the same time the debt is being created**, there is no problem of consideration because the guarantor is bargaining for the loan (even though the loan is given to someone else).

    ☞ When the guaranty is given **after the underlying debt has been created**, see if there is any independent consideration. If not, point out that most modern courts hold that the guaranty is enforceable if it's in writing and includes a **recital** of consideration — even if no consideration is actually paid.

Promissory Estoppel

☞ **General:** In the absence of consideration, a contract is enforceable if the promisee *foreseeably and reasonably relies* upon the promise to her detriment.

☞ **Powerful business strings along an underdog:** Look for fact patterns in which a *powerful business* (call it *A*) *"strings along"* a less powerful business or consumer (*B*), by indicating over a period of time that if *B* takes various actions, *A* will consider forming some business relationship with *B* to *B*'s benefit. (*Example: A* is a bank, and promises *B*, a borrower with a cash shortage, that if *B* stops making payments, *A* will consider modifying the mortgage.) Courts are especially likely to order P.E. in this "stringing along" situation.

☞ **Reliance:** Most tested issue: Has there been *actual reliance*? Look for these common scenarios where reliance has occurred:

  ☞ **Intra-family promises:** When one family member promises something to the other, the latter may materially change his position in reliance, making the promise enforceable under p.e.

    Example: After being told of Daughter's engagement, Father promises her a new home as a wedding present. He shows her the plans and promises that he will build the house on a lot which he owns. Daughter is so pleased with the plans that she immediately cancels a contract which (as Father knows) she has already made for the purchase of a different home, forfeiting a $20,000 deposit. After Father has caused the home to be halfway built, he refuses to complete it or to convey the land to Daughter.

    Father's promise (to make a gift) is unenforceable as a contract, since it was given without consideration (Father didn't bargain for Daughter to cancel her prior contract.) However, Daughter may be able to use promissory estoppel to argue that the agreement should be enforced, at least to the extent of reimbursing her for the lost $20,000 deposit, since her reliance on Father's promise seems to have been reasonable, and foreseeeable to him.

  ☞ **Oral promise to convey land:** An oral promise to *convey land* may become enforceable by the promisee's reliance (e.g., the promisee gives up a job and moves on to the property, plus improves it).

  ☞ **Promise of pension.** If an employer promises an employee a *pension* that is effective as soon as the employee should decide to retire, the promise will be enforceable if and only if employee *relies on it* in some objective way (e.g., by in fact retiring under circumstances that prevent the employee from returning to the job).

    Example: Worker, 55, has worked for Company for 30 years on an at-will basis. Worker mentions to Boss (the owner of Company) that he'd like to retire eventually and travel throughout the U.S. (though he has not decided yet when this will be.) Shortly thereafter, Boss hands Worker a letter on Company stationery saying, "If at any time you choose at your sole discretion to retire, Company will pay you a pension of $3,000 per month for the rest of your life." 6 months later, Worker announces his retirement, gives up his rent-controlled apartment, and buys a $40,000 RV in which to travel. One year later, Company terminates the pension on cost-savings grounds. Can Worker recover for breach?

Yes. First, notice that the pension promise wasn't supported by consideration — Worker didn't do anything to his detriment or Company's benefit in exchange for the promise. (For instance, he didn't agree to stay on the job longer in exchange for the promise.) On the other hand, this was a promise that the promisor (Company) should reasonably have expected to induce reliance (retirement) by the promisee, and it did induce such reliance (not just Worker's giving up the job, but also his giving up the apartment and buying the RV). (Note that the buying of the RV is *foreseeable* reliance from Company's perspective, since Worker had previously said he'd like to travel widely when he retired.) Therefore, the pension promise will be enforceable without consideration under promissory estoppel, since that's the only way to avoid injustice.

☞ **Sub-contractor's bid:** If a *sub-contractor's bid* is relied upon by the general contractor when he submits his overall bid to the customer, the sub-contractor is promissorily estopped from revoking the bid for the time necessary for the general contractor to receive the job and accept the sub-contractor's bid.

☛ *Exception 1:* There's probably no promissory estoppel if the general contractor would still have *time to revise its bid* to the potential customer.

Example: C, a general contractor, has a 3:00 pm deadline for submission of a bid to a potential customer and he solicits bids from sub-contractors for the job. S, a sub-contractor, submits his bid to C at 1:30 pm. C, relying on S's bid, immediately submits his overall bid to the potential customer. S, realizing he has made a mistake in calculating, calls C at 2:58 to withdraw the bid and revise it. S is promissorily estopped from revoking his bid because C reasonably relied on it in submitting his overall bid to the customer. However, if the revocation call from S had come in at 1:40, and there was time for C to revise his bid by taking the next-lowest sub-bid, then C's promissory estoppel argument would probably not work.

☛ *Exception 2:* The sub-bid (like any promise covered by promissory estoppel) is only enforceable "to the extent *necessary to avoid injustice.*" So if the next-lowest bidder is only $x more, the general contractor's recovery will presumably be limited to $x (and the general won't have the right to recover expectation damages as in the ordinary case of breach).

☛ In any p.e. fact pattern, after you have spotted reliance, make sure it's *justified,* i.e., *reasonable.* Confirm that there has been an *express or implied promise.*

> **Example:** Sub, a sub-contractor, submits a bid to General, a general contractor on a project. General responds, "Right now you're the low bidder, so if nothing changes and I get the contract, you'll get the work." Sub then reads in the paper that General got the contract. Therefore, Sub buys $30,000 of materials for the job, which have only scrap value if not used on the job. General gives the job to X, a different sub-contractor who bid $1 more than Sub. Probably Sub's reliance on continuing to be the low bidder, and thus getting the job, wasn't reasonable. If so, she won't collect the $30,000 she spent (let alone the profits she would have made had she gotten the job and performed).

☛ Remember that a *promise to donate money to charity* is generally not supported by consideration. However, most courts will apply the doctrine of promissory estoppel — even if there *hasn't been detrimental reliance* — if the promise to donate is *made in writing.*

Exam Tips on *MISTAKE*

Mistakes as to Existing Fact

☛ Use the term "mistake," and the analysis in this chapter, only to cover those situations involving a mistake as to the facts *as they existed just prior to the contract.* Where the parties are operating under a mistaken assumption about *future* events (e.g., future market prices), use the Impossibility/Impracticability analysis given in Ch. 12.

Mutual Mistake

☛ The topic most frequently tested from this chapter concerns a mistaken assumption made by *both* parties to the contract (mutual mistake). Before concluding that there has been a mutual mistake — and that the contract can therefore be avoided by a party who is injured by the mistake — make sure that all 3 requirements are met:

(1) Mutuality. Make sure that *both parties* made the same (ultimately wrong) assumption when entering into the agreement.

(2) Materiality. Make sure the assumption was ***"basic"*** to the bargain, and that the mistake had a ***material effect*** on the agreed-upon exchanges. Watch for these situations:

☛ **Real estate transactions.** Look out for a sale where there has been a ***mistaken acreage count*** and the total acreage contained in the contract can't be conveyed by the seller.

    ☞ If the portion of land that cannot be conveyed is large or otherwise significant, then its inclusion was probably a basic assumption of the contract. But if the parcel that cannot be conveyed is insignificant (e.g., a 3-foot-wide strip along one end of a 50 acre parcel), then it probably would not be considered a basic assumption of the contract.

☛ **Purchase of a unique good.** Look for the purchase of a unique work of art where the parties are mistaken as to its origin or creator. These will probably be basic assumptions.

Example: D, an art dealer, receives from one of her purchasing agents a painting entitled "Sunset" which she is informed was painted by Van Goon. C, an art collector, sees the painting at D's gallery and says to D, "What an interesting Van Goon." D responds (honestly believing that he's telling the truth), "Yes, it is." C pays $50,000 for the painting, its worth had it been a genuine Van Goon. C later finds out that the painting is a forgery worth only a few hundred dollars and stops payment on her check. The assumption about authorship was almost certainly a basic assumption, so C's nonperformance is probably not a breach.

(3) Allocation of risk. Make sure the parties did not explicitly or implicitly ***allocate the risk*** of the mistake to the party who is now trying to avoid the contract. (If they did so allocate the risk, that party can't use the doctrine.) Also, remember that the court can allocate the risk of mistakes wherever it is "reasonable" to do so.

Examples of situations where courts usually find an implicit allocation of risk of mistake:

☛ **Minerals in the land:** The risk that there will turn out to be valuable mineral deposits is allocated to the ***seller***. (*Example:* S and B enter into an agreement for the sale of Farmland for $8 an acre. Oil is then discovered under the land. S may not avoid the contract, because he'll be found to have implicitly borne this risk, assuming the contract is silent.)

☛ **Auctions with object of unknown characteristics:** At an ***auction***, the risk that the item won't have some desired attribute — where both the auctioneer and the buyer know that the existence of that attribute is ***unknown*** — is allocated to the buyer.

Example: Auctioneer offers a 2-month-old calf at auction. Breed buys the calf for $1,000, believing that the calf will prove fertile (as most calves are). No express warranty is made about fertility. Two years later, the calf is conclusively shown to have been born sterile, making it useless for Breed's purposes (of which Auctioneer was aware). Had this fact been known at auction-time, the calf would have been worth $150. Both parties knew at auction time that the fertility of a calf can't be measured until it is at least 1 year old.

Breed can't rescind for mutual mistake. That's because both sides knew that the fertility of the item couldn't be known, and the circumstances implicitly allocated to the buyer the risk of a mistake on this point.

☛ **Building conditions:** In a construction contract, the risk of undiscovered unfavorable building conditions is normally allocated to the *contractor.*

Example: X is hired to drill a well for Y, to be completed by June 1. Two hundred feet down X's drill strikes a solid layer of rock and breaks, plugging the hole. It's no longer possible for X to complete the drilling of the well by the agreed-upon date. Even though the accident may have been unavoidable and neither party was aware of the rock which caused the drill to break, X may not rescind the contract, because the contractor implicitly bears the risk of such conditions if the contract is silent.

However, always make sure that the contract language or surrounding circumstances don't effectively allocate the risk in a different way.

Unilateral Mistake

☛ Where only *one party* has made a mistake (unilateral mistake), he is excused from performance *only if the other party knew or should have known of the mistake.*

☞ If you don't know whether the other party knew or should have known of the mistake, argue the evidence in support of each view, and then state that the result depends on which way the "knew/should have known" issue is resolved.

☞ **"Too good to be true":** Here's a common fact pattern: *A* makes *B* an *offer* that *B* realizes (or should realize) is *"too good to be true"* (e.g., because it looks like *A* made a computational error). If *B* tries to "snap up" the offer, *A* will likely to able to get the contract rescinded or reformed for unilateral mistake.

☛ **Distinction:** On the other hand, if the error in an offer or bid is *not obvious* to one in the offeree's position, then when the offeree accepts, unilateral mistake probably *won't* apply.

Example: C, a contractor, solicits bids from sub-contractors for a construction job to be performed for X. S, a sub-contractor, delivers a bid for the foundation work in the amount of $140,000. The next lowest bid that is submitted to C is $150,000. Relying on S's bid, C immediately submits its overall bid to X. Fifteen minutes later, S telephones C and says that there was a mistake in the calculation and revises its bid to $170,000. Since the next lowest bid was only $10,000 more than S's bid, C probably did *not* have reason to know that S's bid was a mistake, in which case S will be not be able to rescind based upon unilateral mistake.

Reformation

☛ If there is a clerical error and a written agreement ***doesn't accurately reflect the parties' agreement,*** the aggrieved party can have the contract ***reformed*** to reflect the prior agreement. This usually occurs regarding price: the contract states a different price than the one agreed upon, or leaves out the agreed-upon price altogether.

Exam Tips on
PAROL EVIDENCE AND INTERPRETATION

☛ **Overall rule:** Remember the standard parol evidence rule:

> Evidence of a prior (oral or written) agreement may ***never*** be admitted to ***contradict*** any ***final writing*** (integration), and may not even ***supplement*** a final writing that was intended to constitute the ***complete*** agreement (total integration).

> (For more about making the distinction between partial integrations and total ones, see the last three paragraphs of these tips, on p. 192.)

☛ **Focus on exceptions:** Most exam questions involve not the standard parol evidence rule (or at least not just that rule), but situations where the rule does not apply. Look for the three most-often-tested such situations:

(1) Clarification of ambiguity: Evidence of prior or contemporaneous negotiations *is* admissible to properly ***define*** an ***ambiguous*** term, even one contained in a total integration. The ambiguity may either be apparent on the face of the contract or derive from the underlying circumstances.

> **Example:** A written contract between *C*, a building contractor, and *S*, a carpentry sub-contractor, states that *C* agrees to "reimburse *S* for all material purchased by *S* for the job." *S* purchases $5,000 worth of lumber and only uses $3,000 worth of it. (Assume that the writing is intended as the final and complete expression of the parties' agreement.) *C* refuses to reimburse *S* for more than $3,000 worth of lumber. *S* may testify to a conversation which took place prior to the signing of the contract in which *C*

agreed that he would pay for materials purchased but not actually used —
this evidence will not contradict or supplement (add a term to) the agreement, it will merely aid in the interpretation of the ambiguous phrase "purchased for the job."

☞ *Hint*: Some ambiguities will only become apparent after you analyze
the unique circumstances surrounding the contract. The above example is an illustration.

☞ **Can't change the meaning:** Be sure that the extrinsic evidence is
truly offered for the purpose of interpreting an ambiguous clause, *not
adding or changing* an unambiguous one (in which case the standard
parol evidence rule applies).

Example: In a contract between a laboratory and a disposal company,
the disposal company agrees that "the specified waste products are to
be removed from the site within 48 hours of our being notified that the
waste containment vessel is 80 percent filled." On one occasion, the
waste container isn't emptied until 96 hours after notification because
notice was given the day before a holiday weekend. The disposal company may not show that during contract negotiations, the parties
agreed that the 48-hour deadline wouldn't apply to holiday weekends.
This is so because the language isn't ambiguous ("48 hours" can only
have one meaning) and the evidence the company seeks to introduce
would *change* rather than *clarify* the terms of the writing.

☞ Remember that ambiguities are construed against the party who prepared the contract.

(2) Custom: There are several ways in which *"customs"* may be introduced to
interpret the meaning of a contract. When one of these ways applies, there is
no parol evidence problem, because the custom is being introduced for interpretation, not in order to vary the writing. The two most frequently tested
types of custom:

☛ **"Course of dealing":** This is evidence about a *pattern of performance
between the two parties under past contracts.* (Distinguish this from
"course of performance," which is how the parties have behaved under the
current contract — the same rule allowing proof applies to course of performance.) Evidence of how the parties acted with respect to the past contracts may be used to show how a term in the current contract should be
interpreted.

Example: *B*, a retail florist, has been ordering roses from *S*, a flower
wholesaler, for more than a year. The orders are for "roses," and have
always been filled with roses of assorted colors. Evidence of these past

transactions can be introduced by *B* to show that when she placed her present order for "roses," she did not want (and the "contract," — i.e., the present order — didn't call for) only red roses.

☛ **"Usage of trade":** This is evidence of a ***generally accepted practice*** or method of dealing in a ***given industry or field.*** This can be introduced to clarify an otherwise ambiguous term.

   Example: *S*, a wholesaler of widgets, signs a contract with *B*, a retailer of widgets, for a "gross" of widgets. *B* sends 144 widgets. *S* refuses delivery, stating that "gross" in the widget industry means 100 units, not 144. Even if the writing is a complete integration, *S* will be permitted to show that under a widget-industry trade usage, "gross" means 100 units.

(3) Existence of a condition and/or formation defect. Parol evidence can be introduced as proof of a ***condition*** not included in the writing, as well as proof that the contract ***never legally came into existence.***

   Example of condition: Painter signs a contract in which she agrees to paint Dave's portrait. Painter finishes the work, and demands payment. Dave asserts that he and Painter orally agreed that Dave would not have to pay for the painting unless Dave's wife liked it (which she doesn't). Even if the contract is an integration (final expression of parties' intent), Dave will be permitted to show that the parties agreed to the wife's-satisfaction condition.

   Example of non-formation of contract: X and Y enter into a written contract whereby X agrees to build a brick fireplace for Y, and Y agrees to pay the sum of $1,000 to X's daughter on her birthday, February 12. Before signing the writing, X and Y orally agree that Y will make a reasonable effort to obtain a loan to pay for the work, but that if she is unsuccessful by January 1, the agreement will be canceled. Y is unable to obtain the loan by January 1 and calls off the deal. Y may introduce the evidence of the prior oral agreement, because it was a condition precedent to the formation of the contract.

☛ **Two types of integration:** Where a writing (or group of writings) represents only the entire ***written*** contract of the parties, but not their ***complete*** agreement, it is merely a ***"partial integration,"*** and evidence of ***consistent*** verbal understandings is ordinarily admissible (though evidence of inconsistent ones is not). But if the agreement does represent the complete agreement (***"total integration"***), it can't even be ***supplemented*** by evidence of prior agreements.

   ☞ The more ***informal*** and *shorter* the writing is, the ***more likely*** it is to be found to be ***merely a partial integration*** (which can therefore be supplemented by proof of consistent additional terms).

Example: If the agreement is in the form of a one- or two-sentence letter, its brevity will usually indicate that it wasn't intended to be a total integration.

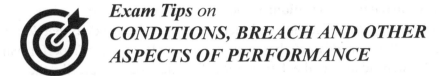

Exam Tips on
CONDITIONS, BREACH AND OTHER ASPECTS OF PERFORMANCE

Analyzing Conditions

☛ When a party's performance appears to be dependent upon the occurrence of a *condition* or event:

  ☞ First, *confirm that there is a condition*. A condition is an *event that must occur* (unless occurrence is excused) *before a party's performance is due.*

  ☞ Second, identify the *type of condition*: there are two types, *express* and *constructive*.

    ☛ **(1) Express condition:** Express conditions are conditions that are *agreed to by the parties.*

      ☞ **Phrasing:** The parties' language can still constitute an express condition even though it doesn't use the phrase "conditional on" or "on condition that." Any phrasing that indicates that the parties have agreed that one party's performance *will not be due unless some event happens* is a condition.

      Example: Painter and Owner agree that Painter will paint Owner's garage. The contract says that Owner will pay $3,000 for the work "when the work is completed to Owner's reasonable satisfaction." Since this language indicates the parties' explicit agreement that Owner will not have to pay until the work is completed to her reasonable satisfaction, such completion is an express condition to Owner's duty of payment.

      ☞ **Strict compliance:** The key thing to remember about express conditions is that *strict compliance* is usually required — "substantial" performance is usually not enough.

      ☞ **Satisfaction of a party:** A clause requiring a party to pay only upon his satisfaction is the most common type of express condition you'll encounter on exams. (The above example is typical.) A satisfaction clause will usually appear in contracts for the creation of an object or painting intended to please the taste of a particular person, so that subjective satisfaction is required.

☞ *Limitation:* A condition requiring subjective satisfaction is **valid** as long as the party's dissatisfaction with the object is in **good faith** (even if unreasonable).

☛ **(2) Constructive condition:** Conditions that are not "express" are *"constructive"* or "implied in law." Here, the court is deducing that **had the parties thought about it,** they would have made one party's performance to be dependent on the happening of some event, typically the other party's prior or contemporaneous performance. The court reaches this conclusion to ensure fairness.

☞ Watch for a situation where, if a condition were not inferred, a party would end up with **so bad a deal** that it's fair to say that she never would have entered the arrangement.

Example: Inventor has invented a better mousetrap. Inventor and Manufacturer have discussions about the terms under which Manufacturer would produce the item and pay Inventor a royalty. Inventor then signs an agreement promising that in 6 months, Inventor will grant Manufacturer a 10-year exclusive license to make the product; in return, Manufacturer promises to tool up immediately to make the item. Manufacturer tools up, but due to technical difficulties in production, he is never in fact able to make any mousetraps.

Inventor will have a strong claim that her duty to issue the license was subject to a constructive condition that Manufacturer be capable of and willing to actually produce the item. (Inventor will be arguing that she never would have agreed to issue a license that would not be exploited.) If the court agrees, Inventor's duty to issue the license will be discharged for failure of the constructive condition.

☞ Third, after identifying the condition, *confirm that the condition has been satisfied*.

☛ *Trap:* Be careful of fact patterns with multiple conditions. Be sure they have *all* been satisfied.

☛ Distinguish between express conditions, which must normally be strictly satisfied, and constructive conditions, as to which substantial performance is usually enough. (See the next section for more about the distinction.)

Strict Compliance and Substantial Performance

☛ **Express conditions:** Remember that if the condition is an "express" one (explicitly agreed to between the parties), *strict* compliance with it is normally required.

> **Example:** Portraitist agrees to paint Sitter's portrait, with payment to be conditional on Sitter's actual good-faith satisfaction. Since this is an express condition, the court will strictly construe the condition — if Sitter is subjectively unsatisfied, the court will not deem the condition met merely because Portraitist "substantially" performed (e.g., painted a portrait that most people would say looked a lot like Sitter.)

☞ **Forfeiture:** But the court can wriggle out of strict compliance if an *excessive forfeiture* would result.

> *Typical scenario for forfeiture doctrine:* Owner takes out a property insurance policy with Insurer, requiring Owner to give notice within, say, 10 days of any loss. Owner is slightly late in giving notice of loss, but in a way that does not cause actual prejudice to Insurer's ability to investigate or defend. The court will hold that strict enforcement of the condition would cause a substantial forfeiture (a damage to Owner out of all proportion to the prejudice caused to Insurer by the lateness), and will excuse the condition.

☛ **Constructive conditions:** Where one party's duty is subject to a *constructive* condition, however, strict compliance with the condition will normally *not* be required.

☞ **Material breach / substantial performance:** Instead, the condition will be deemed satisfied if there was *"substantial performance"* by the party who had to satisfy the condition. Or, to put it conversely, the condition will only be deemed unsatisfied if there was a *material breach* on the part of the party who had to satisfy the condition.

☛ **Generic example:** So you're looking for fact patterns where *A* doesn't want to pay or perform because he says *B* breached first. You'll first have to check whether *A*'s duty of payment/performance was expressly conditioned on *B*'s performance. If not, you're dealing with a constructive condition. Then, you'll analyze the materiality of the breach: *A* won't be relieved of his own duty unless *B*'s breach was material (i.e., *A* won't be relieved if *B* substantially performed).

☛ **Factors making a breach material:** Here are the *3 main factors* you should look at in deciding whether the breach was material:

❑ How completely was the party who benefits from the condition (*A* in the above generic example) *deprived of her expected benefit* in entering the contract? The more complete the deprivation, the more likely the breach is to be material.

❑ Can *A* be *adequately compensated* for the breach by *money dam-*

ages, instead of being relieved of performance? If damages will suffice, the breach is more likely to be non-material.

❑ Was the breach *willful* (intentional)? If so, it's more likely to be found material.

> **Example:** P, an equipment company, promises to deliver and install 6 coolers for the grand opening of D, a meat market, on Sept. 1. The price is quoted on a per-cooler basis. P only gets 5 coolers installed by Sept. 1. On Sept. 3, D refuses to pay for any coolers, demanding that P remove the 5 since it breached. D offers to install the 6th cooler by Oct. 1, but P refuses. D sues for the pro-rata contract price. (Assume that because of the large amount of installation services required, this is not a UCC sale-of-goods contract.)
>
> Unless there is a showing that the 5 coolers were rendered much less valuable by the temporary absence of the 6th, the court will hold that the breach was non-material (i.e., that P substantially performed). In that event, D will not be entitled to cancel the contract, and P will be entitled to collect the pro-rata contract price for the 5 coolers, less money damages for the delay on the 6th.

☛ **Divisibility:** Always be alert to the possibility that the contract is *"divisible"* into multiple pairs of corresponding part-performance (e.g., multiple services, each with its own price quoted in the contract). If the contract is truly "divisible," remember that a party who has **substantially performed one piece** is entitled to **recover the contract price** for that piece, even if that party materially breached as to all other pieces.

> **Example:** In a single document, Paint agrees to paint Owner's kitchen for $1,000 and the master bedroom for $1500, both payments to be made at the end of the whole job. Paint paints the kitchen in substantial conformity with the specs, then unjustifiably walks off the job and never paints the bedroom. If the court is convinced that the two prices corresponded to the relative values the parties placed on each component, then Paint can recover at the contract price for the kitchen, even though he didn't substantially perform the overall contract. (But Owner can counterclaim for damages for the bedroom, if any.)

☞ **Clues to divisibility:** To set up a question that turns on divisibility, the professor will have to make it clear that each piece, and the price for it, forms a separate *"agreed equivalent."* To do this, the professor will usually have to make it clear that there is *no "cross-subsidizing,"* i.e., that each separately-quoted price is *fair for the corresponding deliverable*. (So in the above Example, you might be told that the kitchen accounted for 40% of the total labor and materials cost, and the bedroom 60%. This would be a clue that each room, and its listed price, were "agreed equivalents," making the contract divisible.)

☞ **Order of performance:** Pay attention to *order-of-performance* issues: you can't say that someone is in breach unless you first determine that her performance came due.

   ☛ **Service contracts:** The most important rule to remember: In *service* contracts, unless otherwise specified, the *total performance must be done before any payment is due.*

   Example: Painter agrees, in a single writing, to paint 3 barns for Farmer, for a total of $9,000. The contract is silent about when payment is due. After Painter paints 2 barns, he demands $6,000. Is Farmer required to pay this money now? Answer: no — Painter must paint all three barns first, then be paid all of the money.

☞ **Sale of goods:** The issue of substantial performance/material breach most often arises in fact patterns involving the *sale of goods.*

   "Perfect tender" rule: The UCC imposes the *"perfect tender"* rule: if the goods deviate from the contract even in just a *non-material* way, the buyer can *reject them*, i.e., send them back and refuse to pay.

   Example: CompCo. contracts to deliver a high-priced computer to Bank, customized to Bank's precise needs. The contract calls for delivery on May 31. CompCo. encounters some manufacturing problems, and is unable to deliver until June 30.

   Because the lateness meant that the tender failed "in any respect to conform to the contract" (UCC §2-601), Bank will be entitled to reject the computer (see next Par. below), and recover damages. That's true even if the delay did not result in material damage to Bank's economic interests. (But if CompCo. can show that by a trade usage in the custom-computer industry, a specific date for delivery is interpreted to give a 30-day leeway, then there won't be any default, and Bank can't reject.)

   ☛ **Nonbreaching party has several options.** If a buyer receives a shipment made up of both *conforming* and *defective* goods he may: *reject the whole* shipment, reject *just the part* of the shipment that's defective, or *accept the entire shipment* and sue for damages.

   ☛ **Exceptions to perfect-tender rule:** But be on the lookout for the many *exceptions* to the UCC's perfect-tender rule. Most important:

☞ **Cure:** The seller usually has a right to try to *"cure"* the non-conformity after the rejection. (But there's no right to cure a late delivery, as in the above Example.)

☞ **Revocation of acceptance:** If the buyer has *already "accepted"* the goods (e.g., paid for them, or inspected them and remained silent), the buyer may *revoke* the acceptance only if the non-performance is *substantial*.

☞ **Installment contracts:** If it's an *installment contract*, even if one installment is substantially non-conforming the buyer may not cancel the entire contract unless the problem with the one installment substantially impairs the value of the *entire* contract — instead, the buyer must *give the seller the chance to cure* the defective installment. Beware of facts that signal that the non-conforming installment doesn't impair the whole.

Example: Bathrooms 'R Us contracts to sell Apartments 40 identical sets of bathroom sinks and toilets (collectively, "fixtures"), for the renovation of a 40-unit apartment building owned by Apartments. 20 sets are due on May 1, and the other 20 on June 1. On May 1, Bathrooms tenders 19 sets, and explains that the remaining one was damaged in transit from the manufacturer to Bathrooms. Bathrooms promises to delivery a replacement for the missing one within 5 days.

Apartments must take (and immediately pay for) the 19 sets, and must give Bathrooms the chance to replace the missing one within the promised 5 days. That's because there are two strong indications that the anticipated 5-day delay in one set doesn't impair the overall value of the contract to Apartments: (1) none of the sets relies on the presence of any other sets to work (unlike, say, a missing piece of a complex machine); and (2) the circumstances indicate that the renovation project is being split into two pieces anyway, so having a slight delay on the 20th unit (which would be installed in the middle of the overall job) is very unlikely to make Apartments late in finishing the whole job. So Apartments can't cancel the whole contract, or reject the 19 sets that have been tendered.

Excuse of Conditions

☛ **Hindrance:** A party can't *willfully prevent* the occurrence of a condition. If she does, the condition is *excused*.

☞ Look for a seller of real estate who purposely thwarts the sale of the property (e.g., by placing a mortgage on it after a contract of sale has been signed). This will result in her owing the real estate commission to the broker despite the fact that the sale doesn't go through — the seller's thwarting of the sale causes the condition to the commission (sale of the property) to be excused.

☞ **Waiver:** Where a party benefits from a condition (i.e., his duty is conditional on the condition's fulfillment), always be on the lookout for a *waiver* by him.

   ☞ **Party begins to perform:** For instance, if a party *begins performance after* learning that a condition to his performance has failed to occur, he may be held to have waived the benefit of the condition.

   ☞ **Knowing and intentional:** However, don't find waivers to have occurred unless you're sure that the buyer *knowingly and intentionally* declined to take the benefit of the condition's non-occurrence.

   ☞ **Retraction:** Also, keep in mind that a waiver can always be *retracted* if the other party hasn't yet *materially relied* on it.

   Example: In a house-sale contract, assume it's a condition of S's duty to convey that B be ready to close by April 1 (and time is made "of the essence"). On March 15, S tells B, "I won't insist on an April 1 closing, May 1 is good enough." S has waived the April 1 condition. But suppose on March 17, S says, "I've changed my mind — you must close by April 1." If B hasn't materially relied on the waiver, S has successfully retracted it, and has reinstated the original condition.

Requests for Assurances of Performance

☞ **Requests generally:** If a party has reason to worry that the other party won't perform, the insecure party may *demand assurances* that the other party will be able (and willing) to perform all its obligations. The demanding party may then suspend his own performance until he receives the assurances. A failure to provide assurances is a breach.

☞ **UCC:** Remember that the "demand for assurances" procedure is expressly codified in UCC § 2-609. You should try to remember, at least approximately, this part of the section's text:

> When *reasonable grounds for insecurity* arise with respect to the *performance of either party* the other *may in writing demand adequate assurance* of due performance and until he *receives* such assurance may, if commercially reasonable, *suspend any performance* for which he has not already received the agreed return.

☞ **Writing:** Note that under the UCC, the demand for assurances must be *in writing.*

☞ **Contents of demand:** The writing can probably qualify even though it does *not use* the precise words "demand" or "assurances." It's enough if the worried party (*A*) tells the other party (*B*), in effect, "Here's why I'm worried that you won't perform. [explanation of grounds for worry] Be on notice that if you don't perform in a timely way, I will *exercise all my legal rights,* including canceling the contract."

☛ **Silence as repudiation:** Remember that, at least under the UCC, the party who receives a properly-issued demand for assurances *must* give those assurances within a reasonable time. If the recipient doesn't do this, the sender is likely to be justified in *treating the silence as a repudiation*, and therefore *canceling the contract* even *before it's time for the recipient to perform.*

☛ **Delegations and Assignments:** Demands for assurances often occur in situations where a contract has been delegated and/or assigned to another. An obligee party has a right to demand assurances from the delegate that the delegate is capable of performing under the contract, and the delegate will be deemed to have breached the contract if she does not provide such assurances.

Exam Tips on *ANTICIPATORY REPUDIATION AND OTHER ASPECTS OF BREACH*

☛ An anticipatory repudiation occurs when, *before performance is required,* a party to a contract says or does something which indicates that she *will not perform* as required. The other party's obligations are discharged, and that party may immediately sue for breach of contract.

   ☞ **Words or action:** Look for an indication by the promisor that she won't be able to perform her promise, either through a reasonably clear *statement,* or a voluntary *action* which renders performance impossible.

      Example: Sue owns a farm in County. She hires Driller to drill a well to supply her with better tasting drinking water than the County water she has been using. The contract provides for a guaranteed completion by June 1. Two hundred feet down Driller's drill strikes rock and breaks, plugging the hole. Driller tells Sue that he won't be able to complete a substitute well any earlier than August 1. Sue refuses to let Driller start the drilling of a new well, cancels the contract, and hires someone else. Sue's refusal/cancellation was not a breach of the agreement because Driller's acknowledgment that he couldn't complete the job except two months late was an anticipatory repudiation.

   ☛ **Breach must be clear:** Make sure that performance has been made *impossible* and/or that the statement of intention not to perform is *reasonably clear.*

      ☞ **Temporary inability not enough:** Remember, if the promisor takes an action which makes her only *temporarily* unable to perform, performance isn't *impossible*, just improbable. In that case, the other party's obligation is usually merely **suspended**, but not actually discharged.

Example: On the facts of the above Example, suppose that after the first hole got plugged, Driller said, "I don't think I'll be able to finish by June 1." This statement is not a repudiation, so Sue can't cancel the contract. But she could **demand assurances of performance** — for instance, she could demand that Driller explain how he plans to overcome the problems. If Driller doesn't give the explanation, she can then cancel. Also, while she's waiting for the explanation, she can **suspend** her own performance (e.g., any progress payments that the contract said she must make while the work progressed).

☞ **Statement of unhappiness not enough:** Remember that the repudiator's statement must **unequivocally** communicate that she can't or won't perform — a statement that the promisor is **unhappy** at the contract, or wishes she had an escape from it, won't suffice.

Example: *B* agrees to buy a cattle ranch from *S*. Two months before the scheduled closing date, *S* tells *B*, "I'm very unhappy I made the deal to buy your ranch, because the cattle market has weakened a lot since then. I don't intend to complete the purchase unless I'm legally obligated to do so." This won't be a repudiation, because *S* hasn't said she won't perform.

☛ **Delegation:** Watch for a fact pattern where there is a delegation of a contract for **personal services** or one calling for **special, unusual skills**. These types of contracts usually cannot be delegated; doing so probably constitutes an anticipatory repudiation.

Example: Client hires Lawyer to handle a tort suit. It is clear that Client is relying on Lawyer's particular trial skills, which are well known. Lawyer sells his practice to Barrister, a much less well-known lawyer with lesser credentials, and tells Client that Barrister will handle the case. The delegation is probably an anticipatory repudiation; if so, Client may immediately cancel the contract.

☞ **Retraction:** Remember that a repudiation, an anticipatory repudiation, or an indication of prospective unwillingness/inability to perform can initially be **retracted (withdrawn)** by the repudiator, in which case the contract is restored.

Example: In the above example, suppose that after Client objects to the delegation, Lawyer says, "OK, I'll stay on to handle your case." At that moment, Client can no longer cancel the contract, because Lawyer has retracted the repudiation. (But see immediately below for how the repudiator may lose the right to retract.)

☛ **Loss of right to retract:** The repudiation *can no longer be retracted* if any of these things happens:

❑ The other party *materially (and reasonably) relies* on the repudiation (e.g., by procuring a substitute contract).

❑ The other party *sues for breach*.

❑ The other party says that she *regards the repudiation as final.*

Example: In August, Pete enters into a written contract with Resort, a corporation that owns and operates a summer resort, providing that Pete will work as the caretaker of the hotel from the following October through April. Two weeks later, Pete enlists in the U.S. Navy for a three-year period beginning in September. Resort's owner sees notice of Pete's enlistment in the local newspaper; Resort therefore enters into a substitute contract with Mark that is identical to the one previously entered into with Pete. In September, Pete fails the navy physical examination and is rejected for service. He then tells Resort he's still counting on showing up for work. Resort has justifiably relied on the repudiation (the enlistment), so Pete cannot retract it by saying he's available; therefore Pete can't sue for breach.

☛ **Immediate suit for breach:** Remember that when a party learns of a repudiation, she may *immediately sue for breach*, even if damages have not yet accrued.

Example: In January, Buyer and Seller enter into a contract whereby Seller is to deliver 10,000 bolts per month to Buyer for a ten-month period, beginning March 1, at a cost of 10 cents per bolt. On Feb. 1, Seller notifies Buyer that he will not be delivering the bolts to Buyer because he has just contracted with another buyer for the sale of his entire output of bolts at a higher price. On Feb. 10, Buyer enters into a cover contract at a cost of 10.5 cents a bolt. Buyer may sue immediately for the cover/contract differential, even though the time for Seller's performance has not arrived, and even though Buyer has not yet laid out any money under the cover contract.

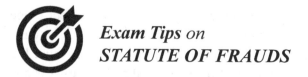

Exam Tips on
STATUTE OF FRAUDS

☛ When you come across an *oral agreement*, always ask yourself whether the agreement should be in writing. The possible violation of the **Statute of Frauds** is frequently tested and can be easily overlooked by students preoccupied with more obvious issues. Look for the following types of contracts:

Guaranty or Surety Agreement

☛ Look for a party's agreement to *pay the debt of another party* ("answer for the debt of another") in case that party defaults. *Confirm that the guaranty is in writing*.

   ☞ **"Main purpose" exception:** The most frequently tested aspect of the guaranty/surety provision is the *"main purpose"* rule: Where the guarantor's *main purpose* for entering into the guaranty agreement is to benefit *herself*, the guaranty *doesn't* have to be in writing.

      Example: Manco, a chair manufacturer, and Distribco, a company that distributes chairs, have a five-year written contract whereby Manco furnishes Distribco with chairs on credit. Distribco orders 150 chairs to be delivered by Manco directly to Cust, Distribco's customer. However, Distribco is already in arrears for 30 chairs, so Manco calls Cust and explains to Cust that, due to Distribco's outstanding bills, Manco won't provide the chairs to Cust unless Cust guarantees payment for them. Cust responds, "OK, I'll pay promises you directly for the chairs if Distribco doesn't pay." Since Cust's main purpose in making the guaranty was to ensure that he got the chairs, his guaranty promise is enforceable even though it wasn't in writing.

Land Contract Provision

☛ Remember that the Statute of Frauds applies not only to the sale of realty, but also to the transfer of *any interest in land*, such as *leasehold* interests.

   ☞ **Price required:** In a fact pattern involving a written land contract, be sure that the document includes the *price*. This is an *essential term* in a land contract and its omission will violate the Statute of Frauds.

   ☞ **Exception for part performance and detrimental reliance:** Remember that there's an exception where one party (usually the buyer) *detrimentally relies* on the oral agreement in a way that is *"unequivocally referable to the agreement"* — i.e., conduct that *would not have been undertaken had the oral contract not existed.* Most commonly on exams, this takes the form of moving on to the property and making improvements.

      Example: At X and Y's wedding, X's father, F, tells them that if they agree to live with him and take care of him for the rest of his life, he will deliver the deed to his home to them within a year. X and Y accept the offer, move into F's home, and beginning caring for him. They use their own money to add a new wing to the house, to pay off the mortgage and to pay the outstanding property taxes. After a year, *F* refuses to deliver the deed and asks *X* and *Y* to leave his home.

X and *Y* should be able to enforce the oral agreement because their actions of adding a new wing, paying off the mortgage and paying the property taxes are actions which are "unequivocally referable" to the oral agreement — that is, there's no other logical explanation for why *X* and *Y* took these actions than that the alleged oral agreement really existed.

☞ **Construction contract not covered:** A trap professors love to spring is where the contract is to ***build a structure*** on land. This is not covered by the Statute — even though it's a contract involving land, it's not a contract for the "transfer of an interest in land."

> **Example:** Contractor agrees to build a house on vacant land owned by Ohn. The contract is in writing, and calls for the house to match certain written specs, and to be completed for $100,000. While construction is in progress, Ohn orally asks for an extra room to be added, at an extra cost of $15,000. Contractor agrees, but Ohn changes his mind before the work starts. The modification will be binding even though oral, because the contract (and the modification) are not covered by the statute of frauds — this was not a contract for the transfer of an "interest in land."

One Year Provision

☛ Look to see if it would be ***impossible*** for the contract to be ***"fully performed" within a year of the time it was made.*** If so, the contract has to be in writing.

> **Example of a promise that can't be fulfilled within a year:** On August 1, 1999, Mom orally promises Daughter that if Daughter gets an average of better than 3.5 in her first year in college, Mom will pay for Daughter's second year of school. Grades for the first year won't be reported until late August of the following year. Mom's promise falls under the one-year provision (and is therefore unenforceable since not in writing), because it can't possibly be fully performed within a year of August 1, 1999.

☞ **Lifetime employment and other indefinite promises:** Don't be fooled by a party's promise to do something for an ***indefinite*** period of time — if he could die within the year yet still fully perform his promise, the contract doesn't fall within the one-year provision. For this reason, a contract for ***"lifetime employment"*** is ***not*** within the statute — the employee might die within the year, and courts look on this as being "full performance."

> **Example:** Son, S, asks his mother, M, to lend him $10,000 with which to pay past due bar bills. On September 1, M orally agrees that if S promises to go to law school and to stop drinking for the rest of his life, she will give

him $10,000 on July 1 of the following year. Because it's possible that S could die within the year and still fulfill both promises, the contract is enforceable.

☞ **Discharge:** But if a contract can only be *"discharged,"* rather than "fully performed," within a year, it *does* fall within the statute.

Example: Boss hires Worker on a 5-year oral contract. This contract is invalid because it can't be "fully performed" within one year of its making — it's true that if Worker dies, the contract will be discharged, but a discharge is not deemed to be a full performance.

Sale of Goods or Personal Property

☞ This is the most frequently tested application of the rule. Several pointers:

☞ **$500:** The Statute of Frauds comes into play — thereby requiring a *written* contract — when the agreement is for the *sale of goods for the price of $500 or more*.

☞ **Personal property:** A contract for the sale of *personal property* that is not goods (e.g., assignment of the right to receive payment under a contract) must be in writing if it's for a price of *$5,000* or more.

☞ **Goods, not services:** Make sure the contract at issue is one for goods and *not services*.

☞ A contract that's *primarily* for the provision of services doesn't fall under the sale-of-goods S/F even if goods are, as an incidental matter, to be provided by the person performing services.

☞ **Modifications:** If a fact pattern involves an oral modification of a written contract, *calculate the total value of the contract as modified,* to see whether the $500-threshold is met. If it is, the modification won't be enforceable.

Example: A written contract for the sale of 2,000 widgets at $1 per widget is orally modified for the sale of 1,000 widgets at the same price. The modified contract amount is $1,000 and must be in writing. Probably the pre-modification contract remains in force.

Trap: Watch for an initial oral contract that doesn't fall under the Statute of Frauds (because it's for less than $500), followed by an oral modification that raises the total price beyond $500. The modification won't be enforceable (and probably the original oral deal remains in force).

☞ Three important *exceptions* applicable only to UCC cases:

☞ **Acceptance or payment:** Remember that if the buyer *"accepts"* the goods (e.g., receives them and keeps them without complaint for a significant time) or ***pays*** for them, the buyer can't assert the Statute as to the accepted or paid-for goods.

Example: Over the telephone, B agrees to buy from S 1,000 widgets at $2 per widget. Several days later S sends an initial installment of 200 widgets to B. B inspects the goods and puts them in his warehouse. One week later, B calls S and says that he never had a firm contract with S and that he is going to ship the 200 widgets back to S; he also warns S not to ship the 800 remaining.

B accepted the 200 widgets (by inspecting them and not complaining), so he's bound to keep and pay for them notwithstanding the S/F. But B is not obligated to accept or pay for the other 800.

☛ **Admission:** Also, look for a statement under oath (i.e. in a pleading, during a deposition or in court testimony) in which a party ***admits*** that a contract was made. In UCC cases, the Statute of Frauds doesn't apply to the extent of such an admission (but *does* apply notwithstanding the admission in *non-UCC* cases).

☛ **Written confirmation between merchants.** Pay attention when one merchant has sent a ***written confirmation*** of the oral agreement to the other merchant. This ***memorandum*** can of course satisfy the Statute of Frauds to enforce the contract against the party who sent it, if the document contains the essential terms of the agreement. More important, it can also be used to enforce the oral agreement against the party ***receiving*** the memorandum if that party ***does not object*** to its terms within 10 days of receipt.

   ☞ **Limited to quantity in confirmation:** However, remember that under UCC §§ 2-201(1) and (2), the confirmatory memorandum is ***not binding beyond the quantity stated in it.***

   Example: StoreCo phones Manco, a manufacturer of towels, and offers to buy between 100 and 200 large beach towels (Manco's choice as to quantity), delivery to occur within 30 days, for $20 each. Manco orally agrees, without saying what quantity it will ship. Manco then immediately sends a confirmation (which StoreCo receives three days later) which says, "This confirms our agreement to sell you 100 large beach towels for 30-day delivery. /s/ Manco." 26 days later, Manco delivers 200 (not 100) large conforming beach towels to StoreCo, all of which StoreCo rejects because it has gotten a better deal on price and terms elsewhere. The price of such towels has fallen in the interim.

   Manco can enforce a contract for 100 towels, but not 200, against StoreCo. Even though StoreCo never signed anything, the confirmatory memo is binding against it, because the confirmation was: (1) between merchants; (2) signed by the sender; (3) received within a reasonable time of the oral agreement; and (4) not objected to by the recipient within 10 days of receipt. However, the memo is only binding as to the quantity stated in it — 100 — not as to the greater quantity that StoreCo orally authorized.

The Memorandum Requirement

☞ Watch out for the following testable issues regarding the *signature requirement* in order for a writing (a "memorandum" of the agreement) to satisfy the Statute:

☛ Look for a *stamped* signature. A handwritten signature isn't necessary and a stamp (or typewritten signature) is sufficient as long as it was stamped *after* the document was written. All that's needed is an "*an intent to authenticate* the document," and a stamped or typewritten signature will do that, as long as it's affixed after the document was written.

☛ The absence of a signature isn't necessarily fatal. Look for other signed documents to which the *unsigned document relates.* A majority of courts hold that when it's apparent that two or more documents refer to the same transaction, one that's unsigned may be considered part of the memorandum if there is external evidence demonstrating that the parties assented to the unsigned document.

Example: *O* contracts in a signed writing to sell Greenacre to *B*. *B* doesn't sign this writing. *B* and *X* later enter into a written agreement where *B* assigns to *X* all his rights under the contract with *O* and *X* agrees to pay the contract price for Greenacre to *O*. *B*'s signature on the assignment to *X* probably satisfies the Statute of Frauds in the *B-O* contract, and *B* is therefore bound under that contract.

Reliance as Nullifying the Statute

☛ **Estoppel:** Watch for a party who has *relied* on the oral agreement to his detriment. Some courts allow for an *estoppel* that blocks application of the Statute, where there would be great injury to the plaintiff or unjust enrichment of the defendant.

☞ **Trap:** But make sure the reliance is more than just *de minimis,* or estoppel won't apply.

Example: Over the telephone, *B* agrees to buy from *S* 1,000 widgets at $2 per widget. *S* then orders 1,000 clips from *X*, which are to be incorporated into the widgets he agreed to sell to *B*. The clips cost S $.04 a piece. *B* later cancels the contract.

S will not likely be successful if he claims detrimental reliance as a way around the Statute of Frauds problem. Although *S* relied on the contract with *B* when he ordered the 1,000 clips, his injury is not significant because the total cost of the clips was only $40. (*Note:* But this argument, though weak, is still worth making on an essay exam — you'd be showing that you are able to spot an issue and discuss its pros and cons.)

Exam Tips *on* REMEDIES

The three most frequently tested subjects from this chapter are the equitable remedy of *specific performance*, suits in *quasi-contract*, and damages in *sales contracts*. Be sure to bone up on these important topics.

Specific Performance

☛ Specific performance is the most important *equitable* remedy for test purposes. When reading a fact pattern, remember that the most important issue is *whether money damages would be adequate to protect the injured party* — if they would, that party can't get specific performance.

   ☞ **Unique good:** Look for a *rare or unusual object* that's the subject of the con-tract — money damages are less likely to be adequate, because exact substi-tutes can't be found. (*Examples:* An antique car; a highly unusual ring; a work of art.)

   ☞ **Speculative damages:** Look for cases where *damages* would be *hard to mea-sure*. This is especially likely where the contract involves a *new business or new product.*

      Example: *S* agrees to sell *B* the rights to make commercial use of a new secret-formula sauce for hamburgers. If *S* reneges and *B* sues for specific performance, *B* will have a good chance of prevailing. This is so because, due to the formula's newness, it will be hard to predict what *B*'s profits or losses would have been for the formula, making it hard for *B* to recover money damages.

   ☞ **Land contract:** In a straight contract for the sale of land in return for money, specific performance will normally be granted *to the buyer,* because courts consider each piece of land to be unique, so that the buyer can't adequately be compensated by a money-damage award.

      ☛ If the suit is brought by the *seller* (i.e., it's the buyer who refuses to close), note in your answer the possibility of several outcomes:

         ❏ Some states *allow specific performance* to be ordered on behalf of the seller.

❏ Of those who don't, some permit the seller to collect only the out-of-pocket costs incurred in making the agreement. Others permit the seller to recover only the difference between the contract price and the market price, which is often zero.

☞ **Employment contract:** An *employment contract* is *not* usually enforceable (on either side) by specific performance. This is so because employment contracts are a form of personal service contract, and enforcement would violate the public policy against involuntary servitude (if the employee is the defendant) or against forcing an employer to accept services of an unwanted worker (if the employee is the plaintiff).

☛ **Liquidated damages available:** Remember the majority rule that the existence of a *liquidated damages* award does not bar the remedy of specific performance.

> **Example:** Buyer, a corporate transferee from out of town, contracts with Seller for the purchase of Seller's house. Because Buyer plans to move her family on April 20, the contract provides that the house is to be vacant and ready for occupancy by that date. The contract also contains a liquidated damages clause and provides for payment to Buyer of $75 for each day after April 20 that the house isn't ready for occupancy. On April 20, Buyer moves her family into town and the house isn't vacant, so they stay at a motel. On May 1, Seller informs her that he doesn't intend to go through with the contract. Buyer may sue *both* for specific performance of the land contract and for liquidated damages — since specific performance would be otherwise appropriate (it's a contract for the sale of land), the court won't deny that remedy merely because Seller is also subject to a liquidated damages clause.

Expectation Damages

☛ This is the *standard measure of damages* for breach of contract. Expectation damages are awarded to *put the plaintiff in the position she would have been in had the contract been performed.*

☞ **Formula:** Expectation damages are usually calculated as:

> the *value of defendant's promised performance* (generally the contract price) *less*

> the *benefits to plaintiff* (i.e., money saved) from *not having to perform* her end of the contract.

Hint: You should always discuss expectation damages in any fact pattern where the contract was valid and one party materially breached.

☞ *Common scenario*: A contractor **partially performs,** and either the hiring party obtains a substitute performance, or the contractor wants to be reimbursed for his partial work.

> ***Substitute performance example:*** Owner owns a farm in County. She hires Driller to drill a water well. The contract provides for a guaranteed completion by June 1. The contract price is $10 a foot and Driller is to be paid $3,500 in advance, with any refund or additional payment to be made on completion. Two hundred feet down, Driller's drill strikes rock and breaks, plugging the hole. Driller refuses to start a new hole. Owner hires Dan to drill the well for $4,500. Dan strikes water at 300 feet.
>
> Because of Driller's repudiation of the contract, Owner may recover the $3,500 advanced to Driller (since she got no value for that advance) *and* the $1,500 difference between the price for the substitute performance and the contract price (which would have been $3,000 for a 300-foot well).
>
> ***Reimbursement example:*** Contractor, a building contractor, enters into a contract with Manco, a manufacturer, for the construction of a two-story factory on Manco's parcel of realty for $250,000, to be paid upon completion. When the factory is partially completed, Manco decides to retire from the manufacturing business, and tells Contractor to stop work. Contractor has already spent $180,000 on the construction and would need to spend another $35,000 to complete the building.
>
> Contractor can collect expectation damages of $215,000, calculated as the contract price ($250,000) minus the cost to him of completion ($35,000).

Reliance Damages

☞ Reliance damages come into play when expectation damages would not adequately compensate the plaintiff, or where there is no enforceable contract, but plaintiff is entitled to some protection anyway. Most commonly, reliance damages generally appear on exams in questions involving **promissory estoppel.**

☞ **Example:** Buyer and Seller orally agree that Seller will sell Blackacre to Buyer for $200,000, with Seller to deliver the property with a presently-existing unsightly shed at the back removed. Seller spends $5,000 to remove the shed. At the time for closing, Buyer fails to tender the purchase price. Seller won't be able to recover contract damages, since the contract is for the sale of an interest in land, and thus was required to be in writing. However, Seller will probably be able to recover on a promissory estoppel theory, in which case he'll recover the $5,000 spend on shed-removal, since that cost was incurred in direct and reasonable reliance on the oral agreement.

Restitution Damages

☞ Restitution damages are defined as the value *to the defendant* of the *plaintiff's performance*. (Think *unjust enrichment*.) Restitution damages can be awarded in a suit *on the contract,* or in a suit brought in *quasi-contract.*

> **Example (suit on the contract):** Duster, the owner of crop-dusting planes, enters into a contract with Farmer, a farmer, for the dusting of Farmer's crop four times a year for four years for a total of $10,000, which is paid upon the signing of the contract. After two years, Duster sells her business to Newco, assigning the contract with Farmer to Newco.
>
> If Newco fails to perform, Farmer may collect as damages from Duster the $5,000 unearned portion of the money paid to Duster, since Duster has been enriched by not performing the final two years. (Alternatively, Farmer could try to recover the "benefit of her bargain" — the amount, if any, by which the $10,000 contract price was less than Farmer's total payments would be by the time she procured a substitute duster for the last 2 years. But the point is that even without proof of cost-of-substitution, Farmer can recover the unpaid deposit on a restitution-damages theory.)

Quasi-contract

☞ Quasi-contract recovery is an important possibility to keep in mind whenever you are discussing the possible remedies available. Always consider relief based on quasi-contract when the *aggrieved party is not entitled to damages for breach of contract.* Remember that recovery will be the *reasonable value of the services rendered.* Watch for these situations:

☞ **Contract never formed:** Look for a fact pattern where an enforceable contract was never formed. The party providing the services may be entitled to recover in quasi-contract if he had a *reasonable expectation of payment* for those services (i.e., he did not intend them as a gift).

> ☞ **Common trick scenario:** A party performs *emergency services* for a person in peril. *Usual conclusion:* The savior has performed *without an expectation of payment* for services or for losses incurred as a result, and therefore *may not recover* in quasi-contract.

☞ **Contract rendered unenforceable:** Look for an originally-enforceable contract that only later *becomes* unenforceable, i.e., where a party is *excused* from performing for some reason. Although the performing party isn't entitled to contract damages, he may still be able to recover in quasi-contract. This is most likely in cases of *impossibility/impracticability* and *frustration of purpose.*

> **Example:** Owner owns a piece of undeveloped land adjacent to City

Airport. On January 2, Owner enters into a contract with Architect, an architect, whereby Architect agrees to produce and deliver by May 1 a design of a ten-story hotel which Owner wishes to build on that land. On March 31, it's announced that City Airport flight operations will cease at the end of the year, making it pointless for Owner to build the hotel. Owner refuses to accept the completed hotel design from Architect on May 1.

If Owner is excused from performing because of frustration of purpose, Architect will still be able recover the reasonable value of services rendered up until March 31, when the event excusing Owner's performance occurred.

☛ **Building destroyed before completion:** Look for a fact pattern where, through no fault of either party, the structure that is being built is *destroyed* and the contractor refuses to begin work again:

❑ If the construction is of a *new* structure, the contractor is usually allocated the risk, so he isn't excused from performing, and therefore *may not collect damages in quasi-contract* for the value of the services performed through the time of destruction.

❑ If the construction involves a repair of an *existing* structure, then the contractor will probably be *excused* from performing because of frustration of purpose and/or impossibility, since the continued existence of the building is a basic assumption upon which the contract is based. The contractor may, in that case, recover in quasi-contract for the value of the work performed up until the time of the destruction.

☞ **Partial performance, then breach:** Quasi-contract remedies are frequently used by the party who has *partially performed* but then breaches a contract, as a way to set-off the damages it owes to the nonbreaching party. Look for a *breaching contractor* who *hasn't substantially performed* but has nonetheless provided the owner with something of value.

Example: O contracts to have C, a contractor, build O a house on O's land. The contract price is $300,000. C does about half the work, then defaults. The reasonable value to O of the work done is $125,000. C has received a $60,000 deposit. It will cost O $225,000 to get another contractor to finish the job (meaning that if O has to pay the full value of C's work less the deposit, O will be $50,000 worse off than had C fully performed). C can recover $15,000, calculated as follows:

> *Reasonable value of work done,* less *deposit received* and less *O's damages for the breach,* or

> $125,000 minus ($60,000 + $50,000) = $15,000

Consequential Damages

☞ **Extra damages:** If the standard expectation measure doesn't fully compensate a party for her losses, remember that the additional damages can also be recovered. These are often called *"consequential"* damages.

> **Example:** C agrees to renovate O's house for $50,000, by March 1. C gets a $25,000 deposit, does half the work, then defaults. O hires a replacement, X, who finishes the job for $25,000. The standard expectation "benefit of the bargain" measure would give O $0 recovery, because there is no difference between the contract and market price. But if X can't finish the job until April 30, and O can't move in during the month of April, O will probably be able to recover the cost of procuring substitute lodging for that month — the lodging costs will be "consequential" damages, and will be on top of the contract/market **differential.**

☞ **Foreseeability:** But remember that consequential damages are subject to an important limitation: the requirement of *foreseeability*. Determine whether the additional losses were either: (1) *reasonably foreseeable* to an objective observer in D's shoes, based on general principles; or (2) foreseeable based on the plaintiff's *special requirements,* of which D had *notice.* (Remember that this is basically the rule of *Hadley v. Baxendale*.) If the losses don't fall into either category, they're not recoverable.

> **Example:** Seller and Buyer enter into a contract for the sale of 10,000 pounds of specifically described bolts each month for a period of ten months beginning March 1; the contract has a total value of $40,000. On March 1, Seller informs Buyer that he will not deliver any bolts to Buyer because he has just contracted to sell his entire output to another buyer for a higher price. It takes Buyer 61 days to find a new supplier; the new supplier charges the same price. Because of the delay in finding a new supplier, Buyer is late in delivering motors to End User, a company with which Buyer has a contract containing a valid liquidated damages clause providing for damages of $10,000 a day for delays in delivery of motors. Although Seller knew that Buyer sold motors, Seller didn't know about Buyer's specific contract with End User. May Buyer recover from Seller the $610,000 he is required to pay End User under the liquidated damages clause?
>
> Probably not, because it probably wasn't foreseeable to Seller that a 2-month delay in delivery on a $40,000 contract would bring about $610,000 in losses. Buyer's needs — in particular his need to avoid heavy liquidated damages — were probably "special requirements" that cannot be the basis for recovery unless Seller knew about them at the time of contracting.

Mitigation

☛ Be sure to discuss whether the nonbreaching party has attempted to *mitigate damages* in a situation where the loss was partially or totally avoidable — if she didn't, any damages that would probably have been avoided by such an attempt are non-recoverable.

   ☞ Look for a *terminated employee,* who fails to make reasonable efforts to find a suitable *replacement job.*

   ☞ Look for a *disappointed buyer or recipient of services.*

> **Example:** *B*, the owner of a furnace-repair company, maintains a fleet of personal trucks for his employees' use and drives his personal station wagon when visiting customers' homes. On February 15, *B* orders a new station wagon from *S*, a car dealer, to be delivered by March 5. On March 4, *B* sells his old station wagon because of the expected delivery of the new car the following day. However, the new car isn't delivered to *S* until March 30. *B* sues *S* for lost profits because of his inability to travel to customers. *B* won't recover for this: although business losses were foreseeable at the time of contracting, *B* could have mitigated his damages by renting a car or using one of the company's trucks.

Liquidated Damages

☛ **Reasonableness:** Remember that the liquidated damages amount will be deemed (in most courts) reasonable if it is a reasonable estimate as of *either* the *time of contracting* or the *time of the actual loss.* Normally, you should try to analyze the reasonableness as of *each* time frame.

☛ Other points to watch for:

   ☞ **Problems not covered by the clause:** Pay attention to what the clause remedies. Even where the clause is enforceable, other types of damages can still be awarded to address *problems not covered by the clause.*

> **Example:** *O* and *C*, a contractor, enter into an agreement for various repairs to be made to *O*'s home. The contract provides that the repairs are to be completed within sixty days, and that if *C* fails to complete the job on time, *C* will pay *O* $50 per day as liquidated damages. After the repairs are finished, *O* discovers that *C* did a faulty job on one aspect, the roof; she has another contractor redo the repair for $1,000. Since the liquidated damages clause only redresses *late* performance, it doesn't eliminate the possibility of *O*'s collecting damages for *defective* performance in the amount of $1,000.

   ☞ **Blunderbuss clauses:** Be on the lookout for *"blunderbuss"* clauses, where the clause gives the *same damage award regardless of the severity* of the breach. Such a clause is likely to be a penalty, at least where it ends up costing D much more than the *actual* damages she's caused.

> **Example:** Boss is a CPA and Emp is his employee (also a CPA) under a two-year contract. As part of the contract, Emp agrees to a non-compete, under which if Emp leaves and does work for any client of Boss during the two years, Emp owes Boss damages equal to three months' salary ($30,000). Emp quits and, with one week left in the two years, does $100 of work for one client of Boss. This "blunderbuss" clause (same $30,000 of damages assessed regardless of how much the competition cost Boss in lost revenues) will be found to be an unenforceable penalty.

Damages in Sales Contracts

☛ **Buyer's damages:** This area is more heavily tested than that of seller's damages. Several reminders:

   ☞ **Standard "contract/market" differential:** If a buyer returns defective goods (or fails to receive any shipment of goods from the seller) and doesn't purchase replacement goods elsewhere, she is entitled to the difference between the *contract price* and the *market price* at the time of breach.

   ☞ **Cover:** If a buyer returns defective goods (or fails to receive any shipment of goods from the seller) and *purchases them elsewhere*, she is entitled to the difference between the *contract* price and the *cover* price.

      ☛ The buyer's *cover price paid by the buyer must be reasonable in the circumstances*. Look the buyer's attempts to find a good price (or at least to verify the true "market" price) — if these are absent, discuss the possibility that the buyer may have behaved unreasonably and should be denied the full contract/cover differential.

   ☞ Remember that if the market price (or the cover price) and the contract price are the *same, there are no damages to collect*, except consequential or incidental ones.

      ☛ *Note:* Where the market price or cover price is *less* than the contract price, the buyer gets the benefit of the difference with no off-setting to what the seller owes for consequential or incidental damages.

   ☞ **Breach of warranty:** If a buyer accepts defective goods the damages are calculated as the difference between the value which the delivered goods had at the time of acceptance and the value which conforming goods would have had at the time.

   ☞ **Specific Performance:** The buyer can only get specific performance if the goods are *unique*.

☛ **Seller's damages:** The most testable issue in this area is whether a seller can be compensated for **lost profits**. *Trick:* The seller appears to have suffered no damage because he resold the item or items for the contract price or for an amount in excess of the contract price. Your inquiry should not end there, however.

    ☞ **"Lost volume" seller:** Look for a seller who has a **supply of goods in excess of the level of demand** (the **"lost volume"** seller). He has lost a sale and is entitled to his lost profits — even if he resold the goods in question — because he could have had *both* sales but for the breach.

        Example: *S*, a computer reseller, contracts to sell a Model 101 Xtra personal computer (made by Xtra Corp.) to *B*, for $3,000, delivery to occur Oct. 1. (The price from Xtra to *S* will be $2,200.) On Oct. 1, *B* unjustifiably repudiates. *S* resells the same computer to *T* for the same $3,000. The Model 101 is a popular computer, and *S* can get as many of it as he wants from Xtra, with rapid delivery. What are *S*'s damages?

        S is a lost volume seller — although he's sold the computer in question to a different buyer for the same price, he's lost one net sale due to *B*'s breach, since *S* could have a different copy of the 101 to *T* if B had honored the contract. Therefore, *S* is entitled to $800 (plus any incidental damages), representing the profit that *S* would have made on the sale to *B* if it had occurred.

    ☛ **Limited supply:** But if the seller resells *all* the available goods of the type that is the subject of the contract, then he is *not* a lost-volume seller and cannot collect lost profits for the breach.

☛ **Deduct costs:** Remember to deduct from all recoveries the **costs** that the aggrieved buyer or seller **didn't incur** as a result of not having to complete his performance.

Punitive Damages

☛ Remember that punitive damages are ordinarily **not recoverable** in breach-of-contract actions. (However, if the breach was also independently a tort — as in fraud — punitives may be recoverable.)

Exam Tips on *CONTRACTS INVOLVING MORE THAN TWO PARTIES*

Material from this chapter is heavily tested. Look for a fact pattern where rights or duties are created in a third person either when or after the contract has been executed.

Assignment and Delegation

☞ Remember that an *assignment* is a transfer of contract *rights,* and a *delegation* is a transfer of contract *duties*.

☞ Be sure to check whether the contract may be assigned, and/or delegated:

When assignment is allowed:

☞ **Consideration:** Don't worry if the assignment isn't supported by *consideration*. Consideration is unnecessary where there's a present transfer of rights.

☞ **Generally permissible:** Where the contract is *silent* on whether assignment is allowed, the contract is *assignable,* even without the obligor's consent.

☞ **Anti-assignment clause:** If a contract contains an anti-assignment clause, an act of assignment gives the obligor a right to *damages* against the assignor for breach, but *does not render the assignment ineffective* (unless the assignment imposes a material additional burden on the obligor, or would be void for some other reason independent of the anti-assignment clause).

When delegation is allowed:

☞ **Nondelegable duties:** In delegation cases, check that the duties are in fact delegable. Remember that the main rule is that delegation is permitted unless the obligee (the one to whom the delegated performance is due) has a *"substantial interest in having the delegator perform."*

☞ **Personal services:** Contracts for performance of *personal services* are generally *not delegable* by the person who would do the work.

Example 1: Contracts of *employment*, which are not be delegable by the employ*ee*.

Example 2: Contracts with *independent contractors possessing special personal skills,* such as musical performers, interior decorators, architects, computer programmers, etc.

Note: In these personal-service circumstances, the delegation may be deemed an *anticipatory repudiation,* in which case the obligee can immediately cancel the contract and sue the delegator for breach.

☞ **Construction contracts:** Generally, an obligation under a *construction contract* is *not* considered a personal service and may be assigned.

☞ *Important distinction:* A *delegation* of the duty to perform personal services is more likely prohibited than an *assignment* of the right to receive the services (which is prohibited only if it materially alters the duty of the obligor).

Example 1: The rights to receive the benefits of a one-year contract for gardening services performed for an owner of a condominium may probably be transferred to the party to whom he sells the condominium. (The duty to make payment may also be assigned, though the assignor remains liable as guarantor.)

Example 2: The rights to a musical performance at one party's wedding may be transferred to another party having a wedding, if all the contract terms (place, time, date, contract price) are the same.

☞ **Waiver:** Remember that even if the contract is nondelegable, the right to object may be *waived*.

> **Example:** Ohn, the owner of a piece of undeveloped land, enters into a contract with Arch, an architect, whereby Arch agrees to produce and deliver by May 1 a design of a ten-story hotel to be built on the land. On January 15, because of health problems, Arch is ordered to take a six-month break from work by his physician. Arch signs a documents "assigning" to Bench — a well-known architect with whom Arch has sometimes collaborated — all Arch's rights and duties under the contract with Ohn. One week later, Bench meets with Ohn to discuss preliminary plans with him. Thereafter, he communicates with Ohn by phone. When Bench submits the completed design on May 1, Ohn refuses to accept it.
>
> Ohn, by failing to object to the assignment during his initial encounters with Bench, has probably waived his right to object.

☞ **Demand for assurances:** When the party who is owed the performance receives notice of a delegation of duties, she may demand *assurances of performance* from the delegate, and may suspend her own performance until assurances are furnished.

☛ **Rights and obligations on assignor/delegator side:** Remember to evaluate the *rights* and *obligations* of the *assignor or delegator.*

Assignor's right to revoke:

☞ **Assignor relinquishes rights:** In an assignment, an assignor's rights are *extinguished* once there has been an effective assignment. Therefore, don't make the mistake of allowing the assignor to sue to enforce rights previously held by her.

☞ **Assignments for consideration are irrevocable:** Also, watch for an assignment that is supported by *consideration* — such an assignment is *irrevocable*, so the assignor can't change her mind and cancel the assignment.

☛ **Gratuitous assignment:** By contrast, a *gratuitous* assignment is *revocable* by the assignor, unless one of the following happens:

❑ the assignor *delivers a symbolic document* evidencing the rights (e.g., hands over a bankbook, which would make assignment of the bank account irrevocable);

❑ the assignor puts the assignment in *writing*;

❑ the assignee *foreseeably relies* to his detriment on the assignment; or

❑ the obligor *gives performance* to the assignee.

Delegator's ongoing liability:

☞ A delegation of contract duties doesn't divest the *delegator* of her obligations to the obligor. Thus, *the delegator can be sued if the delegate breaches.*

Example: Store, a retailer of home gardening supplies, enters into a one-year contract with Seedco, a wholesaler of seeds, whereby Seedco will supply Store with all of its requirements for rye grass seeds on a monthly basis. After delivering one delivery of rye grass seeds to Store, Seedco sells its business to Byer, who fulfills Store's next month's requirement of seeds. Store pays Byer for the seeds, but also demands that Byer assure it that it will be able to meet Store's future rye grass seed needs. Five weeks later Store has still not heard from Byer and notifies Seedco and Byer that it's canceling the contract.

Store may successfully sue *Seedco* for breach of contract — the delegation by Seedco to Byer did not relieve Seedco of liability if Byer should not perform.

☞ *Trap:* A fact pattern may indicate that an obligee has *consented* to the delegation. This consent does *not* relieve the delegator of liability, unless the obligee *explicitly agrees* to release the delegator (in which case there is said to be a "novation.")

☛ **Rights and obligations of assignee:** Also, analyze the *rights* of the *assignee.*

☞ **Assignee's rights:** The assignee is entitled to *enforce the contract rights* to the same extent that the assignor could have — the assignee *"steps in to the assignor's shoes."*

☛ **Subject to defenses:** However, the assignee's right to enforce the contract is *subject to any defenses* which could have been asserted against the assignor, such as *breach* of the assignor's return promise, *lack of consideration*, or occurrence of a *condition* to the defendant's duty.

Example: Pawn, a pawnbroker, sells to Jewel, owner of a jewelry store, a ring for $2,500, representing it to contain a diamond. The following month, Pawn sells Jewel a pearl necklace for $2,200, to be paid for within thirty days. Before Jewel pays for the necklace, he learns that the ring he previously purchased contains a cubic zirconia and is worth only $300. A day later, Pawn assigns his rights to payment for the necklace to Art. Since Art steps into Pawn's shoes, if Art sues Jewel for payment on the necklace, Jewel can successfully assert against Art (at least as a set-off to reduce Art's recovery) the breach-of-contract claim regarding the ring.

☞ **Warranty of no defenses:** An assignor (at least one who assigns for value, rather than as a gift) makes an *implied warranty* that at the time of the assignment, the obligor has *no defenses.*

Example: Thus in the above example, if Pawn assigns to Art for value his right to payment from Jewel, Pawn has impliedly warranted to Art that Jewel has no defenses. Since Jewel has a defense against Pawn, Pawn has breached the implied warranty and is liable to Art for any amount by which Art's claim against Jewel is reduced.

☞ **Modification of assignee's rights by original parties:** In assignment scenarios, professors love to test whether/when the two original parties (the obligor [who owes the duty] and the assignor) may *modify the assignee's rights.* Remember that the assignee's rights depend on whether the modification took place *before or after* the assignee got notice of the assignment:

☛ **Modification before notice:** If the modification takes place *before* the assignee gets *notice of the assignment* (not the scenario that's usually tested), the modification is *binding* no matter what.

☛ **Modification after notice:** But if the modification occurs *after* the assignee has received notice of the assignment, the modification is binding *only if the assignor has not yet fully performed.*

Example: Conti, a contractor, agrees to build a house for Owen, at a price of $300,000. Since Conti owes $400,000 to Bert, Conti's brother, Conti assigns to Bert Conti's right to receive payment from Owen, and immediately notifies Bert of the assignment. Then, Owen and Conti agree to a price reduction to $250,000. If the price reduction occurred before Conti finished the work, Bert is bound. But if the reduction occurred after Conti finished, the reduction is not binding on Bert, and Bert can sue for the whole $300,000.

☛ **Multiple assignments:** Also, look for a fact pattern where there have been *two assignments* of the same right. If the first assignment is irrevocable, then, generally, that first assignee has priority.

☞ **Prior payment as defense:** Remember that timing also counts where the obligor pays (or gives performance to) the assignor instead of the assignee. If the obligor pays the assignor (in part or in full) or gives the required performance *before he has received notice of the assignment*, he may *use this as a defense* against the assignee. But if the obligor renders payment/performance to the assignor *after* learning of the assignment, she may *not* use this as a defense vis a vis the assignee.

> **Example:** In the above example, suppose Owen paid $200,000 to Conti (rather than to Bert) after Owen got notice of the assignment. Owen would not be able to use this payment as a set-off in an action for the $300,000 brought against him by Bert.

☞ **Assignee's obligations:** Typically, the assignee will have *obligations* to *both the assignor and to the original promisee*, since the latter will be a third-party beneficiary. So either can sue the assignee if he breaches.

> **Example:** Chef hires Delegator, a famous interior designor, to have Delegator design Chef's new restaurant. Delegator hires Newdes, another designer, to take over the project. Chef allows the deligation to take place (notice that he doesn't have to, since the contract involves Deligator's unique personal skills). Newdes fails to do the work properly.
>
> Newdes can be sued by both Chef and Delegator. First, Chef can sue Newdes — Chef was almost certainly an intended beneficiary of the Delegator-Newdes contract (Chef was to receive Newdes' performance, and Delegator clearly intended that Chef be benefitted by Newdes' taking over Delegator's role — see the discussion of third-party beneficiaries immediately *infra*). If, instead, Chef chooses to sue Delegator (which he can do because the delegation did not let Delegator off the hook), Delegator can sue Newdes to be made whole — Newdes owed the obligation of performance both to Delegator (the promisee of Newdes' promise to perform) *and* to Chef (the third-party beneficiary of that promise).

Third Party Beneficiaries

☛ This topic is always a favorite on exams. The two most important issues to concentrate on are the distinction between intended and incidental beneficiaries, and the analysis of whether an intended beneficiary's rights have vested.

☞ **Intended vs. incidental:** You must distinguish between these two types of beneficiaries, because the *intended* beneficiary may *enforce* the contract whereas the *incidental beneficiary cannot.*

> ☛ **Creditor:** If the agreement is to *pay money* that one of the original parties owes to a third party, that third party is an intended beneficiary, and may sue. (This is the classic "creditor beneficiary" situation).
>
> **Example:** Own hires Gard to landscape Own's property for $90,000. The

contract provides that Own is to pay $80,000 to Gard and the balance is to paid to Cred, to whom Gard owes money. Cred is an intended beneficiary of the contract between Own and Gard. Therefore, Cred may sue if Own doesn't pay.

☛ **To whom performance runs:** Look at whether the performance *runs directly* from the promisor to the third party. If it does, the beneficiary is probably "intended." If not, the beneficiary is probably incidental.

Example: Whole, a wholesaler, agrees to supply to Ret, a retailer, 100 bicycles made by Manco. Ret is to pay Whole, who will then order from, and pay, Manco. Because Ret's performance (payment) is to run to Whole, not to Manco, Manco is not an intended beneficiary, and may not sue Ret if Ret cancels the contract.

☛ **Promisee's intent:** Pay the closest attention to the intent of the *promisee*, not the promisor — if the promisee didn't intend to benefit the third party, the latter is not an intended beneficiary.

   ☞ *Trap:* The mere fact that a third party is *mentioned* in a contract doesn't automatically mean that he's an intended beneficiary. Analyze whether the promisee really intended to benefit the third party.

   Example: Cli owes Lawr money for legal services. Lawr suggests to Cli, "I'd like you to pay me off by buying my nephew Neff a Goldray Special from the Zebra Car Agency — they've got good prices there." Cli responds, "If that's what you want, I'll be glad to do it." Neff is an intended beneficiary, because it's clear that Lawr (the promisee, to whom Cli owes money) intends to benefit Neff. (The fact that Cli has no particular desire to benefit Neff is irrelevant). On the other hand, there's no indication that Lawr intended to benefit Zebra — Lawr seems to have suggested Zebra by name merely because she wanted a good price, not because she had an affirmative desire to benefit Zebra. Therefore, Zebra is merely an incidental beneficiary.

☞ **Vesting as a bar to modification or discharge:** In exam fact patterns the two original parties often try to *modify or discharge* the obligation after it comes into existence. The general rule is that they may do this, but only until the beneficiary's rights have *"vested."* Vesting occurs when the beneficiary does one of these 3 things:

    ❏ she *manifests assent* to the promise,

    ❏ she *brings suit* on the promise, or

    ❏ she *materially changes her position in justifiable reliance* on the promise.

Examples of justifiable reliance: (1) A freelance book illustrator who is the beneficiary of full-time employment for a year notifies her other clients that she can't work for them. (2) A person who is the beneficiary of a promise to convey land cancels a contract for the purchase of a different parcel.

☞ **Beneficiary doesn't know of contract:** A common exam situation is that the beneficiary *doesn't know of the contract* prior to the time it's discharged or modified. In this situation, the beneficiary obviously can't do any of the 3 vesting events (manifest assent to the promise, bring suit on it, or materially change her position). Therefore, the original parties can modify or discharge the contract with impunity.

Example: Frank, owner of a house, hires Paynt, a painting contractor, to paint Frank's residence. The contract price is $5,000, provided that Paynt delivers a "satisfactory result." A provision in the contract directs that payment be made to Paynt's daughter, Dot (intended as a wedding gift). When the job is completed, Frank says he doesn't find it "satisfactory." Paynt agrees to settle for a lower price of $4,500, provided the money's paid directly to him. Paynt doesn't give any of the money to Dot. Shortly thereafter, Dot finds out about the promise, and sues both Paynt and Frank for breach of the agreement. Dot will lose, because prior to the settlement (a modification), Dot didn't manifest assent to receiving the money, didn't bring suit on the agreement, and didn't materially change her position in reliance. Therefore, Dot's rights never vested.

Exam Tips on IMPOSSIBILITY, IMPRACTICABILITY, AND FRUSTRATION

☞ Exams often hint at the possibility of a defense based on Impossibility/Impracticability/Frustration (we'll call this "I/I/F" for short). Usually, your fact pattern won't mention any of these defenses — it'll be up to you to spot the issue, based on the fact that some unlikely event has occurred that makes it difficult or senseless for one party to perform.

Issues Common to Impossibility, Impracticability, and Frustration

☞ **Failure of basic assumption:** Remember the basic standard for when I/I/F applies: it applies only when the parties made the contract on the *basic assump-*

tion that the contingency in question *would not occur.* When you try to decide whether this test is met, focus on three sub-issues:

(1) Assumptions shared by both parties: Look first to see if *both* parties made this underlying basic assumption — if the party who's trying to avoid a discharge (i.e., who's trying to enforce the contract) *didn't know* that the contract was predicated on that assumption, I/I/F won't apply.

> **Example 1:** Stu, a high school senior, interviews with Count, an accountant, for a position in his firm in January. Count then writes to Stu: "I offer you employment with my firm, beginning August 1, at $25,000 a year." Stu accepts the offer several days later. In March, Count sends Stu a letter stating: "It was my intention in hiring you to have you work with my International Union account. However, the Union no longer retains my firm. Therefore, I lack the funds and will not hire you. Good luck in securing other employment."
>
> If Count asserts the defense of frustration, Stu can successfully contend that he wasn't apprised of the special reason for hiring him. Therefore, the keeping of the account wasn't a "basic assumption" of the contract, and Count can't be excused on grounds of frustration.
>
> **Example 2:** In January, *O* and *A* enter into a contract under which *A* will design a ten-story hotel to be built on a piece of land owned by *O* adjacent to City Airport. The design is to be delivered on or before May 1. *A* is aware that *O*'s interest in building a hotel is on account of the business that will come from travellers using the airport. In March, the government announces that the airport will shut down at the end of the year.
>
> *O* will probably be able to argue successfully that the continuation of the airport's operation was a basic assumption under both parties made the design contract. If he can show this, he'll probably be able to have the contract excused on frustration grounds.

(2) Foreseeability: Remember that the more *foreseeable* the contingency was, the *less like* it is that the contingency represents the failure of a basic assumption.

> ☛ Circumstances which *are* usually foreseeable, and that therefore probably won't lead to discharge:
>
> > ☞ **Increase in costs.** Look for a sudden large increase in the *cost* of labor or materials which the seller of goods or services claims makes it impossible to perform. Usually, such difficulties were relatively foreseeable when the contract was made, in which case they probably *won't* excuse performance. (But this won't always be true: if the cost increase is due to a truly unforeseen type of event — a sudden industry-wide strike, outbreak of war, etc. — impossibility will generally apply.)

☞ Circumstance which *may or may not* be deemed foreseeable:

☞ **Weather conditions.** Look for bad storms that either push off the date of completion of performance or destroy a crop. Note in your answer that foreseeability probably depends upon whether that type of weather was usual for that time of year in that region.

(3) Risk allocation: The last step in determining whether a party's obligations have been discharged because of I/I/F is to make sure that the *risk* of one of these outcomes wasn't implicitly *allocated to that party* by the contract.

☞ **F.O.B. contracts:** Watch for "F.O.B." and the name of a location in an agreement for the sale of goods. The phrase means that the parties agreed that the risk of loss would not pass to the buyer until the goods were delivered to a carrier at the location specified. Thus if the location specified is the *buyer's* factory ("F.O.B. buyer's plant"), the buyer does not assume the risk until the goods arrive at her factory.

Example: *B* agrees to purchase fifty gallons of chemicals from *S* at $5 a gallon "F.O.B. *B*'s factory." *S* delivers the chemicals to *T*, a trucking company, which loads it onto its truck. While en route to the city where *B*'s factory is located, the truck is hijacked by thieves. *B* doesn't have to pay for the chemicals (she's discharged from the contract), because the risk of loss didn't yet pass to her.

☞ **Fixed-price contracts:** When *S* agrees to sell goods to *B* at a *fixed price,* the existence of the fixed price usually means that the parties have agreed to allocate the risk of an *increase* in market prices to the *buyer*, and of a *decrease* in market prices to the *seller*. However, a truly unforeseen many-fold market-price increase (e.g., 10x) might be sufficient.

☞ **Technology breakthroughs:** If *S* agrees to develop a customized product for *B*, and both parties understand that the product will need to develop or use *new, unproven, technology*, the court will almost certainly find that the parties allocated to *S* the risk of an inability to develop the needed technology. (*Example:* CompCo agrees to develop a new type of computer to meet Bank's special needs. If CompCo can't develop the new computer, it can't rely on impracticability to escape the deal, even if CompCo's failure comes despite its having made all reasonable development efforts.)

☞ **Supervening illegality:** When you find a fact pattern where parties have entered into an *illegal contract,* pay attention to *when* it became illegal. If it became illegal because of a change in law that took effect after the formation of the contract, then the frustration or impossibility defenses may apply. But if the illegality existed before the contract was signed, and one or both parties were unaware, analyze the problem under illegality (next chapter), not I/I/F.

Example: In February, *L*, a landlord, and *T*, a tenant, enter into a written lease agreement for two years beginning April 1 whereby *T* is to rent a building for use as a "sports book," an establishment where bets are made on horse races and other sporting events. The rent is $1,000 per month and 20 percent of *T*'s gross profits. *T* gives *L* a $2,000 deposit. Between the time of the signing of the lease and April 1, a law is passed which makes the operation of sports books illegal.

T may sue for the refund of his deposit and the parties will be excused from performing. This is so because *T*'s purpose, of which *L* was aware, has been frustrated by the supervening illegality.

Distinguishing between Impracticability and Frustration

☞ Both impracticability and frustration involve a significant event whose ***non-occurrence*** was a ***basic assumption*** on which the parties based the agreement. So it can be confusing to know which one to apply on given facts. Here's an easy way to tell which doctrine probably applies:

❑ where it is the ***seller or supplier*** of goods, land or services who wishes to escape the bargain, that party typically claims ***impracticability***; whereas

❑ where it is a ***buyer or recipient*** of goods, land or services who wishes to escape the bargain, that party typically claims ***frustration***.

Frustration of Purpose — Special Issues

☞ **Total frustration required:** When dealing with a fact pattern where one party claims frustration of purpose, make sure the purpose is ***totally*** (not just partially) ***frustrated***.

☞ **Illness:** For instance, in cases not involving personal services, a party's ***serious illness*** may not lead to total frustration, in which case it probably won't lead to excuse for frustration.

Example: Sol, a homeowner, enters into a written contract with Byer for the sale of Sol's house in Illinois. Three months later Byer informs Sol that he's retiring down South because he has suffered a heart attack, and that he therefore won't be going through with the deal. If Sol sues Byer for breach of contract, Byer won't be excused from performing because of frustration — Byer could still buy the house and re-sell it, so his illness and retirement probably haven't totally deprived him of all possible benefits from the transaction.

☞ **Extreme drop in market value:** Look for situations in which a buyer who has agreed to pay a ***fixed price*** for goods, land or services relies on ***an extreme drop in the market value of the contracted-for item*** as the reason she should be allowed to escape the contract by use of frustration.

☞ **Claim usually fails:** In such a situation, you should probably say that the buyer's claim of frustration will *fail*. Point out that where buyer and seller agree on a *fixed price* or fee for a good or service, allocating the *risk of a plunge* in market prices to the buyer is probably the *very purpose* of the contract.

Impossibility — Special Issues

☛ When you're dealing with a fact pattern where one party claims impossibility, make sure performance is *totally impossible*, and that the event creating the impossibility was *unforeseeable* at the time of formation.

  ☞ **Destruction of subject matter:** Destruction isn't always an excuse.

  ❑ First, determine whether the parties *allocated* the risk to the party seeking to be excused — if it was, then impossibility/impracticability won't apply.

  Example: Where a builder agrees to build a new structure, most courts say that the builder implicitly assumes the risk of total destruction of the structure during construction (unless the contract expressly says otherwise).

  ❑ Next, if the risk remained with the party claiming impossibility, determine whether the subject matter is *replaceable* on a commercially sensible basis — if so, impossibility won't apply.

  Example: *B* enters into a written agreement to purchase 100 standard air conditioning units from *S*, F.O.B. *B*'s warehouse. While the truck carrying the units is en route to *B*'s warehouse, it overturns and the shipment is destroyed. Because *S* could readily obtain replacement units, *S* won't be excused on account of the destruction. (But *S would* be excused if what was being delivered was, say, a one-of-a-kind painting.)

  ☛ Also, make sure that the impossibility isn't due to the *fault* of the party claiming impossibility.

Impracticability — Special Issues

☛ **Increased expense:** Although an *increased expense* generally doesn't rise to the level of fulfilling the requirements for an impossibility defense, some jurisdictions sometimes allow a party to use the increased costs as an *impracticability defense*.

  ☞ **Extreme increase:** In addition to ensuring that the parties didn't allocate the risk (e.g., an explicitly fixed-price sales contract), make sure that the impracticality is *extreme.* Probably the cost of performance should be a minimum of five times the anticipated cost.

☞ **Slight reduction in profitability:** Also, make sure that the increase wouldn't just make performing *slightly* unprofitable. (For instance, even a 10x increase in the cost of one component wouldn't suffice, if the component was only a very small percentage of the seller's overall costs.)

Consequence of Excuse

☞ Remember that *if parties are excused from performing, contract damages aren't awarded, because there hasn't been a breach*.

☞ However, *quasi-contractual remedies* for the value of *work performed* (or benefits rendered) may be appropriate. (See the chapter on Remedies).

Exam Tips on
MISCELLANEOUS DEFENSES

☞ The defenses in this chapter don't appear as frequently on exams as do those that are covered in the previous chapter. Basically focus your efforts on capacity, illegality and unconscionability.

Capacity

☞ **Disaffirmance generally:** Where one party was *under 18* at the time of the contract, remember that the minor has the power to "*disaffirm*" (avoid) the contract, whether before or shortly after reaching 18.

☞ **Who may disaffirm:** Pay attention to who's attempting to disaffirm. *Only the minor may disaffirm*, not the other party.

> **Example:** Myner, a minor, and Deal, a motorcycle dealer, enter into a written agreement for the sale of a new motorcycle to Myner for $1,000, to be paid on delivery within two weeks. One week later, Deal notifies Myner that the motorcycle is ready for delivery, but that Deal will not deliver it unless Myner shows proof of majority or brings an adult as a co-purchaser. If Myner sues Deal for breach of contract, Myner will be successful because Deal is obligated to perform — only Myner can disaffirm the contract.

☞ **Offset:** If the minor is suing for rescission or restitution, her recovery is *offset by the reasonable value of the benefit* which she has received.

> **Example:** Mine, a minor, purchases a used car from Carman for $3,000. After two months, the steering fails, and Mine decides that the car is

unsafe to drive. Therefore, she returns it to Carman and demands her money back. If the reasonable rental value of the car is $300 a month, Mine is entitled to $2,400 (purchase price less 2 months' rental value) when she returns the car.

☛ **Recovery of value of "necessaries":** Furthermore, even if it's the non-minor who is suing, if the non-minor supplied *"necessaries"* to the minor (e.g., badly-needed food, shelter or medical care), then the supplier can recover in *quasi-contract* for the fair value of the supplies, even if the minor disaffirms the actual contract.

Illegality

☛ Make sure *both parties are aware of the purpose* of the contract (though not necessarily aware of the illegality of that purpose). If only one party is aware, that party won't be able to claim illegality.

> **Example:** Tenn enters into a 2-year lease for premises from Land. Tenn intends to use the premises for an illegal bookmaking operation. At the time of the lease, Land has no idea that this is Tenn's purpose. Tenn will not be able to have the agreement declared void for illegality, because Land did not know of the illegal purpose; however, Land will probably be able to void the agreement.

☞ **Severable:** Look for a contract whose primary purpose isn't illegal, but which contains an illegal provision. Argue that the illegal provision should be *severed* and the remaining provisions enforced if these condition are all met:

❏ the contract is *divisible* (i.e. there are corresponding pairs of part performances),

❏ the illegality doesn't affect the *entire agreement*, and

❏ the party seeking performance *hasn't engaged in serious misconduct*.

> **Example:** A premarital agreement is signed by Wilma, a pregnant woman, and Alan, the man with whom she lives. The agreement provides, among other things, that in case of divorce, Alan will not be responsible for payment of child support for the unborn child, in return for the Alan's advance relinquishment of custody and visitation rights. A state statute says that mothers may not agree to waive the right to child support.
>
> The "no child support" provision is arguably severable, since: (1) the child support and custody provision are arguably a "corresponding pair of part performances; (2) other aspects of the agreement (e.g., division of property) are not affected by the illegal provision; and (3) signing the clause does not constitute serious misconduct by either party. If the court agrees, either Wilma or Alan may enforce the con-

tract, except that the court will not enforce the child-support provision (or, probably, the custody/visitation waiver, since that was part of the illegal trade).

Unconscionability

☛ Look for a contract involving a ***consumer***. The unconscionability defense is rarely applied to a contract between businesspeople.

   ☞ Consider applying the doctrine in any non-UCC context involving a consumer contract, where the party seeking to use the doctrine has **substantially weaker bargaining power** and the contract or clause seems substantively or procedurally "unfair" to you.

      Example: Same facts as the above example (the premarital agreement between Wilma and Alan). Now, assume that Wilma has been living with Alan for 15 years, and that in the agreement she has agreed to waive not only her rights to child support but also her rights to alimony and to her share of any earnings by Alan during the forthcoming marriage. Alan is a wealthy businessman, and Wilma is unemployed as well as pregnant. Assume further than Alan told Wilma that if she didn't sign the agreement as drafted, he wouldn't marry her.

      On these facts, you should argue that Wilma should be given the benefit of the unconscionability doctrine as to the entire agreement, since it is substantively unfair, and the product of the parties' very unequal bargaining positions.

☛ Gauge for unconscionability ***at the time the contract was made,*** not later on.

☛ In order for a ***price*** to be unconscionable, it must be very excessive (e.g., two to three times the market price), not just substantially higher than the prevailing market price.

 *Exam Tips on*
WARRANTIES

☛ **Express warranty:** Be on the lookout for descriptions of goods or services to be furnished, since such descriptions are usually express warranties. For instance, a ***description of goods in a sales contract is an express warranty that the goods will have those qualities.***

   Example: *B* agrees to purchase 250 2" x 4" "construction grade" wooden studs from *S* by a written contract in which she agrees to tender payment on delivery prior to inspection. After paying for the studs, *B* inspects them and discovers that they're utility grade instead of construction grade. *B* sends a letter notifying *S* that the studs are defective, but keeps them and uses them anyway. *B* is entitled to damages for breach of express warranty, since the description of the goods as "construction grade" amounted to an express warranty that the goods would have this feature, and *B*'s use of the goods after inspection did not serve as a waiver of the warranty.

☞ **Implied warranty:** Remember that a contract providing that goods are to be sold *"as is"* serves to impliedly disclaim all implied warranties (including the warranty of merchantability and the warranty of fitness for a particular purpose). But such language does not exclude express warranties.

> **Example:** Seller offers, on e-bay.com, a "1951 Barbie & Ken matching 'Beach Party' doll set, sold as is." The words "as is" would prevent the buyer from suing on account of the poor condition of the set, even if a sale of dolls on e-bay would normally include an implied warranty that the goods were in good enough condition to be worth collecting. However, the words would not prevent the buyer from suing if the dolls turned out to be a 1980 set, because the description "1950" constituted an express warranty that the dolls were from that year, and the words "as is" do not modify or disclaim express warranties, only implied ones.

Exam Tips on ### DISCHARGE OF CONTRACTS

Discharge of Obligations Through Accord and Novation

☞ Watch for a fact situation in which both parties agree to perform *differently* than originally agreed, or agree to the substitution of a party to the contract.

     ☞ **Accord:** This is an agreement to accept a lesser obligation than the one which existed under the original contract. Watch for a *substituted performance* by both parties.

         ☞ **Consideration:** Be sure to identify the *consideration* given by both parties for the change in obligations. If there is no consideration, the new agreement is not binding and either party can try to enforce the original contract terms.

         ☞ **Satisfaction:** Look for a situation where there hasn't been "satisfaction" (performance) of the new obligation. If the accord has been breached by one of the parties, the other party can sue on the ***original obligation.***

Example: *S* and *B* sign a contract for the sale of 500 bicycles to *B* for $50,000. The contract requires delivery prior to June 1 and payment within 30 days after delivery. *S* delivers the bicycles on May 15 and asks if *B* can pay immediately. *B* promises to pay within five days if *S* will accept $45,000 as payment in full. *S* agrees. By June 20, *B* has made no payment at all. *S* sues *B* for $50,000. Since there was no satisfaction of the accord by payment of $45,000, *B* is obligated to pay the original contractual amount, $50,000.

Caution: Be sure to distinguish between an accord and a substituted agreement: In an accord, *A* can still sue on the original deal if *B* breaches the accord. In a substituted contract, *A* can only sue on the substituted deal, not the original one, if *B* breaches the substituted deal. The more informal the new deal (e.g., it's oral), the more likely it is to be an accord, not a substituted agreement.

☞ **Check cashing:** Look for a fact pattern where a debtor sends to a creditor a check for a lesser amount than the creditor thinks is due him and it's clearly marked ***"payment in full."*** Even if the creditor marks the check "under protest," the recently-revised UCC rule (§3-311) is that the creditor's act of cashing it constitutes an enforceable ***discharge*** of the debtor as long as:

❑ the amount of the debt was ***unliquidated*** (not fixed) or subject to a ***bona fide dispute***; and

❑ the debtor acted in ***good faith***.

☞ **Novation:** Look for a ***delegation of duties*** where the obligee under the original contract agrees to ***relieve the obligor of liability*** and to hold ***only*** the delegate liable. This is a "novation."

☞ **Consent to novation:** Make sure there has been consent by all parties. Although a novation can be implied, this will happen only if the facts indicate that the obligee has intended to ***release the delegator from his obligations***. The mere fact that the obligee ***remains silent*** when told of the delegation and/or assignment (or even the fact that the obligee ***consents to the delegation***) is ***not enough*** to constitute a novation.

Example: Contractor agrees to remodel Ohn's kitchen for $50,000. Before work begins, Contractor sells the assets of his business to Remodeler, and "assigns" the Contractor-Ohn contract to Remodeler as part of the sale. Simultaneously, Contractor notifies Ohn in writing about the assignment, and says, "Remodeler will be carrying out the contract instead of me, if you have no objection." Ohn says nothing, and allows the work to proceed. Remodeler does the work incompetently, and Ohn sues Contractor for damages.

Ohn will probably be able to recover from Contractor for Remodeler's poor performance — the mere fact that Ohn knew of and consented to the "assignment" (and delegation) doesn't constitute a novation. Only a direct indication by Ohn that he was relieving Contractor of liability could have done that. (On the other hand, suppose Contractor had written to Owner, "If you allow Remodeler to do the work, I will consider myself discharged." Here, Contractor would have a good chance of arguing that Ohn agreed to a novation, even if Ohn never explicitly responded but merely stood by and allowed the work to be done.)

SHORT-ANSWER QUESTIONS

Note: These questions are selected from among the "Quiz Yourself" questions in the full-length *Contracts Emanuel Law Outline*. We've kept the same question numbering here as in the *Outline*. Since some questions have been omitted here, there are gaps in the numbering.

CHAPTER 2

OFFER AND ACCEPTANCE

1. Dorothy, owner of the Wizard of Odd-Sizes Shoe Store, is chatting with the Wicked Witch about her ruby slippers. Dorothy says, "I'm planning on selling my ruby slippers for $50." Wicked Witch says, "Here's my check. I accept." Is there a contract? _____

2. CityWatt, an electric utility serving the city of Metro, posts the following notice on its website on January 1, 2015:

To All CityWatt Homeowner Customers — Solar Rebate Program

If you placed a Qualifying Solar Panel Installation ("QSPI") [a term carefully defined elsewhere in the website] in service at your home during calendar year 2014, under our Solar Rebate Program you are eligible for a 10% credit against the cost of your QSPI. Submit the information required in the application form below, and our home office will determine your eligibility; if you are approved, we will contact you with the amount of your Rebate.

Gary Green, a CityWatt customer who made what was in fact a Qualifying Solar Panel Installation during 2014, submits on Jan. 15, 2015 all information required by the online application form. However, before CityWatt makes any further contact with Green, the company on Jan. 17 posts this notice on its website: "We regret to say that the Solar Rebate Program has been canceled. All pending applications are null and void." Green asserts that he accepted CityWatt's offer of a rebate on Jan. 15. Is there a contract between CityWatt and Green whereby City-Watt is obligated to pay Green the QSPI Rebate? _____

3. Einstein, intending his statement as a joke, tells Oppenheimer, "I'll sell you my chemistry set for $50." Oppenheimer, who has no idea that the set's plutonium alone is worth many times the $50 price (or that Einstein is joking) says, "I accept." Is there a contract? _____

The Camelot Army/Navy Surplus Store advertises in a local circular, "Magic Swords, Excalibur model, for sale @ $24 ea." Lance walks into the store, and says "I accept your ad; here's my $24, give me 1 sword." Is there a contract? _____

Same basic facts as prior question. Now, however, assume instead that the ad reads: "Sale — Saturday only — Excalibur, the magic sword. Only one left. Was $500, now only $24. First come, first served." Lance walks in and makes the same response as in the prior question. Is there a contract? _____

Prince Charming finds a glass slipper on the sidewalk in front of his house. Unbeknownst to him, Cinderella has offered $1,000 as a reward for the slipper's return. Charming goes from house to house, looking for the slipper's owner. He finally finds Cinderella and returns the slipper to her. Is there a contract between Cinderella and Charming for payment of $1,000? _____

Fern owns an antique shop, Junk Is Us. She makes a written offer to buy Euphrates Antique Wholesalers' entire inventory of old string over a period of months. Fern's offer promises that she'll pay any invoice within 30 days, but says nothing about what happens if Fern doesn't pay on time. Nor does the offer says anything specific about what kind of response by Euphrates will constitute an acceptance. Euphrates immediately sends a written response that says, "We accept your offer." The response includes an extra clause providing for 8% interest (a rate typical in the industry) on overdue invoices. Fern makes no response to the overdue-invoices clause, receives the first shipment of string and places it into her inventory.

(A) Is there a contract? _____

(B) If your answer to (A) is yes, is the overdue-invoices clause part of that contract? _____

11. Willie Wonka places an order with Nuts To You for 1,000 pounds of Grade A almonds at $1.25/pound, to be delivered in five days to his chocolate factory. A clause in the boilerplate of the order form states that Willie Wonka will be entitled to recover his reasonable attorney's fees should he have to sue over a problem with the contract.

(A) Nuts To You sends an acknowledgement form in which it states that it will sell Willie Wonka 1,000 pounds of Grade A almonds, to be delivered in five days to his chocolate factory. In the boilerplate language in the acknowledgement form, Nuts states that each party will be responsible for its own attorney's fees should a suit arise from the contract. Is there a contract? If so, what does the contract say about who will pay Willie's attorney's fees if he has to sue? _____

(B) Same as part (A), except now assume that the Nuts To You acknowledgement form, instead of mentioning attorney's fees, changes the grade of almonds to Grade B at a $1.25/pound price. (Grade B almonds are perceived in the marketplace as being significantly less good-tasting than Grade A ones, and typically sell for about 10% less.) Is there a contract? If so, what does the contract say about the Grade? _____

12. On Feb. 10, Chris Columbus offers to sell his powerboat, the Santa Maria, to Leif Ericson, and tells Leif that Leif has until March 1 to decide. On Feb. 20, before Leif has responded, Chris sells the boat to Isabella instead. On Feb. 25, Leif overhears of the sale from two

strangers at the local tavern, Newe Worlde. On Feb. 26, Leif sends an email to Chris, "I accept your offer, here's my credit card number." Is there a contract between Leif and Chris? _____

13. Washington decides he wants his new house at 1500 Pennsylvania Ave. painted barn red. On June 20, he send a letter to Potomac House Painters that says, "I'd like you to paint my new house. If you're willing to do the work for $1500, just show up and start painting by July 4. No written contract necessary."

    (A) Assume that on June 30, Potomac buys (expressly for this job) the requisite red paint, at a cost to it of $500. On July 3, Washington decides he likes the mansion in its present color (white), and sends Potomac a telegram, "I revoke my offer." Potomac would have made a profit of $750 on the job (it would have had to spend $250 more in labor charges to finish the job). The red paint is valueless to Potomac if the paint won't be used on this job. Is there a contract in force, and if so, how much may Potomac recover?

    _____

    (B) Same basic facts. Now however, assume that Washington waits until Potomac arrives at the house and spends one day sanding it (a necessary part of the painting job); Washington then says, "I revoke." Is there a contract in force, and if so, how much may Potomac recover? _____

14. Jessica Rabbit's Microbrewery sends the following letter to Toontown Tavern: "We hereby offer to sell you 50 kegs of beer at a price of $40 per keg. This offer shall remain open for 2 months from the date of receipt." Toontown does not give or promise anything of value in return for this offer. After six weeks, Jessica Rabbit's Microbrewery sends another letter that says, "As we have not heard from you in all this time, we revoke our offer." A week later, Toontown Tavern faxes a letter to the Microbrewery saying, "We accept your offer of 50 kegs at $40 per keg." Is there a contract? _____

15. The Founding Fathers select Ben Franklin to choose a king for the newly-formed United States. He sends an offer in the mail to Prince Henry of Prussia.

    (A) Assume for this part that a few days after the offer is sent by Ben, the Founding Fathers decide that having an American king isn't such a hot idea after all. They therefore tell Ben to send a revocation of the offer. Ben mails the revocation on July 4. Prince Henry mails an acceptance on July 6. The Prince receives the revocation on July 7. Ben receives the acceptance on July 8. Is there a contract? _____

    (B) Assume for this part that Ben never sends a revocation. The Prince mails an acceptance on July 4 (while the offer is still open). He then changes his mind, and mails a rejection on July 7. Due to the vagaries of the Pony Express, the rejection arrives at Ben's house on July 10, and the acceptance arrives on July 11. Is there a contract?

    _____

    (C) Same basic facts as (B). Now, however, assume that the Prince mails a rejection on July 4, then changes his mind and mails an acceptance on July 6. The rejection arrives on July 8, and the acceptance arrives on July 10. Is there a contract? _____

17. Samantha's House of Magic agrees to buy 50 silk top hats from Esmerelda's Supply.

(A) Assume that the parties never discuss the time for shipment. Is there a contract? If so, for what time of shipment? _____

(B) Assume instead that Samantha's order form says that shipment will be made in 5 days, and Esmerelda's acknowledgement form recites that shipment will be made in 90 days. Neither party notices the discrepancy until one month after Samantha receives Esmerelda's acknowledgement form, when Samantha wonders where the shipment is. Is there a contract? If so, for what time of shipment? _____

19. Tweedle Dee enters into a contract with Mad Hatter Catering to purchase some pies for a party he is giving. The contract specifies that Mad Hatter will provide 10 "moon pies" for the occasion. Prior to the contract, Tweedle Dee was at a friend's house and was served an unusual pie made out of chocolate and green cheese, and the friend told him it was a moon pie — this is what Tweedle Dee meant to be ordering. Unbeknownst to Tweedle Dee, the pie Mad Hatter calls "moon pie" is made with ollaliberries and tang. The night of the party, Mad Hatter delivers his version of moon pies. Tweedle Dee is stunned when he sees the fruity concoction and refuses to accept them.

(A) Assume Mad Hatter had no reason to know that Tweedle Dee thought moon pies were made out of cocoa and green cheese, and Tweedle Dee had no reason to know that Mad Hatter thought moon pies were made with fruit. What result? _____

(B) Now assume that, just prior to their first meeting, Mad Hatter had heard Tweedle Dee tell Cheshire Kitty, Mad Hatter's receptionist, about the delicious chocolatey-cheesy moon pies he was hoping to serve at his party. What result? _____

CHAPTER 3

CONSIDERATION

20. George Washington's friend Benny Arnold tells him, "If you walk across the street with me now and go into the hardware store, I'll buy you an axe." Washington crosses the street and enters the store. Arnold reneges. Has Arnold breached a contract?

_____

21. Lion Hart is walking through the woods when he steps on a thorn. He languishes in pain for hours, screaming. Furdley Naturelover walks by and sees Lion's predicament. Acting as a good samaritan, without any expectation of payment, Furdley removes the thorn. Lion, immensely relieved, says, "Boy, am I grateful. I'm going to send you $1,000 a month as long as I live." Is Lion's promise supported by consideration?

_____

23. The Trianon Bakery has a contract with Marie Antoinette to deliver 1,000 cakes for a Bastille Day Party Antoinette is conducting. Trianon fails to deliver, and Antoinette threatens to sue. Trianon says, "If you agree not to sue, I'll give you a strand of priceless black pearls." Antoinette agrees, and accepts the pearls. Both parties reasonably believe that Antoinette's claim may be valid.

(A) Assume that Antoinette's claim is in fact valid. Is Antoinette's promise not to pursue her claim enforceable? _____

(B) Now assume that Antoinette's claim is invalid, because the jurisdiction just shortened the statute of limitation for food-related contracts to five days, and that period has already lapsed. Assume further that neither Antoinette nor Trianon knows about this change, and that their lack of knowledge is reasonable. Is Antoinette's promise not to pursue her claim enforceable? _____

24. The New World Cruise Company hires Christopher Columbus to perform a publicity stunt for them — Columbus promises to sail due West to discover America, in return for which New World promises to pay $5,000 on completion, plus a lifetime supply of dramamine.

   (A) Just before Columbus is set to sail, he decides that the payment isn't big enough, and refuses to go unless New World ups the ante. New World says, "OK, we'll also name the capital of Ohio after you if you're successful." Columbus agrees, sails, discovers America, and collects his $5,000 + dramamine. New World refuses to name the capital after him. Under common-law principles, can Columbus enforce this capital-naming promise? _____

   (B) Same facts, but assume that the original agreement called for Columbus to leave Genoa on April 1. Assume further that when Columbus balked at starting the trip, New World said that it would name the Ohio capital after Columbus if he left on March 30 instead of April 1, and successfully completed his mission. Columbus leaves on March 30, completes the mission, and now wants to compel New World to honor the capital-naming promise. Is that promise enforceable? _____

25. Charlie Tuna's Fish Shack contracts to buy 100 pounds of fresh salmon over the next month at $3 a pound from Chicken of the Sea, a fresh fish wholesaler. After the contract is entered into, an unexpected freeze affects the salmon migration and makes it more difficult (and more expensive) for Chicken of the Sea to obtain the fish. Melissa Mermaid, president of Chicken of the Sea, calls Charlie and says, "We've got to talk. I'm going to lose money if I sell you the salmon at $3 a pound. Let's make it $4 and we'll still both come out ahead under the present market conditions. Agreed?" "Agreed." One day later (at a time when Melissa hasn't yet relied on the higher price in any way), Charlie says, "Sorry, I won't pay the $4. We've got a contract at $3/pound; I'll expect you to deliver."

   (A) Can Melissa enforce the modification to the contract? _____

   (B) If the contract was governed by the Restatement and not by the UCC, could Melissa enforce the modification? _____

26. E.T. signs up for a long distance calling service with MCI (Make Calls Intergalactically). The calling plan says that calls made "between 7 and 11" will be 10 cents a minute, and calls made at all other times will be 15 cents a minute. E.T. gets a bill for $187 for one month's calls, properly computed based on MCI's assumption that "between 7 and 11" means between 7 and 11 p.m. E.T. thinks that "between 7 and 11" should also apply to the 7-11 a.m. period. (Assume that a court would probably find for MCI on this issue, but that E.T.'s reasoning is not crazy, and is done in good faith.) E.T. decides to pay only what he thinks he owes, and sends in a check for this lesser amount ($125). At the bottom of the check he writes, in neon green ink, "Paid in Full." He sends the check, along with a note explaining why he believes this is all he owes, to MCI. MCI cashes the check but writes next to its endorsement, "Under Protest, and With Reservation of Rights." MCI then sues

E.T. for the $62 difference. Can MCI recover? _____

27. Princess promises to sell her golden ball to Frog for $200 "unless I change my mind." Can Frog enforce Princess's promise? _____

29. Hercules Manufacturing agrees to buy "all the thing-a-ma-bobs we need to produce our what-cha-ma-callits for the next year" from Zeus Metalworks. Zeus declines to deliver.

(A) Is Zeus bound? _____

(B) Assume instead that the agreement was for Hercules to buy "all the thing-a-ma-bobs we order for the next year." Is Zeus bound? _____

30. Papa Bear agrees to sell, and Goldilocks to buy, four bushels of oats from the next season's harvest. The agreement further provides that Papa Bear's duty will be conditional on Papa's planting of one more acre of oats than he planted the prior season. (Papa's decision on whether to plant the extra acre will be based solely on his decision about how hard he wants to work.) Papa Bear in fact plants the extra acre, and tenders the resulting four bushels to Goldilocks. Is Goldilocks bound to accept and pay for them? _____

CHAPTER 4
PROMISES BINDING
WITHOUT CONSIDERATION

33. Opie became extremely ill one day while visiting his Aunt Bee. Aunt Bee, a retired nurse, ended up nursing him back to health for several days and spent $200 on medications for him. When Opie recovered, he said, "Aunt Bee, I know you devoted several days of your time to caring for me, and I appreciate it greatly. I promise to repay you by giving you $500 for your services, plus an additional $200 to reimburse you for the medications." Opie never pays up. According to the modern view, can Aunt Bee enforce the promise? If so, to what extent? _____

34. The Great Philosophers Mint offers to consumers a collection of commemorative plates, each with the likeness of a great philosopher on it. Plato, an amateur collector of plates, signs a contract with Great Philosophers to purchase the entire 12-plate set for $300, payment to be at the rate of $10 a month for 30 months, no interest. The contract contains a clause in the boilerplate (which Plato never noticed) saying that no modification will be effective unless it's in a writing signed by both parties. Plato gets the plates, makes the first 2 months' payments, then loses his job writing philosophy tracts. He and Great Philosophers orally agree that he can pay just $5/month til the debt is paid off, still no interest. After one month of this arrangement, Great Philosophers says, "We want the original $10/month." Is Plato obligated to resume paying $10/month? _____

35. Jerry Seinfeld is a part-owner of a soup store called The Soup Nazi. On Aug. 1, Jerry and his friend George Costanza sign an option agreement that reads as follows: "In consideration of $10 paid this day by Costanza to Seinfeld, Seinfeld hereby grants to Costanza an option to purchase Seinfeld's interest in The Soup Nazi for $10,000 cash, this option to be exercised no later than Sept. 1." ($10,000 would be a fair price for Jerry's interest.) George never in fact paid Jerry the $10 for the option, as Jerry knew when he signed the option agreement. On August 15, Jerry tells George that the option is terminated, because he has decided his interest is worth more than $10,000. Will a court enforce the option?

_____

37. Ali Baba is out hiking on his property one day and stumbles into a hidden cave that is stuffed with ancient treasure. He runs home and calls his girlfriend, Scheherezade. She is thrilled. Ali tells her, "Naturally, I'll split it with you." The value of Scheherezade's 1/2 of the treasure would be $1 million (in 1999 dollars).

(A) One hour after making the promise, before Scheherezade has even really started to think about what the treasure will mean to her life, Ali has a change of heart. He immediately calls Scheherezade back and reneges on his promise to split the treasure with her. Can Scheherezade recover anything from Ali, and if so, what amount?

_____

(B) Assume that during his initial phone call with Scheherezade, Ali adds, "I know how much you have been wanting that 200-camel-power convertible Porsche. Now you will be able to buy it." As soon as she hangs up the phone, Scheherezade races over to the Porsche dealer and puts a down a $25,000 deposit on the car of her dreams, which has a market value of $250,000. Ali then decides to keep the treasure all for himself. The dealer refuses to refund any part of the deposit, and Scheherezade can't afford the car without the treasure. Can Scheherezade recovery anything from Ali, and if so, what amount?

_____

38. Hound Dogg, a general contractor, wants to bid on a construction project to be done for casino magnate Steve Winner: a hotel in the shape of Elvis Presley. Hound solicits subcontract bids from a number of electrical sub-contractors, including Elektra Cution. Elecktra's sub-bid on the electrical work comes in the lowest, $1 million. (The next lowest bid, by Juice Corp., is $1.2 million.) Hound figures in Electra's sub-bid into Hound's own master bid, and bids a total of $10 million, on which Hound projects a profit of $300,000 (it's a low-margin industry, unlike operating casinos). Two hours after Hound submits its bid, Elecktra phones Hound and says, "My bid was due to a terrible computational error. I can't do the job for less than $1.25 million. I revoke my offer to do the job for $1 million." Hound tells Elektra that Elektra must perform if Elektra is awarded the job, but Elektra still insists on revoking.

The terms of Winner's bid-solicitation say that all master bids are final, and that all such bids must be backed by a construction-completion bond (as Hound's bid is.) Hound is awarded the job at $10 million. When Elektra persists in refusing to honor its original $1 million bid, Hound gives the job to Juice for $1.2 million. What, if anything, can Hound recover against Elektra? _____

CHAPTER 5
MISTAKE

39. Jack agrees to sell Giant a goose for $20. Both parties think the goose is a regular goose, which Giant wants for breeding.

(A) Before the goose is transferred or the $20 paid, the goose begins laying golden eggs, which makes her priceless. Jack refuses to uphold the agreement, and Giant sues to enforce the contract. Will a court force Jack to sell for $20? _____

(B) Assume instead that before the goose is transferred or the $20 paid, both Jack and Giant witness the goose laying eggs that are gold in color. Giant says, "Wow, that's bizarre. What do you suppose those eggs are made of?" Jack replies, "I don't know, but I think it's some alteration of the albumin content. Anyway, you can still have her for $20 if you want her." Giant, who believes Jack's assessment, agrees to go through with the deal. Shortly thereafter, Jack finds out the eggs are actually made of gold and refuses to consummate the sale. Will a court enforce the agreement? _____

40. After doing some spring cleaning in his wine cellar, Gatsby decides to sell several bottles of wine from the Magenta region of France. He enters into a contract with Daisy to sell the wine for $250. Both believe this to be the fair market value of the wine at the time. In actuality, wines from the Magenta region have gone up in value recently and the collection is really worth $500. Gatsby learns of this just before the sale is completed, and he seeks to avoid the sale. Can Daisy enforce the contract? _____

41. Mike Angelo, newly arrived in the United States from Italy, develops an immediate fascination with baseball. He visits "Leo's Locker," a baseball memorabilia store, to check out some baseball cards. The owner, Leo diVinci, has a slogan, "I love to dicker" — so he doesn't put a price tag on anything. Mike spots an old card with a famous name on it, and offers Leo $5,000 for it. Leo realizes that Mike has mistaken the player on the card — Babe Root, of the 1929 New York Spankies (an amateur team) — for Babe Ruth, whose card *would* be worth $5,000. Leo quickly accepts Mike's offer, knowing the card is worth about fifty cents. Leo writes up a contract that they both sign, and Mike goes to the bank to get the $5,000. When he tells the bank teller about his find, the teller laughs hysterically, telling him of his mistake. Mike reneges on the deal. Leo sues. Mike defends on grounds of mistake. Who wins? _____

44. Oliver Douglas enters into the following contract with Arnold Ziffel: "Douglas hereby agrees to sell and Ziffel hereby agrees to buy Green Acres, a 10-acre parcel, at the price of $600 per acre for a total of $6,000." Ziffel plans to use the property as a country home, as Douglas knows.

(A) Before the deal is completed, Lisa, a county surveyor, measures the property and informs the parties that it is only nine acres. Ziffel wants out of the contract. What relief, if any, would a court likely grant? _____

(B) Assume instead that the survey showed the property was really only five acres, and that this would be insufficient for Ziffel's stated purpose for the land. Before the parties learned of this mistake, Ziffel invested in farming equipment at a cost of $3,000. He bought the equipment used at an "As Is" sale, cannot return it, and is not likely to buy a comparable property any time soon at which he could use the equipment. What relief, if any, would a court likely grant? _____

45. Little Jack Horner enters into an oral agreement with Big Bad Wolf ("BBW") whereby, if BBW can obtain two blackberry pies baked by Little Red Riding Hood's mother within the next two weeks, Little Jack Horner will buy them for $3 a pie. BBW has his attorney draft up a written confirmation of the agreement. The attorney mistakenly writes up the contract as being for three pies at $2 each. No one notices the problem until after the contract is signed; both parties are equally at fault in this. A week later, BBW wants to enforce the terms of the agreement. Little Jack Horner reviews the contract and offers either to take the pies for $2 apiece or rescind the contract. BBW refuses to do either, and seeks the court's assistance to enforce the terms of the oral agreement ($3 price for 2 pies). What result? _____

CHAPTER 6

PAROL EVIDENCE AND INTERPRETATION

46. Washington and Adams agree for Adams to sell Washington 1000 Declaration of Independence Commemorative Placemats, which Washington intends to re-sell. They sign a written contract, which both parties intend to represent all aspects of their agreement, and which both parties intend to be final. One day after the writing is signed, the parties orally agree that the price to Washington will be adjusted from $ .40 per mat to $ .30. The writing says nothing about subsequent oral agreements. Adams ships the mats, and bills at the $ .40 price. If Washington refuses to pay more than $ .30 and Adams sues, may Washington prove in court that the oral modification occurred? _____

47. Cagney and Lacey enter into a written contract to open "Tried and True," a store specializing in used guns recovered from murder scenes. The writing is a 2-paragraph handwritten document, prepared during a 1-hour meeting. The writing states that each party will receive 50 percent of any net profits and that each will devote 30 hours a week to the venture. Both parties regard the writing as a final expression of their deal.

(A) Subsequently, Cagney sues Lacey for breach because Lacey has been working only 20 hours per week over the last few months, which are summer months. In defense, Lacey attempts to testify that just prior to the parties' signing of the writing, Cagney orally agreed that for the approximately four months a year when Lacey's young children were on vacation from school, Lacey could work only 20 hours a week. Is Lacey's testimony admissible? _____

(B) Assume that in the same lawsuit, Lacey counterclaims for lost profits due to certain small merchandise discounts that Cagney gave to her adult children. Cagney tries to testify that before the writing was signed, the parties orally agreed that each party could sell up to $500 per year in merchandise, at a 20% discount, to members of that party's immediate family. The writing says nothing about whether and when such merchandise discounts will be given. Is Cagney's testimony admissible? _____

48. Marshall and Blackstone have a written contract whereby Blackstone will sell Marshall 10,000 "Scales of Justice" candy dishes. Marshall subsequently sues Blackstone, alleging breach of what Marshall says was an express oral warranty by Blackstone that the dishes would appreciate in value by 30% in the first year, and that if they did not, Marshall could return them.

(A) Marshall wishes to demonstrate that both he and Blackstone regarded the written contract as covering only some aspects of their deal, and that warranties were not one of the aspects intended to be covered by the writing. May Marshall, consistent with the parol evidence rule, testify to this effect, for purposes of showing that the writing is not a total integration? _____

(B) Assume this is a jury trial. Further assume, for this part only, that the evidence in part (A) is admissible. Who (judge or jury) will decide each of the following issues: (i) whether the writing is a "final" integration; (ii) whether the writing is a "total" integration (in which case it cannot even be supplemented by prior or contemporaneous oral agreements); and (iii) whether the oral warranty that Marshall is alleging supplements, or instead contradicts, the writing? _____

49. Enrico Fermi patents a new invention: a solar-powered flashlight. He enters into a written agreement to sell the patent to Albert Einstein. The parties orally agree that the contract will not become effective until the patent is reviewed and approved by a patent expert, Moe Howard, of the patent law firm Larry, Moe, and Curly Joe, P.C. Howard reviews the patent and tells Einstein, "It's bogus. Only a stooge would buy this." Fermi sues Einstein, seeking to enforce the contract. Einstein wants to introduce evidence of the oral condition. Will the parol evidence rule prevent him from doing so? _____

50. Gary Gullible enters into a contract with Sam Slick, owner of the "Better than New" used car lot, for the purchase of a used car. While examining the car, Gary asks Sam if it had ever been in any accidents. Sam says, "Absolutely not. This car is in the same condition it was in the day it left the assembly line." On the sales contract, Gary is required to initial a clause stating as follows:

> "Buyer has had an opportunity to inspect this vehicle and to satisfy himself of its condition prior to the purchase. Buyer accepts this vehicle in its current condition. Buyer is not relying in any way on any oral representations concerning the vehicle's condition that may have been made by Seller."

A few months later, during a routine service, a mechanic points out some obvious repair work indicating the car has been in a major accident sometime in the past. Gary sues to have the contract rescinded. At trial, may Gary enter evidence that Sam knowingly lied about the accident issue? _____

51. Wally, Eddie and Lumpy are members of a secret club. They use a secret code to help keep their communications private. As part of their code, "red" really means "blue," and "shirt" really means "sweater." Wally and Lumpy enter into a written contract whereby Wally is to sell to Lumpy his "red shirt" for $5. Wally tenders his red shirt and Lumpy sues for breach, claiming that he is supposed to get Wally's blue sweater for the $5. Under the modern view towards such matters, can Lumpy introduce evidence about the boys' secret code? _____

CHAPTER 7

CONDITIONS, BREACH AND OTHER ASPECTS OF PERFORMANCE

53. Noah is to buy a boat from Acme Houseboats. Noah agrees to pay "40 days after the boat is delivered to me." Is Acme's delivering the boat an express condition or a constructive condition? _____

54. Santa and Rudolph agree that "If it snows before 9 am on Dec. 24, Rudolph will plow Santa's driveway by 5 pm, in which event Santa will pay Rudolph $25." Is Rudolph's plowing of the driveway by 5 pm a promise, a condition, both or neither?

_____

57. Tuileries Construction Company agrees to build a house for Madame de Pompadour for $500,000. The contract states, "Owner's duty to pay anything under this contract shall be expressly conditional upon Contractor's strict compliance with the specifications for materials and workmanship in this contract." The house as built conforms strictly to specifications, except for the Maison de Whoopee mirror tiles on the bedroom ceiling — de Pompadour had specified Brand X mirror tiles, and Tuileries intentionally used Maison de Whoopee tiles because they were available with a shorter delivery time. Brand X and Maison de Whoopee tiles look nearly the same, are of the same general quality, and cost the same. It would cost over $100,000 now to rip out the Maison de Whoopee tiles and substitute Brand X ones.

de Pompadour refuses to pay Tuileries anything due to the contract deviation. de Pompadour's anger over the deviation is genuine, although probably unreasonable. The contract as written contains a substantial profit margin for Tuileries ($100,000), in part because a comparable house would only have a market value of $450,000. If Tuileries sues de Pompadour for payment, may Tuileries recover under the contract? _____

58. Queequeeg agrees to swab the decks on Ahab's boat once a month between the months of February and August for $10 a swab. Queequeeg's fee is payable within 30 days of his performance. In June, Queequeeq swabs the deck, as required under the agreement. In July, Queequeeg does not swab the decks. On August 1, can Ahab withhold payment to Queequeeg for the June swabbing on account of Queequeeq's failure to swab in July?

_____

59. Mr. Peabody contracts with the Nutty Professor to have Nutty build a "Way Back Machine" to Mr. Peabody's specifications so that Peabody and his trusty sidekick, Sherman, can travel back in time. To save money, Nutty will send the component parts to Mr. Peabody as he creates them, and Mr. Peabody will put it all together himself. It will take 10 months to make all the parts. Nutty agrees to send the parts as they are ready on the first of each month for the next ten months. Mr. Peabody agrees to break up the $50,000 total cost into 10 monthly installments of $5,000 each, with each payment due upon receipt of that month's parts. After three months of exchanging parts for dollars, Nutty sends the April parts shipment three days late. Mr. Peabody, charging that Nutty has breached their agreement, cancels the agreement and refuses to pay for the April shipment. What are the rights of the parties? _____

60. The Grinch hires Pollyanna to undertake a broad public relations campaign to try to improve his public image. He agrees to pay her $3,000 for the work. Nothing is said in their contract about timing of payment. When Grinch calls for a progress report a few weeks later, Pollyanna tells him she hasn't begun work because she is waiting for the money. Grinch sues for breach. What result? _____

61. Sylvester Stallion, an action flick icon, decides to leave the film industry and open up "Boys Will Be Boys," a toy store specializing in toys of mass destruction. He orders a gross of Mighty Might Super Hero action figures from Action Plastics. Stallion specifies that he wants red-caped figures. Action Plastics, however, sends a gross of blue-caped figures.

(A) Assume that color of the cape distinguishes the various super heroes' identities in the Mighty Might family; the one with the red cape is named "Destructo Man" and the one with the blue cape is named "Emotionally Sensitive Man." The figures are otherwise identical in looks, and identical in cost and in market value. May Stallion send the toys back and refuse to pay for them? _____

(B) Now assume that the figures come in a variety of colors, but that the color differences have no particular significance to most consumers. As before, Stallion specifies red-caped figures, but receives blue-caped ones. Assume further that in the action-toy industry, manufacturers frequently send whatever color toys they recently have produced to fulfill a purchase order, and that small deviations from buyer-specified colors are deemed insignificant. May Stallion send the blue-caped figures back and refuse to pay?

_____

(C) Same basic facts as part (A). Now assume that the date for delivery is September 15 and that Stallion receives the blue figures on September 5. Assume further that Stallion rightfully considers the shipment to be defective, that he rejects the shipment that same day, and that he immediately notifies Action Plastics of the rejection. That same day, may Stallion cancel the contract? _____

(D) Assume the same facts as in part (C) above, except that the delivery of the original shipment takes place on September 15. Assume further that Action Plastics: (i) knew it was shipping goods that were non-conforming because blue; and (ii) believed, reasonably though erroneously, that Stallion would accept the blue figures. After Stallion rejects the goods on Sept. 15, may he immediately cancel the contract? _____

62. Humphrey Bogart's granddaughter, Helen, opens up a chain of kitchenware stores called "Here's Cooking At You, Kid." She orders 100 blenders from the Whirlie Bird Co., to be paid for two weeks after delivery. The blenders arrive in individual boxes. She takes one out, plugs it in and tries a few cycles. Everything seems just fine, so puts the shipment in inventory, and signs the delivery receipt "received, HB." Two weeks later, Helen uses one of the blenders in an in-store demonstration. When she pushes the button for frappé, the blade spins so fast that it flies out of the bowl and across the room, nearly injuring several patrons. Helen calls Whirlie Bird back, describes what just happened, and says, "I'm sending these goods back to you, and I won't pay a penny." Assume that the blenders in fact breached Whirlie Bird's implied warranty of merchantability. What are the rights of the parties under contract law? (Ignore tort issues.) _____

63. Michael Corleone contracts to buy a house from his brother Sonny for $2 million. The contract contains the following clause: "Provided, however, that Michael shall have no obligation to consummate the purchase unless he receives by Sept. 1 a commitment for mortgage loan, at a rate of no more than 8%, from the Cosa Nostra Savings & Loan." Michael applies for such a loan, but fails to comply with the bank's reasonable request for a certified copy of his most recent tax return. The bank refuses to issue the loan by Sept. 1, and Michael refuses to close on the purchase of the house. May Sonny recover against Michael for breach of contract? _____

64. On August 1, Marie Antoinette contracts in writing to buy a diamond necklace from Bohmer for $500,000, the closing to take place on Sept. 15. The market value for large diamond necklaces is changing rapidly, due to the unstable political climate. On Sept. 1, Antoinette calls Bohmer and says she's having trouble getting the money together. Bohmer orally promises not to insist on the Sept. 15 date, as long as Marie pays within 30 days thereafter.

(A) For this part only, assume that on Sept. 2, Bohmer phone Marie and says, "I've changed my mind. If you can't come up with the money by the original Sept. 15 date, I'm cancelling the contract." Marie can't get the money by then, and Bohmer cancels. (Assume that Marie would not have been able to raise the money by Sept. 15 even if Bohmer had never promised an extension.) Marie sues for breach, and shows that she would have been able to arrange to borrow the money by Sept. 30. Can Marie recover? _____

(B) Same basic facts. However, for purposes of this part, assume that: (1) Bohmer still phones Marie to retract his promise of an extra 30 days, but does this on Sept. 13, not Sept. 2; (2) Marie tries, but cannot arrange the loan by the Sept. 15 deadline; (3) if Bohmer had never promised the extra 30 days in the first place, there's a 40% chance that Marie could have and would have had time to arrange the loan so as to be able to close on Sept. 15. May Marie recover for breach? _____

66. Larry Flynt is holding a stag party for his buddy Hugh and on Sept. 1 hires Bunny, an exotic dancer, to perform at the bash. The party is set for October 15, with Bunny to be paid $250 after her performance. On Sept. 15, Flynt hears plausible-sounding rumors that Bunny has recently cancelled several other bookings at the last minute.

(A) You represent Flynt. Would you advise Flynt that he may immediately cancel the contract and hire someone else? _____

(B) Same facts as (A). Assume that you believe, or fear, that the answer to (A) is no. What would you advise Flynt to do? _____

(C) Assume the same facts as in (B), except that Flynt knew of Bunny's tendency to cancel at the last minute before they entered into their agreement, and has learned nothing new in this respect since the contract was made. Does this change your advice in (B)? _____

CHAPTER 8

ANTICIPATORY REPUDIATION AND OTHER ASPECTS OF BREACH

67. On Jan. 15, Dahlia and Agatha sign a written agreement wherein Dahlia promises to sell her estate, Totleigh Towers, to Agatha for $100,000. The property is to be conveyed on February 25. Agatha goes ahead and withdraws her bids on other pieces of property. On January 30, Dahlia sells Totleigh to Tom. May Agatha sue Dahlia for breach on Feb. 1?

_____

68. Connie Tractor enters into an agreement to construct a custom home for Frank Lee Unreezonable. As part of the contract, Tractor is to use pale blue caulking around the master tub. Shortly after construction begins, Tractor says to Unreezonable, "I absolutely refuse to use pale blue caulking because I think it looks tacky and I don't want to blemish my reputation. I will use navy blue instead." (Assume that the difference in practical effect between pale blue caulking and navy blue caulking is minor.) Unreezonable is offended by Tractor's unwillingness to follow the terms of the contract, and wants to cancel the contract and sue immediately on an anticipatory repudiation theory. Can he do so?

_____

70. Blanche agrees to buy Kowalski's bar, A Streetcar Named Desire, for $50,000. The transaction is to take place July 15. On June 10, Blanche calls and says she's changed her mind and that she intends to move away and get married. Kowalski says, "I hope you change your mind, and I'll have to sue you if you don't go through with the deal." Blanche says, "I have always depended on the kindness of strangers, and therefore I don't think that you'll sue me, stranger."

(A) On June 20, Blanche calls Kowalski back and says the engagement is off, and that as far as she's concerned, the deal is still on. As of the 20th, Kowalski has re-listed the bar with a broker, but hasn't done anything else in response to Blanche's June 10 phone call. On the 21st, Kowalski gets an offer for $60,000. Can Kowalski take the higher offer, or must he sell to Blanche? _____

(B) Same basic facts as (A). Now, however, assume that during the June 10th conversation, Kowalski says to Blanche, "OK, I'm interpreting this as a breach of contract. I have nothing further to say to you, and I'll see you in court." However, Kowalski has not yet sued Blanche (or listed the bar with a broker) when she calls back on June 20 to reinstate the contract. Can Kowalski take the $60,000 offer, or must he sell to Blanche?

_____

71. Spock contracts to buy a tribble fur coat from the Klingon Fur Company. Spock prepays the $2,000 purchase price on March 1; Klingon is to deliver the coat April 1. On March 15, Klingon calls Spock and says it will not deliver the coat. Does Spock have an immediate cause of action on the basis of anticipatory repudiation? _____

CHAPTER 9

STATUTE OF FRAUDS

74. Marie Antoinette is having Tuileries Construction Co. build a new palace for her. The contract calls for a gold-plated mirror. The only place around that stocks such a mirror is the local No Value Hardware store, which sells it for $399. Tuileries hasn't been paying its bills to No Value recently, so No Value is unwilling to extend credit to Tuileries unless someone with good credit gives a guarantee. Marie therefore orally says to No Value, "Put the mirror on Tuileries' account. If they don't pay promptly, I will." No Value does so, and Tuileries doesn't pay promptly. Must Marie pay the bill? _____

75. Witch orally agrees to sell her home, Gingerbread House, to Hansel, for $10,000. An hour later Gretel comes along and makes Witch a better offer — $15,000. Witch calls Hansel and tells him the deal is off. Can Hansel enforce the $10,000 deal? _____

77. Pope orally agrees to sell his country place, Santa Maria del Grazie, to da Vinci. da Vinci gives Pope a down payment and Pope conveys the property to da Vinci. da Vinci moves in and begins to paint a giant mural, "The Last Supper," on one of the walls. da Vinci subsequently decides he doesn't like the décor of the place and moves out without paying another lira. Can Pope enforce the agreement? _____

78. Same basic facts as prior question. Now, however, assume that the parties orally agree on a purchase price and terms, and further agree that da Vinci will move onto the property and perhaps "do some painting and decorating there" in advance of the conveyance." (Pope knows that da Vinci paints great murals and ceilings.) No money changes hands, and da Vinci moves in and paints the mural. He then demands the conveyance, and Pope refuses to make it (though he's willing to pay da Vinci the fair market value of the mural). Will a court order Pope to make the conveyance? _____

79. The Ramm Beau Weaponry Company hires Einstein as its research director. The term of the employment contract is five years. As Ramm Beau knows at the moment of signing, Einstein is terminally ill when the contract is created, and is not expected to live more than nine months.

(A) Must the contract be in writing to be enforceable? _____

(B) Assume instead that Ramm Beau hired Einstein as an employee for the rest of his life. Must the contract be in writing to be enforceable? _____

80. Lear agrees to lease his Castle to Cordelia for nine months, with the lease to begin six months from the signing of the contract.

(A) Must the lease be in writing under the Statute of Frauds? _____

(B) Say instead that the lease is to begin immediately, and to last for nine months. Must the lease be in writing? _____

81. Charlie Tuna orally agrees to supply Chicken of the Sea with all the fish bait she requires over the next 18 months. Charlie fully performs his end of the agreement, but Chicken of the Sea fails to pay up. Charlie sues. Chicken of the Sea defends by arguing that the contract is unenforceable because it falls within the one-year provision of the Statute of

Frauds. (Ignore the UCC's Statute of Frauds provision, governing goods sales for more than $500; just concentrate on the one-year provision). Who wins? _____

82. Kamp E-Kwipment Inc. agrees to sell fifteen pairs of hip boots to the Our Lady of 115th Street Convent for its annual retreat. The contract price is $700, although the merchandise has a wholesale price of $120. Must the contract be in writing to be enforceable?

_____

83. Rosebud General Contractor agrees to build a fabulous home, Xanadu, for Charles Foster Kane in return for $750,000. The contract price includes all materials, which will have an aggregate value of $200,000. Must the contract comply with the Statute of Frauds?

_____

84. Minnie and Mickey decide to get married. The Etty-Kette Paper Goods Company orally agrees to custom-make 350 party hats with Minnie and Mickey's names printed on them for the wedding for $675. After Etty-Kette begins to manufacture the hats, Minnie decides Mickey is a rat, and cancels the wedding. She also tries to cancel the hat contract. Can Etty-Kette enforce the oral agreement? _____

85. Flybye Nite Co. orally agrees to sell the Fix-M-Up Hardware Store 500 electric-powered generators at $100 each. In a subsequent confirmation sent by Flybye Nite to Fix-M-Up, the deal is correctly recited, except that the quantity term is erroneously typed as "50." Fix-M-Up makes no response during the next two weeks, and at the end of those 2 weeks Flybye Nite ships 500 generators. Fix-M-Up returns all 500, and refuses to pay anything. How many generators, if any, was Fix-M-Up contractually obligated to take?

_____

87. On January 20, 2009, Miss Piggy enters into a written contract with the producers of The Nighty Night Show, a late-night talk show, to appear as a guest host on February 15, 2010. The show's standard contract includes a clause that gives the producers the right to select the other guests who will appear on the show. The document does not include a "no oral modifications" clause. Several days later after the document is signed, the parties orally agree that Miss Piggy will be given a veto power over which guests will appear the night of her performance. The following month, the producers sign a contract with Jessica Rabbit, Miss Piggy's arch rival, to be a guest on the show Miss Piggy will be hosting. Miss Piggy is furious and sues to enforce the oral modification. What result?

_____

CHAPTER 10

REMEDIES

88. Acme An-teeks offers to sell Marge Scavenger the squirting rose boutonniere that George Washington wore to his Inaugural Ball for $5,000, and Marge agrees. Before the transaction takes place, Acme gets another offer for $7,000, which it accepts, thereby breaching the contract with Marge. Marge really wants the boutonniere itself (not just damages), because she's a collector of boutonnieres. Is there any remedy available to her?

_____

89. Sisyphus is a well-known expert on hauling rocks. He enters into an employment contract with the Rocco Rock Hauling Co., in which he agrees to work for three years as Chief Operations Officer. His relationship with Rocco brings great prestige to the company; however, after six months Sisyphus finds the work unbearable and quits.

(A) When Rocco sues Sisyphus for breach of contract, will it be entitled to an order compelling him to come back to work and finish the contract? _____

(B) Assume for this part only that your answer to (A) is no. What other equitable remedy might be available to Rocco, and on what showing? _____

(C) Assume for this part that after six months, it's Rocco who's unsatisfied, and Rocco gives Sisyphus the heave-ho. Can Sisyphus obtain an ordering compelling Rocco to reinstate him? _____

90. Drew Idd hires the Landmark Construction Co. to build the Stonehenge Resort on Idd's property. The contract price is $500,000. When the frame is complete, Idd commands Landmark to stop work, and he refuses to pay for the building. Up to that point, Landmark has spent $100,000, and would have needed to spend another $200,000 to complete the job. Idd paid $250,000 up front.

(A) How much will Landmark be able to recover if it sues on the contract?

_____

(B) Assume that Landmark is unable to determine what its cost of completion would have been. Can it still recover its expectation damages? _____

91. Bo Peep decides to get out of the sheep business and open up a business selling household cleaners door-to-door. She enters into a contract with Mr. Clean in which he agrees to supply her with household cleaners at wholesale cost for the next 12 months. Before Bo Peep gets her first shipment, Mr. Clean breaches the agreement. Bo Peep figures that with her pretty face and smooth-talking style, she could have made $1,000 a month in profits from her new venture.

(A) When Bo sues for breach, can she recover the $1,000/mo. she believes she would have made, for the 12 months covered by the contract? _____

(B) Now assume that Bo Peep had been in her new business for three years before she entered into her agreement with Mr. Clean, during which she had purchased comparable supplies at similar pricing from a different supplier. She can show that she made a profit of $1,000/mo. in the last year of that arrangement, and that she cancelled that arrangement to make the new one with Mr. Clean. She can further show that when Mr. Clean cancelled, any other then-available arrangement would have been so much more expensive (due to changing industry conditions) that she would have made no profit. May Bo recover the $1,000/mo. she believes she would have made from the contract with Mr. Clean, for the 12 months covered by the contract? _____

93. Neulla Rich enters into a contract with the Rococo House of Design to redecorate her New York penthouse. Rococo designers set to work immediately. They install new wallpaper and lighting in Neulla's house, and paint a mural of little cherubs on her dining room ceiling. Shortly thereafter, Neulla breaches the agreement by refusing to pay for anything.

Rococo has spent $10,000 (including labor) on the installation of the wallpaper, lighting and mural, and the market value of these items is $15,000. The total redecorating contract was for $50,000.

(A) Assume that Rococo cannot estimate with specificity what its cost of completion would have been. If Rococo sues, what damages can it collect? _____

(B) Now assume that the total contract price was $12,000. How much may Rococo recover? _____

(C) Now assume that Rococo has fully performed under the contract, and Neulla has refused to pay anything. Rococo spent $25,000 to perform. The market value of the new décor (what a reasonable home owner would expect to pay for it) is $60,000. The total contract price was $50,000. What damages can Rococo recover? _____

94. Plato agrees to build a gazebo on Agamemnon's property in Pompeii, in return for $25,000. Plato spends $10,000 on materials and labor before Agamemnon's property is buried in lava from the Mount Vesuvius eruption. At the moment of the eruption, the partly-completed gazebo had a market value of $15,000. Will Plato be entitled to anything? If so, on what theory, and in what amount? _____

95. Dr. Welby is walking down the street when he sees a car hit Old Man River. Old Man River is lying unconscious in the street. Dr. Welby runs over and immediately begins CPR. He then pulls out his Swiss Army Knife, sterilizes it with a match and performs emergency surgery, saving Old Man River's life. Dr. Welby is a high-class Beverly Hills doctor who would normally charge $4,000 for the type of work he performed on Old Man River. The reasonable (market) value for this type of services, however, is $2,000. Dr. Welby sends Old Man River a $4,000 bill. Old Man River refuses to pay, arguing he never consented to have the work done and would not have done so had he been conscious at the time. Dr. Welby sues. How much, if anything, can Dr. Welby recover? _____

96. Scarlett O'Hara contracts to have Wilkes Construction to build a dream home for her, for a total cost of $1 million. The specifications include clay bricks and leaded glass windows. Wilkes decides to increase his profit margin a little by using plastic bricks and plain window panes; he figures Scarlett won't notice. When the work is about one-eighth done (and Wilkes has made outlays of $75,000), Scarlett notices the sub-standard work, and cancels the contract. It is not feasible to restore the house to the contracted-for specifications, since the bricks cannot be replaced without essentially demolishing what has already been built. The market value of the partly-completed house is $100,000. Scarlett has not paid anything yet on the contract price. If Wilkes sues Scarlett for the partly-done work, what (if anything) can he recover, and on what theory? _____

97. The Three Little Pigs Cement Co. ("TLP") needs its main cement mixer to be taken back to the manufacturer for repairs. TLP calls the B. B. Wolf Transport Co. ("Wolf") and says, "How much would you charge to send a pair of drivers to drive our cement mixer to the manufacturer?" Wolf quotes a price of $500. TLP agrees, and says nothing else to Wolf. Wolf delivers the mixer to the wrong address, and it takes five days for the mistake to be tracked down. As a result, TLP must close down for those days, resulting in TLP's having $100,000 less of profits than had the delivery been done properly.

(A) Can TLP recover the $100,000 losses from Wolf? _____

(B) Now, assume that the day after the parties entered into the shipping deal and before the mixer was delivered anywhere, TLP called Wolf and said, "By the way, be extra careful to get the mixer to the right place at the right time, because we can't operate without it and every day until it's fixed, we lose about $20,000." Wolf mis-delivers the mixer anyway, with the same results as in part (A). May TLP recover its $100,000 losses from Wolf?

_____

98. Anna Passemova is a prima ballerina for the 2 Left Feet Dance Company, a major company located in (and performing exclusively in) New York City. She has a three-year employment contract at $100,000 per year. Two years into the contract she is wrongfully dismissed.

(A) For this part only, assume that Passemova sits at home for the remaining year, eating cheese puffs and watching soap operas. If Passemova had notified her agent that she was again available to dance, there is a better-than-50% chance that Passemova would have secured comparable roles paying her at least $40,000 during the remaining year of the contract. At the end of the year, Passemova sues 2 Left Feet for $100,000, the amount she would have earned had 2 Left Feet honored the contract. Will Passemova's recovery be reduced by $40,000? _____

(B) For this part only, assume that Passemova, acting promptly after the firing, notifies her agent that she is again available. The only offer that comes in is from a major San Francisco opera company, offering a two-month guest engagement paying $15,000. Passemova declines the offer, preferring to stay in New York City where she can be near her two small children. Will the $15,000 that Passemova could have earned from San Francisco be deducted from her recovery against 2 Left Feet? _____

99. The puppetmaker Geppetto hires Jiminy Cricket to be a full-time tutor to teach Geppetto's puppet, five-year-old Pinocchio, how to speak and write English. The contract is for one year, at $3,000 per month, and may not be terminated by Geppetto except for cause. After Cricket has been on the job for five months with adequate performance, Geppetto, acting without cause, fires him in a drunken rage. At the end of what would have been the year of employment, Cricket sues Geppetto for breach, seeking $3,000 times the seven months post-firing. At the ensuing bench trial, Geppetto offers testimony that English teachers qualified to teach five-year-old puppets usually earn about $2,000 per month in that locality. Geppetto also shows, without contradiction from Cricket, that following the firing Cricket sat at home all day for the next seven months singing songs, made no effort to find replacement employment, and earned no income. Neither side offers any evidence about whether any particular jobs teaching English to five-year-old puppets were available locally during the seven-month period at issue, or about whether Cricket's credentials would have been sufficient to obtain any such job if there one had been open. How much, if anything, should the judge award Cricket in damages? _____

100. Scarlett owns a saw mill. Cal Carpetbagger contracts to deliver 40 tons of pine logs to the saw mill, at a total cost of $20,000, payable cash on delivery.

(A) For this part, assume that Cal fails to deliver the logs as promised. Scarlett could procure comparable logs on short notice from an alternative source for $30,000, in which case she could keep the mill running without interruption. However, the other supplier would require that the logs be paid for in cash. Because Scarlett's business has been poor, and because she was budgeting just the $20,000 that was to be charged by Cal, Scarlett does not want to (though she could) lay out the $30,000 the new supplier demands. Scarlett therefore instead closes down the mill for a week, until she can procure supplies priced at the same $20,000 as in the deal with Cal. Closing down the mill for the week results in $15,000 of losses to Scarlett. How much, if anything, may Scarlett recover from Cal?

_____

(B) For this part, assume that Cal is willing and able to deliver, but that before he can do so, Scarlett wrongfully repudiates. On the day for delivery, the 40 tons have a market value of $20,000. These logs, like all the logs that Cal sells, come from his own land (he sells all the logs from his land as they mature). Cal could sell the 40 tons earmarked for Scarlett on the day she repudiates, but Cal holds on to them, thinking the market price will rise. Instead, the price falls, and Cal continues to refuse to sell. He still owns the logs when he sues Scarlett for breach. At the time of trial, the logs are worth $9,000. How much may Cal recover from Scarlett? (Ignore storage and other incidental costs caused by the breach.) _____

103. Ben Hur contracts with Athena contractors to construct a shopping mall, the Parthenon, on his property. To take advantage of the Christmas shopping season, the contract stipulates that the mall must be completed by November 1.

(A) For this part only, assume that the contract provides that if the mall is not done by November 1, Athena will be liable for a flat-fee liquidated damages amount of $100,000. (The amount does not change with the length of the delay.) Viewed as of the moment of contracting, the $100,000 is a good estimate of the damages likely to be caused by a delay of between 1 and 2 weeks, but is not a good estimate of damages from a delay of less than 1 week, or more than 2 weeks. In reality, the mall opens on November 8. If Ben Hur presents evidence that his actual damages from the delay are $80,000, how much will the court award? _____

(B) For this part, assume the same facts, except that the delay is 2 days, and Athena shows at trial that Ben's damages are only $20,000. How much will the court award?

_____

(C) Assume instead that the contract states as follows: For every calendar day completion is delayed by Athena, Athena will pay $10,000 in liquidated damages, which is what Ben reasonably anticipates earning in gross profit on a daily basis. Athena slips behind schedule and the mall is not complete until November 15. Ben's actual damages turn out to be $75,000. How much may Ben recover? _____

104. Batman thinks the Batmobile is a little too ostentatious for everyday use, and contracts to buy a new car from the Superhero Car Dealership. He chooses a Penguin Swinger, a popular sub-compact. The cost to the dealer is $9,500, and the sticker price is $10,500, which Batman has agreed to pay. Superhero orders the Swinger from the factory, but when it arrives, Batman repudiates the contract. Superhero sells many Swingers, and it has no trouble selling the one Batman ordered to Spiderman. (Supplies of this model are freely

available, and Superhero can get as many as it can find buyers for.)

(A) Under the UCC, is Superhero entitled to damages from Batman? (Ignore incidentals, reasonable overheads and saved expenses from breach.) _____

(B) Assume instead that Batman had custom-ordered a car with a turbo-charged ejection button and hot pink leather seats. The contract price is $20,000 and the cost to the dealer is $19,000. After Batman repudiates the contract, Superhero decides to place the vehicle up for auction and gives Batman notice of the sale. The car goes for $19,500. The auction costs Superhero $250. What damages can Superhero collect from Batman now?

_____

107. Princess Mary is about to get married, and orders her wedding dress from the tailor who clothes her entire family, Savvy Row. The dress is to cost $3,000. When the dress is delivered, two weeks before the wedding, Mary is horrified to find that Savvy Row has cut the dress to the measurements of her grotesquely fat father, King Henry VIII, by mistake. She immediately ships the dress back (at a cost of $20) and orders the same type of dress from another tailor, Saville-Bassoon (who does not charge for shipping). Because of the short amount of time available, the replacement dress costs her $5,000.

Assuming Mary didn't pay Savvy Row anything up front, how much, if anything, will she be able to recover from them in damages? _____

CHAPTER 11
CONTRACTS INVOLVING
MORE THAN TWO PARTIES

108. Noah Webster sells the movie rights for his dictionary to Sammy Goldfish for $2,000. Webster assigns his right to payment under the contract to his nephew, Spyder, without receiving any compensation from Spyder.

(A) After assigning his payment rights to Spyder, Webster assigns those rights to Webb Foote, a friend, before Spyder has collected anything. Webb Foote knows nothing of the prior assignment to Spyder. Webb Foote does not given any consideration to Webster for the assignment. As between Spyder and Webb, who has superior right to the $2,000?

_____

(B) Same basic facts. Now, however, assume that Webster made the original assignment to Spyder in return for a cash advance of $1,000. He makes a subsequent assignment of the same right (fraudulently) to Webb Foote, in return for another advance, of $500. Webb did not know of the prior assignment to Spyder. Webster is not owed money by anyone else. The $2,000 has not been paid by Goldfish. As between Spyder and Webb, who has priority? _____

(C) Same facts as part (B). Now, however, assume that at the time of the second assignment (Webster to Webb), Webb knew of the prior assignment to Spyder. Who has priority, Spyder or Webb? _____

109. Euphrates Faceless claims to have Napoleon's diary in his possession. He sells it to the

Liberté Publishing Company in return for royalties, on Euphrates' promise that the diary is genuine. The publishing contract calls for Liberté to make an advance of $50,000 against royalties one month after signing. Euphrates assigns this right to an advance to his nephew, Irving. Euphrates does this as a gift. Before Liberté pays the advance, the company learns that the diary is forged — for one thing, it's written in felt-tip pen — and Euphrates admits to the forgery. Liberté refuses to honor the contract.

(A) Does Irving have a valid contract claim against Liberté? _____

(B) Does Irving have a valid contract claim against Euphrates? _____

111. Madame Gioconda contracts to pay Leonardo da Vinci $10,000 to paint her portrait. Da Vinci delegates his duties under the contract to Picasso. Gioconda shows up at da Vinci's studio for her first sitting for the portrait, and is shocked to find Picasso instead of da Vinci waiting for her. She's familiar with Picasso's work, which is very different from da Vinci's.

(A) Suppose that Madame Gioconda immediately objects to the switch, and insists that da Vinci do the portrait. da Vinci refuses, claiming that Picasso's work is at least as good. Will Madame G. be in breach if she refuses to let Picasso do the work? _____

(B) For this part only, suppose that Madame Gioconda, though upset at the switch, nonetheless sits for her portrait, while Picasso paints it. May Madame G. recover against da Vinci for breach of contract? _____

112. Robert E. Lee agrees to lend Abe Lincoln $1,000. The loan agreement contemplates that in return for the money, Lincoln will execute a promissory note. Before Lee makes the actual loan or Lincoln signs the note, Lincoln signs a document that says, "I hereby assign to Jefferson Davis my loan agreement with Robert E. Lee, with the intent that Davis be substituted for me as borrower in said loan agreement." Lincoln hands this assignment document to Davis, who indicates his approval by signing his initials. Davis presents the assignment document, together with Davis' own promissory note, to Lee, and demands the $1,000.

(A) Assume that Lee does not want to go along with the assignment of the contract. Must Lee make the loan to Davis? _____

(B) For this part only, assume that the original Lee-Lincoln loan agreement does not call on Lincoln to execute a future promissory note. Instead, the loan agreement recites that Lincoln "shall be liable for any advances made by Lee to Lincoln pursuant to this agreement," and provides that Lee will make advances of up to $1,000. Before Lee has made any advances, Lincoln says to Lee, "I've assigned to Davis my right to receive the $1,000, so pay that sum to him." Lee does so. Davis does not sign any agreement with Lee. He does, however (just before receiving the $1,000) receive from Lincoln a document that says, "Lincoln hereby assigns to Davis Lincoln's loan agreement with Lee." Davis initials this document. If Davis does not repay the $1,000 to Lee, may Lee recover this sum from Davis? _____

(C) Same facts as part (B). Now, assume that Lee makes the loan to Davis, and Davis defaults, because he's broke after the Civil War. May Lee recover the $1,000 from Lincoln? _____

113. Khufu has Valley King Architects design a pyramid for him. Khufu takes the plans to Cheops General Contractor, and contracts to have Cheops build the pyramid for him. The contract says nothing about whether delegation by Cheops is permitted. Cheops delegates its duties under the contract to Tut General Contractors, a reputable contractor with reasonable experience in projects of this kind.

    (A) Suppose Khufu objects to the delegation as soon as he learns of it. Cheops insists that it is permitted to make the delegation, and that Khufu must accept performance from Tut or be in breach. Khufu remains firm. Which, if either, original party (Khufu or Cheops) is in breach? _____

    (B) For purposes of this part only, assume that the original Khufu-Cheops contract contains the following language: "Cheops hereby agrees to personally perform its duties under this agreement, and not to delegate or attempt to delegate those duties." As soon as Khufu learns of the attempted delegation, he objects. Assume that in the absence of the just-quoted clause, the attempted delegation would be invalid. Cheops refuses to do the work, and insists that its delegation is valid. Which, if either, original party is now in breach? _____

    (C) Same basic facts as (B). Now, however, assume that the Khufu-Cheops contract's only provision relating to assignment or delegation says, "This contract may not be assigned." If Cheops insists on delegating its performance to Tut, and Khufu objects, who is breach, Cheops or Khufu? _____

114. O'Hara owns Tara, a plantation. She hires Selznick to build a movie set in the backyard, which will enhance the value of the property next door, Twelve Oaks, owned by Wilkes. When Wilkes learns of the pending set project, Wilkes adds a souvenir hut to his front yard. Selznick breaches the contract with O'Hara and the set is never built. May Wilkes sue Selznick as a third party beneficiary to the O'Hara-Wilkes contract?

    _____

115. Gretel eats $500 worth of gingerbread from the walls of Witch's home, and Witch demands $500 from her. Shortly thereafter, Hansel, Gretel's brother, enters into a contract with Mother Goose Publishing to write his autobiography. In the publishing contract, at Hansel's request, Mother Goose agrees to pay part of the royalties to Witch to pay for the damage caused by Gretel. (Hansel doesn't like to see his sister burdened down by debt.) If Mother Goose doesn't pay the royalties to Witch, can Gretel sue Mother Goose?

    _____

116. Dorothy contracts to appear in Wizard's play. The agreement provides that Wizard will also tender a standard Actors Equity acting contract to Dorothy's friends Scarecrow, Lion and Tin Man, for co-leading roles in the production. Dorothy shows her friends her contract with Wizard. They express to her their delight that they'll be getting roles, and they all buy new wardrobes to be worn in the show. Subsequently, Wizard decides not to produce the play, and he and Dorothy agree to rescind the agreement.

    (A) Assume that the contract says nothing about whether or when the parties may modify or rescind the agreement. May Dorothy's friends recover against Wizard for failing to tender them contracts? _____

(B) Assume, for this part only, that the Dorothy-Wizard contract contained the following provision: "The parties may at any time, by mutual agreement, modify or rescind this agreement without consideration." If all other facts are the same, may Dorothy's friends recover against Wizard for failing to tender them contracts? _____

117. Betsy Ross contracts to deliver 50 hand-sewn Stars and Stripes flags to Washington. Washington promises Betsy in return that once he receives the flags, he will pay off Betsy's $500 debt to Singer. Betsy tells Singer about the agreement. Betsy delivers the flags, but unfortunately the flags are red, white, and chartreuse instead of the contracted-for red, white and blue. Betsy refuses to correct the defect, and Washington refuses to pay Singer. Singer sues Washington for the $500. Does Washington have a valid defense?

_____

CHAPTER 12

IMPOSSIBILITY, IMPRACTICABILITY AND FRUSTRATION

118. Whinney sells Hoof Hearted, her prizewinning horse, to Grunt for $50,000. Before Hoof Hearted changes hands, it dies from eating a bad batch of Purella Horsey Chow. Grunt tenders the $50,000 and then sues Whinney for breach. Will Grunt recover?

_____

119. Polly Plastiskin contracts to buy 50 gallons of mineral water from the Pisarro Water Supply Co. The contract merely specifies that the water will be "pure mineral water." Pisarro gets its mineral water from several sources, but it primarily relies on the Fountain of Youth, and plans to fill Polly's order with Fountain of Youth water. (Polly doesn't know this — she's never heard of the Fountain of Youth.) Before Pisarro fills Polly's order, the Fountain of Youth is destroyed in an earthquake.

(A) May Polly recover damages from Pisarro for breach of contract?

_____

(B) Same basic facts. Now, however, assume that the contract provides that Pisarro will deliver "pure mineral water from the Fountain of Youth." May Polly recover damages from Pisarro for breach of contract? _____

121. The Colossus Construction Company contracts to build a palace in Rome, on land owned by Emperor Nero. The job is to be paid for in full at the end of construction. Six months into the construction, during a terrible lightning storm, the building catches fire and is destroyed.

(A) Suppose that Colossus is now unwilling to start the work from scratch, unless Nero pays extra. Nero refuses, and tells Colossus that he expects it to do the work for the original contract amount, which Nero promises to pay on completion. May Nero recover against Colossus for breach? _____

(B) Assume instead that the palace was already in existence at the time of the Colossus-

Nero contract. Assume further that Colossus had contracted to do an extensive remodeling job. The half-renovated palace is destroyed by a fire caused by lightning. Colossus has been paid the pro-rata contract amount for all work completed as of the moment of the fire, on which it earned half the total profit it would have made had the contract been completed. Nero rebuilds the palace from scratch, but has a different contractor (one specializing in palaces-from-scratch) do the rebuilding. Colossus therefore loses the chance to do the second half of the renovation project, and loses the profit it would have made ($100,000) on that second half. May Colossus recover any damages from Nero, and if so, what amount? _____

123. Super Bowl XLVII is to be held in New Orleans on February 3, 2013. In April 2012, Rabb Id Fann signs a contract for 3 large suites at the Swank Hotel in New Orleans, for the week that ends on Super Bowl day. The price is twice as high as the Hotel usually charges for those suites for that week in a non-Super Bowl year. At the time of booking, there has been labor peace in pro football for several years, and few observers expect that to change. In December 2012, the NFL Players Association goes on strike, and the 2013 Super Bowl is cancelled. The Hotel demands that Fann pay for the suites anyway.

(A) If you represent Rabb Id Fann, what doctrine will you assert on his behalf?

_____

(B) If you assert the doctrine listed in your answer to (A), will Fann be required to pay for the suites? _____

124. Bay Area Design ("BAD") contracts with Rich N. Tasteless to redecorate his San Francisco home. The contract is for $50,000, to be paid upon completion of the project. After BAD has finished about one-third of the project, a terrible earthquake destroys the home. At the moment of the earthquake, BAD has spent $12,000 on labor and materials. The market value of the work done to that point is $18,000. The contract is discharged due to impossibility. However, BAD wants some compensation anyway. Is it entitled to any recovery, and if so, how much? _____

CHAPTER 13
MISCELLANEOUS DEFENSES

125. Hy Nickin sells Bud Wizer his small beverage store in New York City for $25,000. As part of the deal, Hy promises that for the rest of his life (he's 32), he will never compete in the retail beverage business anywhere within 20 miles of the shop being sold. Eight years later, Nickin opens a beverage store of his own, six miles from Wizer's. Can Wizer enforce the covenant not to compete? _____

126. The U.S. has a ban on trade with Iraq. The Snakeoil Pharmaceuticals Company gets an unsolicited order for $100,000 worth of medicine from Abdul Hussein. It ships the medicine on credit to Hussein in New Jersey, knowing Hussein intends to smuggle it into Iraq. Hussein doesn't pay. Can Snakeoil recover the $100,000 due under the contract?

_____

128. Kermit takes his livestock to the county fair in hopes of selling it. Fozzie Bear shows a

particular interest in one of Kermit's sows, "Miss Piggy." Kermit says the pig will cost Fozzie $10,000 because it is a special dancing pig. Fozzie asks for a demonstration, and he sees what he thinks is Miss Piggy dancing. In fact, Kermit has her pen electrified, and a few well-timed shocks are what create the appearance of "dancing." Fozzie buys Miss Piggy, and subsequently finds out she can't dance. He seeks his money back on grounds of misrepresentation. Assume that a person of ordinary credulity attending the fair would not have believed that Miss Piggy was dancing, but that Fozzie did believe that she was. May Kermit have the contract rescinded? _____

129. Gail Ible meets with her long-time stockbroker, Bully Bear, for some investment advice. Bully advises Gail to invest $2,000 in a local biotechnology company. Bully knows, but carelessly fails to mention, that the president of the company was just indicted on fraud charges and that no successor has yet been picked. (The news is not yet public — Bully knows the info through his contacts at the company.) Gail signs a contract to buy the stock through Bully's firm. After the news becomes public, the stock price falls by 50%. Gail sues Bully for contract damages based on misrepresentation.

(A) Will the fact that Bully's misstatement was negligent rather than intentional make a difference in the outcome? _____

(B) If you're representing Bully's firm, what defense will represent your best shot at getting him off? _____

(C) Will the defense you asserted in part (B) work? _____

130. The Krullen Heartless Appliance Store is located in a poor neighborhood. Sam Shyster is the sales manager. He puts a sign in the window reading, "New Dishwashers — only $19." Fred Farkus, fourth-grade dropout, sees the sign and asks, "Is it really $19?" Sam says, "Yeah — take a look at this contract. See? $19!" What Sam doesn't point out is that it's $19 a month for ten years, chargeable to a credit card. This is in small print buried toward the bottom of a 10-page contract. Sam tells Fred to sign, and he does, although he doesn't really understand the contract since it's all words and no pictures. The actual cost of the dishwasher under the contract, expressed as a present value, is $1,900; the same model is on sale nearby at an all-cash price of $600. Fred soon goes into default, and Sam not only seeks to repossess the dishwasher but also to collect the balance owed.

(A) If you represent Fred, what defense should you assert on his behalf?

_____

(B) Will the defense you assert in (A) be successful. _____

131. Krullen Heartless, the same appliance store featured in the prior question, offers the same "$19/month for 10 years" deal, on the same dishwasher, to Pete, owner of Pete's Tavern. (Pete's tired of having to wash glasses in his bar by hand all night.) Sam Shyster, Krullen's sales manager, doesn't make any factual statements about the provisions of the contract — he just hands it to Pete and says, "Look, you can buy for no money down." Pete glances at the contract, doesn't realize that he'll be paying triple the cash price, signs, and then soon goes into default. Krullen sues on the contract. If Pete defends on grounds of unconscionability, what result? _____

132. Roger Thornhill, teetotaler, is at a party one night. He's delighted that there's a big punch

bowl full of fruit punch. He drinks a lot of it, not realizing that it's *Electric Kool Aid*, a very potent brew indeed. He gets completely intoxicated, and in a drunken state calls Windshear Airlines and puts a plane ticket to South Dakota on a credit card. (The ticket agent thinks Roger sounds a bit weird, but doesn't realize he's dead drunk.) The ticket is not refundable. Before Roger's due to leave, he sobers up and wants to get out of the purchase. Can he disaffirm the purchase? _____

133. Zeus, an adult, sells his chariot to Apollo, aged 17, for $50 down and $50 a month until the $2,000 purchase price is paid off. Apollo, while still 17, rides the chariot much too fast one day, and crashes it into a wall. It bursts into flames and is destroyed; Apollo jumps free, unhurt. He then disaffirms the contract with Zeus, and returns the remnants of the chariot in a shoebox.

(A) Can Zeus recover the remainder of the purchase price? _____

(B) Say instead that Apollo immediately sells the chariot to an acquaintance, Mars, for $1,000. (Mars thinks Apollo's 18, which is the age of majority in the jurisdiction.) Apollo then disaffirms the contract with Zeus, at a time when he still owes Zeus $1,950. Can Zeus recover any of the unpaid balance from (i) Apollo or (ii) Mars? If recovery from either is possible, how much will Zeus recover? _____

(C) Now assume that Apollo pays $2,000 cash for the chariot, and totally wrecks it so that it has no value. He then disaffirms the contract, and sues Zeus to get back the $2,000. How much, if anything, may Apollo recover? _____

(D) Now assume that, after the agreement for an all-cash sale is signed, but before Apollo has received possession or title to the car, Zeus realizes he can get more for it by selling it to someone else and tries to get out of the contract. Assume that Zeus realized, at the time of the agreement, that Apollo was a minor. Can Zeus escape the contract? _____

(E) Same facts as part (D), except now assume that before the contract is signed, Zeus is worried that Apollo may be underage. He asks Apollo his age, and Apollo falsely replies, "18." After the contract is signed, and before delivery, Zeus learns that Apollo has lied about his age; Zeus also realizes that he can get more money for the chariot from someone else. He therefore purports to rescind the contract on account of Apollo's underage status. If Apollo sues to have the contract enforced, will he prevail? _____

134. Lizzie Borden axe murders her parents when she is sixteen years old. She is acquitted of the crime on a technicality. While still a minor, she contracts with Shyster & Shyster Publishers to write her memoirs for $500,000. When she turns eighteen, she writes to Shyster & Shyster, reaffirming her acceptance of the contract terms. Shortly thereafter, Lizzie gets religious and decides she doesn't want to relive the horror of her past. Can she avoid the contract on the grounds that she was a minor when she made it? _____

CHAPTER 14

WARRANTIES

135. Delilah wants to cut Samson's hair. She goes to Medusa's Beauty Supply Store to buy some shears. Medusa shows her a sample of the Exacto-Chop, manufactured by Exacto Corp. Exacto-Chop is a newly-invented hair-cutting machine that attaches to a vacuum cleaner hose; the device cuts the hair and sucks up the trimmings at the same time. Medusa tells Delilah, "This machine is foolproof: You just program in the style you want and it does all the work for you, with extreme accuracy." Delilah decides to buy one.

(A) Delilah takes home the box containing the Exacto-Chop, opens it, and finds an owner's manual. The manual contains the following statement (which Delilah reads before she uses the device): "Exacto-Chop cannot guarantee satisfactory results. Use at your own risk. ALL WARRANTIES ARE HEREBY DISCLAIMED." (Assume that the outside of the box contains no relevant information.) Delilah tries the machine on Samson, using it according to the instructions, and with the intent of giving Samson a regular crew-cut. Instead, Samson ends up looking like a cross between a bald eagle and a mangy sheep. If you represent Delilah, what type(s) of warranty action would you advise, and against whom? _____

(B) Will Delilah succeed in the action(s) you recommended in (A)? _____

(C) Now assume that Medusa does not make any express statement about the device, but that she simply shows the box to Delilah as something she might be interested in. The advertising copy on the outside of the box says, "Precise and Automated Hair Cutter!" Delilah buys one. (Assume that there's no disclaimer in or on the box.) When Delilah tries the machine on Samson, it has the same bad results as in parts (A) and (B). What successful warranty claim(s), if any, can Delilah bring against Exacto Corp? _____

136. Saul Practitioner is an attorney in practice for himself. He decides it is time to update his computer system, but he knows very little about the latest technological options. He goes to a local computer dealer and consults with Tammy Techno, the owner. Saul explains that he needs a computer to keep track of his billable time, to generate his invoices, to do his accounting work and to do his word processing. Tammy shows him a computer that is "on special." Saul buys it, but when he gets it back to the office and sets it up, he discovers that the computer is completely inadequate for his needs. There is nothing inherently wrong with it, however — it is a perfectly fine computer for most kinds of tasks for which people customarily use a PC.

(A) Assuming the sale price meant he could not return the PC, can Saul recover for some kind of breach of warranty? If so, what kind, and what will he have to prove?

_____

(B) Now assume that when Saul signed the sales slip, it contained the following language: "There are no warranties which extend beyond the product descriptions on the packaging of the items you are purchasing." This statement was printed in red ink (the rest of the sales slip was in black). Assume that in the absence of this statement, Saul would have a valid claim for breach of some sort of warranty. How does the clause affect Saul's rights?

_____

CHAPTER 15

DISCHARGE OF CONTRACTS

137. Calvin hires Hobbes to build a treehouse out of cherry wood for him for $1,000. Hobbes builds the treehouse, but uses particle board instead. Calvin refuses to pay, despite Hobbes' frequent entreaties. Calvin finally says, "I'll give you $750 next Tuesday, and that's it. Do you accept?" Hobbes says, "Yes." On Tuesday, Calvin tenders the $750. Hobbs, however, says, "I've changed my mind, I want the full $1,000," and refuses to take the $750. If Hobbes sues for the full $1,000, can he recover this sum?

_____

138. Mrs. O'Leary buys a cow from the Here-A-Moo Cow Farm on February 25 for $100, payable March 25. On March 10, she writes and says she is having a hard time coming up with the money. Here-A-Moo writes back a one-line letter: "We'll take a goat from your farm, instead of $100, if you deliver by April 15." Mrs. O'Leary writes back a 2-word response: "I agree."

(A) For this part only, assume that on April 1, Here-A-Moo announces to Mrs. O'Leary that it has changed its mind, and will require cash. On April 15, Mrs. O'Leary tenders a goat. May Here-A-Moo reject the goat and successfully sue for $100?

_____

(B) For this part only, assume that Here-A-Moo never announces any change of mind. April 15 comes and goes, but Mrs. O'Leary never tenders her goat. What remedies can Here-A-Moo seek? _____

139. Stanley and Ollie enter into an agreement whereby Ollie will detail Stanley's car for $150. Ollie gets started, but doesn't do more than spit-shine the chrome around the headlights (a service worth about $10 on the open market) when he realizes this is not his cup of tea. He tells Stanley he wants out of the agreement. Stanley decides he should probably trust his car to a professional anyway, and agrees. Can Ollie sue to recover the $10 value of the partial performance he has rendered? _____

ANSWERS TO
SHORT-ANSWER QUESTIONS

1.   No, because Dorothy's statement was not an offer, but rather a statement of her intention to contract in the future. An offer requires the present intention to enter into a contract; here, Dorothy did not intend to create in Wicked Witch the immediate power of acceptance. Therefore, no contract results.

2.   No, because a reasonable person in Green's position would have understood that CityWatt did not intend to be bound until its home office determined an applicant's eligibility. Rest. 2d, § 26 says, "A manifestation of willingness to enter into a bargain is *not an offer* if the person to whom it is addressed knows or has *reason to know* that the person making [the manifestation] *does not intend to conclude a bargain* until [the maker] has *made a further manifestation of intent*." Here, the communication that Green asserts was an offer — the Jan. 1 website notice — tells customers to submit an "application form," and says that CityWatt's "home office will determine your eligibility." These references to an application and a determination of eligibility would give the customer reason to know that (in the Restatement's words), CityWatt did not intend for any "bargain" (agreement to award a rebate) to be concluded until CityWatt had made a "further manifestation of intent," namely at least a determination of eligibility, and probably also contact with the customer. In other words, the website made it clear to one in Green's position that the customer's application would be the *offer*, and that acceptance would not occur until the home office's determination of eligibility and notice of such to the customer. Cf. *McAtee v. City of Austin*, 2013 Tex. App. LEXIS 12518 (Ct. App. Tex. 2013) (same basic facts as this question).

3.   Yes, probably. If a reasonable person in Oppenheimer's position would have no reason to know of the value of the plutonium (or any other reason for thinking that Einstein was joking), then under the *objective theory of contracts,* Einstein's offer would create an immediate power of acceptance in Oppenheimer. The fact that Einstein actually was joking is irrelevant; it's the *appearance* of a valid offer that counts. If, however, Oppenheimer *knew* that Einstein had a very dry sense of humor, and realized at the time that Einstein was joking, there'd be no valid offer and thus no contract. (An "offer" which the offeree *knows* is made in jest is not a valid offer, regardless of what any other "reasonable person" might think.)

4.   No. Mass-market advertisements are generally construed as invitations for offers, not offers themselves, because they do not contain sufficient words of commitment to sell.

5.   Yes, because under these facts, Camelot's offer was specific as to quantity ("one left"), price ($24), and the person to whom the offer was made ("first come"), and was, in general, worded as a *commitment* to enter into a deal on proposed terms. As such, it created an immediate power of acceptance in anyone who chose to purchase the sword under the terms advertised.

8.   No. An offer can generally be accepted only by a person who knows of the offer and intends to accept. This rule applies to rewards. Charming didn't know about the reward, so his actions of returning the slipper did not constitute a valid acceptance.

9.   (A) Yes. This is a contract covered by Article 2 of the UCC (since it's for the sale of goods). Under §2-207(1), the fact that an "expression of acceptance" "states terms additional to or different from those offered or agreed upon" does not prevent that expression from operating as an acceptance, unless the expression is "expressly made conditional on assent to the additional or different terms." Since Euphrates' response didn't indicate that Euphrates was unwilling to enter the deal if Fern wouldn't agree to the overdue-invoices clause, the response was not "expressly made conditional on [Fern's] assent" to the overdue-invoices clause, and that response therefore served as an acceptance.

(B) Yes. Unlike at common law, under the UCC terms in an acceptance that fail to match those in the offer can nonetheless become part of the contract in some circumstances. Under §2-207(2), if both parties are merchants, an "additional" term in the acceptance will become part of the contract unless either: (a) the offer expressly limits acceptance to the terms of the offer; (b) the additional term "materially alters" the offer; or (c) the offeror gives notice of her objection to the additional term either before the acceptance, or within a reasonable time after the offeror receives notice of the additional term.

Here, Fern and Euphrates are both merchants. (Since we're told that Fern has an antique shop, we know she's in the business of dealing in the type of merchandise in question, i.e., antiques.) The facts make it clear that neither (a) nor (c) applies — Fern didn't indicate in advance that Euphrates had to accept exactly on the offer's terms, and she remained silent after she got notice of the new clause in the acceptance. As to (b), The overdue-invoices clause is probably not a material alteration to the contract, since: (i) it will apply only if Fern fails to do what she's already promised she'd do (pay on time), and (ii) a charge for overdueness that's of a size typical for the industry probably isn't a material change to the overall agreement. Therefore, §2-207(2) says that the clause became part of the contract.

11.   (A) Yes, there is a contract; Willie will have to pay his own fees. Under the UCC, the fact that documents purporting to be an offer and an acceptance deviate from each other does not prevent the two documents from forming a contract (assuming they agree on essential points). §2-207(1) (see previous question, part (A), discussing this aspect.) When a term differs between the offer and acceptance, most courts apply the "knockout" rule. Under this approach, both conflicting terms are knocked out of the contract and replaced with a UCC gap filler, if one applies, or with a provision derived from the common law. Here, the parties have agreed on all major terms of the contract and disagree only as to who will be responsible for attorney's fees should a conflict arise. The conflicting terms will be knocked out and replaced with the common-law rule that each party to a commercial transaction is responsible for his own fees should a dispute arise.

(B) There is no contract. Under these facts, the parties significantly disagree over a material term of the contract: the Grade (quality) of product to be shipped. As a general rule, when the purchase order and acknowledgement forms differ significantly as to price, quality, quantity, or delivery terms, courts will hold that the acknowledgement diverges so materially from the offer that it is not an acceptance at all but rather a counter-offer. Therefore, no contract has been formed yet, and Willie Wonka can either choose to accept Nuts To You's counter-offer or reject it.

12. No. An offer is terminated when the offeree learns of an act by the offeror that is inconsistent with the offer. Selling the subject of the offer to someone else would certainly qualify as a revocation (though merely looking for other potential buyers would not). Consequently, Chris' offer was revoked at the moment Leif learned of the sale. Therefore, there was no live offer for Leif to accept as of the moment he sent his "acceptance" telegram, and that telegram had no effect.

13. (A) No conventional contract is in force, but Potomac can recover its $500 reliance damages, since this sum will be needed to avoid injustice. First, notice that the offer by Washington was for a ***unilateral*** contract (since it was to be accepted by Potomac's performance, not by its promising to perform.) Under Rest. §45, once Potomac started to actually perform on a unilateral contract, it would have had a temporary option to enter into a fully-binding contract (see part (B) below). But the buying of the red paint would probably be held to be a mere ***preparation*** to perform, not the commencement of performance; in that case, §45 wouldn't apply. However, under Rest. 2d §87(2), "an offer which the offeror should reasonably expect to induce action … of substantial character on the part of the offeree before acceptance and which does induce such action … is binding as an option contract to the extent necessary to avoid injustice." This would apply here. Since giving Potomac the $500 it spent on paint would be enough to "avoid injustice," this is all the court will do — Potomac won't be entitled to true enforcement of the contract (i.e., to recover the $750 it profit it would have made on top of the $500 it spent).

(B) Yes; Potomac can recover $1250. Once the offeree under an offer for a unilateral contract commences ***actual performance***, the offer gives rise to an option contract, i.e., it becomes ***temporarily irrevocable*** for the time needed for the offeree to promptly performance in accordance with the terms of the offer. Rest. 2d §45. The sanding represented a true commencement of performance (not just preparations to perform), so the offer became temporarily irrevocable when the sanding was done. Consequently, Washington lost the ability to revoke. Potomac will be entitled to full contract damages of $1250, which is the sum needed to give it the profit it would have made had the job been completed (i.e., the $1500 contract price less the $250 cost saved by Potomac in not having to perform).

The key point is that in part (A), Potomac didn't have a true contract, and gets only its reliance damages to avoid injustice; here, since performance began, Potomac gets true contract remedies.

14. Yes. At common law, there would be no contract, because the Tavern gave no consideration for the promise of irrevocability — at common law, offers are revocable even if they say otherwise, unless separate consideration has been given for an option. But the UCC provides for what it calls *"firm offers"*; under UCC §2-205, a merchant will be held to have made an irrevocable offer — even though no consideration is given by the offeree — if the merchant makes the offer in writing and with explicit assurances that the offer will remain open for a specified period of time. That's what the Microbrewery did here. Therefore, the Microbrewery had no ability to revoke its offer before the two-month time period had lapsed, and the offer was still open when Tavern accepted.

15. (A) Yes. Under the mailbox rule, the acceptance was *effective upon dispatch* (July 6), provided that at the time it was dispatched, the offer was still open. A revocation does not become effective until it is received by the offeree; so the revocation could not have become effective until July 7. By then, the contract was already in force (it came into force on July 6), and the revocation was of no effect.

(B) Yes. Again by the mailbox rule, the acceptance became effective on dispatch, July 4. The subsequently-dispatched rejection did not change this, even though Ben received that rejection before he received the acceptance.

(C) No. Where a rejection is dispatched before an acceptance, there is an exception to the usual mailbox rule for acceptances: in this situation, the acceptance is effective if and only if it *overtakes the rejection*, which did not happen here. (This makes sense — once Ben got the rejection, he ought to have been entitled to assume that the deal was dead, and to make other arrangements.)

17. (A) Yes, for shipment at a "reasonable" time. There is a contract because the UCC will provide a "gap filler" to complete a contract when it is otherwise clear that the parties intended to be bound. Here, the time for shipment will be a "reasonable time" (§2-309(1). What is a reasonable time will be determined based upon looking at the parties' prior course of dealing, if there is any, or by looking at trade usage (what is customary in the industry).

(B) No, probably. The fact that the order and acceptance (or, more generally, the parties' beliefs about the deal) diverge somewhat does not prevent a contract from coming into existence. But if the parties are in substantial disagreement about an essential term of the contract, their expressions of intent to contract will be deemed to be so divergent that no contract was ever formed (i.e., there never was a "meeting of the minds.") A discrepancy between 5 days and 90 days on the shipment date would probably be found to be major enough to block formation of a contract.

19. (A) There is no contract, so Tweedle Dee can refuse to accept the pies. When the parties to a contract have a misunderstanding about a material term in the contract and neither party knows or has reason to know of the misunderstanding, there is no "meeting of the minds" and therefore no contract.

(B) There is a contract, on the terms as understood by Tweedle Dee, and Mad Hatter is liable for breach. Unlike the facts in (A), here Mad Hatter *did* know that the parties had different interpretations of the term "moon pie." Where one party knows that his interpretation of a term is different from that of the other party, he is considered to be more "at fault" for not clearing up the misunderstanding. In that event, a contract will be found to exist and it will be on the terms understood by the *other* party. So there was a contract for the chocolate-style pies, which Mad Hatter breached by preparing fruity ones. Mad Hatter not only can't get the contract price from Tweedle Dee, but he's liable to Tweedle Dee for consequential damages for the non-delivery (e.g., damage to the quality of the party, stemming from the lack of appropriate food).

20. No, because there was no consideration, and promises without consideration are generally unenforceable. These facts highlight the difference between: (a) consideration, and (b) a condition on a gift. In these kinds of cases, you have to look at whether the detriment in question is something the promisor *bargained* for (a requirement for consideration). In other words, did the promisee's detriment *motivate* the promisor to make the promise? Here, Arnold wasn't really motivated by a desire to have Washington cross the street and enter the store; instead, these acts were merely a condition to facilitate Arnold's making of the purchase. Since Arnold didn't bargain for Washington's crossing the street, there was no consideration for Arnold's promise. Therefore, that promise was an unenforceable promise to make a gift.

21. No. Consideration requires a bargained-for exchange. If the promisee's detriment occurred *before* the promise was made, then the promisor could not have bargained for that detriment. Here, Furdley has already performed by pulling out the thorn, so his performance wasn't bargained for in exchange for Lion's promise to pay him $1,000 a month. As such, Lion's promise is not supported by consideration. (But the promise might be enforceable without consideration, especially if Furdley somehow relied on the promise; see the next chapter.)

23. (A) Yes. The agreement is supported by consideration in the form of Antoinette's promise not to assert her claim. When a party promises to waive a valid claim, that is sufficient "detriment" to constitute consideration for the other party's promise to pay a settlement (here, the pearl necklace).

(B) According to most courts, yes. Even though Antoinette's claim is not valid — and she is therefore actually giving up nothing (i.e. suffering no "detriment") — the majority rule is that her promise not to sue will be sufficient consideration if (1) she had a *bona fide* subjective belief that her claim was valid, and (2) that belief was reasonable. Both appear to be the case under these facts. (Some courts, and the Restatement, go further: they'll enforce the settlement if it's the case that *either* the promisor had a subjective believe that her claim was valid, *or* such a belief would have been reasonable.)

24. (A) No, because New World's promise to do so was not supported by consideration. Consideration requires a bargained-for exchange, and either detriment to the promisee or benefit to the promisor. At the moment New World made its capital-naming promise, Columbus was already obligated to sail West and discover America. Therefore, he was promising merely to do exactly what he was already obligated to do. A promise to perform a ***pre-existing duty*** does not involve a detriment to the promisor.

(B) Yes, because he did something beyond what he was originally obligated to do. Even in courts following the majority/common-law rule that a promise to do what one is already obligated to do cannot be consideration, the promisor's promise to undertake different or additional duties (no matter how slight the difference) is consideration for the return promise. So Columbus' agreement to leave 2 days earlier was consideration for the capital-naming promise, making that promise enforceable.

25. (A) Yes. Under the common-law "pre-existing duty rule," contract modifications generally require independent consideration to be enforceable. However, the UCC abolishes this rule with respect to contracts for the sale of goods. Under §2-209(1), sales contracts can be modified without any additional consideration, even if the other party merely promises to do exactly what it had previously promised to do. So even though Melissa is merely promising to supply the same quantity of fish she was already required to supply, Charlie's agreement to raise the price was binding. Once he made that agreement, he couldn't retract it, even though Melissa hadn't relied on the modification yet.

(B) Yes. Under Rest. 2d §89, a modification of a contract that has not yet been fully performed on either side is binding, if the modification is "fair and equitable in view of circumstances not anticipated by the parties when the contract was made." The freeze and consequent price run-up certainly qualify as such an unanticipated circumstance.

26.   No. Under UCC §3-311 (added in 1990), a creditor who cashes a check thereby surrenders his underlying claim, provided that: (a) the check or accompanying written communication contains a "conspicuous statement" that the check is being tendered in full satisfaction of the claim; (b) the claim is either unliquidated, or subjected to a bona fide dispute; and (c) the debtor acted in good faith. (a) is clearly satisfied by the "Paid in Full" notation and the accompanying letter. (b) is probably satisfied, since we're told that E.T.'s reasoning is plausible, though not necessarily likely to prevail. (c) is also satisfied, since we're told in the facts that E.T. is acting in good faith. So when MCI cashed the check, this act released E.T. (it acted as an accord and satisfaction), and nothing MCI wrote on the check could change this result.

27.   No, because Princess's promise is illusory. An illusory promise is one unsupported by consideration due to one party's completely unrestricted right to renege on her promise. Here, there is no restriction whatsoever on Princess's freedom of action — she can change her mind at will. Therefore, her promise is illusory and unenforceable.

29.   (A) Yes. This is a typical "requirements" contract. Both requirements and output contracts are enforceable under the UCC, because they are deemed to be supported on both sides by consideration. This is so because the UCC imposes an implied obligation of good faith upon the parties, as well as one of exclusivity, in such output and requirements contracts. That is, Hercules has implicitly agreed to run his business in a good-faith way, so that he will continue to have a need for thing-a-ma-bobs. This (together with his agreement that he will not buy any thing-a-ma-bobs from anyone but Zeus), provides sufficient consideration to make the contract enforceable. Since Hercules has bound himself, Zeus' return promise is supported by consideration, making Zeus also bound.

(B) No. Under these facts, Hercules has not restricted his freedom in any way — he can choose to buy one unit, 100 or none. His promise is therefore illusory, and does not constitute consideration. Consequently, that promise cannot serve as consideration for Zeus' return promise, and Zeus is therefore not bound.

30.   No, because Goldilocks' promise was not supported by consideration, in that Papa Bear's return promise was illusory. An illusory promise is one that does not constitute consideration because the promisor has an unrestricted right to renege on his promise. One type of illusory promise is a promise that is conditional upon an event, which event is solely within the promisor's control. That's what we have here: Papa's duty to sell was subject to a condition (his planting of the extra acre), but Papa was solely in control of whether that condition was satisfied. Now, the doctrine of "mutuality of consideration" says that one party's illusory promise (here, Papa Bear's) cannot serve as consideration for the other party's return promise (here, Goldilocks' promise to buy). So Goldilocks' promise was not supported by consideration, and she's therefore not bound.

33.   Yes, but probably only for the $200 spent on drugs. Under the modern and Restatement view, a promise to pay someone for benefits received is enforceable without consideration — but only to the extent necessary to ***prevent injustice.*** Here, Aunt Bee would likely be able to enforce the promise to reimburse her for the medicines, since it's probably unjust that she be left with this out-of-pocket expense after Opie promised otherwise. However, she would probably *not* be able to enforce the promise for the additional $500 for the value of her services: since Aunt Bee is not only a *retired* nurse but also a relative of the recipient, it's highly likely that a court would conclude that Bee intended the services as a gift, not as something for which she expected to be paid. If she intended a gift, prevention of injustice would not require that she be paid.

34. No. First, the fact that Plato is not giving consideration in return for Great Philosophers' concession is irrelevant: under UCC §2-209(1), "an agreement modifying a contract within [Article 2] needs no consideration to be binding." Next, §2-209(2) generally enforces No Oral Modification clauses, such as the one here. However, where the deal is between a merchant and a consumer, an N.O.M. clause on a form supplied by the merchant is not enforceable against the consumer unless the clause has been separately signed by the consumer. Since the facts tell us that Plato didn't even notice the clause, he clearly didn't "separately sign" it. Therefore, the clause isn't enforceable, and the modification was effective, under the general rule that oral modifications are enforceable.

35. Yes. Under the Restatement and prevailing modern view, an option does not need consideration to be binding, provided that the option is in writing, recites a purported consideration (whether actually paid or not), and proposes an exchange on fair terms within a reasonable time. Rest. 2d, §87(1)(a). All of these conditions are satisfied here, so the option is enforceable. The significance of the option's enforceability, of course, is that Jerry cannot revoke the option (in contrast to the usual rule making offers that are not supported by consideration revocable even where the offer recites that it's irrevocable).

37. (A) No, because Scheherezade did not suffer a detriment in reliance on Ali's promise. First, remember that of course promises to make gifts are generally not enforceable, because they're not supported by consideration. Promissory estoppel can overcome this problem, but p.e. only protects against the promisee's reasonable and foreseeable detrimental reliance on the promise. Here, the facts tells us that Scheherezade did not take any action in reliance on the promise before it was retracted. Therefore, there is nothing on which the promissory estoppel doctrine could operate, and the usual "promises to make gifts are not enforceable" rule applies.

(B) Yes, but only $25,000. Here, unlike in part (A), Scheherezade has reasonably and foreseeably relied on Ali's promise to her detriment. She will therefore be able to enforce his promise under a theory of promissory estoppel. However, the promise will only be enforceable to the extent necessary to prevent injustice, which means that only Scheherezade's reliance expenditures will be protected. In this case, that will mean that Ali will have to reimburse Scheherezade for the forfeited deposit money, since this is the only respect in which Scheherezade has actually relied on the promise.

38. $200,000. Most courts treat sub-contractors' bids as offers that are temporarily irrevocable for the period necessary to allow the contractor to obtain the job and accept the sub-contractor's bid. The reasoning is based on the theory of promissory estoppel, since the contractor justifiably relies on the sub-contractor's bid. That's what happened here. (If Hound had had the chance to withdraw or amend his own bid to Winner, his failure to do so would have made his continued reliance on Electra's offer unreasonable; but the facts tell us that Hound was stuck with his bid.) The recovery will protect Hound's reliance interest, i.e., the amount by which he was worse off than had Elektra honored her offer. That amount is the difference between Elektra's bid and the next-lowest bid that Hound ended up using, or $200,000.

39.   (A) No, due to the parties' mutual mistake. A mistake by both parties, which goes to a *"basic assumption"* on which the contract was made, will generally be grounds for avoidance. Here, this standard is satisfied: the parties thought they were bargaining for a regular goose when in fact they were bargaining for a vastly more-valuable goose that lays golden eggs. Were the court to enforce this contract, Giant would wind up with a tremendous windfall and Jack would suffer a significant loss. Although the court will not allow rescission if it's proper to allocate the risk of the mistake to the party seeking avoidance, nothing in these facts makes it appropriate to allocate the risk of this mistake to Jack. Therefore, the court will allow Jack to rescind.

(B) Yes, under these facts, the court *would* enforce the contract. Even where a mistake is mutual, a court will not allow a party to avoid the contract if the risk of the mistake is properly allocated to that party. One of the ways such allocation will occur is if a party is aware that he has only *limited information* regarding some aspect of the deal, but treats his limited information as sufficient. (This is sometimes called "conscious ignorance.") Here, Jack knew that there was an issue as to whether the eggs were different from the usual goose eggs, but chose to rely on what he knew was his own imperfect (and wrong, as it turned out) assessment. Having made that choice, he's stuck. (But the result would be otherwise if Giant *knew* that the eggs were gold; this would be a unilateral mistake, of which the non-mistaken party was aware — see the treatment of unilateral mistake later in this chapter.)

40.   Yes. Even a mutual mistake will not be grounds for rescission if the mistake is one the risk of which is properly allocated to the party now seeking rescission. A mistake about the general state of market conditions will almost certainly fall into this category, since a contrary rule would give parties an incentive to remain ignorant of something they could easily check. Therefore, Daisy can enforce the contract as it is written.

41.   Mike. The issue here is the effect of a unilateral mistake. In addition to the requirements necessary in a mutual mistake situation (mainly that the mistake must relate to a "basic assumption" and the risk must not be one properly allocated to the party seeking to avoid it), a party who wants to avoid a contract based on unilateral mistake must also prove that *either:* (1) enforcement of the contract would be unconscionable, *or* (2) the other party **knew** or **should have known** of the mistake or somehow was *at fault* for creating the mistake. Here, Leo was aware from the get-go that Mike was mistaken about the value of the card, but failed to correct Mike. Mike is therefore able to satisfy requirement (2), and can avoid the contract.

44.   (A) Adjustment of the price to $5,400. Although the parties were under a "mutual mistake" with respect to the size of the property, the court will probably not allow the contract to be rescinded, because: (1) the 10% deviation in the size of the property does not have a "material effect on the agreed exchange of performances" (a requirement for relief under the doctrines of both mutual and unilateral mistake); and (2) an adjustment to the contract could alleviate any unfairness created by the mistake. The court will therefore probably adjust the contract to reflect the actual size of the parcel: $600 per acre for *nine* acres, for a total of $5,400.

(B) Rescission, plus a splitting of Ziffel's out-of-pocket loss. In contrast to the facts in (A), here the mistake appears to go to the very purpose of the contract. Therefore, a court would likely grant rescission of the contract. Rescission, however, will not be sufficient to put the parties back in the positions they were in before the contract was made, since Ziffel has incurred $3,000 in reliance expenses which he cannot avoid by returning the equipment or using it somewhere else. A court will try to split the loss the best it can. Reliance damages may probably appropriate here, and would likely take the form of an order for Ziffel to sell the equipment and then, if there is a shortfall, recover half that shortfall from Douglas.

45. The court will reform the contract to reflect the intended price and quantity. When parties have reached an oral agreement and then the agreement is incorrectly reflected in a written document, the court will in essence re-write the agreement to make it conform to the original agreement. This is called a *"reformation."*

46. Yes. The parol evidence rule would prevent Washington from showing an oral agreement that occurred prior to or contemporaneously with the writing, and that either contradicted or supplemented the writing. But the parol evidence rule doesn't prevent (or even deal with) *subsequent* oral modifications to contracts. Since the writing has no No Oral Modification clause, the oral modification may be proved (and will be enforced).

47. (A) No. The parol evidence rule bars any evidence of a prior or contemporaneous oral agreement where such evidence would ***contradict*** a term of a written contract that was intended as a "final" (even if not "total") integration, i.e., expression of the parties' agreement. The facts tell you that the writing is a final integration, so this rule applies here. The writing specifically requires both parties to work 30 hours a week, and an oral clause that would reduce Lacey's time by 1/3 for 1/3 of the year certainly seems to be a contradiction of the agreement, not a mere supplementation or interpretation of it.

(B) Yes, probably. The merchandise-discount clause merely supplements the writing, and doesn't contradict it, since the writing is silent on the subject. The parole evidence rule provides that a final integration may be supplemented (not contradicted) by prior oral agreement if and only if the integration is partial rather than total (that is, only if the writing was *not* regarded by the parties as covering all aspects of the deal). Here, the relatively short length of the writing, the fact that it was handwritten, and the fact that it was entirely drafted in one hour, all make it likely that the parties intended the integration to be merely partial. If so, the supplementary oral term will be admissible.

48. (A) Yes. The parol evidence rule only forbids introduction of prior agreements or contemporaneous oral agreements that vary, modify or contradict a "totally integrated" contract — one intended by the parties to be the final and complete expression of their agreement. Therefore, evidence that the writing was not intended to be a total integration is always admissible on this threshold issue that determines whether and how the parol evidence rule will apply.

(B) The judge will decide all of these issues. All of these issues are viewed as being essentially procedural ones that involve primarily legal reasoning. Therefore, all are unsuitable for the jury. The jury will consequently be left with at most the job of determining whether Blackstone made the alleged oral warranty, and whether the goods breached that warranty. (The jury won't even get to decide these issues unless the judge first decides either that the integration was not total, or that it was total but that the alleged warranty only supplements the writing.)

49. No. The parol evidence rule only operates when a contract is *effective*. This means that anything showing it's *not* effective — fraud, a lack of consideration, duress, mistake, or, as here, failure of a condition to the contract's effectiveness — *is* admissible. Here, the allegation is that the agreement is only binding if Howard approves the patent. If true, this would be a condition to the contract's effectiveness, so Einstein *can* introduce evidence to prove the condition was agreed upon.

50. Yes. Even though the disclaimer states that Buyer assumed the risk of the car's condition and that Seller made no oral representations, Gary will be able to introduce evidence of his conversation with Sam during the negotiations for the sale. The parol evidence rule does not ar evidence designed to prove fraud, such as that the other party ***intentionally misrepresented*** an aspect of the deal otherwise covered by a disclaimer clause.

51. Yes. Under the *traditional* view to parol evidence and interpretation, the *"plain meaning"* rule (which says that terms and provisions that on their face are unambiguous may not be altered by parol evidence) would apply. In that event, Lumpy would be out of luck, since there is nothing ambiguous on its face about the term "red shirt." The modern approach, however, is to reject the plain-meaning rule, and allow testimony about what the parties intended by any term or provision, even if that term or provision, viewed solely in the context of the document's "four corners," seems unambiguous. So under the modern approach, Lumpy will be entitled to testify that he and Wally were applying their secret-code meaning to the terms, not using these terms' ordinary-language meaning.

53. It's an express condition, of the implied-in-fact variety. Although the parties did not explicitly state that Acme's payment duty would not arise until 40 days after delivery, a court would probably find that the parties in fact intended the payment duty to be conditional upon delivery 40 days before. If so, this is an express condition, because it's one the parties actually intended (not one imposed by the court for fairness, which would make it a constructive condition). But this express condition is of the "implied in fact" variety, because we have to look at the surrounding circumstances, not just at the language, to know whether the parties intended a condition.

54. It's both a condition and a promise. It's a promise, since it's a commitment by Rudolph to perform (even though the promise is itself conditional on snow falling before 9 am); so if Rudolph doesn't perform, Santa can sue for breach. But it's also a condition on Santa's duty of payment: if Rudolph doesn't plow by 5 pm, Santa doesn't have to pay. In fact, the condition is probably an express (intended) one; if so, Rudolph will have to strictly comply with the deadline, and substantial performance (e.g., plowing, but doing it 3 hours late), won't suffice.

57. Yes. The condition here is obviously an express one. And it's true that express conditions generally require "strict" compliance. However, courts will usually wriggle out of the strict-compliance requirement and settle for substantial compliance if enforcing the strict terms of the contract would result in a large ***forfeiture***. See Rest. 2d §229: "To the extent that the non-occurrence of a condition would cause *disproportionate forfeiture*, a court may *excuse* the non-occurrence of that condition unless its occurrence was a *material part* of the agreed exchange." Here, the substitution of mirror tiles did not materially impair the overall purpose or value of the contract. It's true that if Tuileries were deprived of the right to recover under the contract, it would still be entitled to recover under quasi contract for the fair value of the house; but Tuileries would lose much of the benefit of its bargain (its profit margin), and this would amount to a "disproportionate forfeiture." Therefore, the court will likely let Tuileries recover under the contract. However, de Pompadour will be allowed to assert a counterclaim for any actual damage (typically loss of market value) that the substitution of tile has cost her.

Note that this result is somewhat unfair to de Pompadour – she bargained specifically for Brand X tiles, but ends up being forced to accept Maison de Whoopee, with just a trivial price allowance for any diminution of market value. But avoidance of massive forfeiture is deemed more important than honoring de Pompadour's right to get exactly what she bargained for.

58. No, because the contract is "divisible" into one-month sub-contracts. Usually, each party's substantial performance of his promise is a constructive condition to any subsequent duty of the other party. However, this rule does not apply where a contract is "divisible," i.e., properly viewed as a series of *agreed-upon pairs of part-performance.* That's what happened here: the parties divided up their performances into one-month installments, with each monthly swabbing by Queequeeg paired in value with Ahab's payment of $10. In this divisibility scenario, the court will treat the arrangement largely as if it were a series of individual contracts, each for one month. Queequeeg did not breach the contract to swab in June, and his failure to swab in July won't prevent the June swabbing and the June payment from being agreed-upon equivalents.

Therefore, Ahab must pay for June, and his only recourse is to: (1) sue Queequeeg for breach of the July installment, provided he can prove he suffered any damages; and (2) cancel the remainder of the contract, if the July failure substantially impaired the value to Ahab of the remaining monthly performance (e.g., Ahab had to hire a replacement because he couldn't safely rely on Queequeeg anymore).

59. Nutty can recover for material breach, and may also cancel the whole contract if he wishes. Mr. Peabody has only the right to recover damages for non-material breach, not the right to cancel or withhold his own performance.

When parties have structured a contract to require periodic payments or alternating performances, a party's duty to perform a portion of the contract is constructively conditioned upon the other party's having substantially performed any prior corresponding duties. The issue under these facts is which party was the first to fail to *substantially* perform. It is true that Nutty was the first to deviate from the terms of the contract. However, his sending parts only three days late, when there was no evidence that time was of the essence under the contract, is unlikely to amount to a material breach. Therefore Mr. Peabody was the first to materially breach (i.e., fail to materially perform) when he refused to pay that month's installment. Consequently, Nutty can not only recover for the breach, but can also elect to cancel the contract if he wants. By contrast, all Mr. Peabody has is a claim for non-material breach, not the right to cancel or to withhold payment for April.

60. The Grinch wins. Where the performance of one party requires a period of time to complete and the performance of the other party does not, the court will hold that the performance requiring time must occur first and that its completion is a constructive condition to the other party's duty to perform. Here, performance of Pollyanna's duties will take time and Grinch's payment will not. Since the parties did not agree otherwise, Pollyanna has to perform her PR services before Grinch has to pay. Pollyanna's refusal to do so was therefore a breach, for which Grinch may recover.

61. (A) Yes. Under the UCC's "perfect tender" rule, a buyer has the right to reject goods if they fail to conform to the contract in any respect. Stallion has the right to reject the blue figures even though they are of equivalent value (and almost equivalent looks) to the red figures, especially since they represent a different character from the one Stallion wanted to sell at his store.

(B) No. Although the "perfect tender" rule states that a buyer can reject goods if the goods are defective in any way, the court will look to such things as course of performance, course of dealing and usage of trade to help define the term "defective." Here, usage-of-trade evidence will prove that the figures are fungible goods regardless of color. As such, Action Plastic's shipment will likely be considered substantial performance, despite the fact that the shipment deviates from the specific terms of the contract!

(C) No. A party who has received a defective shipment may reject the goods, and may suspend his own performance (here, payment). But if the time for performance has not yet expired, the seller has a statutory right to *cure* within the contract period, no matter how severe the breach, provided that he gives prompt notice of his intention to cure. UCC §2-508(1). Therefore, Stallion must give Action a reasonable opportunity to say that it intends to cure by shipping conforming goods. If Action says it will do so, Stallion may not cancel until the delivery time expires without Action's having in fact shipped conforming goods. Until then, Stallion must simply wait until such time as Action's failure to give reassurances of cure itself amounts to a new act of material breach (which would justify Stallion in cancelling immediately).

(D) No. Even if the time for performance under the contract is up, under §2-508(2) a buyer has to give the seller a reasonable extension of time to cure a defective shipment if the seller shipped nonconforming goods that it thought were going to be acceptable to the buyer (called an "accommodation shipment"). That's the case here, so Stallion has to give Action Plastics one more shot. Once again, however, Stallion's duty to pay is suspended until he receives the right stuff. Note that there is no evidence that time is of the essence in this contract. If it were, then Stallion would not have to grant any extension.

62. Helen has the right to do what she did; Whirlie won't be able to collect anything, and Helen can recover for material breach.

Helen's act of signing the delivery receipt and putting the goods in inventory constituted an *"acceptance"* of the goods, as that term is used in the UCC. Once a buyer has accepted, she normally loses her ability to reject the goods (i.e., her ability to throw them back on the seller), even if they're non-conforming. However, a buyer who has accepted may "revoke" the acceptance (and then reject the goods) if two things are true: (i) the buyer did not know of the non-conformity at the time of acceptance, and the acceptance was induced by the difficulty of discovering the defect or by the seller's assurances; and (ii) the nonconformity substantially impairs the value of the goods to the buyer. §2-608(1). Since the problem couldn't easily have been discovered (and, indeed, wasn't discovered during Helen's brief initial test), (i) is satisfied. The physical dangers suggest that the goods' value to a professional merchant such as Helen has been substantially impaired, thus satisfying (ii). Therefore, Helen was entitled to revoke her acceptance and to send the goods back. She's also entitled to sue for breach, as anyone receiving (and even accepting) nonconforming goods may do.

63. Yes, because the condition will be excused. Where a party's duty is conditional on an event, and that same party's wrongful conduct prevents the occurrence of the condition, the non-occurrence of the condition will be excused. Michael will be held to have impliedly promised to use his reasonable efforts to ensure that the bank issues a loan on the stated terms. Since Michael did not make such efforts, his conduct will be deemed wrongful. Since that wrongful conduct prevented the condition from occurring, the condition will be excused.

64. (A) No, because Bohmer was permitted to retract his waiver. A party whose duty is subject to the occurrence of a condition can waive the benefit of the condition, by indicating that he won't insist on strict compliance with it. That's what Bohmer did here, by saying Marie could have the extra 30 days. However, if the condition is a meaningful part of the deal (as it probably was here, due to the fast-changing diamond market), and the other party has not yet materially relied on the promise not to insist on the condition, the waiving party can *retract* the waiver. Bohmer's Sept. 2 phone call was such a retraction. The facts tell us that Marie couldn't have materially relied on the waiver, because we're told that Marie wouldn't have been able to meet the Sept. 15 date anyway. So the retraction was effective.

(B) Yes, because Marie materially relied on the promise to waive the condition. As described in the answer to part (A), a party who has waived the benefit of a condition (here, Bohmer) may ordinarily retract that waiver. However, retraction is no longer possible once the other party has *materially and detrimentally relied* on the waiver. Here, the facts tell us that Marie would have had a 40% chance of meeting the original Sept. 15 date (the condition) if Bohmer had not promised the extra 30 days. Marie's giving up of this chance is probably enough to constitute "material" reliance, even though there was a less-than-even chance that the waiver changed the outcome. If so, this reliance prevented Bohmer from retracting.

Bohmer might argue that his original promise to waive the condition was void for lack of consideration, since Marie didn't give Bohmer anything of value (or suffer any legal detriment) in return for that promise. Under this view, the promise to waive was in effect a modification of the contract. However, Bohmer's argument will be unsuccessful, for at least one of these two reasons: (1) the UCC would regard the modification as binding without consideration, provided that the need for it was dictated by events unanticipated at the time the contract was formed (something that Marie may be able to establish); and (2) even if consideration were ordinarily required for such a modification, a court would almost certainly hold that Marie's justifiable reliance on the modification acted as a substitute for consideration, under the promissory estoppel doctrine.

66. (A) No. When a party makes an anticipatory repudiation — an advance, *unequivocal* refusal to (or manifestation of inability to) perform her contractual duties — the other party is permitted to cancel the contract immediately, without waiting for the time for performance to arrive. (He may also sue immediately for breach, as covered in the next chapter.) However, under these facts, Bunny's unreliability is not unequivocal, and Flynt cannot be certain or almost certain that Bunny will breach the agreement. Therefore, he cannot treat Bunny as having anticipatorily repudiated. Consequently, he has no immediate right to cancel the contract or sue.

(B) Advise Flynt to demand reasonable assurances of performance from Bunny. A party who after formation of a contract learns facts leading him to reasonably fear that the other party will be unable or unwilling to perform has the right to demand reasonable assurance of performances from that other party. If Bunny fails promptly to provide adequate assurances (probably either a demonstration that the reports of earlier cancellations are wrong, or an explanation of why it's unlikely to happen again), Flynt can treat this as an anticipatory repudiation. At that point, he would have the right to cancel the contract, sue her for any damages he may have suffered, and hire someone else.

(C) Yes. If a party already knew *at the time of entering into the contract* of facts indicating that the other party may be unwilling or unable to perform, he cannot rely on those facts as the basis for a demand for adequate assurances. Under this scenario, Flynt will just have to keep his fingers crossed and hope Bunny comes through as promised — he can't cancel, and can't sue for breach unless and until she actually fails to perform on the scheduled date.

67.   Yes. It is a constructive condition of each party's duty to perform that the other party not manifest an unwillingness or inability to perform. If a party does manifest such an unwillingness or inability, the other party can suspend her own performance and, under the doctrine of *Hochster v. De La Tour*, sue *immediately* for breach. Here, Dahlia's own conduct (selling Totleigh to Tom) has created her inability to perform under the contract. Therefore, Agatha's duty to perform is suspended and she can sue immediately, even though the time of performance is still several weeks away.

68.   No. Even though Tractor has made is clear in advance that she intends to breach the caulking part of the contract, this would only amount to a minor ("partial") breach of contract, since the facts tell us that choice of the caulking color doesn't have much impact. In order for a party to sue prior to the date of performance based on anticipatory repudiation, the breach in question must be *material* — i.e., a total breach. Unreezonable will just have to wait to get his day in court on this one.

70.   (A) Kowalski must sell to Blanche. A repudiation may be *retracted* until the aggrieved party has done one of three things: (1) sued for breach; (2) changed his position materially in reliance on the repudiation; or (3) stated that he regards the repudiation as final. Rest. 2d, §256(1). Kowalski has done none of these things by the time he gets Blanche's retraction call on the 20th. (His mere re-listing the bar with a broker isn't likely to be found to be a "material" change of position.) Therefore, Blanche is entitled to retract her repudiation, in which case the contract is reinstated as if there had been no repudiation.

(B) He may take the $60,000 offer. As the answer to part (A) shows, one of the ways in which a repudiator loses the ability to retract the repudiation is if the aggrieved party states that that party regards the repudiation as final. Kowalski's statement to Blanche that he'd see her in court probably qualifies as such a statement, so at that point Blanche lost the ability to retract. Consequently, the breach was complete and final on June 10, making Kowalski free now to regard the contract as cancelled and to make other arrangements.

71.   No. Ironically, when it comes to suing after an anticipatory repudiation, a party who has fully performed has lesser rights than a party whose performance has not yet come due: there is a special rule that says that when the party aggrieved by an anticipatory repudiation has already given all the performance he was required to give, that party may not sue immediately, and must instead wait for the time for performance before suing. So Spock may not sue until Klingon actually fails to deliver the coat on April 1.

74.   Yes. Marie has agreed to pay the debt of another person, so ordinarily her promise would have to be in writing, under the suretyship provision. But the most important exception to the suretyship provision is the *"main purpose"* rule, which says that if the promisor's chief purpose in making his promise of suretyship is to further his own interests, his promise does not fall within the suretyship provision. That's the case here: Marie's main reason for guaranteeing Tuileries' debt is not to help Tuileries, but because she, Marie, wants the mirror installed. Therefore, Marie's promise is enforceable even though not in writing.

75. No, because it violates the Statute of Frauds. Contracts for the sale of "an interest in land" require a writing to be enforceable.

77. Yes. It's true that contracts for the sale of land normally require a writing. But where the seller has made the contracted-for conveyance, he can recover the contract price even though the original agreement was not in writing.

78. Probably not. The land-sale provision applies here, unless some exception to it applies. The only exception that might apply is the doctrine that where the vendee relies to his detriment, this may entitle him to specific enforcement. However, this exception applies only where the vendee's conduct is ***"unequivocally referable"*** to the alleged oral contract of conveyance (i.e., the vendee's conduct would never have occurred unless the alleged contract of conveyance actually occurred). Here, da Vinci, given his profession, might have moved temporarily onto the property just to paint the mural as a contract painting job for Pope, so it probably can't be said that da Vinci's acts of moving in and painting the mural are "unequivocally referable" to the alleged contract of conveyance. Therefore, the detrimental-reliance exception probably doesn't apply, and the oral contract is unenforceable.

79. (A) Yes, because by its terms, the contract cannot be fully performed within one year, and so falls within the Statute of Frauds. Any contract that by its terms cannot be "fully performed" within one year from its making must be in writing. Ramm Beau's principal purpose in making the contract is to have a research director for five years; therefore, if (as seems almost inevitable), Einstein dies before the end of the five years, the contract will have been "discharged," not "fully performed."

Note, by the way, that it doesn't matter what *actually* happens (i.e., whether Einstein in fact lives and works for the five years). What counts is the terms of the contract, and whether, analyzed as of the moment the contract is made, there is any possible way that the contract could be fully performed within one year. Since the answer is "no" even to this easier-to-satisfy question, the contract falls within the Statute and must be in writing.

(B) No. Now the contract is removed from the Statute of Frauds and does not have to be in writing, because it is capable of being "fully performed" in less than one year. That's because the contract is, by its terms, for Einstein's "life" — if Einstein dies in less than a year, the contract will nonetheless have been fully performed.

80. (A) Yes. What counts is not the length of the lease once it begins, but the time from the making of the lease until its full performance (its expiration). Although the lease itself is only for nine months, the contract cannot be performed within one year from the execution of the contract, so a writing is required.

(B) No. Now no writing is required because the contract can be fully performed within one year of its making. (Remember that leases for one year or less in duration do not constitute an "interest in land," so the "Land Contract" provision of the Statute of Frauds would not come into play here, either.)

81. Charlie, according to most courts. Most courts (and the Second Restatement) now hold that *full performance* by one party removes the contract from the one-year provision of the Statute of Frauds — even though the contract could not have been (and was not) fully performed within one year of its making.

82. Yes. According to UCC §2-201, a contract for the sale of goods priced at $500 or more must be in writing. The wholesale cost of the goods is irrelevant — what matters is the contract price.

83. No. Where, as here, the contract is primarily for the provision of services, the contract is not within Article 2 of the UCC, even though it also involves the sale of goods worth more than $500. Services contracts — no matter how large — need not be in writing (unless they cannot be completed in less than one year).

84. Yes. There is an exception to the "sale of goods" provision of the Statute of Frauds for goods that are "specially manufactured." §2-201(3)(a). As long as the seller has made a "substantial beginning" on their manufacture, or has made "commitments for their procurement," the oral agreement will be enforceable. Since the facts tell us that Etty-Kette has begun manufacture, this condition is satisfied.

85. 50. First, the fact that Fix-M-Up never signed any document doesn't matter: when a deal is between merchants, UCC §2-201(2) says that if one sends the other a confirmation that is "sufficient against the sender" (i.e., signed by the sender, and containing the essential terms), and the recipient fails to make written objection within 10 days, the recipient is bound as if she had signed that confirmation. So Fix-M-Up is bound the same way Flybye Nite is bound, whatever that is.

Next, a separate provision of the UCC, §2-201(1), says that in a deal for more than $500, the Statute of Frauds must be satisfied by "some writing sufficient to indicate that a contract for sale has been made between the parties." The section also says that "A writing is not insufficient because it omits or incorrectly states a term agreed upon but the contract is not enforceable under this paragraph beyond the quantity of goods shown in such writing." So the error doesn't prevent the confirmation from being a writing that satisfies the memorandum requirement, but Flybye Nite can't enforce the deal beyond the quantity shown on the confirmation, 50.

87. Miss Piggy loses this round. When a contract undergoes an oral modification, courts will look to see if the new contract, as modified, falls within the Statute of Frauds. If it does, the modification will be ineffective, and the original contract will be left standing. Here, even with the additional term, the contract falls within the Statute because it is a contract incapable of being performed in less than a year from its making. Therefore, the court will enforce the original contract, the one with no veto clause.

88. Yes, an order for specific performance (i.e., a court order compelling Acme to honor the original deal with Marge). Where the subject matter of the contract is unique, as here, the court will likely grant specific performance, since damages will not be adequate to compensate Marge for the breach.

89. (A) No. Because of the personal relationship involved and the constitutional prohibition of involuntary servitude, courts will generally deny specific performance as a remedy for breach by an employee of an employment contract.

(B) An injunction against worker for a competitor of Rocco, for the remaining length of the contract. Rocco can receive an order enjoining Sisyphus from working for a competitor for the remaining 2.5 years, if it can prove the following: (1) that Sisyphus has a special skill (which he does, since we know he is an expert on hauling rocks); (2) that Sisyphus will not be left without any other reasonable means of earning a living (the injunction would most likely be limited in geographic scope so that he can get a job *somewhere* in his field); and (3) that if the probable result of the injunction would be that Sisyphus would just decide to come back to work for Rocco, Rocco would be ready, willing and able to take him back.

(C) No. The general rule against orders of specific performance in personal-services (i.e., employment) contracts applies to both employers and employees. Therefore, Sisyphus will not be able to require Rocco to take him back — his only recourse is to sue for damages for the breach.

90. (A) $50,000 — that is, the balance of the contract price ($250,000) less Landmark's remaining cost to complete ($200,000).

(B) No. If a contractor cannot show with some specificity what it would have cost him to complete the job, he will not be able to recover his expectation damages. Under these facts, Landmark will likely only be able to recover the value of the benefit it has conferred upon Idd (restitution damages).

91. (A) No. A plaintiff can only recover damages that she can prove with reasonable certainty. Lost profits on a brand new business venture are normally too speculative.

(B) Yes. The fact that Bo has previously made $1,000/mo. under a similar arrangement means that there is a "reasonable certainty" that she would have made this amount in the new venture. Therefore, unless Mr. Clean can show some reason why past conditions would not have applied to the new contract, Bo will be able to recover, as expectation damages, $1,000 x 12 months, or $12,000.

93. (A) $15,000. Where, as here, a party can't estimate her expectation damages with sufficient certainty, the party may recover restitution damages. Therefore, Rococo can collect restitution damages to compensate it for the benefit it has conferred upon Neulla. These damages will be $15,000, or the market value of the work it has done.

(B) $15,000. With restitution damages, a party who has not yet fully performed can collect an amount *in excess of* the total contract price. (Yes, this is paradoxical, but the law is pretty clear on this point.) So Rococo will be entitled to its $15,000 even though the contract price was only $12,000.

(C) $50,000. Ironically (in light of the answer to (B)), when a party has *fully performed* under a contract and the other party's breach amounts to a failure to pay money, most courts will *limit* the plaintiff's recovery to her expectation damages, even where the restitution damages would have been greater. So here, Rococo will be entitled to collect only the $50,000 contract price, not the $60,000 market value.

94. Yes, in quasi-contract, probably for $15,000. Where impossibility prevents the fulfillment of a partially-performed contract, the court will normally allow the party who has performed work to recover in quasi-contract. The court will choose between reliance damages (here, $10,000) and restitution damages (here, $15,000). Probably the court will allow restitution, even though Agamemnon got no *lasting* benefit from the gazebo — the court will likely reason that Agamemnon received a temporary benefit worth $15,000, and that he could have (and should have) carried insurance to cover the value to him of partly-completed construction work.

95. $2,000. Dr. Welby cannot recover his expectation damages ($4,000) because no contract was ever attempted under these facts. He can, however, recover the reasonable value of his services ($2,000) in quasi-contract. It is irrelevant that Old Man River claims after-the-fact that he didn't want the services performed — in emergency situations, the person who provides the services with a reasonable expectation of being compensated for them will be able to recover the reasonable value of the services.

96. Probably nothing. A plaintiff who materially defaults is not by that fact alone prevented from recovering; he will usually be permitted to recover in quasi-contract for the market value of the partial performance. But in most jurisdictions there is an exception: if the plaintiff willfully (i.e., intentionally) breaches, courts will often deny *all* recovery, especially where the breach was done to save money, and done in a deceptive manner. Wilkes' motive to save money by substituting inferior materials would fall into this category, so Wilkes will probably be denied all recovery. This is especially likely since there is no way for Scarlett to pay a reasonable amount to have the work transformed to something that meets her specifications.

97. (A) No, because the lost profits were not reasonably foreseeable. In order to recover consequential damages (i.e., damages resulting as a consequence of the breach), the plaintiff has to show either that a *reasonable person* in the defendant's position would have foreseen the damages as a *logical and ordinary result* of a breach, or that the defendant had *actual notice* that this type of damage could occur. (This is the rule of *Hadley v. Baxendale*.)

Here, there's nothing to suggest that Wolf should have known that Three Little Pigs would have to shut down if the mixer was misdelivered: Temporary unavailability of a mixer wouldn't ordinarily cause this magnitude of losses (especially since a business that was so dependent on such machinery would ordinarily have a spare), so the loss wasn't reasonably foreseeable to one in Wolf's position. And the facts, by saying that TLP said nothing to Wolf except a description of the job and a request for a quote, show us that TLP didn't give Wolf actual notice of the danger of loss. As a result, the lost profits will be considered unforeseeable, and Wolf won't be liable for them.

(B) No. Foreseeability will be measured as of the time the contract was made. It is irrelevant that Wolf *subsequently* learned about the danger of extensive damages, even though it got this knowledge before it breached. (This makes sense, since Wolf had already quoted a price calculated based on the absence of any exposure to large business-interruption losses.)

98. (A) Yes. A party who suffers a breach of contract must make reasonable efforts to mitigate her damages. The duty to mitigate extends to employment contracts: wrongfully dismissed employees must look for comparable work (just as employers whose employees have wrongfully quit must look for comparable replacements).

(B) Probably not. It's true that a party must make reasonable efforts to mitigate damages. However, where the contract is for personal services, courts are quite lenient towards the plaintiff, and do not require her to accept any position that is substantially different from (even if not necessarily inferior to) the one contracted for. Here, the San Francisco position was much shorter than, and more importantly, 3,000 miles away from, the one Passemova had with 2 Left Feet. Especially considering Passemova's family reasons for not leaving New York for extended periods, it is very likely that a court would conclude that the San Francisco position was substantially different from the contracted-for one.

99. $21,000, i.e., no deduction for failure to mitigate damages. Courts generally view the so-called duty to mitigate as an affirmative defense, and therefore impose on the breaching party the **burden of producing evidence** that the non-breaching party / plaintiff failed to mitigate. In an employment case, this placement of the burden of proof usually means that it's not enough for the employer to show that the employee failed to act reasonably in seeking substitute employment. Instead, the employer must also: (1) **identify one or more positions** that the employee would likely have succeeded in obtaining, and (2) show **how much** the employee would likely have earned had she been offered and taken one of these suitable replacement positions. Here, Geppetto has made showing (2) (that a comparable position, if available, would have paid about $2,000 per month); but he has not satisfied (1) (i.e., he has not identified any particular comparable position that Cricket would likely have been able to obtain during the relevant time-frame). Therefore, the court will likely hold that Geppetto has failed to bear the burden of proving his failure-to-mitigate defense, and is not entitled to any reduction at all in damages. See *Maness v. Collins*, 2010 WL 4629614 (Tenn. Ct. App. 2010).

100. (A) $10,000, probably. A buyer of goods must make reasonable attempts to mitigate damages, just as most other types of victims of breach must do. It is likely that a court would conclude that Scarlett's unwillingness to come up with an extra $10,000 to avoid $15,000 in losses was unreasonable. If so, the court will limit her to the amount she would have lost had she reasonably mitigated (i.e., the $10,000 differential between Cal's price and the new supplier's price), not the $15,000 she actually lost.

(B) Nothing. When goods are resaleable and the seller does not choose to resell, his recovery is normally limited to the difference between the contract price and the market price on the day for delivery. §2-708(1). (A "lost volume" seller can recover his lost profits under §2-708(2) even if there is no contract-market differential, but the facts tell us that Cal is not a lost-volume seller, since he's already selling all the mature logs on his own land.) That differential is $0, which is all Cal can recover. The fact that the contract-market differential widened after the delivery date (to $11,000 by the time of trial) is irrelevant — Cal bears the risk of such a widening, giving him in effect a "duty to mitigate."

103. (A) Probably $100,000. A liquidated damages clause will be struck down (under the modern approach) unless it meets either of two tests: (1) it is a reasonable forecast viewed as of the time of contracting; or (2) it is a reasonable estimate, viewed after-the-fact. Here, the clause amount satisfies (2), since it is reasonably close to the actual loss. Therefore, the court will probably uphold the award.

(B) Probably $20,000. As we explain in the answer to part (A), a liquidated damages clause will be valid if it's a reasonable estimate of likely damages, viewed as of the moment of the contract, even if the estimate turns out to be quite badly off. However, a *"blunderbuss"* clause that assigns the same damage award regardless of the severity of the default will generally not be considered a reasonable advance estimate, considering the variation in scenarios (and damage amounts) that the clause will cover. The clause here, which is invariant to the length of delay, would probably be considered a blunderbuss clause. Even a blunderbuss clause will be saved if it turns out to be reasonably accurate. But the estimate of $100,000 is not reasonably close to the $20,000 actual delay, so there is no after-the-fact accuracy to save the clause. Consequently, the court will probably strike it down, and award just the actual damages suffered by Ben.

(C) $150,000, i.e., the amount called for by the clause. As noted in the prior parts, a damages clause will be valid if it's a reasonable forecast viewed as of the moment of contracting, even if the estimate turns out to be quite inaccurate. That's what happened here: keying damages to the number of days of delay, multiplied by a reasonable estimate of each day's damages, is certainly a reasonable method of forecasting loss. Therefore, the clause won't be rendered invalid by the fact that the actual damages turned out to be much less than the forecasted ones. (Note that the per-day calculation method is what prevents this from being a "blunderbuss" clause like the one in parts (A) and (B).)

104. (A) Yes. Superhero is a "lost volume" seller — a seller whose supply is greater than the demand. That's because Superhero will likely be able to prove that it would have made the sale to Spiderman regardless of Batman's breach: had Batman not breached, Superhero would have made *two* sales. Under §2-708(2), a seller who would not be made whole by the contract/resale differential may recover his lost profits; lost-volume sellers are prime examples of persons entitled to use 2-708(2). Therefore, Superhero is entitled to collect its lost profits from Batman's breach. Those profits equal $1,000 (the list price less the wholesale price).

(B) $750. Under these facts, the car in question is a unique item. Therefore, Superhero is no longer a "lost volume" seller — he could sell the custom car only once. Consequently, Superhero is no longer entitled to collect its lost profit. Superhero is now limited to more traditional seller's remedy: the difference between the contract price and the resale price, plus incidentals. Here, that is ($20,000 - $19,500) + $250 in auction costs, for a total of $750.

107. $2,020. A buyer has the right to cover by procuring substitute merchandise. In that event, buyer's damages equal the different between the contract price and the cover price, plus any incidentals. So Mary will recover the $2,000 contract-cover differential, plus the $20 shipping expenses as incidental damages.

108. (A) Webb Foote. The assignment to Spyder was gratuitous (not made for consideration). A gratuitous assignment is automatically revoked by, inter alia, the assignor's subsequent assignment of the same right to someone else (even if the second assignment is also gratuitous). That second assignment therefore left Webb Foote with the only remaining rights to the assigned money.

(B) Insufficient facts, because we don't know who filed first under Article 9. This is something of a trick question. Where both assignees of the same claim took for value, and the assignment was a financing device, Article 9 normally governs. Therefore, whichever party first files an Article 9 security interest in the public records will win, and the facts don't tell us who did this first. (Normally, before a litigated controversy between the two, at least one would have filed.)

(C) Spyder. Where the first assignee gives value, and the second one knows of the prior assignment, the first assignee has priority. Many courts base this result on an estoppel theory:

the second assignee is "estopped" from taking ahead of the first one, because his own knowledge of the prior right would make it unfair for him to have priority.

109. (A) No. The assignee stands in the shoes of his assignor. This means that Irving takes subject to all the defenses, set-offs, and counterclaims which Liberté could have asserted against Euphrates. Here, Euphrates guaranteed that the diary was genuine and then later admitted it was forged. Euphrates' breach of the contract nullifies Liberté's obligation to pay.

(B) Probably not, because the assignment was gratuitous. The maker of a gratuitous assignment does not make an implied warranty of the assigned claim's validity, as the maker of an assignment-for-value does. Therefore, the mere fact that the claim turns out to be invalid won't be enough to allow Irving to recover against Euphrates. However, if Irving can prove that he relied to his detriment on the assignment (e.g., that he charged an expensive vacation in reliance on it), it is conceivable that Irving may be able to recover under a kind of promissory estoppel theory against Euphrates; that is, Irving would claim that the assignment was an implicit promise by Euphrates that Irving would in fact collect the money, and that Irving's reliance was foreseeable and reasonable.

111. (A) No. Duties to be performed under a contract are generally delegable. But where a contract calls for the performance of personal services by a person with particular personal skills, those services normally may not be delegated. Since portrait-painting involves personal skills that vary significantly from one person to another, such services may not be delegated without the consent of the person who is to receive the services. Therefore, Madame Gioconda can refuse to let Picasso paint her portrait and can insist that da Vinci do it. If she refuses to accept Picasso and da Vinci refuses to paint her portrait, he's breached the contract by repudiating it, and she can recover damages from him.

(B) No. If she sits for the portrait, she will be held to have implicitly assented to the delegation. She will thereby have waived her right to complain about the delegation, and must pay the contract price.

112. (A) No. To begin with, a document that purports to assign "the contract" will generally be interpreted as being an attempt at *both* an assignment of rights *and* a delegation of duties. Therefore, Lincoln's execution of the assignment document, and Davis' initialling of it, will constitute both: (1) an assignment by Lincoln to Davis of Lincoln's right to receive the money; and (2) an attempted delegation to Davis of Lincoln's obligation to tender a promissory note in return for the money.

The attempted delegation will be invalid, if Lee objects to it. That's because a duty as to which the promisee has a substantial interest in having only the original promisor perform is non-delegable. A promise that calls for the promisor's use of his own particular, unusual skills generally falls into this category. This principle is commonly applied to promissory notes: the promisee is not required to accept a promissory note from someone other than the original promisor, because the delegatee's creditworthiness will not be the same as the promisor's. Therefore, if Lee objects, he need not accept Davis' promissory note as a substitute for Lincoln's, and he may refuse to lend the money to Davis.

(B) Yes, probably. As noted in the answer to part (A), a document that purports to assign "the contract" will generally be interpreted as being an attempt at both an assignment of rights and a delegation of duties. So Lincoln has, as in part (A), assigned his rights to the loan, and has attempted to delegate his duty (of repayment). Davis, by initialing the assignment document and receiving the money, has implicitly promised Lincoln that Davis will repay Lee. The more interesting question is whether Lee may sue on this promise, since Davis didn't make the promise to Lee, just to Lincoln. The answer is that Lee may sue if he was a ***third party beneficiary*** (a concept discussed below) of Davis' promise to Lincoln. A court will probably hold that Lee was an "intended" beneficiary of Davis' promise (since Lincoln wanted Lincoln's repayment obligation to Lee to be discharged); in that case, Lee may sue Davis.

(C) Yes. Unless the promisee expressly indicates his consent to a ***novation*** (a complete substitution of one promisor for another), the mere fact that the promisee consents to an assignment and delegation does not discharge the assignor/delegator from liability. So here, the fact that Lee allowed the "assignment" of the contract (and made the loan to Davis) will not be interpreted as Lee's consent to substituting Davis for Lincoln. Therefore, Lincoln will remain liable, and may be sued if Davis defaults.

113. (A) Khufu, probably. Where the contract is silent, delegation is normally permissible unless either: (1) the promisee has a ***substantial interest*** in having the delegator perform (usually due to the delegator's unusual personal skills); or (2) the surrounding circumstances indicate that the parties both intended that the duty in question not be delegated. The facts indicate that (1) is not satisfied, since we're told that Tut is competent at work of this type, and the promisee's mere preference that the work be done by the promisor is not enough to constitute a substantial interest in having the work done by the promisor. As to (2), there's nothing in the surrounding facts to indicate that the parties ever thought about delegability, let alone implicitly agreed to forbid it. Therefore, as in most construction contracts, the duty of performance here will probably be found delegable.

(B) Cheops. A contract provision stating that the duties are not delegable will be enforced, even if the duties are ones that would, in the absence of the provision, be delegable. Therefore, Cheops is insisting on doing something that it has no right to do, and that insistence would be a breach (a repudiation).

(C) Cheops. A contract provision that prohibits "assignment of the contract" will, unless the circumstances indicate otherwise, be prohibited as barring the delegation of duties, but not the assignment of rights. (See UCC §2-210(3), so stating, for sales-of-goods cases.) Here, there are no circumstances indicating otherwise. Therefore, Cheops' attempted delegation will be a breach of the "anti-assignment" clause (but Cheops' assignment of, say, its right to be paid for its work would not be.)

114. No. A beneficiary may sue the promisor only if the beneficiary was an "intended" beneficiary. A beneficiary is "intended" if the circumstances indicate that the promisee intended to give the beneficiary the benefit of the promised performance. Here, there is no evidence that O'Hara (the promisee) intended to give Wilkes the benefit of the promised set — Wilkes was essentially a bystander whose very existence was probably not even considered by O'Hara when O'Hara made the set deal. Therefore, Wilkes was an "incidental" (not "intended") beneficiary, and as such, has no right to sue on the promise.

115. Yes. A non-party who would benefit by performance of a contractual promise may sue if the non-party is found to be an "intended" beneficiary. Where the promisee's purpose in bargaining for the promise is, at least in part, to confer a benefit on the beneficiary, the beneficiary is "intended." Here, although Hansel doesn't personally owe money to Witch, he clearly has a desire to see his sister's debt repaid. Therefore, he's intentionally attempting to confer a benefit on her by extracting the promise from Mother Goose that she'll part off the debt. Consequently, Hansel is an intended beneficiary, and may sue.

Note that these facts present an exception to the general rule-of-thumb that when performance does not run directly to the beneficiary, the beneficiary is probably not "intended" — here, the payment will go to Witch, not Gretel, but Gretel is still an intended beneficiary since Hansel intends that Gretel benefit by having her debt be extinguished.

116. (A) Yes, probably. The rule is that a beneficiary's rights "vest," making his rights irrevocable, when one of three events occurs: (1) the beneficiary materially changes his position in justifiable reliance on the promise; (2) he brings suit on it; or (3) he manifests his assent to the contract at the request of one of the parties. Here, the third party beneficiaries have materially relied on the contract to their detriment, by buying expensive wardrobes. Assuming that their reliance was reasonable, they will be able to recover in their suit. (An alternative rationale is that when the friends were shown the agreement by Dorothy and expressed their delight, this constituted their "assent" to the contract at Dorothy's request, making their rights irrevocable.)

(B) No, probably. Although a beneficiary's rights normally vest upon any of the three types of events described in the answer to part (A), the original parties are always free to retain the right to vary this rule. Here, Dorothy and Wizard's retention of the right to modify or rescind the contract (even though they don't mention the effect this will have on the three friends) will probably be interpreted as an implicit variation of these normal vesting rules. If so, the fact that the friends materially relied on (or manifested their assent to) the promise will be irrelevant.

117. Yes. When an intended beneficiary (Singer) sues the promisor (Washington) under a contract, the promisor has the same defenses as he would have against the promisee (Betsy Ross). Thus, breach of contract (as here), lack of mutuality or consideration, fraud, duress, or mutual mistake will all be valid defenses against the beneficiary.

118. No. The contract will be discharged due to the doctrine of impossibility. Here, the essential subject matter of the contract, Hoof Hearted, was destroyed through no fault of either party. Therefore, the contract cannot possibly be performed, and both parties are discharged from their obligation to perform.

119. (A) Yes. In impossibility and impracticability cases, discharge will occur only when three main conditions are satisfied: (1) the event relied on was one whose non-occurrence was a "basic assumption" on which the contract was made; (2) the event was not the fault of the party seeking discharge; and (3) the language or circumstances don't indicate that the parties allocated the risk to the party now seeking discharge. On these facts, test (1) is not satisfied — since Polly didn't know that Pisarro was contemplating using Fountain of Youth water, and since Pisarro could fill the order with other water, it's very unlikely that the unavailability of Fountain of Youth water would be held to be an event the non-occurrence of which was a basic assumption on which the contract was based.

(B) No. The fact that the contract specifically mentions Fountain of Youth as the source of supply indicates that the unavailability of Fountain water was an event the non-occurrence of which was a basic assumption on which the parties based their deal. Thus condition (1) listed in part (A) is satisfied. Since the earthquake was not Pisarro's fault (condition (2) from part

(A)), and since there's no evidence that the parties intended Pisarro to bear the risk of such an event (condition (3)), Pisarro will be discharged.

121. (A) Yes, probably. The majority view is that when a contractor is to build a structure from the ground up, the contractor will normally *not* be excused from performing even if the partially completed building is destroyed by no fault of the contractor. Therefore, Colossus must start over for no additional compensation, or be declared in breach.

(B) No, Colossus may not recover anything. Where a party contracts to repair or remodel an existing building owned by another, *each party* will normally be discharged from its duty to perform by the doctrine of impossibility if the building is destroyed throughout fault of either. That is, in a repair or renovation contract, the destruction of the structure is normally deemed to be an event the non-occurrence of which is a basic assumption on which the contract was based. Since there's nothing to indicate that Nero and Colossus bargained for a different allocation of the usual allocation of risks (discharge for both in the event of destruction), they'll both be discharged. Discharge here means that Nero doesn't have to put Colossus in a position to finish the contract, or to pay Colossus what it would have earned from full performance.

123. (A) The doctrine of frustration of purpose.

(B) No. The frustration-of-purpose defense allows a party (usually a buyer of goods or services) to cancel the contract if: (1) the buyer's primary purpose in making the agreement has been completely or almost-completely thwarted by an event the non-occurrence of which was a basic assumption of both parties to the contract; (2) the parties did not allocate the risk of that event to the party seeking discharge; and (3) the party seeking discharge wasn't at fault for causing (or failing to guard against) the event.

Here, these conditions are satisfied. As to (1), the Hotel obviously knew that Fann was probably planning on attending the Superbowl (the Hotel's double room rates show it knew that that was the purpose of most guests booking for that week), so both parties knew that the playing of the game was a "basic assumption" behind the contract. As to (2), there is no evidence that the parties intended Fann, as opposed to the Hotel, to bear the risk that something would happen to prevent the game. Also, the relative unforeseeability of the event (continued labor peace was expected at the time the contract was signed) makes it even more likely that a strike was not an event the risk of which the parties thought about imposing on the party whose purpose would be thwarted by that event. As to (3), Fann hasn't been at fault in failing to guard against the strike, since there's little he could have done to protect himself against the strike's occurrence.

124. Yes, $18,000. Where a contract is discharged under impossibility, impracticability or frustration, a party who has already rendered a benefit to the other will normally be entitled to restitution damages. Restitution will usually be computed based on the market value of the benefit rendered (not the cost to the discharged party of rendering the benefit, which would be a reliance measure.) Therefore, BAD will receive the market value of the work done to that point, $18,000. Notice that it's irrelevant that Tasteless did not receive any long-term benefit from the partly-done work — courts figure that Tasteless could *buy insurance* to cover loss of partly-done renovation more easily than BAD could, so it's economically efficient to impose the burden of the loss on him.

125. Probably not, but it depends on the court's precise approach to non-competes that

are unduly broad as drafted. A person's promise not to compete, entered into as part of that person's sale of a business, will be enforceable if (but only if) the non-compete is ***not unreasonably broad*** as to either: (1) the type of activity constrained, (2) the non-compete's duration, and (3) the non-compete's geographic reach. Here, requirement (1) is no problem: the business being sold and the activity proscribed are in the same industry (retail beverage sales). But requirement (2) is probably a problem: Hy has an estimated remaining working life of over 30 years, which is longer than Bud's store's goodwill is likely to last, so a court will probably conclude that the lifetime duration is unreasonable. Requirement (3) is probably also a problem: it's unlikely that a small beverage store in a populous place like N.Y.C. has a 20-mile radius within which it competes with other similar stores; therefore, the 20-mile radius provision is probably unduly broad.

However, a court might enforce the non-compete up to reasonable limits. That is, if the court believes that an 8-year non-compete, applicable to, say, a 6-mile radius, would have been reasonable (which the court might well conclude), the court might choose to bar Hy even though the non-compete as written is way too broad. But not all courts will perform this task of "editing the contract down to reasonable limits." Some won't enforce an unduly-broad-as-written non-compete *at all*. Others will do so only if a hypothetical "blue pencil" could remove the offending provision and leave something left to enforce; since no amount of excision — as opposed to rewriting — can turn a lifetime limit into an 8-year limit, or a 20-mile radius into a 6-mile radius, a court following the blue-pencil rule would refuse to enforce this agreement no matter how reasonable it thought an 8-year or 6-mile-radius limit would be.

126. Yes, probably. Normally, neither party to an illegal contract may recover. But where only one of the parties has an illegal purpose, the other party may be able to enforce the contract, under the "pari delicto" doctrine. Under that doctrine, the "innocent" party can recover, even if it knew about the other party's illegal purpose, as long as: (1) the innocent party is not guilty of moral turpitude; and (2) the innocent party is less blameworthy than the party with the illegal purpose. That's probably the case here: Snakeoil's behavior probably isn't deeply blameworthy (since it involves medicine), and Snakeoil is clearly less blameworthy than Hussein, who's the one who's doing the smuggling.

128. Yes, probably. Courts have traditionally said that a party may recover for contractual misrepresentation only if the party's reliance on the misrepresentation was "reasonable." However, the modern trend is to hold that if the misrepresentation was intentional, and the party asserting misrepresentation honestly believed the misrepresentation, the fact that the reliance was "unreasonable" will not bar recovery. Therefore, a court following the majority approach will find in favor of Fozzie, and allow rescission.

129. (A) No A contract action for misrepresentation can be based on a negligent (or even non-negligent but incorrect) misrepresentation of a matter of material fact — unlike a tort action for fraud or deceit, there is no particular mental-state element in a contract misrepresentation action.

(B) That Bully never made any affirmative misrepresentation; he merely failed to make a disclosure.

(C) Probably not. It's true that as a *general* rule, a party's failure to make a disclosure won't be treated as equivalent of an affirmative misstatement, and therefore won't serve as the basis for a misrepresentation action. But there are a number of exceptions to this general rule. On of those exceptions is that if there is a relation of *"trust and confidence"* between the plaintiff and the defendant, the defendant's failure to make disclosure will be treated as the equivalent of an assertion. Since the facts tell us that Gail has used Bully for a long time, and has come to him for advice, a court would probably hold that the requisite relation of trust and confidence existed between them.

130. (A) That the contract is unconscionable.

(B) Yes. A consumer contract will be held void for unconscionability under UCC §2-302 if it is unduly one-sided under the circumstances existing at the time of signing. The fact that the party opposing a finding of unconscionability concealed the true nature of the contract from the other party will strongly militate towards a finding of unconscionability. So will the weaker party's lack of sophistication or education, as will the extreme substantive unfairness of the terms. Here, all of these factors work in favor of a finding of unconscionability, so that's what the court will probably do. As a remedy, the court will then probably either order the contract rescinded (in which case Fred would give back the used dishwasher and be relieved of the need to make further payments), or will "rewrite" the contract so that the payments due will approximate the dishwasher's fair value.

131. Pete will probably lose. Where the buyer is a business or a businessperson, it's exceptionally rare for the court to find the contract unconscionable. Here, where there's been no affirmative misstatement of the contract's terms — and the only unfairness is the substantive one of an excessive price — the court is unlikely to depart from this general refusal to use unconscionablity in commercial disputes.

132. No. A party seeking to avoid a contract that he entered into when drunk must show *both* (1) that he was so intoxicated that he couldn't understand the nature of his transaction, and (2) that the other party knew, or had reason to know, that this was the case. Here, the airline had no reason to know that Roger was drunk, so the second requirement isn't met.

133. (A) No. Apollo, as a minor, has a right to disaffirm the contract. An infant who disaffirms a contract and still has the consideration in his possession must return it. If the goods have been disposed of or destroyed, the infant has no obligation to pay for them. Since Apollo destroyed the chariot, he doesn't owe Zeus anything.

(B) Probably, but just the $1,000, and just from Apollo. When a minor doesn't have the item in question anymore because he *sold* it, the UCC doesn't let the original seller recover from the good-faith third-party purchaser for value; UCC §2-403. However, a court will probably require the minor in such a situation to return to the original seller whatever the minor received (and still has) for selling the item. So here, Apollo will probably have to fork over the $1,000 in sale proceeds, if he still has it.

(C) Nothing. When the disaffirming infant is the plaintiff, most modern courts will cut his recovery by the diminution in value of the item. Since the chariot is worthless, what would otherwise be a $2,000 recovery will be reduced by the full $2,000 in diminished value, leaving Apollo with a $0 recovery.

(D) No. Contracts that infants enter into are voidable at *their* option *only* — the other party does not have the option of voiding the contract.

(E) No. Virtually all jurisdictions hold that where the infant lies about his age to induce the transaction, the other party may avoid the transaction. So the usual rule — that only the infant may disaffirm — does not apply to the fraud-by-the-infant scenario.

134. No. Lizzie's initial promise was voidable at her option due to her infant status. However, once she reached the age of majority, she had the right to reaffirm the contract. Once she exercised that right of reaffirmation, the contract became fully enforceable as if she had been an adult at the time the contract was made.

135. (A) An express-warranty action against Medusa, and a claim for breach of the implied warranty of merchantability against Exacto Corp.

(B) Probably yes, as to both defendants. First, Medusa, by telling Delilah that the machine is "foolproof" and cuts with "extreme accuracy," has made an *express warranty* as to these performance attributes. And Exacto Corp., by manufacturing and selling the machine at all, has made an *impliedly warranted* the machine's "merchantability," which means that Exacto has implicitly said that the goods are, among other things, "fit for the ordinary purposes for which such goods are used." (§2-314(2)(c).) It seems highly likely that the machine doesn't in fact satisfy either of these warranties, so unless there has been an effective disclaimer, both defendants will lose.

The question, then, is whether the disclaimer statement in the owner's manual will be effective. The answer is that it will probably not be. The problem for both defendants is that the only disclaimer was contained in the owner's manual, which was inside the box. Since Delilah was not given an opportunity to read the manual before she made the purpose (and was not, so far as the facts tell us, otherwise aware of the disclaimer), a court will probably hold that the disclaimer was a post-contract fact, which had no impact on the parties' bargain.

(C) Breach of both an express warranty and the implied warranty of merchantability. The description on the outside of the box would constitute an express warranty that the machine will indeed precisely and automatically cut hair. Since it doesn't, that's grounds for recovery. And any good is impliedly warranted by its seller (Exacto is a "seller" for this purpose, even though it didn't sell directly to Delilah) to be "merchantable," which under UCC §2-314(2)(f) includes conforming to promises or affirmations of fact made on the container or label.

136. (A) Yes, for breach of the implied warranty of "fitness for a particular purpose." In order to succeed, Saul will have to prove three things: (1) that Tammy knew what he needed the computer to be able to do, (2) that Tammy knew Saul was relying on Tammy's skill and judgment to recommend a suitable computer, and (3) that Saul did in fact rely on Tammy's advice.

(B) This statement will work as an effective *disclaimer* of the implied warranty of fitness for a particular purpose. UCC §2-316(2) allows a merchant to disclaim implied warranties, provided that the merchant follows some specific rules. In the case of a warranty of fitness for a particular purpose, the rules are that the disclaimer must be: (1) in writing, and (2) "conspicuous." The statement on the sales slip will likely pass the test, because it is in writing and is conspicuous (due to the contrasting ink color).

137. No. In answering this question, you should first try to figure out whether the parties intended to make a "substituted agreement" (in which the new deal, as soon as it's agreed to, completely extinguishes the old deal) or instead an "executory accord" (in which the new deal does not extinguish the old deal until the terms of the new deal are fully performed.) The most important single factor in distinguishing between the two types of deals is the level of formality: the more *in*formal, the more likely it is that the parties intended an accord. So here, the fact that the deal is oral suggests that it's an accord.

Therefore, if Calvin had not tendered the $750, Hobbes would have been able to sue for the full, original $1,000. But when Calvin tendered the $750, he was fulfilling the terms of the accord. Once performance (called "satisfaction") under the terms of the accord was tendered, this was enough to extinguish Hobbes' right to sue for the original amount.

138. (A) No. As in the prior question, the new deal here was probably an accord, not a substituted agreement. (That's because it was relatively informal, as manifested by the extreme brevity of the writings, and the fact that there's no indication of any intent by the parties to replace the prior agreement.) However, although an accord does not immediately extinguish the prior agreement, the accord is still a binding contract: each party has the right to tender performance in exchange for extinguishment of the original deal. So Mrs. O'Leary had a contractual right to tender a goat in full performance by April 15, and Here-A-Moo's announcement of a change of mind could not and did not remove that right.

(B) Here-A-Moo has a choice: it can sue on *either* promise — the original promise for $100, or the substituted one for the goat. As we indicated in part (A), the agreement here was probably an accord, not a substituted agreement. Therefore, the mere making of the new deal did not extinguish Here-A-Moo's rights under the original deal (that extinguishment would have occurred only if Mrs. O'Leary tendered a goat by April 15.) Once Mrs. O'Leary breached her promise under the accord, Here-A-Moo got the right to sue under either the old deal or the new deal.

139. Probably not. What has happened here is that the parties entered into a "mutual rescission" — an agreement to cancel the whole contract. When this happens, most courts hold that neither party is obligated to pay for any benefits already received under the contract, unless there is some affirmative evidence that the parties intended otherwise. There is nothing under these facts to indicate that the parties intended to compensate Ollie for his spit shine, so he's out of luck.

MULTIPLE-CHOICE QUESTIONS

Here are 30 multiple-choice questions, in a Multistate-Bar-Exam style. They are taken from *Strategies & Tactics for the Finz Multistate Method*, a compendium of over 1100 questions in the Multistate subjects by the late Professor Steven Finz and published by Aspen Publishing. To learn more about this book and other study aids, go to www.AspenPublishing.com.

1. Immediately after his graduation from college in June, Stuart announced his plan to begin law school the following September and to marry Sue in December. Stuart's father, Farrell, was afraid that marriage during Stuart's first year of law school might cause him to fail or drop out of school. He called Stuart on the phone and said that if Stuart postponed his wedding plans until after the completion of his first year of law school, Farrell would give him a cash bonus of $1,000 and would pay Stuart's tuition for the second year of law school. Stuart agreed, and called Sue to tell her that he wanted to postpone the wedding. She became so angry at him that she broke off their engagement. Two months later, Sue married someone else.

   Farrell died soon after Stuart began school, but Stuart successfully completed his first year. Although Stuart earned excellent grades, he decided that he was not really interested enough in the law to want to continue his legal education. After failing to register for a second year of law school, he notified Farrell's administrator of his decision. Stuart said that although there would be no tuition expense, he expected to be paid the $1,000 cash bonus which his father had promised him. The administrator refused to pay anything.

   If Stuart brought suit against the administrator of Farrell's estate for $1,000, Stuart would probably be

   (A) unsuccessful, because his contract with Farrell violated public policy.

   (B) unsuccessful, because Stuart failed to register for a second year of law school.

   (C) unsuccessful, because Farrell's death terminated his offer.

   (D) successful.

2. Corman was the owner of a condominium which consisted of an apartment with a patio and a small backyard. When he moved in, he entered into a written contract with Lansman. Pursuant to its terms, Lansman was to perform certain specified gardening services in the yard of Corman's condominium each week for a period of one year, for which Corman was to pay the sum of $50 per month. The contract contained a clause which stated, "Corman hereby agrees not to assign this contract without the written permission of Lansman." Three months after entering into the

agreement, Corman informed Lansman that he was selling the condominium to Antun, and asked Lansman to consent to Corman's assignment of the contract to Antun. Because the costs of landscaping materials had increased dramatically in the last three months, Lansman was glad for an opportunity to be relieved of his obligations under the contract, and refused to consent to the assignment. Corman assigned the contract to Antun anyway, but Lansman refused to perform any further work on the yard. After formally demanding performance from Lansman, Antun hired another gardener to do the same work for $75 per month which was the best price Antun could negotiate.

In an action by Antun against Lansman for breach of contract, the court should find for

(A) Antun, because Lansman had no right to unreasonably withhold consent to the assignment.

(B) Antun, because the assignment was valid in spite of Lansman's refusal to consent.

(C) Lansman, because the contract prohibited assignment by Corman without Lansman's consent.

(D) Lansman, because the contract was for personal services.

3. On June 1, after arson fires had damaged several city buildings, the City Council of the city of Metro voted to offer a reward to aid an apprehension of the arsonists. On June 2, by order of the City Council, signs were posted in various locations throughout the city. The posters identified the buildings which had been burned, and stated: "$1,000 REWARD is hereby offered by the City of Metro to any person furnishing information leading to the conviction of persons responsible for setting fire to said buildings." Curran, a police officer employed by the City of Metro saw the posters on June 5, and resolved to make a special effort to catch the arsonists. Although he was not officially assigned to the case, he notified his fellow police officers and his usual underworld informants that he was especially interested in the case. As a result, Marino, a police officer, and Pidgeon, an underworld informant, passed information to Curran which they thought might relate to the arson crimes. The tip which Curran received from Marino proved to be of no assistance, but that which he received from Pidgeon led him to conduct a further investigation. His efforts eventually resulted in the arrest of two men who pleaded guilty to setting fires in public buildings. Curran demanded that the City Council pay him $1,000 but the council refused.

If Curran institutes a lawsuit against the City of Metro for the $1,000 reward offered in the signs posted on June 2, which of the following would be the City's most effective argument in defense?

(A) The reward should go to Pidgeon, since it was his information which eventually led to the arrest of the arsonists.

(B) The reward was not accepted, since the arsonists were not convicted but pleaded guilty.

(C) Curran gave no consideration for the City's promise to pay a reward, since he was already obligated to attempt the apprehension of the arsonists.

(D) There was no enforceable promise by the City, since the offer was for a gratuitous cash award.

4. X-tendo contracted to add a room to Homer's house for $3,000, with the understanding that the materials used by X-tendo were to be included in that price. The day before work was to begin, Homer wired X-tendo, "The deal is off. Do not begin work, Homer." X-tendo subsequently asserted a claim against Homer for breach of contract. Homer raised non-compliance with the Statute of Frauds as a defense. Which of the following statements is most correct about the application of the Statute of Frauds to the contract between Homer and X-tendo?

I. The contract was required to be in writing if the materials which would have been required had a price in excess of $500.

II. The contract was required to be in writing if, at the time of contracting, the parties intended that the materials required would have a price in excess of $500.

(A) I only.

(B) II only.

(C) I and II.

(D) Neither I, nor II.

5. On August 1, Wells, a wholesaler of office supplies, contracted by telephone to sell 50 cases of typewriter ribbons to Ronson, a business equipment retailer, at a total price of $450. On August 15, Wells telephoned Ronson and told him that because of a shortage of materials, the price which Wells had to pay for typewriter ribbons had increased drastically. Wells said if he delivered the ribbons at the price of $450, he would lose a great deal of money. He asked Ronson to consent to a higher price, suggesting that Ronson pass the increase along to his customers. After further discussion, Ronson and Wells agreed to change the price of the order $450 to $650. On August 18, Ronson succeeded in purchasing fifty cases of typewriter ribbons from another supplier for $500. On September 1, Wells delivered fifty cases of typewriter ribbons to Ronson together with a bill for $650. Ronson rejected the delivery.

In an action by Wells against Ronson for breach of contract, which of the following would be Ronson's most effective argument in defense?

(A) Ronson's demand for more money was unconscionable, since typewriter ribbons were available at a lower price.

(B) The August 15 agreement increasing the price was not in writing.

(C) Ronson's promise to pay $650 was unsupported by consideration.

(D) An increase in Well's cost resulting from a shortage of materials was forseeable on August 1.

6. On March 22, by a written memorandum signed by both parties, Varsey agreed to sell and Pantel agreed to buy a described parcel of realty. The contract called for closing of title on May 30, and fixed all other terms, but did not indicate the price to be paid. On May 30, Pantel tendered $60,000 cash, but Varsey refused to convey the realty. Pantel subsequently instituted an action against Varsey for specific performance of the contract, and offered evidence that $60,000 was the fair market value of the realty, both on March 22 and on May 30. In defense Varsey asserted that the memorandum failed to satisfy the requirements of the Statute of Frauds. Pantel's suit against Varsey should

(A) succeed, if Pantel and Varsey are both in the business of buying and selling real estate.

(B) succeed, because under the Uniform Commercial Code a contract which is silent as to price is presumed to call for payment of fair market value.

(C) fail, because the written contract did not fix the price to be paid.

(D) fail, unless the evidence establishes that the parties orally agreed that the price to be paid was the fair market value of the realty.

7. In preparation for the annual convention of the Association of Life Insurance Agents which was to be held on January 9, Committee ordered 500 ball point pens from Penco at a total price of $285, paying for them in advance. Because the pens were to be given to conventioneers as souvenirs, they were to be imprinted with the name and slogan of the association, and were to be delivered to Committee on or before January 8. Penco and Committee entered into a written contract containing the above terms on November 16. Penco tendered 475 ball point pens to Committee on January 8.

Which of the following correctly states the legal relationship between Committee and Penco on January 8?

(A) Committee must accept the tendered delivery of 475 pens, but may successfully sue for damages resulting from breach of contract.

(B) Committee may elect to accept the tendered delivery of 475 pens, but may not successfully sue for breach of contract if it does so.

(C) Committee may reject the tendered delivery of 475 pens, but may successfully sue only for the return of its advance payment if it does so.

(D) Committee may reject the tendered delivery of 475 pens, and may successfully sue for the return of its advance payment and for damages resulting from breach of contract if it does so.

8. Ace, a construction contractor, was planning to submit a bid for the renovation of a county office building. Ace called Wire, a subcontractor who had done electrical work for Ace in the past, and described the proposed project. Ace told Wire about the electrical work that would be required, and asked Wire to state the price that Wire would charge to do the electrical work for Ace. Wire inspected the office building on which the work was to be performed, and spent six hours estimating the cost of the job. Wire mailed Ace a letter describing the work to be performed, and containing the following statement: "I will do the work described for a total price of $16,000. This price is not subject to change until one week after the county awards the contract." Wire subsequently purchased materials in anticipation of the job.

Ace submitted a bid for renovating the building, and was awarded the contract. Ace called Wire, offering to pay $12,000 for the electrical work. When Wire refused to accept anything less than $16,000, Ace hired Lectric to do the work instead of Wire.

If Wire sues Ace for the cost of the materials which Wire purchased in anticipation of the job, the court should find for

(A) Wire, if Ace relied on Wire's offer in bidding on the job.

(B) Wire, if the materials which Wire purchased will not otherwise be used in the ordinary course of Wire's business.

(C) Wire, if he purchased the materials in reliance on the belief that Ace would hire him upon receiving the contract from the county.

(D) Ace, because he had no agreement with Wire concerning the electrical work.

9. Solder and Brandeis entered into a written contract for the sale of five hundred bicycles at a total price of $50,000. The contract required delivery by Solder prior to June 1, and payment by Brandeis within 30 days after delivery. On May 15, Solder delivered the bicycles to Brandeis, who received and accepted them. On May 21, Solder was having cash-flow problems, he telephoned Brandeis asking whether Brandeis could pay for the bicycles immediately. Brandeis said that he would pay by May 25 if Solder was willing to accept $45,000 in cash as payment in full. Solder agreed, but by June 20 Brandeis had made no payment at all. Solder subsequently instituted an action against Brandeis for $50,000. Brandeis admitted the existence of the contract, the delivery of the bicycles, and his non-payment; but asserted that he was liable for only $45,000 because of the agreement which he made with Solder on May 21.

Is Brandeis's assertion correct?

(A) No, because Brandeis did not pay $45,000 by May 25.

(B) No, because a promise to perform a pre-existing obligation is not valuable consideration.

(C) Yes, because there has been a valid novation.

(D) Yes, because there has been a valid agreement of accord.

10. In response to an advertisement which he saw in the newspaper, Huner telephoned Screner and asked him to come to Huner's home to estimate the cost of providing and installing new aluminum screens for all of Huner's window's. After taking measurements, Screner returned to his shop and prepared a written estimate, in which he said that he would do the entire job for $350. When Huner received Screner's written estimate, he wrote across it with a red felt-tipped pen, "I'll pay $300, but not a penny more," and mailed it to Screner. When Screner received the estimate with Huner's statement written on it, he wrote "I'll do it for $325." He sent the estimate back to Huner on September 5, but on September 12, having received no response, he sent Huner another note. The note said, "All right, you win. I'll do the job for $300. Unless I hear from you to the contrary, I'll be there with the new screens on September 28. Signed, Screner." Huner received the note on September 14, but made no response. On September 28, without Huner's knowledge and while Huner was at work, Screner went to Huner's home and installed new aluminum window screens.

Which of the following best characterizes the legal relationship between Huner and Screner AFTER installation of the window screens on September 28?

(A) A contract was formed when Huner failed to respond to Screner's letter of September 12 within a reasonable time after he received it.

(B) A contract was formed when Screner began to install the screens on September 28.

(C) A quasi contract was formed when Screner finished installing the screens on September 28, obligating Huner to pay a price equivalent to their reasonable value.

(D) No contractual relationship existed between Huner and Screner.

11. Hostel Corporation was seeking a contractor to build a hotel on realty which it acquired near the seashore. Hostel sent copies of its plans to several builders with whom it had done business in the past, and asked them to submit bids for construction of the building. Coast Construction, one of the builders, assigned an employee, Edwards, to prepare an estimate of the job. Although Hostel's plans called for construction of a twenty-seven story building, Edwards mistakenly believed that the building was to be seven stories. He estimated the costs accordingly, and submitted the estimate to Coast, the owner of the company. Based on Edwards's figures, Coast prepared and mailed to Hostel a letter offering to build according to Hostel's plans for $1,000,000 and setting forth all other necessary terms. Hostel had already received four other bids on the job, each for a figure far in excess of $1,000,000. Upon receiving Coast's bid, Hostel immediately telegraphed Coast, "we accept your offer to build according to the plans which we sent you. Entire job to be completed for one million dollars. Hostel." Before Coast began construction, he learned that

Hostel's building was to be 27 stories, and that Edwards had calculated in the mistaken belief that bit was to be seven stories. Coast wrote to Hostel asking for renegotiation of the contract, but Hostel indicated his intent to hold Coast to his original offer. Coast advised Hostel that he regarded the contract as a nullity, and would not perform according to its terms.

In an action by Hostel against Coast for breach of contract, the court should find for

(A) Hostel, if Coast's mistake was the result of negligence by Coast's employee.

(B) Hostel, because Coast's mistake was unilateral.

(C) Coast, because it would be unfair to require Coast to complete construction at the contract price.

(D) Coast, if the reasonable person in Hostel's position would have known that Coast's bid was the result of a mistake.

12. Bott was the owner of a large yacht which he usually kept moored in Shimmering Bay, On August 15, Fixer agreed to repair Bott's yacht for a fee of $2,000, and to have all work completed by November 1. Because of the yacht's size, it would have been impractical to take it out of the water for repairs, and it was understood that all work would have to be performed while the boat was moored in the bay. There were heavy storms all during the month of October, however, and the waters of the bay were too choppy to permit any work on the yacht. As a result, on October 28, Fixer notified Bott that he would be unable to complete repairs by November 1.

If Bott asserts a claim against Fixer for damages resulting from breach of contract, the court should find for

(A) Fixer if Fixer's prior commitments made it impossible for him to work on Bott's yacht at any time other than during the month of October.

(B) Fixer if Bott's prior commitments made it impossible for Bott to use the yacht until the following March.

(C) Bott if Shimmering Bar was frequently subject to storm conditions and choppy waters in the month of October.

(D) Bott if Fixer could have completed the work in time by removing the yacht from the water during the month of October.

13. In an agreement made on April 15, Carver agreed to design a coat of arms for Houser to fabricate a wooden door with the coat of arms carved into it for the front of Houser's home. Houser agreed to pay $650 for the door, but it was understood that if Houser was not completely satisfied with the coat of arms and the door, he would be under no obligation to go through with the deal. Before Carver completed the door, Houser came to the conclusion that he did not really want a coat of arms. When Carver brought the finished door to Houser, Houser took a quick glance at it. Although the coat of arms was properly designed and carved, and although the door

had been fabricated in a workmanlike manner, Houser said, "I just don't like it," and refused to accept it.

In an action by Carver against Houser, which of the following would be Houser's best defense?

(A) The agreement was not in writing as required by the Statute of Frauds.

(B) The door, objectively viewed, was not satisfactory.

(C) The door, subjectively viewed, was not satisfactory

(D) Since the coat of arms was not yet associated with Houser, it was possible for Carver to find another buyer for it.

Questions 14-16 are based on the following fact situation.

On September 10, Pubco, a well known publisher of law books, posted the following notice on the bulletin board at University Law School:

As an incentive to research and scholastic excellence, Pubco announces the institution of the Pubco Award. The award will consist of a complete set of the Pubco Encyclopedia, and will be presented to the student in each graduating class of the law school who attains the highest overall cumulative Grade Point Average. In the event two or more students graduate with the same Grade Point Average, the dean will be asked to select the winner from among them based on school service and community involvement.

Val, who had just begun her final year at the law school saw the notice. Her grades already placed her toward the top of her class, but she resolved to work harder than ever before in an attempt to win the Pubco Award. On September 20, she mailed a letter to Pubco saying. "I accept your offer for the Pubco Award, and will do my best to win it." Her letter was received by Pubco, but lost in the mail department before any Pubco officials had an opportunity to see it.

The following May, because of budget cutbacks at Pubco, the following notice was posted at University Law School:

The Pubco Award program is hereby discontinued. Pubco will be unable to present any prize or award to students of this law school.

The week after the second notice was posted, Val took her final examinations. Her scores on those examinations made her grade point average the highest in the class, and resulted in her being declared Valedictorian at her graduation. She subsequently wrote to Pubco demanding her prize, but Pubco refused to award it.

14. Which of the following statements is most correct about Pubco's first notice?

(A) It was an offer for a unilateral contact.

(B) It was an offer for bilateral contract.

(C) It was an offer for either a unilateral contract or a bilateral contract at the offeree's option.

(D) It was an offer for a unilateral contract which ripened into a bilateral contract when Val achieved the highest grade point average in her class.

15. In a jurisdiction which applies the *Restatement of Contracts, 2nd* rule, a court's decision as to whether Pubco's offer was effectively revoked by the notice posted in May (the second notice) will most likely depend on whether

(A) Val saw the second notice before taking her final examinations.

(B) the second notice was a large, and as conspicuously posted as the first.

(C) Val's letter of September 21 was effective when mailed or when received.

(D) Val made extra efforts in her studies in reliance on the offer contained in the notice of September 10.

16. In an action by Val against Pubco, a court is most likely to find promise contained in the September 10 notice

(A) enforceable, on a theory of promissory estoppel.

(B) enforceable, because Val's performance was consideration for it.

(C) unenforceable, since Val was already legally obligated to use her best efforts while in law school.

(D) unenforceable, since it was a conditional promise to make a future gift.

17. Susan and Barbara had been friends for years. Susan was the owner of a rare antique sports car, which Barbara had offered to buy from her on several occasions, but which Susan had never been willing to sell. On Barbara's birthday, Susan and Barbara went out for dinner and drinks. After dinner, Susan continued drinking until she was somewhat intoxicated. During their conversation, Susan said, "Barbara, as a birthday present, I've decided that I'm going to sell you my sports car for five hundred dollars. And just to make sure that I don't change my mind after I sober up, I'll put it in writing." With that, she wrote on a paper napkin, "We agree to the sale of my sports car to Barbara for five hundred dollars, COD," and signed her name at the bottom. Barbara also signed the napkin and put it in her purse. The following day Barbara tendered five hundred dollars in cash to Susan but Susan refused to sell her the car, claiming that she had been drunk when she made the offer.

In an action by Barbara against Susan for breach of contract, which of the following additional facts, if it was the only one true, would be most helpful to Susan's defense:

(A) that she was so drunk when she wrote on the napkin that she did not know the legal consequences of her act.

(B) that she would not have offered to sell the car to Barbara for five hundred dollars if she had not been drunk.

(C) that she made the offer to sell as a joke.

(D) that she changed her mind about selling the car before Barbara tendered the cash.

18. Beatrice received an advertising brochure from Selco in the mail. The brochure contained a photograph of a Peechie 401 computer, and above it the statement, "While they last. All Peechie computers on sale at 25 percent below manufacturer's list price." Beatrice immediately contacted the Peechi Computer Company which manufactured the computer pictured in Selco's brochure, and determined that Peechie's list price for the 410 was $1,000. She then sent her check for $750 ($1000 less 25 percent) to Selco with a covering letter which stated "I hereby accept your offer for the sale of a Peechie 401 computer. My check is enclosed herewith." Selco threw Beatrice's letter and check away.

The brochure which Selco sent Beatrice is best described as

(A) an invitation for offers.

(B) an invitation for offers which ripened into an offer when Beatrice learned the Peechie Computer Company's list price for the 401 computer.

(C) an invitation for offers which ripened into an offer when Beatrice relied on it by sending her check and covering letter.

(D) an offer for the sale of a Peechie 401 computer.

19. When Salzburger's employers transferred him to the west coast, they promised to pay all his relocation expenses, including any commission which he might have to pay for the sale of his home. Salzburger contacted Ritchie, a real estate broker, and entered into a written contract with her on September 1. Under its terms, Salzburger agreed that if the house was sold to any buyer who made an offer during the following two months, he would pay Ritchie upon the closing of title a commission equivalent to 6 percent of the actual selling price of the house. In return, Ritchie agreed to make reasonable efforts to find a buyer for the house at a price of $80,000.

On September 15, after Ritchie showed Salzburger's home to Barnaby, Barnaby offered to purchase it for $75,000, on condition that title would close on or before December 1. On September 18, Salzburger accepted Barnaby's offer. On September 19, Barnaby gave Salzburger $10,000 as a deposit.

On November 15, Barnaby notified Salzburger that he had changed his mind, and would not go through with the purchase of the house, agreeing to forfeit the deposit which he had paid in return for Salzburger's agreement not to sue for damages. The following day, Salzburger entered into a contract to sell the house to another buyer for $80,000. Salzburger subsequently rejected Ritchie's demand for payment.

If Ritchie institutes a claim against Salzburger for her commission, she is entitled to collect

(A) $4,800 (6 percent of $80,000).

(B) $4,500 (6 percent of $75,000).

(C) $600 (6 percent of $10,000).

(D) Nothing.

20. Bildco was a construction company which had been awarded a contract to build a transmission tower for the United States government. Sue Supervisor was a well-known architect and managing partner of S&M Architectural Specialists. On October 20, Bildco wrote to S&M Architectural Specialists indicating that Bildco was interested in retaining the firm to supervise the building project on condition that Sue Supervisor undertake the job personally. On October 28, S&M responded with a letter stating, "Sue Supervisor receives $50,000 for every project which she personally supervises. Our fee for such a project is normally $60,000." Bildco received the letter on October 31. On November 5, after a telephone conversation between Bildco officers and the president of S&M Architectural Specialists, Bildco wrote to S&M,"Terms in your letter of October 28 are acceptable to us."

After Bildco completed the project under the supervision of Sue Supervisor, S&M Architectural Specialists rendered a bill for $110,000, indicating that of this sum $60,000 was the fee charged by S&M, and $50,000 was an additional sum for the personal services of Sue Supervisor. Bildco refused to pay, asserting that the agreement called for a total fee of $60,000, of which $50,000 was to be paid to Sue Supervisor for her services. S&M Architectural Specialists subsequently sued Bildco for breach of contract. At trial S&M's president attempted to testify that in her November 5 conversation with Bildco officers, she had explained that Sue Supervisor's fee was in addition to the $60,000 charged by S&M Architectural Specialists. On timely objection by Bildco's attorney, the testimony of S&M's president should be

(A) excluded, under the parol evidence rule.

(B) excluded, unless it is regarded as evidence of a prior course of dealing between the parties.

(C) admitted, only if S&M's billing arrangement was consistent with customs and procedures normally followed in the construction and architectural industries.

(D) admitted, because it does not contradict a term of any written agreement.

21. Boss and her assistant Edward were working alone late one night when Boss had a heart attack which rendered her unconscious and caused her to fall down an airshaft.

Edward believed Boss to be dead, but called for an ambulance, and leaped into the airshaft, sustaining serious injury himself. Finding that Boss was still alive, Edward gave her first aid consisting of cardio-pulmonary resuscitation. When the ambulance arrived, paramedics used stretchers and pulleys to get Boss and Edward out of the airshaft, and then brought them to the hospital. Several days later while she was still in the hospital, a doctor told Boss that she would probably have died if not for Edward's quick and effective action. Boss wrote Edward a note, which said,"In return for your saving my life, I'm going to pay all your hospital bills. In addition, I'm going to add a bonus of $3,000 per month to your salary for the rest of your life. If you choose to retire right now, I'll pay you $3,000 per month for the rest of your life as a retirement pension." Boss paid Edward's hospital bills, but because her business took an unexpected downturn, she never paid him $3,000, and subsequently informed him that she would not be able to pay him a bonus or a retirement pension. If Edward asserts a claim against Boss for her failure to pay him the bonus of $3,000 per month, which of the following would be Edward's most effective argument in support of his claim?

(A) Boss's promise to pay the bonus was in writing.

(B) Edward detrimentally relied on Boss's promise.

(C) Boss's promise was supported by an underlying moral obligation.

(D) Edward's rescue of Boss resulted in a contract implied-in-fact.

22. Gail, an art dealer, employed several agents who traveled throughout the world purchasing art for her to sell in her gallery. One of her agents sent her a painting entitled "Sunset," informing her that it had been painted by Van Gook. Gail had just received the painting and was about to place it on display when Bertrand, a collector of art, came into the gallery. Seeing the new painting, he said, "An interesting Van Gook." Gail replied,"Yes, it is. I'm asking $50,000 for it." Bertrand agreed to the price, and immediately wrote a check for the sum of $50,000 payable to the order of Gail, writing the words "Payment in full for Sunset" on the back of the check. Gail accepted the check and delivered the painting to Bertrand. If the painting had actually been by Van Gook, it would have been worth $50,000. The same day, however, Bertrand discovered that the painting was a forgery, worth only a few hundred dollars, and stopped payment on his check before Gail could cash it.

If Gail asserts a claim against Bertrand for breach of contract, which of the following would be Bertrand's most effective defense?

(A) The contract of sale was not evidenced by a writing signed by both parties.

(B) At the time of sale, Bertrand and Gail both believed that the painting was by Van Gook.

(C) It is unconscionable to make Bertrand pay $50,000 for a painting worth only a few hundred dollars.

(D) The painting known as "Sunset" was not adequate consideration for Bertrand's promise to pay.

23. Owen was the owner of two adjoining parcels of unimproved realty. Although she was interested in improving and selling the realty, she did not have the necessary capital. After negotiation, Owen entered into a written contract with Barksdale, a building contractor. According to the terms of the contract, Barksdale was to provide labor and materials for the construction of a building on one of the parcels according to certain specifications. All construction was to be completed by a certain date, at which time Owen was to convey the other parcel of realty to Barksdale as his sole compensation for the labor and materials supplied. The contract contained a clause providing for liquidated damages in the event of a breach by either party.

After Barksdale completed construction as agreed, Owen refused to convey the other parcel of realty to him. As a result, Barksdale appropriately asserted alternative claims for relief against Owen demanding liquidated damages as provided in the contract, or actual damages, or an order directing Owen to perform as agreed.

Which of the following correctly describes Barksdale's rights against Owen?

I. If the liquidated damages clause established a penalty, the court can properly enter judgment for any actual damages which resulted from Owen's breach.

II. If the liquidated damages clause did not establish a penalty, the court can properly direct Owen to perform as agreed.

(A) I only.

(B) II only.

(C) I and II.

(D) Neither I nor II.

24. Sandez was an investor who frequently bought and sold real estate on his own account. He had purchased a parcel of realty known as Sandacre for for $100,000 and was considering selling it. On September 1, Bethel asked whether Sandez would be willing to accept $125,000 for the property. Sandez said that he would, but only if payment was in cash. When Bethel said that he would need a month or two to raise that kind of money, Sandez wrote the following on a sheet of paper and signed it:

> I hereby offer to sell my realty known as Sandacre to Bethel for the sum of $125,000 cash. I promise to hold this offer open until November 1, and I further promise that I will not sell the property to anyone else before then. This is a firm offer.

Subsequently, but prior to November 1, Sandez sold the property to Duncan for $110,000 and wrote Bethel a note in which he said, "I hereby withdraw my offer to sell you Sandacre for $125,000." On October 25, Bethel purchased Sandacre from Duncan for $135,000.

If Bethel asserts a claim against Sandez for damages resulting from Sandez's sale of Sandacre to Duncan, the court should find for

(A) Sandez because he received no consideration for his promise to keep the offer open.

(B) Sandez only if he sold the realty to Duncan more than thirty days after promising Bethel that he would keep the offer open.

(C) Bethel because the document which Sandez signed on September 1 was a firm offer in writing.

(D) Bethel only if Bethel customarily engaged in buying and selling real estate.

25. Sorrento, a furniture dealer, had 500 barrel chairs for sale. The chairs had a fair market value of $100 each. The manufacturer had discontinued production of the chairs, however, and they were the last ones Sorrento had. For that reason, Sorrento advertised them at $75 each, even though at that price her profit would only be $10 per chair. Barrie, an interior decorator, had contracted to provide furniture for a new hotel. On May 4, after seeing the barrel chairs advertised, Barrie wired Sorrento, "please ship me 500 barrel chairs as advertised at $75 per chair COD." On May 5, immediately upon receipt of the telegram, Sorrento wired Barrie, "Accept your offer. Will ship 500 barrel chairs tomorrow." Barrie telephoned Sorrento immediately upon receipt of Sorrento's telegram on May 6, saying that after discussing the chairs with his client he had decided to cancel the order. On May 7, Barrie sold all the chairs to Meyers at $75 each. If Sorrento sued Barrie for breach of contract, the court should award Sorrento

(A) $5,000 (500 chairs at $10 profit per chair).

(B) $37,500 (500 chairs at $75 per chair).

(C) $12,500 (fair market value of $100 minus contract price of $75 times 500 chairs).

(D) nothing, since Sorrento sustained no damage.

Questions 26-28 are based on the following fact situation.

Boswell agreed to purchase 250 2" x 4" construction grade wooden studs from Stilton by a written contract which provided that Boswell would make payment prior to inspection. The studs were delivered to Boswell by truck, and were covered with a canvas tarpaulin when they arrived at Boswell's worksite. The driver demanded payment before he would unload or uncover the studs.

26. Assume for the purpose of this question only that Boswell refused to pay for the studs before inspecting them, and that the driver returned them to Stilton. If Stilton asserts a claim for breach of contract against Boswell, the court should find for

(A) Stilton, because Boswell's refusal to pay prior to inspection was a breach.

    (B) Stilton, because Boswell's refusal to pay prior to inspection was an anticipatory repudiation.

    (C) Boswell, because the contract provision calling for payment prior to inspection was unconscionable.

    (D) Boswell, because Stilton failed to deliver the studs.

27. Assume that Boswell paid the driver before inspecting the studs. Upon subsequent inspection, however, Boswell discovered that the studs were utility grade instead of construction grade. Assume for the purpose of this question only that he then telephoned Stilton, offering to return the studs and demanding the return of his money, but Stilton refused to take the merchandise back or to return Boswell's money. Which of the following is most correct about the effect of Boswell's payment prior to inspection?

    (A) The terms of the contract required an unconditional acceptance prior to inspection, and payment constituted unconditional acceptance.

    (B) Even if the contract provision calling for payment prior to inspection was invalid, payment resulted in a waiver of the right to inspect prior to acceptance.

    (C) Payment did not impair Boswell's right to inspect the goods prior to acceptance.

    (D) Payment constituted acceptance, but Boswell was entitled to revoke acceptance within a reasonable time thereafter.

28. Assume for the purpose of this question only that after discovering that the studs were utility grade instead of construction grade, Boswell sent Stilton a letter notifying him that the studs did not conform to the contract. Assume further that Boswell kept and used the studs. If Boswell asserts a claim against Stilton for breach of warranty, the court should enter judgment if favor of

    (A) Boswell, for the difference between the value of utility grade studs and the value of construction grade studs.

    (B) Boswell, for return of the price which he paid.

    (C) Stilton, because Boswell used the studs.

    (D) Stilton, because he might have been able to sell the studs elsewhere for a higher price.

Questions 29-30 are based on the following fact situation.

Honniker's hobby was restoring and collecting antique automobiles. After acquiring a 1919 Bensonhurst Bullet automobile, she contacted Carl's Custom Body Shop about having the car repainted. Carl said that he would paint the Bullet for $700, and would sell Honniker a new bumper for an additional $150. Using an order blank from a pad which he purchased at a stationary store, Carl wrote out all the terms of their agreement. On a printed line marked, "PAYMENT" he wrote, "Paint job -- $700, payable $300 in advance and $400 on completion. Bumper -- $150 payable on delivery." Both Carl and Honniker signed at the bottom of the form.

29. Which of the following statements most correctly describes the obligations set forth in the writing signed by Honniker and Carl?

    (A) Payment by Honniker of the initial $300 is a condition precedent to Carl's obligation to paint the car, and Carl's painting of the car is a condition precedent to Honniker's obligation to pay the additional $400.

    (B) Payment by Honniker of the initial $300 is a condition by precedent in form and substance to Carl's obligation to paint the car, and Carl's painting of the car is a condition precedent in form, but subsequent in substance to Honniker's obligation to pay the additional $400.

    (C) Payment by Honniker and painting of the car by Carl are concurrent conditions.

    (D) Neither party's obligation to perform is conditioned upon performance by the other party.

30. Assume for the purpose of this question only that Carl notified Honniker that he would not deliver the new bumper as agreed, and that Honniker succeeded in buying one like it in another town for $130, but that her reasonable travel expenses in finding and purchasing it amounted to $20. In an action by Honniker against Carl, the court should find for

    (A) Honniker, in the sum of $20.

    (B) Honniker, in the sum of $40.

    (C) Honniker, in the sum of $170.

    (D) Carl.

ANSWERS TO MULTIPLE-CHOICE QUESTIONS

1. **D** Farrell's offer was for a unilateral contract — his promise to pay in return for Stuart's postponing the wedding. When Stuart postponed the wedding, he accepted Farrell's offer, and a contract was formed.

   Some cases have held that an agreement never to marry violates public policy, but there is no reason why an agreement to postpone a marriage would do so. **A** is, therefore, incorrect. **B** is incorrect because Farrell's promise was to pay if Stuart postponed the wedding. His language did not make payment conditional upon Stuart's registration for a second year. Although an offer terminates upon the death of the offeror, **C** is incorrect because Stuart accepted the offer by postponing the wedding, and once accepted, an offer is no longer revocable.

2. **B** Damages are available as a remedy for the breach of a promise not to assign a contract. Assignments made in violation of such a promise are usually regarded as valid, however.

   A is incorrect because a contract which prohibits assignment without the consent of one of the parties does not require that party to act reasonably in deciding whether or not to consent. **C** is incorrect because although Corman might be liable for damages, the assignment will probably be regarded as valid. The only thing that the contract required Corman or his assignee to do was make payment. **D** is incorrect because that is hardly a personal service.

3. **C** Consideration is a benefit to the promisor or a detriment to the promisee which was bargained for and given in return for the promisor's promise. For this reason, if Curran did something which he was already obligated to do, his act could not be consideration for the City's promise to pay since no new benefit was given to the City and no detriment was sustained by Curran in return for that promise. A police officer's obligation to his employer includes the duty to attempt to apprehend criminals; so Curran's performance was of a pre-existing duty.

   A is incorrect because establishing that Pidgeon is entitled to the reward does not necessarily establish that Curran (or anybody else) is not entitled to it also. **B** is incorrect because a guilty plea is regarded as a conviction. Since the City's promise was to pay in return for information leading to a conviction, it was an offer to pay for something of value, not an offer for a gratuitous cash award. **D** is, therefore, incorrect.

4. **D**   The Statute of Frauds requires a contract for the sale of goods with a price of $500 or more to be in writing, but does not apply to a contract for services, even if goods are to be provided by the person performing the services. **I** and **II** are, therefore, incorrect.

5. **B**   The UCC treats a modification of a contract as a new contract. For this reason, if the contract as modified falls within the provisions of the Statute of Frauds, the modification must be in writing. Since the modification resulted in an agreement to sell goods with a price of $500 or more, the Statute of Frauds requires a written memorandum. The absence of a writing makes the contract unenforceable over the objection of Ronson.

    A is incorrect because the fact that the typewriter ribbons were available at a lower price is not enough to make Wells's demand unconscionable. **C** is incorrect because under the UCC an agreement to modify a contract may be enforceable even though unsupported by consideration. **D** would be relevant if Wells attempted to excuse his own non-performance by asserting impossibility or frustration of purpose. Since Ronson agreed to the modification, however, Wells's reason for requesting it is irrelevant to its enforceability.

6. **C**   Under the Statute of Frauds, a contract for the sale of any interest in real estate must be in writing, and the writing must contain all the essential terms. The price is an essential term in a contract for the sale of realty, since the court will be unable to fashion a remedy without it.

    Although the UCC makes special provision for contracts between merchants, providing that a contract silent as to price is presumed to be for a reasonable price, these provisions do not apply to the sale of land, but only to the sale of goods. **A** and **B** are, therefore, incorrect. Since this contract does not satisfy the requirements of the Statute of Frauds regardless of which party tries to enforce it, it is unenforceable over the objection of either party, even though oral evidence might establish the intentions of the parties with respect to missing terms. **D** is, therefore, incorrect.

7. **D**   The seller's obligation under a contract of sale is to deliver goods which conform in every way to the terms of the contract. Since the contract called for delivery of 500 pens, delivery of anything less is a breach. Since Penco failed to perform as promised, Committee is entitled to the return of all money already paid. In addition, since Penco breached the contract, Committee is entitled to damages resulting from the breach.

A is incorrect because the buyer is not required to accept a non-conforming tender. If a buyer chooses to accept a non-conforming tender, it must pay at the contract price, but is entitled to sue for damages resulting from the seller's defective performance so long as it notifies the seller of its intention to do so. **B** is, therefore, incorrect. On the other hand, if the tender does not conform to the seller's promise, the buyer may reject it. Having done so, the buyer is entitled to damages which resulted from the seller's breach. **C** is incorrect because return of Committee's advance payment may not be sufficient to compensate Committee for other damages which it sustained. (***Note:*** Damages are traditionally measured by the difference between the contract price and the "cover price" or the fair market value of the goods involved.)

8.   **D**   An unaccepted offer binds neither the offeror nor the offeree. There is nothing to indicate that Ace accepted Wire's offer to do the job for $16,000.

Ace's reliance on Wire's offer might entitle Ace to enforce it, but **A** is incorrect because Ace's reliance does not confer any right on Wire. Wire's reliance on the belief that Ace would hire him confers no right on Wire unless that reliance was justified. Since there is no indication that Ace promised the job to Wire, Wire's reliance was not justified. **B** and **C** are, therefore, incorrect.

9.   **A**   An accord is a new obligation intended to take the place of an existing one. To be enforceable, it must be supported by consideration. To discharge the original obligation, it must actually be performed. Performance of the new obligation is known as "satisfaction," and it is the satisfaction rather than the accord which discharges a contractual obligation. The agreement of May 21 constituted an accord, but since Brandeis did not pay $45,000 in cash by May 25 there has been no satisfaction and thus no discharge of his obligation to pay $50,000 as originally agreed.

While a promise to perform a pre-existing obligation is not valuable consideration, **B** is incorrect because Brandeis's original contractual obligation was to pay before June 14, and his May 21 promise was to pay by May 25. A novation is an agreement to substitute a third party for one of the parties to the contract. **C** is, therefore, incorrect. **D** is incorrect because accord without satisfaction does not work to discharge contractual obligations.

10.   **D**   The note which Screner sent on September 5 demanding $325 was a rejection of Huner's offer to pay $300. An offeree who has killed an offer by rejecting it does not have the power to resurrect it by a subsequent acceptance. Screner's note of September 12 was thus no more than a new offer. Since an offer may not make the offeree's silence an acceptance, Screner's offer to September 12 was never accepted

because Huner did not respond to it.

A is, therefore, incorrect. Since there was no existing offer which could be accepted by performance, Screner's commencement of performance on September 28 could not have resulted in the formation of a contract, making **B** incorrect. Since Huner did not know that Screner was installing the screens, and since Screner did not have a reasonable expectation of compensation at the time he installed them, Screner has no quasi-contract remedy, and **C** is incorrect.

11. **D** Ordinarily, a unilateral mistake does not excuse performance and is not grounds for rescission. Where the other party knew or reasonably should have known of the mistake, however, the mistake may be asserted as an excuse for non-performance.

A is incorrect because even though the mistake resulted from negligence by Coast's employee, the difference between Coast's bid and all the others received would probably have led the reasonable person in Hostel's position to realize that an error has been made. **B** is incorrect for the same reason. Unless it is found as a matter of law to have been unconscionable at the time it was formed, a contract may be enforceable even though some unfairness will result. **C** is incorrect because unfairness alone is not sufficient to excuse non-performance.

12. **C** Circumstances which make performance of a contractual obligation impossible excuse such performance, but only if the circumstance could not have been foreseen by the contracting parties at the time the contract was formed. If Shimmering Bay was frequently subject to stormy conditions and choppy waters in the month of October, the circumstance which prevented performance was foreseeable and would not excuse Fixer's non performance. **C** is, therefore, correct. Since Fixer must have known of his prior commitments at the time he contracted with Bott, **A** is incorrect for the same reason. **B** is incorrect because Bott may have been damaged (e.g., by his inability to rent it or lend it to friends) even though he himself was unable to use the yacht until March. Since the parties understood that the work would be performed while the yacht was in the water, Fixer cannot be required to remove it from the water. **D** is, therefore, incorrect.

13. **C** A contract making the buyer's satisfaction a condition precedent to his obligation is usually held to require that the goods be satisfactory to the reasonable person (i.e., viewed objectively). But where, as here, the agreement calls for the design of something to be personally identified with the buyer, it is more likely that the parties intended subjective satisfaction to be the standard.

A is incorrect because Carver's fabrication of a door which was designed especially for Houser and which would not be readily saleable in the ordinary course of Carver's business takes the contract out of the Statute of Frauds. **B** is incorrect since the parties apparently intended subjective satisfaction to be the test. **D** is incorrect because even though it might have been *possible* for Carver to sell the door to another, the coat of arms would obviously have prevented the door from being readily saleable in the ordinary course of Carver's business.

14. **A**   An offer for a unilateral contract involves an offer to exchange a promise for an act. Since the notice offered a prize to the student achieving the highest GPA and did not ask students to make any promise or agreement that they would do so, it was a promise offered in return for an act.

B is therefore incorrect. **C** is incorrect, since the offeror has the sole power to decide whether its offer can be accepted by an act or a promise. **D** is incorrect since once Val achieved the highest GPA in her class, there was nothing further for her to do, and so it could not be said that she was now obligated, as she would be under a bilateral contract.

15. **D**   Although an offer can ordinarily be withdrawn by the offeror at any time prior to its acceptance, the *Restatement* Rule is that an offer for a unilateral contract cannot be withdrawn once the offeree had begun to perform. Thus, if Val began making extra efforts in an attempt to win the prize, Pubco was prevented from withdrawing the offer.

A and **B** are, therefore, incorrect. **C** is incorrect because an offer for a unilateral contract can only be accepted by performance, making Val's letter irrelevant.

16. **B**   Since the promisor in a unilateral contract has called for acceptance by performance of an act, the promisee's performance is regarded as consideration for it. **A** is incorrect, since promissory estoppel applies only where there has been no consideration. **C** is commonly used MBE "red herring." **D** is incorrect since a gift is something given without consideration, and, here, Val's performance was consideration for Pubco's promise.

17. **A**   Since a contract is a meeting of minds, a person who is too intoxicated to know the legal consequences of her act is incapable of contracting.

B is incorrect, since so long as Susan knew the legal consequences of her acts, the fact that the motivation for those acts might result from intoxication is irrelevant. **C** is incorrect because Susan's intent to jest would not, alone, have prevented a contract from being formed, unless Barbara was (or the reasonable person in Barbara's position would have been) aware that she was jesting. Although an offeror may withdraw an offer at any time prior to acceptance, **D** is incorrect for two reasons: first, such withdrawal is not effective until communicated to the offeree;

and, second, the facts suggest that a contract was formed when the napkin was signed, making a subsequent attempt at revocation ineffective.

18.   A   An advertisement is usually regarded as a mere invitation rather than as an offer unless the circumstances indicate that the party who published the advertisement did so with the intent of empowering another to turn it into a binding contract simply by accepting it. Usually, such an intent is found only where the advertisement indicates the number of items on sale, and contains words indicating an intent to be bound. Here, the phrase "While they last" makes clear that a reader of the advertisement does not have the power to turn it into a binding contract by accepting, and so indicates an intent not to be bound.

          B, C and **D** are therefore incorrect.

19.   D   A condition precedent to a contractual obligation is an event which must occur before a party will be under a duty to perform. Real estate brokerage contracts frequently make the broker's commission due upon her producing a buyer who is "ready, willing, and able" to purchase on the agreed terms. In the contract by which Salzburger agreed to pay a 6 percent commission to Ritchie, however, there were two express conditions precedent to Salzburger's obligation to pay. First, the commission was only due if the house was sold to a buyer who made an offer during a two-month period beginning September 1. Second, the commission was only due upon the closing of title. Although Ritchie found a buyer during the agreed period, the house was not sold to that buyer. In addition, title did not close. Since there was a failure of these conditions precedent, Salzburger's obligation to pay Ritchie's commission never became absolute, and Ritchie is entitled to no recovery from Salzburger.

          A, B, and **C** are, therefore, incorrect.

20.   D   Under the parol evidence rule, extrinsic evidence of prior or contemporaneous agreements or negotiations is inadmissible if offered to contradict the terms of an unambiguous written contract which was intended by the parties to be the complete expression of their agreement. If, however, the terms of a writing are ambiguous, evidence of prior or contemporaneous discussions may be admissible to clear up the ambiguity. Since the language of this writing could reasonably be understood to mean what each party claims it means, it is ambiguous. Thus, the evidence is offered to explain rather than contradict the terms of the writing, and is admissible for that purpose.

          A is, therefore, incorrect. Although the UCC provides that evidence of a prior course of dealing or of usage in the trade may be admitted to explain even an apparently *un*ambiguous contract, B and **C** are incorrect because these are not the *only* kinds of evidence which are admissible.

21. **C**   Ordinarily a promise is not enforceable unless there was consideration (i.e., something given in exchange for and to induce the promise) for it. Since Edward's service had already been rendered without expectation of payment, it was not given in exchange for the promise and is not consideration for it. Some cases have held, however, that a promise to do that which the promisor is morally obligated to do should be enforceable. Although this is an infrequently applied exception to the requirement of consideration, it is the only one of the arguments listed which could result in a victory for Edward. **A** is incorrect, because an otherwise unenforceable promise is not made enforceable simply because it is in writing. Sometimes, a promisee's justified and detrimental reliance makes a promise enforceable, serving as a substitute for consideration. Detrimental reliance means, however, that the promisee changed his position for the worse because he believed that the promise would be kept. **B** is incorrect since there is no fact indicating that Edward relied on her promise by changing his position because of it, or that he was worse off as a result. When a person confers a benefit on another with a reasonable expectation of payment, an implied-in-fact contract may result. **D** is incorrect, however, because there is no fact indicating that Edward had any expectation of payment when he rescued Boss.

22. **B**   If, at the time a contract is formed, the parties to it are operating under a mutual mistake, the resulting lack of mutual agreement excuses non-performance by either party. Thus, if both Bertrand and Gail mistakenly believed that "Sunset" was painted by Van Gook, Bertrand's non-performance would not constitute a breach.

        A is incorrect for two reasons: first, the Statute of Frauds requirement that the writing be signed by the party to be charged may be satisfied by Bertrand's check; and, second, delivery by the seller satisfies the Statute of Frauds. The UCC and some jurisdictions hold that if a contract was unconscionable at the time it was made, the court may refuse to enforce it. **C** is incorrect, however, because the equality of bargaining positions in a contract between experts (such as an art dealer and an art collector) prevents a voluntary agreement from being unconscionable unless one of them deliberately withholds knowledge from the other. To avoid interfering with the freedom to bargain, courts rarely consider the adequacy of consideration, except in consumer contracts when equitable relief is sought. **D** is, therefore, incorrect.

23. **C**   A liquidated damages clause is a provision in a contract fixing the amount of damages should a breach occur. Courts enforce liquidated damages clauses so long as the amount set is reasonable, the actual damages are difficult to ascertain, and the contract tailors the liquidated damages to the circumstances. If any of these requirements is unful-

filled, the clause is unenforceable as a "penalty." In that event, the parties may collect only the actual damages which resulted from the breach. **I** is, therefore, correct. The purpose of an agreement as to liquidated damages is to eliminate the problems that may arise in establishing or defending against actual damage claims in certain circumstances. For this reason, if the liquidated damages clause is enforceable, it provides the only *damage* remedy. It does not, however, prevent the wronged party from seeking other *non-damage* relief. Thus, even if the liquidated damages clause did not establish a penalty (i.e., was enforceable), Barksdale may be entitled to the equitable remedy of specific performance. **II** is, therefore, correct.

24.   **A**   Ordinarily, no promise is enforceable without consideration. Consideration consists of some legal detriment suffered by the promisee in return for the promise. Since Bethel suffered no legal detriment in return for Sandez's promise to keep the offer open, Sandez's promise is unenforceable. **A** is, therefore, correct. UCC section 2-205 provides that a promise to keep an offer open for a specified period of time is binding without consideration if made by a merchant, in a signed writing, and the transaction involves the sale of goods. This kind of offer is known as a "firm offer." The section also provides that the maximum time for which a firm offer is binding is three months. **B, C** and **D** are all designed to trap examinees who are confused about section 2-205. All are incorrect because section 2-205 applies only to transactions in goods and has no application to the sale of realty. In addition, **B** is incorrect because the section sets a time limit of three months rather than 30 days. **D** is also incorrect because the section requires only that the offeror be a merchant and fixes no such requirement about the offeree.

25.   **D**   Since Sorrento sold the chairs to another buyer at the same price which Barrie had contracted to pay, Sorrento sustained no damage. Some cases allow a seller to recover lost profits when a buyer cancels, reasoning that even though the seller resold at the same price, she would have made two sales instead of one if the buyer had not breached. Since there were no more barrel chairs to sell, however, Sorrento lost nothing.

A is, therefore, incorrect. An action for the price might be available where traditional calculation of damages would be inadequate, but **B** is incorrect because Sorrento has suffered no damages. **C** correctly states the remedy which would have been available to Barrie in the event of a breach by Sorrento. Because the fair market value exceeds the contract price, however, the formula expressed in **C** bears no relationship to damages actually suffered.

26.   **A**   The UCC provides that where there is no agreement to the contrary, a buyer is entitled to inspect the goods prior to making payment or accept-

ing them. It provides further, however, that the parties may agree that payment is required before inspection. If so, failure to make payment upon delivery of the goods is a breach.

Anticipatory repudiation occurs when, *prior to the time when performance is required,* a party indicates by word or deed that he will not perform. **B** is incorrect because Boswell's refusal to pay occurred at the time payment was required, and therefore constituted a breach. The UCC provides that even if payment is made prior to inspection, no acceptance occurs until after the buyer has had a reasonable opportunity to inspect. In view of this provision, a promise to pay prior to inspection is not unconscionable, and **C** is incorrect. Since Stilton tendered delivery in accordance with the terms of the contract, **D** is incorrect.

27. **C**   Section 2-606 of the UCC provides that unless the buyer does some act inconsistent with the seller's ownership, acceptance of goods occurs only after the buyer has had a reasonable opportunity to inspect the goods and either notifies the seller of his intention to keep them or fails to reject them. Thus, a payment did not constitute acceptance because it was made before Boswell was given a reasonable opportunity to inspect the studs.

A, B and **D** are, therefore, incorrect.

28. **A**   Under Section 2-313 of the UCC, a warranty is made by any description of the goods which is given by the seller and which is part of the basis of the bargain. Stilton thus warranted that the studs delivered would be construction grade. Under Section 2-714 of the UCC, a buyer who has accepted non-conforming goods and who notifies the seller of the non-conformity within a reasonable time is entitled to damages. The measure of damages for breach of warranty is fixed by that section as the difference between the value which the delivered goods had at the time of acceptance and the value which conforming goods would have had at that time.

B is incorrect because it would entitle Boswell to keep the studs without paying anything for them. **C** is incorrect because it would allow Stilton to collect the price of construction grade studs although he delivered utility grade studs. Although Stilton might have been better off selling the utility grade studs to another buyer at a price higher than they were worth, he has breached his warranty that the studs delivered would be construction grade, and will be required to compensate Boswell for what Boswell has lost. **D** is, therefore, incorrect.

29. **A**   Performance of one of a series of mutual promises is a condition precedent to others in the series if the circumstances indicate that it should obviously precede the others. Since the writing called for payment of

$350 in advance it is obvious that the parties intended that it should be paid before the work commenced. Honniker's payment of $300 was thus a condition precedent to Carl's obligation to paint. Since the contract called for the payment of an additional $400 after completion, it is obvious that the parties intended that the paint job should be finished before payment of the additional money was required. Completion of the paint job is thus a condition precedent to Honniker's obligation to pay the additional $400. A condition subsequent is an event the occurrence or non-occurrence of which operates to discharge a duty which had already become absolute. Since Carl was obligated to paint before receiving the additional $400, and since he could not undo the paint job once it was completed Honniker's payment of the additional $400 cannot be called a condition subsequent to Carl's obligation to paint the car. **B** is, therefore, incorrect. Concurrent conditions require the parties to exchange performance simultaneously. **C** is incorrect because the language of the contract makes it obvious that the parties intended a consecutive order of performance (i.e., H pays $300, C completes paint job, H pays $400). Since the agreement required part payment in advance, and completion of the job before the balance was due, **D** is incorrect.

30.   **A**   Upon breach of the sales contract, the non-breaching party is ordinarily entitled to compensatory, incidental, and consequential damages. A buyer's compensatory damages consist of the difference between the contract price and either the fair market value or the "cover" price (i.e., actual cost of replacement, so long as reasonable). If the cover price (or fair market value) is less than the contract price the buyer is not entitled to compensatory damages, but the saving is not credited to the breaching seller. Incidental damages consist of the reasonable costs of repurchasing. Consequential damages are those which foreseeably arise from the special needs or position of the buyer which result from the breach (e.g., seller's non-delivery causes buyer to go out of business). Honniker sustained no consequential losses, and since Honniker's cover price was less than the contract price, she can receive no compensatory damages. Since the repurchase involved $20 in reasonable expenses, she is entitled to $20 as incidental damages.

B is incorrect because it gives her, in addition to her $20 in incidental damages, an extra $20 as if the cover price had been $20 more than the contract price (it was really $20 *less* than the contract price). **C** is incorrect because it would award Honniker the entire contract price in addition to incidental damages, which would overcompensate Honniker, since she would have had to pay $150 for the bumper if the contract had been fulfilled. **D** is incorrect because it would credit Carl with the savings which resulted from his breach, which under the UCC courts do not do.

ESSAY EXAM
QUESTIONS AND ANSWERS

The following questions were adapted from various Harvard Law School First-Year Contracts examinations of the past. The questions are reproduced almost exactly as they actually appeared, with only slight changes to the facts. The sample answers are not "official" and represent merely one approach to handling the questions.

QUESTION 1

David Dole, owner of 75,000 acres of forest land in Dover County, Maine, had attempted for several years without success to persuade state and local authorities to purchase the tract as a wildlife refuge. He was approached by Paul Pinsky, a prominent producer of motion pictures and creator of an entertainment park in California known as Pinsky Land. Pinsky said that he saw great possibilities in Dole's tract of land as a ski area if properly developed with access roads, motels and a summer resort, and if several hundred cottages were built for rental. However, extensive surveys would be needed before he would want to buy. Dole explained that the taxes assessed against the property were delinquent, and that the 2014 tax would be payable Dec. 11, 2014. Dole added: "I simply have to bail out by then." Dole then prepared and gave Pinsky the following document:

Oct. 9, 2014

I hereby give Paul Pinsky the privilege of entering my land in Dover County, Maine to survey and map it as a recreation area. I will sell him the whole tract of 75,000 acres for $7.5 million, provided he accepts this offer by giving me a certified check for $750,000 on or before Dec. 4, 2014.

/s/ Paul Dole

Pinsky sent a crew of surveyors and architects to the Dover County tract, where they worked for four weeks, at a cost to Pinsky of $100,000. Their activities became widely known and on Nov. 12, a group of five wealthy owners of land in Maine approached Dole, who informed them of his offer to Pinsky. They persuaded Dole that the land should be preserved unspoiled if possible. During the next two weeks the five secured pledges totaling $10 million from 500 persons, and on Nov. 30 the five gave Dole a check for $1 million and jointly signed a promissory note for the remaining $9 million. Dole then executed a conveyance of the 75,000 acre tract to the Wilderness Society, a non-profit corporation whose charter authorizes it "to receive and hold land that is still preserved in or can revert to its natural state and to dispose of such holdings only on such terms as will insure that its natural state is preserved so far as possible."

On Dec. 1, 2014, Pinsky called from California to Dole's home in Webster, Mass., gave his name, and said, "I have a $750,000 check for Mr. Dole. Where shall I mail it?"

Acting on instruction from Dole, his wife replied, "He has moved. I don't know where he is." Pinsky arrived in Webster on Dec. 2 with a $750,000 check in his pocket. He inquired around the city and was told that Dole was last seen leaving town by bus with a lot of camping gear. Pinsky, in hot and continuous pursuit, proceeded to the Dover County tract and after searching through the forest finally found Dole in a secluded cabin on Dec. 6. Pinsky said: "Mr. Dole, I believe. Here is your check, well within your Dec. 11 tax deadline." Pinsky tendered a $750,000 certified check but Dole refused to accept it. Pinsky now consults your law firm. The senior partner instructs you to "prepare a memorandum discussing the legal and equitable remedies Pinsky may have against Dole and the Wilderness Society, and stating your best judgment of the likelihood of success concerning each possible remedy." Write the memorandum.

ANSWER TO QUESTION 1

Was there an acceptance while the offer was still in force? I am putting aside until later whether Dole's offer was an ***irrevocable*** one. Assuming that the offer was not irrevocable, the question is whether Pinsky accepted while the offer was still in force.

As a preliminary matter, it is not clear that Dole's offer of October 9th is sufficiently definite to give rise to an enforceable contract upon Pinsky's tender of a check. The offer contemplates that Dole will give Pinsky $6.75 million worth of credit, but does not specify when this large sum must be paid, nor how it is to be secured. Nor does the offer specify a conveyance date. Thus a court might hold that even if we show that Pinsky did accept before Dole revoked or the offer lapsed, there is no enforceable contract for lack of definiteness. But I think we have a fair chance of showing that as of October 9th, the parties fully intended to reach sufficiently definite terms upon Pinsky's tender of a check. The court might therefore be induced to supply the missing terms with respect to time for full payment, conveyance date, security, etc.

Turning now to whether Pinsky did anything to accept while there was still a valid power of acceptance, the general rule is that the offeror has the right to set the time as of which his offer expires. Thus, Dole's October 9th offer created a power of acceptance which lasted no later than December 4th. It is possible that we will be able to show that Pinsky's call to Dole's wife, in which he said that he had the check ready for mailing, constituted an acceptance. However, in all probability Dole will successfully contend that only receipt by him of the check, not a statement of Pinsky's readiness to send it, constituted an acceptance. Dole could point to the general rule that gives the offeror the right to prescribe the exact means by which his offer may be accepted.

It is also possible that Pinsky's act of showing up in Webster with the check constituted a sort of "constructive" acceptance, in that he did everything in his power to give Dole a check at the place where Dole was supposed to be. Again, however, I would imagine that a court would hold that no acceptance could take place until Dole was actually given the check. We could argue that Dole's act of disappearing constituted an intentional interference with Pinsky's right of acceptance, and that therefore Dole has no right to insist upon the precise conditions of his offer (i.e., that the check actually be given to him in person.) However, since I am now assuming that Dole's offer was revocable at any time, presumably Dole had the right to thwart Pinsky by moving, just as he had the right to revoke the offer outright. This would be an indirect communication of revocation.

We might try the argument that Dole in fact made two offers to Pinsky: one was the written offer, which terminated on December 4th, and the other was an oral offer which by its terms was to last until December 11th (Dole's tax deadline). Therefore, we would contend, the oral offer remained in force until expressly revoked, and Pinsky's December 6th tender of a check was a valid acceptance of this offer. (Dole's refusal to accept this check on the 6th probably would not be a revocation of the offer, since I think a court would hold that the tender of the check was sufficient to accept.)

I think, however, that this "two offers" theory is unlikely to prevail. Even if we convince the court that there were two offers, Dole will have a good chance of showing that the oral offer was revoked. An offeror can revoke his offer by indirect as well as direct means. Restatement 2d, §43, states that "An offeree's power of acceptance is terminated when the offeror takes definite action inconsistent with an intention to enter into the proposed contract and the offeree acquires reliable information to that effect." Dole could argue that when he went off into the wilderness without telling anyone of his whereabouts, and Pinsky learned of his having done so, it should have been clear to Pinsky that Dole meant not to accept the offer.

In summary, unless we can show that Dole's offer was irrevocable, I think we will have a very hard time showing that Pinsky accepted it while he still had a valid power of acceptance. I turn now to the irrevocability question.

Irrevocability of the offer: There are a number of theories which we might advance to establish that Dole's October 9th offer was ***irrevocable*** until December 4th. If we can succeed with any of these arguments, I think we will then be able to convince the court that Dole's running off into the wilderness was an interference with Pinsky's right to exercise his option, and that Pinsky should be regarded as having validly exercised the option by arriving in Webster with the check. (If the offer was irrevocable, Dole should not have the right to get around its irrevocability by making it impossible for Pinsky to accept.)

One theory is that the October 9th offer was a validly binding ***option contract.*** Restatement 2d, §87(1)(a), makes an offer irrevocable as an option contract if it "is in writing and signed by the offeror, recites a purported consideration for the making of the offer, and proposes an exchange on fair terms within a reasonable time." The difficulty with this provision is that Dole's October 9th document does not recite a purported consideration. Therefore, unless the jurisdiction in which Pinsky sues has a statute or case law analogous to the UCC "firm offer" provision, §2-205 (by which a merchant's signed offer to sell that states that it will be kept open for a certain time is irrevocable, even without consideration), I don't think a conventional option contract theory will work. We might conceivably be able to show that Pinsky's act of surveying was of benefit to Dole, and bargained for by him, and was therefore consideration for the option. But since there's a good chance that the court will find that Dole didn't care whether Pinsky surveyed or not, and that there was therefore no consideration for the option, I think this whole "binding option" contract theory will probably go down the drain.

A more promising theory is that Dole's offer was for a ***unilateral contract,*** and that when Pinsky began to perform the requisite act of acceptance (i.e., the tender of a check), the offer became temporarily irrevocable. See Restatement 2d, §45. To win with this theory, we would have to convince the court that from the time Pinsky got to Webster, he was engaged in the act of tendering the check (and not merely *preparing* to tender the check.) If we can establish this, we have a good chance of getting the court to follow Restatement §45, and Pinsky will be able to get the full expectation measure of damages.

Promissory Estoppel: If all of the above theories fail, I think we can at least let Pinsky get his $100,000 in surveyors' fees, by use of the doctrine of ***promissory estoppel.*** Restatement 2d, §87(2) provides that "An offer which the offeror should reasonably expect to induce action or forbearance of a substantial character on the part of the offeree before acceptance and which does induce such action or forbearance is binding as an option contract to the extent necessary to avoid injustice." This provision does not require that the offer have been supported by consideration, and seems to fit Pinsky's situation to a "T." Dole certainly knew that Pinsky planned to spend money on surveyors' fees.

The reason that this promissory estoppel theory is less than completely satisfactory is that, as the Restatement puts it, enforcement will be given only "to the extent necessary to avoid injustice." I'm afraid that the court is likely to award Pinsky only his $100,000 in fees, and not to give him the "benefit of his bargain" (i.e., the profits he could have made from Pinsky World, or even the $2.5 million profit he could have made by reselling the land to the wilderness group.) It's possible that we can convince the court that "justice" requires giving Pinsky at least this $2.5 million turnaround profit, but I wouldn't count on it.

Specific Performance Against Wilderness Society: If we can establish, by one of the above theories, that there is a valid contract between Pinsky and Dole, we might be able to get the court to order *specific performance,* in the form of a decree ordering Wilderness Society to convey the land to Pinsky (and a collateral decree ordering Dole to return the money raised to purchase the land for donation to the Society). In support of this request for specific performance, we can point out that the Wilderness Society people are not *bona fide* purchasers, but in fact had knowledge of the offer to Pinsky. But as a practical matter, I don't think we're likely to find a judge who would be willing to turn this land over to a developer like Pinsky, rather than keeping it in its natural state. Specific performance is a remedy very much left to the trial court's discretion, and I wouldn't get our hopes up about it. I think the best we can hope for is a breach of contract verdict against Dole, with damages of the $2.5 million profit that Pinsky could have made by selling the land to the Wilderness people. If we can come up with some very specific figures showing how profitable Pinsky World would have been, maybe we can get some damages for these lost profits as well, but I'm afraid they will be held to be too speculative unless Pinsky has previously operated a similar business.

QUESTION 2

The General Construction Co. of Memphis, Tennessee decided to build for itself a new headquarters building of an original and striking design. It secured much publicity in journals read by architects and builders by printing artists' sketches of the building, located at a dramatic site at a bend in the Mississippi river. In the publicity was included the announcement of a self-imposed deadline for completion, a deadline that was very short by usual standards of the construction industry for a building of that size.

The Frank Corporation is a steel fabricator that buys steel ingots and transforms them into structural steel. On September 1, 2013, the General Construction Co. and the Frank Corporation executed a written contract under which Frank undertook to fabricate and deliver the structural steel called for by General's specifications, which were made part of the contract. The contract provided a delivery schedule with five lots to be delivered as follows:

Lot I	March 6, 2014
Lot II	March 27, 2014
Lot III	April 10, 2014
Lot IV	April 24, 2014
Lot V	May 1, 2014

The contract also provided that although the tonnage and value of the lots would differ somewhat, the total contract price of $10 million would be divided into five installments of $2 million each, and that General would pay Frank $1.75 million "within five days after the timely and satisfactory delivery of each lot. The $250,000 withheld from each payment will be paid by General Co. after complete performance, satisfactory to the General Co., of all Frank Co.'s obligations." The contract also stated: "Because of the importance to the General Co. of completing its own building by the published completion date, time is declared to be of the very essence of this contract and for each day's delay in delivery of any lot General may retain $5,000 as damages."

Lot I was delivered on March 12 (6 days late) and on March 14 General mailed a check for $1.75 million to Frank. Lot II was delivered April 6 (10 days late). On April 9 General's President telephoned Frank's President to express her concern about the timeliness of future deliveries.

> "I know your reputation is on the line, but supplies of steel are getting short. My usual suppliers have failed me and I expect there will be some longer delays. But aren't you worried about the recent river floods?"

General's President replied:

> "Don't you worry about us. You go ahead and deliver or I'm going to saw you off."

By the date of this conversation, April 9, the steel contained in Lot I had been all attached to the foundations of the structure and a few beams from Lot II had been attached (the rest was lying on the ground at the site) when, on the morning of April 11, the levee protecting the area burst and the flood waters of the Mississippi, which were then reaching their greatest height in 100 years, covered the building site to a depth of 15 feet. The Army Corps of Engineers estimates that the water will not subside at the site before the middle of June. Past experience makes it clear that lying under water for two months will make the steel at the site unusable unless cleaned of muck and rust and covered with a special rust inhibitor. The cost of this operation will be at least $1.2 million.

On April 12, Frank faxed General:

> "Have not yet obtained steel for Lot III. Best promise from any supplier is delivery to us on May 25. We can complete fabrication of Lot III and deliver it to you by June 15. After that I will do my best to obtain supplies."

General faxed in reply:

> "You have been late with every delivery. We cannot accept any promises from you. We cancel."

After canvassing all steel fabricators with substantial supplies of steel, General now finds that the best delivery terms are offered by States Steel Corp., which will charge $7.5 million for the balance of the steel due under the Frank contract. States Steel Corp. will promise to begin deliveries July 1 and complete them by August 1. The architects' journals have published pictures of the original model of the General headquarters building and beside it some steel beams projecting from the river, with such captions as

> "Old Man River Rolls Over General And Just Keeps Rolling Along."

The President of General expresses to you her dismay over the effects of these events on General's reputation, and her uncertainty as to whether to complete the submerged structure. She wants to know General's rights against and liabilities to Frank if the building is completed by contracting with the States Steel Corp. for the steel required. What would you advise? Why?

She also asks whether General's rights or liabilities would be altered if the whole building project is abandoned? What is your answer? Why?

ANSWER TO QUESTION 2

I will examine first whether General's cancellation of the contract constituted a breach, and will then discuss the question of damages.

The cancellation: I think General can make a fairly strong case that it was entitled to cancel the contract when it did. For a definite answer, a number of UCC sections, particularly those dealing with installment contracts, must be examined.

The contract was clearly an "installment contract," since it authorized in "separate lots," and since each lot would obviously be "separately accepted" (or rejected), due to the relatively long time periods between them. §2-612(1)). The real crux of the breach issue is presented by §2-612(3): "Whenever non-conformity or default with respect to one or more installments substantially impairs the value of the whole contract there is a breach of the whole...."

Frank will undoubtedly argue that the delay with respect to Lot III did not "substantially impair the value of the whole contract," and that General therefore had no right to cancel. Frank will base this argument on the evidence that General could not have used the steel had it been delivered on time, since it would have been submerged by the flood and would have cost a significant amount to clean. Thus, Frank will argue, the delay did not substantially impair the value of the contract, since it didn't make things any worse for General than they otherwise would have been.

I think General can make a fairly convincing response to this, to the effect that not only the delay on Lot III, but also the ***uncertainty*** about whether Frank could make a timely delivery (or any delivery at all) on Lots IV and V, must be considered in determining whether there was a "substantial impairment" of the whole contract.

Frank in turn can respond that if it was anxiety about Lots IV and V that induced General to cancel, General's proper remedy was to "demand assurances" pursuant to §2-609, and not to cancel. However, I think that General can reply, successfully, that Frank's April 12th fax was itself a failure to furnish reasonable assurances in response to General's request for assurances on April 9th. In that event, General had the right to treat the lack of assurances as a repudiation (§2-609(4)), thus allowing it to cancel §2-711(1)). Alternatively, General can contend that Frank's April 12th fax was an ***anticipatory repudiation*** (§2-610), giving General a right to cancel. However, this is not as powerful an argument, in my opinion, as the "failure to give assurances" argument previously stated.

Frank might attempt to avoid liability for breach by asserting the doctrine of ***impracticability*** or ***impossibility***. He could say that his source of supply dried up unforeseeably, making performance by him "... impracticable [because of] the occurrence of a contingency the non-occurrence of which was a basic assumption on which the contract was made...." §2-615(a). But assuming that the Frank-General contract had not specified a particular source from which Frank was to obtain the deal, and assuming that a shortage of steel ingots is reasonably foreseeable in the industry, it is unlikely that he would prevail with this defense.

In summary, I am fairly confident that: (1) General can establish that it had the right to cancel the entire contract on grounds of Frank's breach; and (2) Frank should not escape liability by virtue of any "impossibility" or "impracticability" defense.

Damages: Under §2-607(1), "[t]he buyer must pay at the contract rate for any goods accepted." Thus General will be liable to Frank for the two lots of steel it accepted, although determination of the "contract rate," and the possibility of a countervailing damage claim by General against Frank, complicate the damage issue.

I suppose that General could argue that the "contract rate" is $1.75 million per lot, and the $250,000 per lot retainage is a separate sum which serves as compensation for completion of the whole project, not as part of the payment for the lot in question. But I don't think we will get far with this argument, since it seems to me that the retainage scheme really relates to the *time for payment*, not the items for which payment is to be made. In any event, I think the question is academic. If the "contract rate" is held to include the $250,000 retainage, we will recover this $250,000 in the form of the contract/cover differential, which is discussed in the next paragraph.

Assuming that General's deal with States Steel is "in good faith" and "reasonable" (§2-712(1)), General can recover from Frank the difference between the cost of the cover contract with States, and the cost of the original contract. Assuming that the court treats the first two installments as having cost a total of $4 million, the difference between the cost of cover and the cost of completion under the original contract is $1.5 million ($7.5 million - $6 million). This recovery must be offset against the remaining $2.25 million which General would owe Frank on the first two lots. If the "contract rate" on the first two lots is held to be $1.75 million, not $2 million, the net result is still the same: General would owe Frank $750,000.

However, General has a right to ***"consequential damages"*** in addition to this cover/contract differential (§2-715(2)). Consequential damages would probably include any *delay* damages suffered by General, as General's need for prompt delivery was a "particular requirement of which the seller at the time of contracting had reason to know." (§2-715(2)). The contract fixes delay damages at $5,000 per day. However, since this contract clause fixes damages at $5,000 for each day *delivery* is delayed, and not every day completion of the building is delayed, it is not clear whether a court would enforce this clause, or would attempt to make its own estimate of damages. Frank will have a good chance of arguing that the damages clause applies only to a slightly delayed delivery, not to breach or other cancellation of the contract, and that ordinary damage rules should apply in the latter event.

Frank will also have a good contention that its non-delivery of Lot III saved General upwards of $1 million, since the steel would have been covered by the flood, and would have cost that much to clean off. Frank could point to §2-715(2), which allows subtraction from the cover/contract differential of any "expenses saved in consequence of the seller's breach."

In summary, I would say that General will owe Frank $750,000, plus any consequential delay damages (probably measured by usual standards, not by the $5,000 per day clause), but that the consequential damages may be reduced by the amount which de-rusting the additional lots would have cost.

If General elects to abandon the building, and not make the deal with States, the only part of the analysis which would be different is that General would use the difference between the contract price and the "market price at the time when [General] learned of the breach," not the contract/cover differential. (§2-713(1)). I have no idea what this market price is. Nor do I know whether the "time when [General] learned of the breach" will be held to be April 10th (when delivery was due), April 12 (when the "repudiation" took place), or whatever the date was on which General cancelled the contract; a good argument can be made that it should be this last date, since that would best protect General's right to have "for a commercially reasonable time await[ed] performance by the repudiating party." (§2-610(a)).

QUESTION 3

The Alumalloy Co., manufacturer of metal sidings for home exteriors, has divided Brighton, a city of 800,000 population, into four districts for assignment of distributorships. The standard form of agreement used with its distributors contains an undertaking by Alumalloy to fill orders secured from customers at prices to be charged to the distributors according to a schedule attached to the agreement. Further, it appoints the distributor for a four year period, "provided, however, and on express condition that Alumalloy may terminate at any time the right of Distributor to sell Alumalloy products." The agreement also provides that the distributor will have the exclusive right for the duration of his appointment to sell Alumalloy products in the geographical district of Brighton to which he is assigned. Moreover, the distributor will purchase at his own expense all equipment required for the installation of Alumalloy products and for their refabrication where this is needed, and "Distributor undertakes for the duration of this agreement not to sell or solicit sales of Alumalloy products outside the area assigned to him by this agreement." [Assume that this territorial confinement clause is consistent with public policy and the antitrust laws.]

On Sept. 10, 2012, Alumalloy and Donald Dirk signed a copy of the Alumalloy standard agreement, assigning to Dirk District II in Brighton, as defined on a map prepared by Alumalloy and attached to the agreement. On Nov. 2, 2012, Alumalloy and Peter Pigeon signed a similar agreement assigning to Pigeon District III, as defined on a map that was similarly attached. Dirk and Pigeon each purchased installation and refabrication equipment at the cost to each of approximately $200,000. During the period prior to May 1, 2014, Dirk prospered while Pigeon suffered a net operating loss of $50,000. The losses by Pigeon were due to sales resistance that he met in District III, which was for the most part a blighted area, and to the high cost of refabricating sidings to fit the old-style houses located in most of the area. During early April 2014, Pigeon's salespeople solicited orders in a 12-square-block area within District III but near its outer edge which adjoins District II. They discovered that Dirk had already invaded this area and sold and installed Alumalloy sidings in 25 relatively new houses in the area. The profit to Dirk on these installations averaged $3,000 per house.

(A) Pigeon inquires of you whether, if Alumalloy cancels his distributorship, he can recover any damages by suing either Alumalloy or Dirk. On the basis of the facts so far stated, what would you advise? Why?

(B) Pigeon then complained to the Alumalloy home office concerning Dirk's invasion of his territory and received the following reply on May 1, 2014: "We do not care that much who sells our products. We are completely satisfied with Dirk, to whom we are sending a copy of this letter. We are notifying him at the same time that, for the remaining period of the contract, we waive the termination condition that we originally reserved in his agreement. We will carry you along and won't cancel you out until you have got back your investment but you will have to work out with Dirk any problems you have with him." Since receiving this letter, Pigeon continued to purchase materials from Alumalloy as he pondered upon his course of action and noted that Dirk continued to purchase and install Alumalloy sidings in ever-increasing quantities. Pigeon now asks you whether this letter improves his chances of securing damages from Dirk for the latter's past invasions of Pigeon's territory. He also asks you whether, in light of all the facts, he would be able to enjoin Dirk from future invasions. What answers would you give, and why?

ANSWER TO QUESTION 3

Part (A): Pigeon has a possibility of recovering damages against either Alumalloy or Dirk.

Pigeon vs. Alumalloy: Pigeon will only have a right of action against Alumalloy if he can show that the latter breached the contract. This will in turn depend principally upon whether the termination clause of the contract ("provided, however, and on express condition that Alumalloy may terminate at any time the right of Distributor to sell Alumalloy products") is to be literally enforced. There are several indications that the parties did not intend (or at least that Pigeon did not intend) that Alumalloy would have the right to terminate the distributorship for no reason at all.

First, the contract clearly contemplated the expenditure of large sums by Pigeon for installation and refabrication. It is unlikely that Pigeon would have agreed to this requirement, and would have in fact spent $200,000, if the understanding was that he could be terminated for no reason at all.

Second, the common practice of businesspeople in distributorship arrangements like this is to make the right of termination available only where the distributor does not perform satisfactorily. Pigeon could probably introduce evidence of this common business practice (a "trade usage" — see UCC §1-303(c)) to show that this is how the termination clause should be interpreted. Such evidence would not run afoul of the parol evidence rule, since Pigeon would be seeking not to contradict the writing, but to "interpret" it.

The termination clause is stated to be an "express" condition of the contract as to which strict compliance would ordinarily be necessary. However, the court has the power to require merely substantial compliance, particularly where, as here, Alumalloy has received benefits under the contract. Thus, the court could hold that the right of termination would be exercisable only if Pigeon did not perform satisfactorily.

Alternatively, the court might hold that the termination clause was **unconscionable**, allowing the court to refuse to enforce it. In support of this contention, Pigeon could point out that the clause was buried in a standard form contract, rather than being included upon the special attached sheets which contain the most important aspects of the deal. Also, Pigeon could obviously point to the extremely one-sided and unfair effect that literal enforcement of the clause would have. Alumalloy, on the other hand, could point to the fact that both parties are businesspeople, and that the unconscionability doctrine has been used relatively rarely in such business contracts.

Assuming that the clause is interpreted to allow a right of termination only if Pigeon performs unsatisfactorily, the satisfactoriness of his performance would be in issue. Since the contract contains no requirement that Pigeon sell a certain number of units, there is no objective standard by which to measure his performance. In view of the fact that the district assigned to Pigeon was an unpromising one, and also considering Dirk's incursion into Pigeon's territory, Pigeon's performance would probably be held to have been adequate. In that event, Alumalloy would be held to have breached by terminating the contract.

Alumalloy might attempt to argue that the entire contract is invalid for **lack of consideration.** In support of this argument, it could point to the fact that Pigeon is not required to make a certain number of sales in the district, and has therefore not really promised to do anything. However, Pigeon could answer by citing *Wood v. Lady Duff Gordon,* and by saying that he had an implied obligation to make a good faith effort to sell the Alumalloy products. In all probability, Pigeon would succeed with this argument.

Damages against Alumalloy: If Pigeon establishes that Alumalloy breached, he could try to obtain either expectation or reliance damages. He will have difficulty establishing with sufficient certainty that he would have made any profits from the enterprise, and even more difficulty establishing a particular dollar amount. Most courts do not permit the plaintiff to prove lost profits from a new business, and where the new business is losing money, the task is even more difficult.

Therefore, Pigeon will be better off trying to get reliance damages. Where expectation damages are difficult to measure, courts often use reliance as a measure of damages. However, if the defendant can prove that the plaintiff was in a "losing contract," the court will not allow a full measure of reliance damages, as this might put the plaintiff in a better position than he would have been in had the contract been performed. However, Alumalloy will bear the burden of proving that the contract would have been a losing one for Pigeon even if no breach by Alumalloy had occurred. Even if Alumalloy does prove that Pigeon would have lost, say, $75,000 over the four-year life of the contract, Pigeon still has a good chance of recovering his $200,000 gross reliance damages minus the $75,000 he would have lost anyway, or $125,000.

Pigeon vs. Dirk: In order for Pigeon to obtain damages from Dirk, he'll have to show that Dirk's promise not to infringe on any other distributor's district created enforceable rights in Pigeon. He can do this only by showing that he was a **third party beneficiary** of the Alumalloy-Dirk contract.

Dirk's promise to Alumalloy created rights in Pigeon only if Alumalloy **intended** to benefit Pigeon by inducing Dirk to make the promise. Pigeon can make a powerful argument that Alumalloy's motive in inducing such a promise of non-infringement from each of its distributors was to be able to offer each distributor an exclusive area — without Dirk's promise of non-infringement, Pigeon might have been unwilling to make his contract with Alumalloy. Therefore, Pigeon can say he was an intended beneficiary.

Dirk can counter this argument by contending that Alumalloy's motive in making him promise non-infringement was to maximize its own sales by making sure that every territory was adequately staffed. But in all probability, Pigeon will succeed in showing that the primary motive of the non-infringement provisions, from Alumalloy's point of view, was to enable it to promise each of the other dealers, including Pigeon, an exclusivity. Pigeon would therefore be able to sue Dirk as a third party beneficiary of Dirk's promise of non-infringement.

Pigeon's damages against Dirk: Pigeon has a fairly good chance of recovering from Dirk the $75,000 in profits which Dirk made by virtue of his infringement. By the expectation measure, Pigeon's damages should be enough to put him in the position he would have been in had Dirk not infringed. Dirk will undoubtedly argue that Pigeon was not as good a salesperson as he, and that Pigeon would therefore have made far less than $75,000 out of the neighborhood where infringement took place. This issue will turn on the facts as they develop at trial, but in view of Dirk's wrongful conduct, Pigeon will have a good chance of recovering the full $75,000.

Part (B): The letter is significant in two respects: (1) It sheds some light on whether Alumalloy originally intended Dirk's promise to benefit Pigeon or not; and (2) If Pigeon did have a right to sue Dirk as third party beneficiary, the letter may constitute a *modification* of Pigeon's rights.

(1) It is hard to say whether the letter makes it more or less ambiguous that the company intended to benefit Pigeon by extracting the non-infringement promise from Dirk. Pigeon can claim that the company's statement that it doesn't care who sells its products shows that its motive, when it made Dirk promise not to infringe, was to be able to offer an exclusive deal to Pigeon and the other potential distributors near Dirk, and not to maximize the company's sales. However, Dirk can just as easily argue that this statement of indifference shows that the company is not out to protect its other distributors (i.e., Pigeon), and that it did not therefore intend to benefit these other distributors by extracting such non-infringement promises.

Conflicting interpretations can also be advanced as to Alumalloy's statement that "You will have to work out with Dirk any problems you have with him." Pigeon can claim that this shows that the company contemplated a potential right of action by Pigeon against Dirk; Dirk can claim that this shows that the company just didn't care.

However, the question is what Alumalloy intended at the time it extracted the promise from Dirk, not what its intentions are currently. Therefore, Pigeon will still probably be able to show that he was (originally at least) a third party beneficiary of Dirk's promise.

(2) Dirk can argue that even if Pigeon originally had a third party beneficiary's rights, these rights have been *altered* (and destroyed) by Alumalloy's letter. He can make a perfectly reasonable argument that Alumalloy's refusal to enforce the non-infringement promise, and its communication of that refusal to Dirk, was an enforceable modification of any third party beneficiary rights Pigeon may have had. The modern view, however, is that once the third party beneficiary *changes his position in reliance on the promise,* his rights are vested, and cannot be altered. Pigeon's signing of the contract, and his making of expenditures, could probably be shown to have been in reliance on the guaranty of exclusivity. Dirk can come back with the contention that Pigeon, by continuing to deal with Alumalloy after the letter, implicitly *assented* to the proposed modification.

Pigeon's right to injunction: If Pigeon can make his way through this thicket of argument and counter argument, and can establish his third party rights, he has a good chance of getting an *injunction*. Because his lost profits are hard to calculate, his legal remedy (i.e., his right to recover damages) is probably not adequate. Furthermore, the injunction sought here is a negative one, and can be much more easily policed by the court than an injunction requiring the defendant to do something affirmatively.

In summary, if Pigeon can prove breach, he can probably get an injunction, to last for the remainder of Dirk's four-year contract, or until Pigeon's own contract is rightfully terminated, whichever happens first.

SUBJECT MATTER INDEX

This index includes references to the Capsule Summary
and to the Exam Tips, but not to Q&A or Flowcharts

ACCEPTANCE
Generally, 48-60, 170-175
By parties' conduct, 53
By shipment of goods, 49
Confirmation, effect of, 53
Definition of, 47
Duration of power of, 54-59, 172-173
Expressly condition on assent to changes, 51
Lost in transmission, 59
Mailbox rule, 59
Method of, 49-50, 170, 175
Misunderstanding as blocking, 61
Notice of, in case of unilateral contract, 50
Offeree must know of offer, 48
Rejection followed by acceptance, 60
Reward, 171
Silence as, 50
Time when acceptance becomes effective, 59-60
Unilateral contract, 171
Varying from offer
Generally, 51-54
Additional term in acceptance, 51, 172
Conflicting terms in documents, 52, 172
Contract formed by parties' conduct, 53
UCC view, 51-54
Who may accept, 48

ACCEPTANCE OF GOODS
Defined, 92

ACCOMMODATION SHIPMENT
As acceptance, 49

ACCORD AND SATISFACTION, 161-162, 231

ACCOUNT STATED, 163

ADHESION CONTRACTS, 152-153

ADVERTISEMENT
As offer, 48

AGREEMENT TO AGREE, 61

ANTICIPATORY REPUDIATION
Defined, 98, 200
Delegation as constituting, 201
Effect of, 96
Insolvency as, 98
Installment contract, 100
Prospective inability to perform, 98

Retraction of, 99, 201-202
Right to demand assurances of performance, 96
Right to sue for immediately, 97, 202
UCC damages for, 101

ARBITRATION CLAUSES
Unconscionability of, 154-155

ASSIGNMENT OF RIGHTS
Generally, 128-135, 217-221
Assignee vs. assignor, 134-135
Assignee vs. obligor, 131-133, 219-220
Counterclaims, set-offs and recoupment by obligor, 133
Assignees, rights of one vs. another, 133, 220
Assignment of "the contract", 136
Consideration for, 184
Contract terms prohibiting, 130-131
Distinguished from delegation, 128
Gratuitous assignments, 129
Revocability of, 129, 219
Impairment of obligor's chance to get return performance, 130
Material alteration of obligor's duty, 130
Material variance of risk, 130
Modification of contract, 132, 220
Payment, assignment of right to, 129
Payment, prior payment to assignor as defense to claim by assignee, 220
Present transfer, assignment as, 128
Request for assurances of performance following, 200
Revocability of, 129-130, 218-219
Rights of successive assignees of same claim, 133
Rights that may or may not be assigned, 130, 217
UCC Article 9 as applying to, 129
Waiver-of-defenses clause, 132
Writing, requirement of, 129

ASSUMPTION OF CONTRACT, 136

ASSUMPTION OF MORTGAGE
Third party beneficiary law and, 139

ASSURANCES
Adequate assurances, defined, 96
Demand for, defined, 97
Grounds for seller to demand, 96